Great American Lawyers

AN ENCYCLOPEDIA

Great American Lawyers

AN ENCYCLOPEDIA

VOLUME ONE A–I

—— *John R. Vile* ——

ABC•CLIO

Santa Barbara, California   Denver, Colorado   Oxford, England

Library of Congress Cataloging-in-Publication Data
Great American lawyers : an encyclopedia / [edited by] John R. Vile.
p.   cm.
Includes bibliographical references and index.
ISBN 1-57607-202-9 (acid-free paper) — ISBN 1-57607-205-8 (e-book)
1. Lawyers—United States—Biography.   I. Vile, John R.
KF353.G74   2001
340'.092'273—dc21
2001000980

06 05 04 03 02 01 10 9 8 7 6 5 4 3 2 1

This book is also available on the World Wide Web as an e-book.
Visit abc-clio.com for details.

ABC-CLIO, Inc.
130 Cremona Drive, P.O. Box 1911
Santa Barbara, California 93116-1911
This book is printed on acid-free paper.

Manufactured in the United States of America

DEDICATED TO
LAWYERS AND OTHER CITIZENS
WHO ARE COMMITTED TO
LIBERTY UNDER LAW

Contents

VOLUME TWO

Preface

FROM COLONIAL TIMES TO THE PRESENT, American attorneys have played significant roles in U.S. history. Lawyers largely drafted early state constitutions, the Articles of Confederation, the Declaration of Independence, the U.S. Constitution, and most of the state and national laws that have been subsequently adopted. When he visited the United States in the 1830s, French writer and politician Alexis de Tocqueville noted that lawyers played roles in the United States similar to those played by the hereditary aristocracy in some European nations. Not only do attorneys fill the judicial branch of the government, but many have been prominent as members of Congress and as presidents.

Courtroom appearances are the most dramatic aspect of most attorneys' lives. Such roles provide continuing grist for the mills of novelists and television producers alike, and lawyers sometimes capture as much attention as the clients or the issues they defend. Although several such books were published in the nineteenth century, no comparable twentieth-century volume focusing specifically on lawyers has attempted to survey more than a dozen or so of the great litigators. *Great American Lawyers*, which provides essays of approximately 2,500 words on the lives and major cases of one hundred great American lawyer-litigators throughout U.S. history, should prove to be useful both as a library reference volume and as a book for lawyers, scholars, and general readers who are interested in the legal profession and in great U.S. trials.

This book is edited by Dr. John R. Vile, a political scientist at Middle Tennessee State University who is author of the *Encyclopedia of Constitutional Amendments* and editor of a CD-ROM, *History of the American Legal System*, both published by ABC-CLIO. It includes contributions from more than fifty lawyers, political scientists, historians, and other scholars from throughout the nation. Lawyers as diverse as John Adams, F. Lee Bailey, Melvin Belli, Johnnie Cochran, Clarence Darrow, Andrew Hamilton, Charles Houston, Abraham Lincoln, Belva Lockwood, Thurgood Marshall, Earl Rogers, Gerry Spence, Kenneth Starr, and George Wythe are among the subjects of this volume.

Introduction

Choosing the Great Attorneys: Neither Legerdemain nor Science

For individuals, like me, who often start their workday by chuckling over a calendar of lawyer jokes or swapping such anecdotes with colleagues, the very idea of compiling a book about great American lawyers may initially seem like an oxymoron, or contradiction. Americans seem to have a love-hate relationship with lawyers, akin to that which they have with their representatives in Congress (who are themselves often lawyers).[1] Most Americans have nothing but praise for their constitutional system,[2] which has arguably spawned such a large number of lawyers, and most Americans appear to respect the lawyers they know and employ. Still, Americans enjoy ridiculing, and sometimes even denigrating, the legal profession as a whole.[3] Moreover, there is a general consensus that the United States has more than enough attorneys and that more attorneys bring still more litigation. Many readers will undoubtedly have heard the story of the small town that could not support one attorney but found that it had more than enough business for two.

Percy Foreman once passed out business cards immodestly listing his partners as "Mose Moses (1297–1202 B.C.), Flavius A. Justinian (A.D. 483–565), William Blackstone (A.D. 1723–1780), and Daniel Webster (A.D. 1782–1852)."[4] Certainly, lawyers, judges, and legal commentators have made their mark throughout history. In addition to the names Foreman mentioned, one could cite the biblical Solomon, the Grecian orators,[5] Rome's Cicero,[6] and England's Matthew Hale and Sir Edward Coke.[7] Eighteenth-century Americans were familiar with great cases in English history, including the trial of William Penn and the trial of John Lilburne.[8] Sometimes conflicting commentaries by Coke, Blackstone, and other English-men played a vital role in educating the generation of American revolutionary lawyers,[9] some of whom had actually attended one of the courts of law in England, but many of whom were largely self-taught through the process of reading law in the office of an established attorney.

Lawyers played a prominent role in the founding of the republic. Although trained lawyers were relatively scarce in seventeenth-century America, where the educated gentry often served in such roles,[10] lawyers were fairly well established by the time that Andrew Hamilton won the 1732 ruling on behalf of John Peter Zenger that helped expand freedom of speech and press in the colonies.[11] Patrick Henry and James Otis argued for colonial rights both in their respective state courtrooms and legislatures. A lawyer named Thomas Jefferson took the lead in crafting the Declaration of Independence (which reads, in part, like a legal brief), and another, John Dickinson, wrote the Articles of Confederation. Lawyers such as Alexander Hamilton, Edmund Randolph, Roger Sherman, John Jay, and James Wilson played prominent roles at the Constitutional Convention of 1787 and in subsequent ratification debates. This Constitutional Convention laid a foundation for a coequal judicial branch of government, in which, as Alexander Hamilton pointed out, legal training would be the unstated sine qua non.[12] Lawyers would also be prominent in the other two branches—with so many lawyers in Congress that a humorist proposed that the country had a government "of lawyers and not men"[13] and with three of the first five presidents (Adams, Jefferson, and Monroe) having been trained as attorneys.[14] Moreover, however familiar educated nonlawyer framers such as George Mason were with the rights of man (Mason largely crafted the Virginia Declaration of Rights, which served as a model for later documents), they themselves generally deferred to lawyers when it came to crafting laws and constitutions.

Early Americans, who had broken from Great Britain, prided themselves on the fact that they had no hereditary aristocracy, but when Alexis de Tocqueville of France visited the United States in the 1830s, he observed that lawyers were filling similar functions.[15] If abstract philosophical debates within the United States sometimes appeared dull when compared with those in other countries (America has arguably never produced a philosopher of the stature of Hegel, Rousseau, or Kant),[16] debates over legal issues—and especially that of slavery—reverberated throughout Congress and the nation.[17] The three most distinguished members of Congress in the mid-nineteenth century, Henry Clay, John C. Calhoun, and Daniel Webster, were all trained as lawyers, and Webster's arguments before the U.S. Supreme Court were among the best-attended social events in the nation's capital. Abraham Lincoln, U.S. president during the dark days of the

Civil War, first distinguished himself as a prairie lawyer and in debates for a Senate seat with another lawyer dubbed "the Little Giant," Stephen A. Douglas.

At the end of the nineteenth century and the beginning of the twentieth, lawyers helped manage and justify the fortunes that American entrepreneurs were making. At times, lawyers defending laissez-faire economics consciously portrayed themselves as defenders of the Constitution against the hoi polloi. Attorney John Randolph Tucker thus posed the following rhetorical question in 1892:

> Can I be mistaken in claiming that Constitutional Law is the most important branch of American jurisprudence; and that the American Bar is and should be in a large degree that priestly tribe to whose hands are confided the support and defense of this Ark of the Covenant of our fathers, the security of which against the profane touch of open and covert foes is the noblest function and the most patriotic purpose of our great profession?[18]

Not long after, a commentator noted that "of no other thing has our country more reason to be proud than of her long list of eminent jurists," and he proceeded to note that "safety of life, liberty of action, increase of wealth, material, mental and social expansion, depend fundamentally upon law—wisely enacted, and administered with impartiality and enlightenment."[19]

The debates between advocates of laissez-faire and the progressives often reverberated in the Supreme Court, where lawyers and justices such as Rufus and Joseph Choate, Stephen Field, Oliver Wendell Holmes Jr., Louis Brandeis, and Benjamin Cardozo articulated a gamut of political and social views. The media brought increased attention to lawyers and their cases, and a number of "trials of the century" propelled attorneys into the public spotlight. Clarence Darrow was but one of a number of modern lawyers who made a name for themselves not only defending the wealthy (which Darrow did toward the end of his career) but also promoting various social issues such as the cause of labor, opposition to the death penalty, and the right to teach evolution in the public schools.

With the rise of the New Deal (inaugurated by lawyer-president Franklin D. Roosevelt) and successive programs that concentrated greater power than ever in the nation's capital, lawyers continued to find themselves at the center of lawmaking, and lawyers continued to serve as key presidential and congressional advisors. Led by the National Association for the Advancement of Colored People and the American Civil Liberties Union, and a host of advocacy groups that would follow, other lawyers found that they could advance civil rights and liberties through courtroom adjudication. Still others continue to be propelled to fame by defending or prosecuting the rich and famous. In the midst of such trials, modern lawyers may garner as much attention as the defendants. During the O. J. Simpson murder trial, it was common for the media to focus on the hairstyle and clothing of one of the prosecutors, Marcia Clark, or on reported tensions within the defense team, while other authors, attorneys, and law professors joined the media spectacle in their daily analyses of the day's proceedings, and *Tonight Show* host Jay Leno presented regular television skits of the "dancing Itos" (after the judge in the case).[20]

If it is undeniable that lawyers have played an important role in civilization generally and in American history in particular, the task of choosing one hundred attorneys for special treatment is not therefore easy. Based on my experience, few individuals are likely to know the names of one hundred great American lawyers, and even legal specialists may lack knowledge of a wide range of famous lawyers throughout American history. Among those scholars and practitioners with such knowledge, no two would be likely to compose an identical list of the top ten, much less of the top one hundred.[21]

From time to time, scholars survey colleagues to assess the greatness of American presidents or Supreme Court justices. As difficult as such jobs are, those who make such assessments do not need to define the initial pool but are drawing from a fixed and relatively narrow category of individuals. By contrast, the American Bar Foundation reports that there were 857,931 lawyers in 1995 alone, averaging one lawyer for every 303 persons.[22] There may be a few presidents who would not rank the attainment of this office as their highest achievement (visitors to Jefferson's Monticello home may remember that being president was not one of the three accomplishments—writing the Declaration of Independence, authoring the Virginia Statute for Religious Liberty, and founding the University of Virginia—for which Thomas Jefferson wished to be remembered), but there must be a very few. Individuals who are appointed to the U.S. Supreme Court hardly ever leave this post for another job, making it likely that, if they serve more than a minimum number of years, they too will be largely remembered for their accomplishments in this position. Again by contrast, a lawyer's reputation as a practicing attorney may well be overshadowed by the lawyer's accomplishments as a judge, an author, an elected officeholder, an advisor, a diplomat, or an entrepreneur, and evaluators might find it difficult to evaluate the worth of an individual as an attorney from his or her reputation in a subsequent position.

If there is anything that distinguishes American lawyers from others and adds drama to their lives, it is the lawyers' legally recognized ability to represent clients in the courtroom.[23] Bar associations ensure that this is a privilege reserved for those with legal educations. Moreover, although lawyers are known for their ability to draft legislation, to give personal counsel in a wide variety of matters, and to draw up contracts, wills, and other conveyances, they are most renowned for their work in the courtroom, or what is generally referred to as litigation. Addressing the nature of a lawyer's work, Arthur T. Vanderbilt wrote, "Lawyers carry on a wide variety of activities but in the final analysis the advocate representing his client in court typifies the profession, for it is in the courts and other tribunals that the rights which the law protects must be vindicated."[24] Noting that litigators are "the closest thing America has to the Knights of the Round Table," Mary Ann Glendon observed that "nearly all of America's legendary lawyer heroes have been litigators."[25] She further noted that trials, rather than the more common legal routines, continue to be the primary subject matter of novels, movies, and television programs:

> Filmmakers, journalists, novelists, and television programmers are fascinated with the activities of the minority of lawyers who are engaged in courtroom work. Don't look soon for a TV sitcom on "Eleanor the Estate Planner," or an action-adventure series titled "This Is Your IRS," or real-life episodes from "Judge Wapner's Conciliation Clinic." Ratings thrive on crime, conflict, and courtroom drama.[26]

Jonathan Turley adds that "the top trial attorneys can become cultural icons."[27]

Although many authors focus on litigators and litigation in identifying outstanding lawyers, such terms can be used in at least two ways. Political scientists such as I tend to associate litigation with any trial appearances, whereas many lawyers tend to associate litigation with trial, rather than appellate, courts.[28] Either type of litigation is likely to receive far more attention than the more daily lawyerly routines; such litigation is accordingly more likely to shape public perceptions of the law.[29]

Having decided that the primary focus of this book would be on litigation (or "trial" work, broadly defined so as to include appellate advocacy) and being informed by my publisher that it was seeking approximately one hundred such individuals, I faced the formidable task of attempting to formulate a list of attorneys who might be considered for inclusion. It seemed clear that, if this book were to cover all of American history, attorneys should be chosen from the colonial and revolutionary period, as well as from the nineteenth and twentieth centuries. Given the obstacles that women and racial minorities often faced in gaining legal educations and/or admission to the bar, it would hardly be possible to include them in equal numbers,[30] but it seemed important to include enough of them to make it clear that such individuals are increasingly contributing to their profession.[31] Similarly, some individuals such as John Marshall, Joseph Story, and Tapping Reeve were included who might not have made it as advocates in their own right but whose influence on the profession was so profound as to mandate their treatment.

A problem with rating presidents and justices is that of introducing a bias when assessing persons who are still alive. Not only are such individuals more likely to be known to the reviewers, but such reviewers' assessments are more likely to be colored by ideological considerations.[32] I accordingly decided that living lawyers would not be excluded from consideration, but that their numbers should be kept relatively small and they should be chosen on the basis of reputation rather than the causes or philosophies with which they are identified. Readers should be warned that an attorney's inclusion or exclusion from this book is not intended as a seal of approval or disapproval of such an attorney's litigation abilities or ideologies, and, although there are entries on attorneys born in every decade from the 1720s forward, no attorneys under age fifty receive a full entry in this book.

Assessing lawyers, like assessing presidents and justices, often requires making complex moral judgments. It is certainly possible to be a virtuous president without thereby being regarded as an effective one (Jimmy Carter is sometimes cited as an example). Similarly, a president whose morality is questionable might be responsible for important accomplishments (Richard Nixon's diplomatic opening to the People's Republic of China or Bill Clinton's handling of the economy). Individuals motivated by the basest motives might profess high ideals; the general lover of humanity might not like, or get along with, any individual in particular. Ultimately, I decided that there would be no moral litmus test for the attorneys discussed in this book. Some such as George Wythe, John Adams, and Abraham Lincoln were individuals of obvious virtue and conviction, whereas others were better known for their trial expertise, and even for legal trickery, than for their moral distinction. Eschewing the notion that lawyers are, as a group, more immoral than others, I also reject the idea that every great practitioner has been a man or woman of virtue. At least for purposes of this book, being listed as a "great" lawyer does not necessarily mean that an individual would otherwise be classified as a "great" or "good" man or woman.[33]

Just as "great" cities often grow along "great" rivers, so too, "great" lawyers, or at least lawyers with great reputations, tend to emerge from "great" cases.[34] The landmark nineteenth-century case of *McCulloch v. Maryland* (1819), dealing with the constitutionality of the U.S. bank, thus featured a veritable "dream team" of six attorneys—William Pinkney, Daniel Webster, and William Wirt favoring the bank and Walter Jones, Joseph Hopkinson, and Luther Martin opposing it[35]—each of whom is the subject of an essay in this book. Individuals participating in a series of such great cases are likely to have been highly regarded in their own day and to have left lasting reputations—although, in what might be an exception that helps prove the rule, I discovered that few modern scholars were aware of Hayden C. Covington, who successfully argued a large number of cases before the U.S. Supreme Court in the 1940s through the 1960s on behalf of the rights of Jehovah's Witnesses. In compiling a list of great lawyers, I have consulted numerous books dealing with noteworthy individual trials,[36] as well as several books that include essays on a number of such great trials.[37] I have tried to take into account the magnitude of the cases that attorneys have taken, while recognizing that one's participation or nonparticipation in such cases may often be fortuitous. Accordingly, I have not considered myself bound to include all attorneys who have participated in a single famous case.

The nineteenth century might have been more conducive to regarding lawyers, and perhaps men and women in general, as heroes than the centuries following have. Thus, in addition to scores of individual biographies, there are several nineteenth-century volumes that provide multiple biographies of leading lawyers, and only lawyers, much along the order of this book.[38] I have made good use of these tomes in identifying eighteenth- and nineteenth-century lawyers for this volume. Similarly, there are several helpful modern volumes, generally less ambitious in scope, that group a dozen or fewer modern lawyers for discussion and/or inspiration,[39] that attempt to assess the legal profession or some part of the profession,[40] or that are helpful in identifying important lawyers in previous time periods.[41] In an essay that I have found to be quite helpful, a student of the ratings of U.S. Supreme Court justices has noted that justices about whom other individuals have written tend to be more highly rated than those about whom little is known.[42] So it is with lawyers. Especially with the rise of radio and television, some great lawyers are good writers and inveterate self-promoters; others are fortunate enough to have argued notorious cases or to have caught the interest of biographers for other reasons. I have generally assumed that lawyers who are the subjects of book-length biographies (many of which I have discovered and purchased during the course of editing this book through sales sites on the Internet) are more likely to have been influential than those who are not so extensively written about—this is one reason I have included an essay on Earl Rogers, even though he was not recommended on the surveys that I sent to scholars. Still, there are undoubtedly many relatively unknown greats (especially those who did not live in large cities where their reputations might have been better known)[43] whose papers may have been destroyed or who have yet to catch the attention of biographers and who have accordingly been missed in this volume.

I compiled a preliminary list of nearly ninety lawyer-litigators, including one or two individuals such as Elbridge Gerry and George Mason who I later discovered were not attorneys. I grouped these attorneys into three periods of American history (colonial and Revolutionary, nineteenth century, and twentieth century) and mailed surveys to more than one hundred individuals. Most were other political scientists, but some were legal historians or practitioners. Respondents were asked to cross names off the list that they did not think belonged and to suggest the names of individuals who were not listed who should be. In hopes of ensuring that I did not miss key lawyers, I also requested that respondents list the twenty-five American attorneys who they thought to be most worthy of inclusion.

Most scholars who responded to the survey also decided to check the names of lawyers whom they apparently recognized and thought should be included. Many respondents, however, simply commended me for my work on the list and indicated their own inability to rank more than a dozen or so lawyers (indeed, such responses suggest that knowledge of great lawyers is not a subject in which there is widespread current scholarly knowledge). At times, respondents included helpful comments. For example, one respondent noted that Justice William O. Douglas had once referred to Robert Jackson (with whom Douglas was not on a particularly friendly basis) as one of the greatest advocates before the U.S. Supreme Court. Another respondent for whom I have great respect questioned what he considered to be the inflated lawyerly reputation of a president, who has nonetheless been included in this volume. Still others questioned the lawyerly skills of individuals such as Roy Cohn and Richard Nixon, whom I had included on the original list but have not dealt with at length in this book. Altogether, nearly one hundred additional names were suggested that were not on my original list, although many received only a single nomination or two.

I have largely worked through this list looking for eligible entries by reading short biographies in the *American National Biography*[44] or other standard general reference works, with a special eye to the individual's courtroom reputation. Although I eliminated most of these individuals on the basis that they were not primarily known for their litigation work (I have covered some of these in shorter sidebars that I have included in this book), in some cases some valuable additions were made. Some individuals have been included in this book largely because of the advocacy of their inclusion by a scholar particularly interested in writing their entry. I believed that such persistence and willingness to write was sometimes a barometer of the strength of such sentiment.

A number of scholars reacted negatively to the suggestion that they rank the top twenty-five lawyers. One even wrote "silly" in response to this part of the survey. Such responses undoubtedly registered a healthy skepticism about the objectivity of such rankings. For what it is worth (and this may be a better indicator of name recognition than of true greatness), the attorney who received the highest number of rankings was Thurgood Marshall (whose ranking, although not unexpected, may reflect a greater knowledge among contemporaries), with Clarence Darrow, Daniel Webster, and Louis Brandeis close behind, followed by F. Lee Bailey, Edward Bennett Williams, James Otis, and John Davis. Other attorneys receiving more than three nominations for the top twenty-five included (in alphabetical order) John Adams, Melvin Belli, Henry Clay, Archibald Cox, Morris Dees, Alan Dershowitz, William Evarts, Davis Dudley Field, Percy Foreman, Abe Fortas, Ruth Bader Ginsburg, Jack Greenberg, Andrew Hamilton, Charles Houston, Robert Jackson, Leon Jaworski, William Kunstler, Abraham Lincoln, Louis Nizer, Edmund Randolph, Laurence Tribe, William Wirt, and George Wythe.

Among scholars who responded to the survey and included their names were Henry J. Abraham of the University of Virginia; Stanley Brubaker of Colgate University; Cornell Clayton of Washington State University; Brannon Denning of Southern Illinois University School of Law; James W. Ely Jr. of Vanderbilt University; Leslie Goldstein of the University of Delaware; Richard Glenn of Millersville University; Ken Gormley of the Duquesne University School of Law; Kermit Hall of North Carolina State University; Peter Handwork of Toledo, Ohio; Kenneth Holland of the University of Memphis; Harold Hyman of Rice University; Ronald Kahn of Oberlin College; David J. Langum of the Cumberland University School of Law; Anthony Lewis of the *New York Times*; Christopher N. May of the Loyola Law School in Los Angeles, California; Bruce Murphy of Lafayette College; Walter Murphy, retired from Princeton University; David Neubauer of the University of New Orleans; Stuart Nagel of the Dirksen-Stevenson Institute; Roger K. Newman of New York University; Mark Pohlmann of Rhodes College; Jack Rakove of Stanford University; John Reid of New York University; Don Roper of SUNY College at New Paltz; John Scheb of the University of Tennessee; Donald Grier Stephenson Jr. of Franklin & Marshall College; and Clyde E. Willis of Middle Tennessee State University.

I have consulted with many of the authors of essays in this book on a more informal basis. I have sought counsel from many others, especially my supportive colleagues in the Political Science, History, and Criminal Justice Administration Departments at Middle Tennessee State University, where I teach, and from colleagues in a wide variety of disciplines whom I see fairly regularly on the undergraduate mock trial circuit. In addition, I received numerous responses to my survey by e-mail, not all of which I recorded. The help I have received from the Middle Tennessee State University library, and particularly the interlibrary loan department (especially Karin Hallett and Rhonda Armstrong), has been indispensable to the writing of this book. An article published by, and correspondence received from, Professor Jerry Uelmen at Santa Clara University School of Law has been useful in focusing on some attorneys with whom I was not familiar.

Ultimately, of course, the decision about which lawyers to include or exclude in this volume is mine and mine alone. I am not including the names of those whom I have consulted as a way of sharing blame but as a way of indicating that, although my selection has not been particularly scientific, I have tried to ensure that the selection was not simply arbitrary. I have also included shorter essays or anecdotes about individuals who have distinguished themselves in one or another area of the law but who have not been included among the hundred who are given fuller treatment in this volume.

More than fifty scholars and practitioners, who are identified and whose credentials are described elsewhere in this volume, have contributed essays to this book. Their interest in and dedication to this project has been a factor that continues to make me believe that this project is a worthy one. In most cases, authors have responsibly met deadlines and have responded positively to my suggestions. Although I provided no template, each writer was asked to include basic biographical information, including positions that lawyers may have held, while keeping the focus as much as possible on a lawyer's litigation skills. As one who has written about eighteen full essays for this volume, including essays of lawyers from each of the last three centuries, I have increasingly recognized that such information is not always easily accessible, and I have been humbled by the dedication that so many of the essayists have shown and I wish to thank each for his or her efforts.

I also wish to thank my friends at ABC-CLIO for suggesting this project and for helping me with it. Special thanks go to Alicia Merritt, Allan Sutton, Michelle Trader, and Liz Kincaid.

Some may question whether someone who is not a lawyer should edit a book like this. Ultimately, others will have to decide whether I have been adequate for the task. It is my hope that my training as a political scientist, my role as an undergraduate pre-law advisor and mock trial coach, and my personal friendships with a number of lawyers have given me both sufficient knowledge of and distance from the subject. That being said, although I have now taught U.S. constitutional law and courses on the judicial process and advised students interested in attending law school for more than twenty years, this book has helped me to realize how little I, and apparently many of my colleagues, actually know about many of the most influential of the legal profession. Like those in other professions, lawyers surely recognize both that fame can be a noble spur to ambition and greatness and that recognition can be ephemeral.

I sincerely hope that this volume will be one way of directing renewed focus on those who have distinguished themselves as litigators and of rekindling serious thought about those qualities that make for a great lawyer. Although this book is intended to be primarily informational, I hope that it will also serve as a source of inspiration for those who are practicing or considering the practice of law and who view the legal profession and its study not simply as a job but as a calling. I enjoy humor too much to stop swapping lawyer jokes, but, contrary to what such jokes may often suggest, I am even more sincerely convinced after editing this book than before that the terms "great lawyers" and "great men (and women)" are not contradictory. Our republic and its citizens owe much to those who have served through our history as legal advocates, and I hope that this book is a worthy tribute to them.

—*John R. Vile*
Middle Tennessee State University

Notes

1. In "What the Public Dislikes about Congress," John R. Hibbing and Elizabeth Theiss-Morse thus note that "the truth is people disapprove of members of Congress as a *collectivity* while approving of Congress as an *institution*, just as they disapprove of the leaders of Congress while approving of their own members." Lawrence C. Dodd and Bruce L. Oppenheimer, *Congress Reconsidered*, 6th ed. (Washington: Congressional Quarterly, 1996), p. 62.

2. See Michael Kammen, *A Machine That Would Go of Itself: The Constitution in American Culture* (New York: Alfred A. Knopf, 1987).

3. This is probably not a new phenomenon. George Wharton Pepper noted both that "lawyers as a class have always been unpopular" and that "as individuals lawyers are as much trusted by their clients as are any other men I know." *Philadelphia Lawyer: An Autobiography* (Philadelphia: J. B. Lippincott, 1944), p. 341.

4. Michael Dorman, *King of the Courtroom: Percy Foreman for the Defense* (New York: Delacorte Press, 1969).

5. A student of the subject notes that Greek citizens were required to defend themselves in court. Although they could get advice from professional rhetoricians, laws prohibited payment for such services. See Robert J. Bonner, *Lawyers and Litigants in Ancient Athens: The Genesis of the Legal Profession* (1927; reprint, New York: Benjamin Blom, 1969), p. v.

6. See Robert N. Wilkin, *Eternal Lawyer: A Legal Biography of Cicero* (New York: Macmillan, 1947).

7. Henry Roscoe, *Lives of Eminent British Lawyers* (London: Longman, 1830).

8. For the influence of these cases, see Robert S. Peck, *The Bill of Rights & the Politics of Interpretation* (St. Paul: West, 1992), pp. 85–87 and pp. 117–120.

9. See Edward S. Corwin, *The "Higher Law" Background of American Constitutional Law* (Ithaca, N.Y.: Cornell University Press, 1965).

10. Charles Warren describes this time as a time of "law without lawyers." Warren notes that a number of colonies actually prohibited lawyers from representing individuals in court for a fee. See *A History of the American Bar* (New York: Howard Fertig, 1966), pp. 3–18.

11. See James Alexander, *A Brief Narrative of the Case and Trial of John Peter Zenger*, ed. Stanley Katz (Cambridge: Belknap Press, 1963).

12. In *The Federalist*, no. 78, Hamilton observed that "there can be but few men in the society who will have sufficient skill in the laws to qualify them for the stations of judges. And making the proper deductions for the ordinary depravity of human nature, the number must be still smaller of those who unite the requisite integrity with the requisite knowledge." See *The Federalist*, ed. Paul Leicester Ford (New York: Henry Holt, 1989), p. 526.

13. Quoted in Roger H. Davidson and Walter J. Oleszek, *Congress and Its Members*, 6th ed. (Washington: Congressional Quarterly Press, 1998), p. 120. Davidson and Oleszek note that 225 members of the 105th Congress were lawyers.

14. Mary Ann Glendon notes that twenty-three of the nation's forty-one presidents have been attorneys. See *A Nation under Lawyers* (New York: Farrar, Straus & Giroux, 1994), p. 12.

15. Alexis de Tocqueville, *Democracy in America*, trans. George Lawrence, ed. J. P. Mayer (Garden City, N.Y.: Doubleday, 1969), pp. 267–269.

16. For a similar observation, see Morton J. Frisch and Richard G. Stevens, eds., *The Political Thought of American Statesmen: Selected Writings and Speeches* (Itasca, Ill.: F. E. Peacock, 1973), pp. 1–2.

17. One scholar who has successfully emphasized the links between American political and legal thought is Alpheus T. Mason. See his *Free Government in the Making: Readings in American Political Thought*, 3rd ed. (New York: Oxford University Press, 1965). Also see Bernard Schwartz, *Main Currents in American Legal Thought* (Durham, N.C.: Carolina Academic Press, 1993), and, more recently, Allen C. Guelzo, *Abraham Lincoln: Redeemer President* (Grand Rapids, Mich.: William B. Eerdmans, 1999), pp. 21–25.

18. Cited in Benjamin R. Twiss, *Lawyers and the Constitution: How Laissez Faire Came to the Supreme Court* (New York: Russell & Russell, 1962), p. 149.

19. Alfred Salem Niles, "William Pinkney," in *Great American Lawyers*, ed. William Draper Lewis (Philadelphia: John C. Winston, 1907), vol. 2, p. 178.

20. Milton C. Cummings Jr. and David Wise, *Democracy under Pressure*, 8th ed. (Fort Worth: Harcourt Brace College Publishers, 1997), p. 262.

21. Thus, although he is not listed among the top one hundred attorneys in this book, Bernard Schwartz lists Thomas Jefferson among the top ten practitioners. See *A Book of Legal Lists* (New York: Oxford University Press, 1997). This author's judgment was based in large part on the fact that Jefferson spent most of his life in politics rather than in the practice of law. In assessing the greatness of Supreme Court justices, William G. Ross, in "The Ratings Game: Factors That Influence Judicial Reputation," points to what he calls "Longevity of Tenure: The Geriatric

Factor" at 411–414 *of Marquette Law Review* (Winter 1996), 79: 401–452. For other studies focusing on the difficulty of rating presidents and justices, see William D. Pederson and Ann M. McLaurin, *The Rating Game in American Politics: An Interdisciplinary Approach* (New York: Irvington, 1987), and William D. Pederson and Norman W. Provizer, eds., *Great Justices of the U.S. Supreme Court: Ratings and Case Studies* (New York: Peter Lang, 1993). The Cultural Center at Hofstra University in Hempstead, New York, sponsored a symposium entitled "The Leadership Difference: Rating the Presidents" on October 11, 2000. For a book helpful in demonstrating how difficult it is even to rank a single justice, see Richard A. Posner, *Cardozo: A Study in Reputation* (Chicago: The University of Chicago Press, 1990). Since I conducted my own surveys attempting to define the top one hundred lawyers, Professor Gerald F. Uelmen has published an extremely useful article entitled "Who Is the Lawyer of the Century?" in the *Loyola of Los Angeles Law Review* (January 2000), 33:613–653. Uelmen, who believes there should be a "Lawyer's Hall of Fame," listed five criteria in attempting to choose the "lawyer of the century." These were: "(1) professional reputation; (2) participation in high-profile trials, especially those ranked as 'trials of the century'; (3) public recognition; (4) current accessibility of information about the individual's career and accomplishments; and (5) adherence to ethical standards" (p. 615). Uelmen focused on twentieth-century defense lawyers in criminal cases, thus excluding from consideration many of the lawyers included in this book. In seeking to identify the greatest lawyer of the twentieth century, Uelmen surveyed three groups, all in California and Arizona. When surveying twenty-five lawyers attending the annual Bryan Scheckmeister Death Penalty College in August 1999 for their top five choices, Uelmen got the following results: Clarence Darrow (19); Thurgood Marshall (10); Steve Bright (7); Gerry Spence (6); Millard Farmer (5); Michael Tigar (5); Johnnie Cochran (4); Earl Rogers (3); Edward Bennett Williams (3); and William Kunstler (3) (see Uelmen, p. 618). Twenty-two respondents from lawyers attending a convention of Arizona Attorneys for Criminal Justice meeting in September 1999 made the following choices: Clarence Darrow (19); Gerry Spence (17); William Kunstler (10); Thurgood Marshall (9); F. Lee Bailey (7); Michael Tigar (5); Alan Dershowitz (4); Leslie Abramson (3); and Johnnie Cochran (3). Twenty-five students in Uelmen's classes came up with the following rankings: Clarence Darrow (13); Johnnie Cochran (10); F. Lee Bailey (9); Alan Dershowitz (8); Gerry Spence (5); Thurgood Marshall (3); Barry Scheck (3); William Kunstler (2); Leslie Abramson (2); and Melvin Belli (1) (Uelmen, p. 618). Uelmen also surveyed contemporary lawyers who might be considered contenders for lawyers of the century, asking them to pick someone other than themselves for such a designation. Leslie Abramson picked Earl Rogers; F. Lee Bailey and Alan Dershowitz chose Edward Bennett Williams; Johnnie Cochran chose Thurgood Marshall; and Gerry Spence and Michael Tigar picked Clarence Darrow. Uelmen believes that Clarence Darrow was the greatest American defense attorney of the twentieth century. Professor Jonathan Turley has tried his hand at identifying the top four trial attorneys of the century in "The Trial Lawyers of the Century," *The Recorder* (December 15, 1999): 4. He lists

F. Lee Bailey, Delphin Delmas, Samuel Leibowitz, and Clarence Darrow. Like Uelmen, Turley believes that Darrow was the greatest of these.

22. Clara N. Carson, *The Lawyers Statistical Report: The U.S. Legal Profession in 1995* (Chicago: American Bar Foundation, 1999), p. 1. A book entitled *The Best Lawyers in America, 1999–2000*, ed. Steven Naifeh and Gregory White Smith, now the eighth in a series (Aiken, S.C.: Woodward-White, 1999), lists thousands of "best lawyers" by state and specialty, apparently based on surveys sent to the more than 14,000 attorneys listed in the previous edition (see p. vii). Entries are limited to names, firms, and addresses.

23. Arguably, good lawyers also know when *not* to go to court. Elihu Root reportedly once said that "about half the practice of a decent lawyer consists in telling would-be clients that they are damned fools and should stop." Quoted in Sol Linowitz with Martin Mayer, *The Betrayed Profession: Lawyering at the End of the Twentieth Century* (New York: Scribner, 1994), p. 4. Similarly, Lincoln advised, "Persuade your neighbors to compromise whenever you can," and once offered not to charge a client if the client agreed to settle his case out of court. See Guelzo, *Abraham Lincoln: Redeemer President*, p. 164.

24. Eugene C. Gerhard, *Arthur T. Vanderbilt: The Compleat Counsellor* (Albany, N.Y.: Q Corporation, 1980).

25. Glendon, *A Nation under Lawyers*, p. 40.

26. *Ibid.*, p. 262.

27. Turley, "The Trial Lawyers of the Century," p. 4.

28. Interestingly, Harvard law professor Alan Dershowitz, who specializes in appellate advocacy, considers himself "a lawyer of last resort." See Dershowitz's *The Best Defense* (New York: Random House, 1982), p. xv.

29. American law does not distinguish between those who do routine legal work advising clients and drawing up documents and those who appear in court (and especially higher courts) on behalf of clients, but in England these tasks are roughly divided between two different groups of lawyers, the solicitors and the barristers. For this distinction, see Henry J. Abraham, *The Judicial Process*, 7th ed. (New York: Oxford University Press, 1998), pp. 91–94. Also see J. H. Baker, *An Introduction to English Legal History*, 2nd ed. (London: Butterworths, 1979), pp. 140–142. Fans of John Mortimer's "Rumpole of the Bailey" stories (some of which have been faithfully produced for television) will recognize that Rumpole, notorious husband of "she who must be obeyed," is an English barrister, who regularly appears, as befits the more formal English setting, in court wearing a white wig. Rumpole was the creation of John Mortimer, a successful English author and barrister born in 1923.

30. See J. Clay Smith Jr., *Emancipation: The Making of the Black Lawyer, 1844–1944* (Philadelphia: University of Pennsylvania Press, 1993); J. Clay Smith Jr., ed., *Rebels in Law: Voices in History of Black Women Lawyers* (Ann Arbor: University of Michigan Press, 2000); Virginia G. Drachman, *Sisters in Law: Women Lawyers in Modern American History* (Cambridge: Harvard University Press, 1988); Geraldine R. Segal, *Blacks in the Law: Philadelphia and the Nation* (Philadelphia: University of Pennsylvania Press, 1983); and Karen B. Morrello, *The Invisible Bar:*

The Woman Lawyer in America: 1638 to the Present (New York: Random House, 1986). More generally, see Linda K. Kerber, *No Constitutional Right to Be Ladies: Women and the Obligations of Citizenship* (New York: Hill and Wang, 1998).

31. The American Bar Foundation reports that the number of women lawyers has increased from 5,540, or 3 percent of the total, in 1951 (the first year in which it apparently began its surveys) to 202,308, or 24 percent of the total, in 1995. See Carson, *The Lawyers Statistical Report*, p. 4. The study does not address the number of racial minorities who are lawyers.

32. In "The Ratings Game," Ross describes the problems of assessment in terms of "Proximity in Time: The Myopia Factor" at 420–423 and "Ideology: The Political Correctness Factor," at 405–411.

33. Uelmen, "Who is the Lawyer of the Century?" cites "adherence to ethical standards" as a key measure of attorneys (pp. 633–642). Uelmen does note that ethical standards for attorneys have changed, and he defends Darrow's role as the premier twentieth-century attorney despite what he believes to have been his ethical lapses.

34. Uelmen's "Who is the Lawyer of the Century?" devotes considerable attention to what he describes as "participation in high-profile trials," identifying in an appendix to his article thirty-seven trials that have been identified as "trials of the century."

35. Robert M. Ireland, *The Legal Career of William Pinkney 1764–1822* (New York: Garland, 1986), pp. 182–183. John Marshall and Joseph Story, also treated in this book, were justices in this case.

36. These books are too numerous to mention here. One outstanding example of such a book is Edward J. Larson's *Summer for the Gods: The Scopes Trial and America's Continuing Debate over Science and Religion* (New York: Basic Books, 1997).

37. These include Bryandt Aymar and Edward Sagarin, *A Pictorial History of the World's Great Trials from Socrates to Eichman* (New York: Bonanza Books, 1967), which, despite its title, includes far more than pictures; Edward W. Knappman, ed., *Great American Trials: From Salem Witchcraft to Rodney King* (Detroit: Visible Ink Press, 1994); Robert D. Marcus and Anthony Marcus, *On Trial: American History through Court Proceedings and Hearings*, 2 vols. (St. James, N.Y.: Brandywine Press, 1998); John W. Johnson, *Historic U.S. Court Cases 1690–1990: An Encyclopedia* (New York: Garland, 1972); John A. Garraty, ed., *Quarrels That Have Shaped the Constitution*, rev. ed. (New York: Harper & Row, 1987); R. Cornelius Raby, *Fifty Famous Trials* (Washington: Washington Laws, 1937); Stories of *Great Crimes & Trials from American Heritage Magazine* (New York: McGraw-Hill, 1973); Michael R. Belknap, ed., *American Political Trials* (Westport, Conn.: Greenwood Press, 1981); and Fred W. Friendly and Martha J. H. Elliott, *The Constitution, That Delicate Balance: Landmark Cases That Shaped the Constitution* (New York: Random House, 1984). Also see the scholarly series published by the University Press of Kansas entitled *Landmark Law Cases & American Society*. I have also drawn from a number of constitutional histories, including Melvin I. Urofsky, *A March of Liberty: A Constitutional History of the United States* (New York: Alfred A. Knopf, 1988), and

Alfred H. Kelly, Winfred A. Harbison, and Herman Belz, *The American Constitution: Its Origins and Developments*, 7th ed., 2 vols. (New York: W. W. Norton, 1991).

38. The most comprehensive of these is an eight-volume work, edited by William Draper Lewis, entitled *Great American Lawyers* (Philadelphia: John C. Winston, 1907). Also see Gilbert J. Clark, *Life Sketches of Eminent Lawyers, American, English and Canadian to Which Is Added Thoughts, Facts and Facetiae* (Kansas City, Mo: Lawyer's International, 1895; reprint, Littleton, Colo.: Fred B. Rothman, 1963); and Henry W. Scott, *Distinguished American Lawyers with Their Struggles and Triumphs in the Forum* (New York: Charles L. Webster, 1891). In a related vein, see William L. Snyder, *Great Speeches of Great Lawyers* (New York: Baker, Voorhis, 1892). For another volume that appears to reflect the nineteenth-century attitude toward great men and includes, but is not limited to, lawyers, see George Cary Eggleston, *The American Immortals: The Record of Men Who, by Their Achievements in Statecraft, War, Science, Literature, Art, Law and Commerce, Have Created the American Republic and Whose Names Are Inscribed in the Hall-of-Fame* (New York: Putnam, 1901). For a book that also includes English greats, see Hamilton W. Mabie, *The Portrait Gallery of Eminent Lawyers* (New York: Shea & Jenner, 1880).

39. See, for example, Marian Calabro, *Great Courtroom Lawyers: Fighting the Cases That Made History* (New York: Facts on File, 1996); Phyllis Raybin Emert, *Top Lawyers and Their Famous Cases* (Minneapolis: Oliver Press, 1996); Daniel J. Kornstein, *Thinking under Fire: Great Courtroom Lawyers and Their Impact on American History* (New York: Dodd, Mead, 1987); Mark Litwak, *Courtroom Crusaders: American Lawyers Who Refuse to Fit the Mold* (New York: William Morrow, 1989); Emily Couric, *The Trial Lawyers, The Nation's Top Litigators Tell How They Win* (New York: St. Martin's Press, 1988); Peter Irons, *The New Deal Lawyers* (Princeton: Princeton University Press, 1993); and Norman Sheresky, *On Trial: Masters of the Courtroom* (New York: Viking Press, 1977). One more ambitious modern volume is Darien A. McWhirter's, *The Legal 100: A Ranking of the Individuals Who Have Most Influenced the Law* (Secaucus, N.J.: Carol, 1998). This volume, which picks out one hundred individuals who have influenced the law in the United States, is not limited to Americans, to litigators, or to lawyers, although it obviously includes some of each. The individual ranked as having the greatest influence on Anglo-American law is nonlawyer James Madison. Others, by order, in the top ten are Alexander Hamilton, John Marshall, Cicero, Daniel Webster, Clarence Darrow, William Mansfield, Thomas Erskine, Edward Marshall Hall, and Earl Warren. For a book that prints closing arguments in ten great cases, see Michael S. Lief, H. Mitchell Caldwell, and Benjamin Bycel, *Ladies and Gentlemen of the Jury: Greatest Closing Arguments in Modern Law* (Touchstone Books, 2000).

40. See, for example, Martin Mayer, *The Lawyers* (New York: Harper & Row, 1967); Joseph C. Goulden, *The Million Dollar Lawyers* (New York: Putnam, 1978); and Mark Baker, *D.A.: Prosecutors in Their Own Words* (New York: Simon & Schuster, 1999). On a related theme, see Sam Schrager, *The Trial Lawyer's Art* (Philadelphia: Temple University Press, 1999). For a helpful treatment of all the U.S. Supreme Court justices, see Clare Cushman, ed., *The Supreme Court Justices: Illustrated Biographies, 1789–1993* (Washington: Congressional Quarterly, 1993).

For a book that describes the work of leading U.S. attorneys general, see Nancy V. Baker, *Conflicting Loyalties: Law & Politics in the Attorney General's Office, 1789–1990* (Lawrence: University Press of Kansas, 1992).

41. See, for example, Benjamin R. Twiss, *Lawyers and the Constitution: How Laissez Faire Came to the Supreme Court* (New York: Russell & Russell, 1962); and G. Edward White, "Prominent Lawyers before the Marshall Court," in *The Marshall Court and Cultural Change, 1814–1835* (New York: Oxford University Press, 1991), pp. 201–291. A more general treatment of the law in American history is Kermit L. Hall, *The Magic Mirror: Law in American History* (New York: Oxford University Press, 1989).

42. Ross, "The Ratings Game," pp. 423–430.

43. There are a number of treatments of state and city bars, as well as reminiscences, often by their children, of "country lawyers." See, for example, Charles H. Bell, *The Bench and Bar of New Hampshire* (Boston: Houghton Mifflin, 1894); Deane C. Davis, *Justice in the Mountains: Stories & Tales by a Vermont Country Lawyer* (Shelborne, Vt.: New England Press, 1980); Milton S. Gould, *The Witness Who Spoke with God and Other Tales from the Courthouse* [discusses the New York City Bar] (New York: Viking Press, 1979); Ben Jones, *Sam Jones: Lawyer* (Norman: University of Oklahoma Press, 1947); John Gwathney, *Legends of Virginia Lawyers* (Richmond: Dietz, 1934); Bellamy Partridge, *Country Lawyer* (New York: Grosset & Dunlap, 1939); James Summerville, *Colleagues on the Cumberland: A History of the Nashville Legal Profession* (Dallas: Taylor, 1996); and W. W. Robinson, *Lawyers of Los Angeles* (Los Angeles: Los Angeles Bar Association, 1959).

44. John A. Garraty and Mark C. Carnes, eds., *American National Biography*, 24 vols. (New York: Oxford University Press, 1999). These volumes, with vital personal information and short bibliographic entries after each essay, have proved almost indispensable. Also helpful has been Dumas Malone, ed., *Dictionary of American Biography*, 10 regular and 10 supplemental volumes (New York: Scribner, 1963).

Great American Lawyers

AN ENCYCLOPEDIA

ADAMS, JOHN

(1735–1826)

JOHN ADAMS
Library of Congress

BEFORE HE WAS A HERO OF THE Revolution, or vice-president or president of the fledgling United States, John Adams was a lawyer practicing in the Province of Massachusetts. His political convictions influenced his approach to law, and his experience at the bar in turn shaped the understanding of politics that he brought to his country's service later in life.

The citizens of Massachusetts in Adams's day were independent in spirit, famously knowledgeable about the law, and notoriously litigious (Burke 1993, 225–226). Then perhaps even more than today, court cases sometimes became the medium through which political controversies were acted out. In addition to being deeply involved in the day-to-day legal business of the colony, Adams tried a number of cases through which the colonists and crown carried out their prolonged struggle in the years before the Revolution. But Adams opposed extremism and believed in the right of legal representation for both sides, so he did not always work for the colonists.

John Adams was born on October 19, 1735, in Braintree, Suffolk County, to John Adams, a farmer, deacon, and shoemaker, and Suzanna Adams. His family never intended for him to practice law, a line of work that was barely respectable in those days. Although they were not affluent, the Adamses managed to send John to Harvard College, with the thought of his entering the clergy, as many of Harvard's graduates then did. Adams graduated in 1755, ranking fourteenth in a class of twenty-five. He agonized between the church and the bar, finally rejecting the former because his unorthodox religious convictions might have caused problems for him as a minister. But he resolved to approach the law in a godly way, to make of it a calling worthy of a religious man.

In 1756, Adams entered into his legal studies under an established lawyer named James Putnam. Although he was disappointed in the rather neglectful and indifferent Putnam, Adams learned a great deal during his time with him. He studied not only the texts of British law but also classics such as Cicero and Justinian (Coquillette 1984, 363–366). Another powerful influence was his acquaintance with JAMES OTIS, a brilliant lawyer who would figure in the struggle with the crown before his growing madness led to his withdrawal from public life. Adams was admitted to the bar in 1758, after the rather informal examination of his knowledge and credentials typical of the time.

When Adams entered the bar, the status of law as a "profession" was still rather doubtful. Not only did lawyers typically engage in other types of business in addition to law practice, but much legal work was done by amateurs, whom the sworn lawyers disdainfully called "pettifoggers" (McKirdy 1984, 313–319). The law in the colony was an amalgamation of English legal traditions and modifications made in light of the very different local conditions in America (Billias 1965, xix), and these modifications sometimes became points of contention between crown and colony.

Lawyers alternately delighted in and derided the baroque technicalities that ensnared unlucky litigants. Indeed, one such technicality met Adams on his first foray into practice. Like many a brilliant young lawyer since, Adams had an excellent intellectual grasp of the law but little practical understanding. His first case was *Field v. Lambert*. Luke Lambert's horse had broken into Joseph Field's enclosure, and Field held the horse as security for the resulting damages. Lambert, however, effected a "rescous," retrieving the horse from Field's property—a legally dubious tactic. Field hired Adams to draw a writ for the resulting litigation. Despite his diligence, Adams fell afoul of the arcana of eighteenth-century writ practice, and the case was dismissed. Crestfallen, young Adams feared that the incident would drive away future business (Peabody 1973, 46–50).

He need not have worried. Adams's practice was to grow into the busiest in the colony. Though law partnerships in the modern sense were unknown, he typically would employ two or three law clerks. In addition, the smallness of the bar and the need for frequent travel on circuit brought Adams close to his fellow lawyers (Williamson 1890). He worked in all areas of law, handling cases involving admiralty and real property, contract disputes and criminal defense.

Adams's political philosophy shaped his understanding of legal practice. Like his nearest counterpart across the Atlantic, Edmund Burke, Adams conceived of political society in terms of an opposition of forces out of which a rough harmony could emerge. This led naturally to his belief in governmental structures that balanced competing interests and political passions. It led him as well to a natural affinity for the adversarial legal system, the theory of which, after all, is that through the clash of interested partisans the objective truth will emerge.

Adams's character controlled his courtroom style. Although he was plagued throughout his life by the fear that he was unduly vain, Adams in practice took a positive pride in eschewing success achieved through mere popularity. Brilliant, argumentative, sometimes caustic or even explosive, he preferred to prevail by sheer superiority of intellect. His courtroom style, accordingly, was heavy on legal substance and convincing argument and was rather lighter on the subrational forms of persuasion that were available to those of more pleasing demeanor.

By 1768, Adams was the busiest lawyer in Massachusetts (Wroth and Zobel 1965, 1:lix). That same year, British troops were garrisoned in Boston in response to the unrest provoked by the Townshend Acts. Despite the troops' presence, Boston in the years before the Revolution was largely in control of mobs—as mobs go, relatively disciplined and restrained and not leaderless, but mobs nonetheless. These mobs terrorized those responsible for enforcement and collection of Townshend duties. In addition to this extralegal pressure, the pre-Revolutionary struggle was played out in the civilian courts, where juries typically favored the patriot cause. The life of the British soldier was endlessly frustrating. He faced abuse and provocation from civilians, but he could not act, other than in cases of self-defense, without orders from civilian authorities. And for any offense, real or imagined, he could be hauled before a civilian court to face a jury full of hostile patriots.

Adams was deep in the politicized legal dramas of the day. In May of 1768, the *Liberty* docked at Boston and unloaded Madeira wine. John Hancock—a prominent merchant, political figure, and flamboyant patriot—owned the ship. Rumors were rife that much more wine had come off the ship than the twenty-five "pipes" (large casks) on which duties had been paid. A month later, Thomas Kirk, a "tidesman" or customs inspector, belatedly reported that on his refusal to allow illegal unloading of wine from the *Liberty* when it docked in May, he had been locked on the ship in steerage, from where he had heard the unloading of a large quantity of goods (Wroth and Zobel 1965, 2:174–175).

On this basis an action was commenced that resulted in forfeiture of the vessel. (The physical seizure of the vessel raised a mob that roughed up the responsible officials, broke the windows in their houses, and burned a ship belonging to one of them.) A later action against Hancock and others sought treble damages—three times the value of the illegally imported goods. Jonathan Sewell, who stood to receive a third of the proceeds as informer, brought suit. Here Adams appeared for the defense.

Trial in *Sewell v. Hancock* began in January 1769 and continued for some weeks. The outcome was legally inconclusive but politically significant. In March, Sewell moved to dismiss the case, for reasons that are still unclear. But by then the case had been widely publicized, presented in colonial newspapers as an example of the corruption and oppression of the enforcement of duties by crown officials. The result was a decided turn of public opinion against those officials (Wroth and Zobel 1965, 2:182–184).

Another politically charged case arose from the impressment of seamen. At that time the Royal Navy sometimes practiced a sort of ad hoc draft, boarding commercial vessels and pressing sailors into naval duty on the spot. As with the issue of taxation, Adams's legal practice led him into the center of the controversy.

Henry Panton was a lieutenant on HMS *Rose*, which on April 22, 1769, stopped the *Pitt Packet*, which carried a load of salt. Panton and others boarded the vessel, apparently looking for sailors to press into service. Michael Corbet and some others holed up in the forepeak to escape impressment. When Panton discovered them, a lengthy effort commenced to induce the men to leave the forepeak. They obstreperously refused, threatening violence to anyone who came near. Panton's men began tearing down a bulkhead to get at the sailors. Although accounts varied to some degree, it is clear that in the ensuing hostilities Corbet stabbed Panton in the neck with a harpoon, an injury from which Panton died two hours later (Wroth and Zobel 1965, 2:276–277).

Thomas Hutchinson, later governor of the colony, presided over the sailors' trial for murder. With Adams on the defense was James Otis (Shaw 1976, 62). There was no question the killing had occurred, so the question became one of justification. A crucial legal question was the legality of the impressment itself. If the impressment lacked legal authority, then the sailors were entitled to use deadly force, if necessary, to defend their liberty against what would be no more than an attempted kidnapping in the eyes of the law.

Adams delivered the closing argument, as Otis at that time was not enjoying one of his lucid intervals. Adams had earlier located an old statute banning impressment of American sailors; its continued validity was in doubt, however (Wroth and Zobel 1965, 2:323). Adams argued forcefully based on this statute, accusing the deceased, Panton, of "an open Act of Pyracy" and calling self-defense "not only an unalienable Right but our clearest Duty, by the Law of Nature" (Wroth and Zobel 1965, 2:324, 326). Perhaps to forestall further provocative statements, Hutchinson suddenly adjourned the trial without allowing Adams to continue. Though Adams later pronounced himself "mortified" at this treatment (Shaw 1976, 62), the court ultimately reconvened to render its verdict in favor of his clients.

Adams's most politically charged legal work was still to come, however, in the trials of the soldiers involved in the so-called Boston Massacre (known in Britain as the King Street Riot). This incident does not correspond to patriotic legend in which soldiers fire on a crowd in response to schoolboys throwing snowballs. In fact, the eight soldiers led by Captain Thomas Preston were besieged by a threatening mob calling for their blood. One of the soldiers had been knocked down, and a club had been thrown at them. In addition, patriots had set the church bells ringing to bring more people out to the mob. But the ringing of the bells usually meant that there was a fire, so the call of "fire" resounded in the streets. And members of the mob itself dared the soldiers to "fire." Finally they did, leaving five dead (Zobel 1970, 180–205). Whether Preston had given the order, or the soldiers had mistaken one of the calls of "fire" for an order, or they had fired on their own was to become an issue at trial, as was the question of whether the shootings were in self-defense.

The soldiers were charged with murder before the civilian legal system of Boston. The legal representation in the case was paradoxical. Prosecuting the soldiers was Samuel Quincy, a Tory. For the defense were Adams and Josiah Quincy, patriots. Various motives have been ascribed to explain why Adams took the case. His own account focused on the sacred right of representation in criminal cases. Others have suggested that the patriots, confident that a Boston jury would convict, believed they had the luxury of allowing the defendants the best defense so as to defuse criticism of the fairness of the trials (Zobel 1970, 220–221).

An important pretrial matter concerned a potential conflict of interest between Preston and his men. Preston had not fired a musket; he was accused instead of having given the order to fire. Obviously it was in his interest to deny having given the order. The men, on the other hand, claimed in their defense that they had fired in response to Preston's order. Because of this conflict of interest, if the trial were held today, Adams would have to withdraw from his representation of either Preston or his men. But there was no such rule of legal ethics accepted in Adams's day, and the problem was handled by severing the trials, with Preston's to be held first (Zobel 1970, 242).

Then, as now, jury selection could be at least as important as the trial itself. Boston and surrounding jurisdictions chose jurymen for the Boston courts. With tensions high, this could have odd results—for instance, the attempt to prosecute those responsible for the riot following the seizure of Hancock's *Liberty* was complicated when the town returned as potential jurors men allegedly involved in the riot. In *Rex v. Preston*, the defense managed jury selection beautifully, packing the jury with Tory sympathizers (Wroth and Zobel 1965, 3:19). This, combined with the likelihood of a royal pardon in case of conviction, made Preston's prospects relatively good, provided he could escape lynching, which loomed as a much-discussed possibility for some time.

The trial lasted five days; it was said that it was the first criminal trial in the province to exceed one day. Testimony concerning whether Preston gave the order was sharply conflicting. Some witnesses said they had heard him give the order, but others said they had heard no order, or that the word "fire" came from another man standing behind the soldiers. The witnesses identifying Preston as giving the order apparently misidentified his clothing, raising the possibility that they had mistaken someone else for him. Under eighteenth-century practice, Preston himself could not testify.

In closing argument, Adams echoed his remark in *Corbet* about self-defense, calling it "the primary Canon of the Law of Nature" (Wroth and Zobel 1965, 3:84; see also Zobel 1970, 260–264). He went on to question whether Preston had in fact ordered the soldiers to fire. Without accusing the crown witnesses of perjury, he suggested that their testimony resulted from "mistakes" or from emotions aroused by the events of that night. With his skillful performance and the contradictory state of the evidence, even a truly impartial jury probably would have acquitted (Zobel 1970, 255). As it was, the outcome was in little doubt. Preston went free.

There remained the trials of the soldiers, a more doubtful matter since at least some of them undoubtedly killed civilians. Once again, the defense impaneled a favorable jury. Conflicting testimony marked this trial as it had Preston's, although this time the focus was more on the degree of threat to which the soldiers were subjected. Josiah Quincy wanted to introduce evidence of the townspeople's unruliness in general, independent of the events on King Street, but Adams stopped him—whether he did this because he wanted to prevent bringing the town into odium even if it meant risking his clients' defense, or because he sincerely believed such evidence would harm the defense, is still disputed (see Zobel 1970, 281–282). The defense did manage to have entered into evidence hearsay uttered by one of the victims before his death to the effect that he did not blame the man who had shot him (Zobel 1970, 285–286).

Adams's closing argument began with a quotation from Marquis Beccaria: "If I can but be the instrument of preserving one life, his blessing and tears of transport, shall be sufficient consolation to me, for the contempt of all mankind" (Wroth and Zobel 1965, 3:242). This statement was said to move his listeners deeply. He went on skillfully to comb both the evidence and legal sources (lawyers at that time argued both law and fact to the jury). He saw no justification for euphemistic efforts to avoid calling those on King Street a mob:

> Some call them shavers, some call them genius's. The plain English is, gentlemen, most probably a motley rabble of saucy boys, negroes and molattoes, Irish teagues, and outlandish jack tarrs. And why we should scruple to call such a set of people a mob, I can't conceive, unless the name is too respectable for them. (Wroth and Zobel 1965, 3:266)

He closed by invoking the inexorable majesty of the law, impartial and austere, oblivious to all pleas except those founded on justice (Wroth and Zobel 1965, 3:269–270).

The jury decided that the soldiers had fired too soon, but that the shootings could at most be manslaughter, not murder. The jurymen were confident that two of the soldiers had fired, so they convicted them of manslaughter. Of the other six, apparently one had not fired, but the jurymen were not sure which one. Accordingly they acquitted all six.

Manslaughter technically carried the same penalty as murder: death. But a relic of feudal law, at once humane and barbarous, saved the two convicted soldiers. This was the legal device of "benefit of clergy," by which clergymen could procure a reprieve from punishment for certain offenses, including manslaughter. At the time the doctrine developed, almost the only literate people were clergy, so one proved that one was a member of the clergy by reading a certain Bible verse (Psalm 51:1, known as the "neck verse"). By a legal fiction, in Adams's day a defendant still could prove himself a clergyman simply by reading the verse in court. This loophole had a barbarous side, however: Benefit of clergy could be pleaded only once in a lifetime, and to ensure that the accused could never plead it again he had to be branded on the thumb. This grisly ritual carried out, the two soldiers joined their comrades in freedom (Wohl 1992, 658).

Adams continued to practice law after the Boston Massacre trials, but his practice gradually declined as he spent more time in the struggle with the mother country. His last appearance in court was in 1777, with the war under way, in *Penhallow v. The Lusanna*, a complex matter involving an attempt to seize a ship allegedly trading with the British enemy (Wroth and Zobel 1965, 2:365). While in the courtroom, Adams received word that he, along with Benjamin Franklin, had been appointed commissioner to France.

There followed years of diplomatic work in Europe on behalf of his new country, the vice-presidency, and finally the presidency of the United States. On leaving that office in 1801, Adams's desire to return to the law apparently was thwarted by an imperfection of speech brought on by the loss of his teeth. So although he would live another quarter century, he never returned to the courtroom. Nonetheless, in his political activities and writings, the impress of his legal learning is clearly in evidence.

—*Tim Hurley*

Sources and Suggestions for Further Reading

Adams, John. *Diary and Autobiography*. Edited by L. H. Butterfield. 4 vols. Cambridge: Belknap Press of Harvard University Press, 1961.

Billias, George Athan, ed. *Law and Authority in Colonial America*. Barre, Mass.: Barre Publishers, 1965.

Burke, Edmund. *Pre-Revolutionary Writings*. Edited by Ian Harris. Cambridge: Cambridge University Press, 1993.

Coquillette, Daniel R. "Justinian in Braintree: John Adams, Civilian Learning, and Legal Elitism." In *Law in Colonial Massachusetts 1630–1800*, edited by Daniel R. Coquillette. Boston: Colonial Society of Massachusetts, 1984, 359–418.

McKirdy, Charles R. "Massachusetts Lawyers on the Eve of the American Revolution: The State of the Profession." In *Law in Colonial Massachusetts 1630–1800*, edited by Daniel R. Coquillette. Boston: Colonial Society of Massachusetts, 1984.

Peabody, James Bishop, ed. *John Adams: A Biography in His Own Words*. New York: Newsweek Book Division, 1973.

Reid, John Phillip. "A Lawyer Acquitted: John Adams and the Boston Massacre Trials." *American Journal of Legal History* 18 (1974): 189–207.

Shaw, Peter. *The Character of John Adams*. Chapel Hill: University of North Carolina Press, 1976.

Williamson, Joseph. "The Professional Tours of John Adams in Maine." *Collections and Proceedings of the Maine Historical Society*, 2d ser., 1 (1890): 301–308.

Wohl, Harold B. "The Boston Massacre Trials." In *Historic U.S. Court Cases, 1690–1990: An Encyclopedia*, edited by John W. Johnson. New York: Garland Publishing, 1992.

Wroth, L. Kinvin, and Hiller B. Zobel., eds. *The Legal Papers of John Adams*. 3 vols. Cambridge: Belknap Press of Harvard University Press, 1965.

Zobel, Hiller B. *The Boston Massacre*. New York: W. W. Norton, 1970.

ADAMS, JOHN QUINCY

(1767–1848)

JOHN QUINCY ADAMS
Library of Congress

JOHN QUINCY ADAMS, THE sixth president of the United States, is remembered today more for his contributions as a diplomat, scholar, and antislavery congressman than for his presidency, in which he failed to persuade Congress to accept his nationalistic program of internal improvements. Until the recent revival of interest in the Amistad case, Adams's legal career was also regarded as being of little consequence. Like many other presidents who were lawyers, Adams found the practice of law boring and frustrating and gladly abandoned it for politics. In many ways, however, Adams had a significant career at the bar, for he argued several landmark cases before the U.S. Supreme Court and was one of only two presidents (the other was William Howard Taft) to receive an appointment to the Supreme Court.

After graduating from Harvard College at age twenty with highest honors, Adams studied law in Newburyport, Massachusetts, in the office of Theophilus Parsons, a distinguished attorney who later served as chief justice of the Supreme Judicial Court of Massachusetts. Adams soon found that he had more taste for literature than for law. The tedium of his legal studies and the drudgery of his clerical work for Parsons led him to despair of his ability to master the vast corpus of the law. Suffering from mental depression and exhaustion, Adams withdrew from Parsons's office after several months and continued his legal studies at the home of his parents in Braintree before returning to Parsons's office to resume his work at a more relaxed pace.

Adams commenced his practice in Boston in August 1790, shortly after his admission to the Massachusetts bar. Contrary to Adams's recollection late in life that he had gone to Boston as "a stranger" and "without support of any kind," Adams enjoyed special prestige as the son of the vice-president, and through his family connections he was personally acquainted with many luminaries of the Boston bar. Moreover, Adams set up his office in a house owned by his father and stocked his office shelves with his father's extensive law library. Despite these advantages, Adams was not able to establish a self-supporting practice for at least two years, during which time he accepted an allowance from his parents. During his first sixteen months in practice, Adams collected only twelve fees, amounting to the equivalent of a few thousand dollars. By 1792, when his practice began to burgeon, Adams received sixty-two fees amounting to £77, roughly the equivalent of $30,000 in today's money. His income increased to a healthy £222 in 1793, and he received £170 during his final six months of practice in 1793.

Like most lawyers of his day, Adams had a diverse practice, dispensing business advice to clients, drafting wills, and handling litigation that required the preparation of writs and frequent court appearances. While most of his business involved commercial matters, Adams assisted at least two clients with naturalization proceedings and prepared petitions to Congress for at least two others.

Even after Adams's practice began to prosper, he remained frustrated with the intellectual aridity of the law. He also continued to question his avocation for the law, and his principal passions remained literary and political. Throughout his first four years in Boston, Adams found ample time to indulge these interests. During 1791, he published eleven anonymous essays in the *Columbian Centinel* attacking the French Revolution. During 1793, Adams published in the same newspaper a series of essays defending President Washington's declaration of neutrality in the war between Britain and France and another series denouncing the intrusion of the French ambassador into American politics. Adams also participated in local politics, serving on committees to change the boundaries of Quincy and to effect police reform.

Adams was delighted to escape the tedium of his law practice by accepting Washington's appointment as minister to the Netherlands in May 1794, even though his practice was swelling and he believed that his diplomatic service would ruin his legal career. Adams doubted whether he could re-

Early Women Lawyers

America's first woman lawyer appears to have been Margaret Brent, a wealthy cousin of Lord Baltimore, who arrived in St. Mary's Parish, Maryland, in 1638 and was addressed in court as "Gentleman Margaret Brent" (Morello 1986, 3). Brent was quite active at the bar but was denied a vote in the Maryland assembly on the basis of her sex. Brent handled the estate of Leonard Calvert and is credited with making the unpopular but prudent decision to pay troops out of Lord Baltimore's estate when Calvert's was found to be deficient. Brent moved to Virginia and died in Westmoreland County in 1671 (Morello 1986, 7).

Although some women apparently represented themselves in court and some may have been practicing at the local level, it was not until 1869 that Belle Babb Mansfield, a woman in Mount Pleasant, Iowa, officially passed that state's bar after graduating from Iowa Wesleyan College and becoming an apprentice in her brother's law firm. She subsequently became a college professor and administrator rather than practicing law.

Although she passed the Chicago bar examination, Myra Colby Bradwell subsequently lost her case seeking admission to the Illinois bar, a decision reaffirmed in 1873 by a 7–1 vote of the U.S. Supreme Court. The year before, Alta M. Hutett had become that state's first female lawyer after she and others worked to adopt state legislation permitting women to be lawyers.

In 1876, the U.S. Supreme Court denied Belva Lockwood's admission to the bar of that court, but in 1879 a bill passed Congress allowing for the admission of women. Lockwood subsequently became a strong advocate of women's suffrage. When Lockwood died in 1917, three years before ratification of the Nineteenth Amendment granting women the right to vote, women had been admitted to the bar in all but four states (Morello 1986, 36).

Long after women had begun practicing law, many men continued to argue that the profession was not suitable for women. Although he led many other reform efforts, Clarence Darrow is quoted as having told a group of Chicago women attorneys that

> You can't be shining lights at the bar because you are too kind. You can never be corporation lawyers because you are not cold-blooded. You have not a high grade of intellect. You can never expect to get the fees men get. I doubt if you [can] ever make a living. Of course you can be divorce lawyers. That is a useful field. And there is another field you can have solely for your own. You can't make a living at it, but it's worthwhile and you'll have no competition. That is the free defense of criminals. (Morello 1986, x)

Reference

Morello, Karen Berger. *The Woman Lawyer in America: 1638 to the Present, The Invisible Bar.* New York: Random House, 1986.

sume the mental discipline required by the law after enjoying the glamour of an ambassador's life, and he feared that he would lose his clients and fall hopelessly behind other lawyers of his own age who had continued to apply themselves to their profession.

Although Adams never again regarded the law as his primary occupation, he continued to practice law sporadically almost until the end of his life. After returning to the United States in 1801 after seven years of diplomatic service in the Netherlands and Prussia, Adams resumed the practice of law in Boston. Contrary to his expectations, he was able to establish a moderately lucrative practice at once, partly because U.S. District Court Judge John Davis appointed Adams as commissioner in bankruptcy as a political favor for Davis's appointment to the bench by JOHN ADAMS. Although Adams continued this practice for eight years, until he was named ambassador to Russia in 1809, he spent most of these years immersed in politics and scholarship, serving briefly in the Massachusetts House of Representatives and later in the U.S. Senate from 1803 to 1808 and as professor of rhetoric at Harvard from 1806 to 1809.

During this period, Adams argued several significant cases before the U.S. Supreme Court. In a number of these cases, Adams espoused positions that were consistent with his advocacy of a strong federal government. One of the cases, *Fletcher v. Peck* (1810), was one of the most important in American history because the Court's decision unequivocally established that the Court had the power to invalidate a state statute. The decision also provided the Marshall Court with another opportunity to defend vested property rights. In *Fletcher*, Adams represented a party who had sold land to a buyer who contended that the seller lacked proper title because the seller had bought the land from the state of Georgia pursuant to a statute that the legislature later rescinded because it had been enacted as the result of bribery. Although the Court ruled against the seller because of a technical defect in his pleading, Chief Justice JOHN MARSHALL indicated in remarks from the bench that he favored the substantive arguments made by Adams. The case remained on the docket and was re-argued a year later by JOSEPH STORY after Adams had become ambassador to Russia. The Court declared in its decision that the rescinding statute was unconstitutional because it violated vested property rights and the Constitution's contracts clause, which prohibits any state from impairing any obligation arising under a contract.

In another case, *Hope Insurance Co. v. Boardman* (1809), Adams successfully argued that insureds who sued an insurance corporation in federal court on the basis of diversity of citizenship between the plaintiffs and the corporation did not need to allege the citizenship of the individual members of the corporation. The Court's decision in favor of Adams's position made it much easier for corporations to be sued in federal court, since diversity of citizenship was much more likely to be present if the citizenship of a corporation's members were not considered.

Adams also won another marine insurance case, *Head and Amory v. The Providence Insurance Co.* (1804), in which Adams argued that an agreement to discharge an insurer's obligation was invalid because it was not in writing and was not executed in accordance with the terms of the insurance company's own rules. Adams lost another insurance case, *Church v. Hubbart* (1804), in which the Court found that Adams's client, a cargo insurer, was not relieved of liability for cargo allegedly seized by Portugal because the insurer had failed properly to establish that the cargo had been seized.

While serving as ambassador to Russia in 1809, Adams was, without his knowledge or consent, nominated by President James Madison and confirmed by the Senate for a seat on the U.S. Supreme Court. Learning of the appointment three months later, Adams rejected it on the grounds that he would not be able to return to the United States for another year and that judicial service did not suit his interests or abilities. Adams also feared that his disdain for the common law made him unfit to serve as an American jurist.

After the termination of his service in Russia in 1814, Adams served as commissioner to the peace conference in Ghent in 1814, as ambassador to Great Britain from 1814 to 1817, as James Monroe's secretary of state from 1817 to 1825, and as president from 1825 to 1829. Although Adams's familiarity with legal terminology and concepts were useful to him in all of these occupations, his legal training and experience do not appear to have profoundly influenced his performance in any of these positions. Adams's legal experience probably was most useful to him in helping him to evaluate the qualifications of candidates for federal judgeships during his presidency. Although Adams made a number of appointments to the lower federal courts, his influence on shaping the Supreme Court was negligible. His first nominee, Robert Trimble, died in 1828 after serving only two years. The Senate indefinitely postponed action on Adams's second nominee, John J. Crittenden, whom Adams named to succeed Trimble after Adams's defeat for reelection in 1828.

After leaving the presidency in 1829, Adams does not appear to have considered the possibility of resuming the practice of law. Instead, he served in the House of Representatives from 1831 until his death in 1848. As a representative from Massachusetts, Adams became one of the most vocal and tenacious opponents of slavery in Congress.

Adams's hostility toward slavery led to the most famous episode in his legal career—his successful representation of thirty-nine Africans who sought freedom from Spanish slave traders after mutinying aboard the slave ship *Amistad* in 1839. The Africans revolted during a voyage between ports in the Spanish colony of Cuba and had ordered their Spanish captives to sail back to Africa. The Spaniards secretly steered the *Amistad* toward the United States, where the Africans were jailed in Connecticut while the courts decided whether to free them or return them to Africa or to send them to slavery in Cuba. Although Spanish law permitted slavery but forbade the importation of slaves into Spanish colonies, the Spanish government demanded the return of the Africans to Cuba. The case soon became a cause célèbre that highlighted the growing conflict between abolitionists and proponents of slavery.

After the proslavery administration of MARTIN VAN BUREN decided to appeal to the U.S. Supreme Court a federal circuit court's affirmation of a federal district court's ruling that the Africans had been illegally kidnapped and must be returned to Africa, an abolitionist defense committee persuaded Adams to work with the abolitionist Roger S. Baldwin in representing the Africans before the nation's highest tribunal.

During several days of oral argument in the case during the late winter of 1841, the government argued that international law required the United States to return the Africans to the Spanish authorities because a Spanish-American treaty of 1795 provided for the delivery of one nation's property on presentation of proper proof of ownership. Arguing for the Africans, Baldwin emphasized that the United States could not give extraterritorial force to a foreign slave law and that the Spaniards had failed to present proper evidence in support of their claims.

Following Baldwin's presentation, Adams delivered a highly emotional argument that stretched over most of two days. Adams eloquently denounced slavery in an appeal to principles of natural law and justice as expressed in the Declaration of Independence, and he attempted to demonstrate that Cuba conducted an extensive slave trade in violation of Spanish law. Drawing on his extensive knowledge of treaty law and practice, he tried to demonstrate that slaves could not be included in cargo as property unless they were specifically denominated as property. Adams argued with vehemence that the government's position would undermine the principle of habeas corpus by placing every American at the discretion of executive caprice or tyranny. Adams also argued at length that the Spaniards had improperly interfered in American domestic affairs by trying to persuade Secretary of State John Forsyth to cooperate in returning the Africans to Cuba, and that Forsyth had violated separation of powers principles in conniving with the Spaniards to circumvent the judicial process.

Although Adams's argument naturally incensed advocates of slavery, even some abolitionists believed that it was too histrionic and lacked legal precision. His role in the case underscored his essential impatience with the law and his tendency to evaluate legal issues from a political perspective. His argument's impact on the Court's seven-to-one decision in favor of the Africans is uncertain. Although Joseph Story, who delivered the Court's opinion, praised Adams's argument for its extraordinary power, he remarked that it covered too many extraneous points. Ignoring Adams's sweeping appeals to justice and his contention that the Van Buren administration had unduly interfered in the case, the Court's opinion largely rested on the narrow ground that the government had failed to prove that the Africans were property. Since they were not proved to be slaves, the Court concluded that the 1795 treaty was not applicable.

While Adams's argument in the case may have lacked intellectual precision, Adams did not need to make a careful legalistic presentation, since Baldwin's argument and legal brief already had informed the Court of the salient legal issues. Adams's contribution was to infuse the case with his passion for justice, to appeal to the justices' sense of history and equity, and to lend the weight of his distinguished name to the case. Adams's argument also called widespread public attention to the shame of American slavery and marked the first time that abolitionist themes were espoused before the Supreme Court. Adams's argument in the *Amistad* case was dramatized in a popular film about the case in 1997.

The *Amistad* case marked the end of Adams's career at the bar, although he continued his antislavery activities. An ardent opponent of the "gag rule" by which proponents of slavery attempted to suppress the controversy over slavery by prohibiting any debate about slavery in Congress, Adams finally secured the repeal of the rule in 1844. The clever parliamentary maneuvering by which Adams was able first to evade the rule and later to secure its repeal may owe much to his legal training and experience.

Although Adams's primary vocation was outside the law, his legal career presents a significant example of how political figures who have legal education and experience can use their legal background to advance political causes.

—*William G. Ross*

Sources and Suggestions for Further Reading

Bemis, Samuel Flagg. *John Quincy Adams and the Foundations of American Foreign Policy*. New York: Alfred A. Knopf, 1949.

Bemis, Samuel Flagg. *John Quincy Adams and the Union*. New York: Alfred A. Knopf, 1956.

Nagel, Paul C. *John Quincy Adams: A Public Life, A Private Life*. Cambridge: Harvard University Press, 1997.

Parsons, Lynn Hudson. *John Quincy Adams*. Madison: Madison House, 1988.

Richards, Leonard L. *The Life and Times of Congressman John Quincy Adams*. New York: Oxford University Press, 1986.

Ross, William G. "The Legal Career of John Quincy Adams." *Akron Law Review* 23 (Spring 1990): 415–453.

Russell, Greg. *John Quincy Adams and the Public Virtues of Diplomacy*. Columbia: University of Missouri Press, 1955.

ARNOLD, THURMAN WESLEY

(1891–1969)

DURING HIS VARIED CAREER, Thurman Arnold wore a variety of hats: small-town lawyer, mayor, law school dean, Yale law professor, New Dealer, federal judge, and founder of the Washington, D.C., law firm Arnold, Fortas & Porter (now Arnold & Porter). Although he was known at the time for his witty critiques of existing institutions in *Symbols of Government* (1935) and *The Folklore of Capitalism* (1937), Arnold's lasting legacies are the reinvigoration of antitrust prosecutions as a tool of governmental regulation and his role in the founding of the paradigmatic "inside-the-Beltway" law firm.

THURMAN WESLEY ARNOLD
Bettmann-UPI/Corbis

Beginnings

Thurman Arnold was born in Laramie, Wyoming. In 1911, he received his B.A. from Princeton University, after first spending a year at Wabash College in Indiana. From Princeton, he matriculated at the Harvard Law School, and he received his LL.B. in 1914. Arnold began his legal career in Chicago, but World War I intervened; his National Guard unit was mobilized and he served in France from 1917 to 1919. After the war, Arnold returned to his native Laramie, where he served one term in the Wyoming legislature and also served for a time as mayor of Laramie.

On the recommendation of legendary Harvard Law School dean Roscoe Pound, Arnold was offered the position of dean of West Virginia's law school in 1927. During his three-year tenure at West Virginia, Arnold's prodigious scholarship earned him the notice of Yale Law School dean (and future Second Circuit Court of Appeals judge) Charles Clark, who lured Arnold to Yale in 1930. At the time, Yale was the epicenter of American Legal Realism, the jurisprudential school that sought to replace arid, formalistic conceptions of the law and legal institutions with more "realistic" ones by, for example, demonstrating the gap between what legal rules on paper purported to direct and how courts actually applied those rules to decide cases. Arnold flourished, writing *Symbols of Government* and *The Folklore of Capitalism*, both of which went through several printings.

The New Deal

Shortly after Arnold's arrival at Yale, Franklin Roosevelt won the presidency and attracted hoards of lawyers and law professors to Washington to participate in the creation and administration of the New Deal. Arnold followed suit, and between 1933 and 1938, he divided his time between government and teaching. His first job was helping prominent Legal Realist and sometime Yale law professor Jerome Frank (who, like Charles Clark, went on to serve on the Second Circuit Court of Appeals) in Frank's Agricultural Adjustment Administration. In subsequent assignments, Arnold served as aide to the governor general of the Philippines; as a trial examiner for former Yale professor and future Supreme Court justice William O. Douglas' Securities and Exchange Commission; in the Department of Justice's tax division; and finally as the head of the department's antitrust division. (In the meantime, Yale, weary of constant sabbatical requests from Arnold, announced in 1938 that he had "resigned" [Arnold 1965, 136].)

It was as the head of antitrust prosecutions that Arnold received considerable notoriety. Although he had poked fun at the uses of antitrust law in *Folklore of Capitalism*, during his tenure he quadrupled appropriations and increased personnel nearly fivefold. Arnold is credited with single-handedly reviving antitrust law as a means of regulating industry. During the period of Arnold's service, he instituted antitrust prosecutions against the oil industry, the American Medical Association, the Associated Press, and General Electric. Arnold professed great disappointment, however, in his inability to employ antitrust laws successfully against labor unions (Arnold 1965, 116–119).

From Bench to Bar

In 1943, as a reward for his tireless efforts, President Roosevelt nominated Arnold for a seat on the Court of Appeals for the D.C. Circuit. Arnold wrote some memorable opinions, including one finding that *Esquire* magazine was not "obscene," and thus holding that the postmaster could not refuse to send it through the mails. Nevertheless, finding the life of a judge unsuited to his temperament, Arnold resigned from the bench in 1945.

Arnold returned to private practice and for a short time was in a partnership with a former Department of Justice colleague, Arne Wiprud. After an unsuccessful attempt to secure control of the Pullman Car Company for a client, that partnership dissolved, and Arnold formed a second partnership with ABE FORTAS, another ex-Yale law school professor and future Supreme Court justice. Arnold and Fortas later added Paul Porter, former ambassador to Greece, creating the firm of Arnold, Fortas & Porter.

The new firm of Arnold, Fortas & Porter, though it would become the very model of the "Washington law firm," was distinguished by "its continuous involvement in civil liberties issues" during the 1950s and 1960s (Kearny 1970, 46). Pro bono, the firm defended many government employees whose loyalty was attacked during the period of virulent anti-Communism led by Senator Joseph McCarthy. The firm's principals sometimes endured criticism for taking these cases. According to one story, Paul Porter was accosted by a fellow member of Washington's exclusive Burning Tree golf club, who accused his firm of defending primarily "Communists and homosexuals." Nonplussed, Porter is said to have remarked, "Yes, that's correct. What can we do for you?" (Gressley 1977, 484). Arnold also successfully defended *Playboy* magazine against an obscenity charge in Vermont, irreverently suggesting that the magazine sought only to prove "the mammalian character of American womanhood" (Rostow 1970, 985). Simultaneously, Arnold was known as a skilled corporate lawyer; the firm claimed among its clients Coca-Cola, Pan American Airways, Lever Brothers, Western Union, Sun Oil, and the American Broadcasting Company.

The Lattimore Affair

Arnold's and his firm's reputation for championing unpopular causes was cemented with its representation of Owen Lattimore, an Asia expert critical of Washington's China policy, in an ordeal that for many symbolized the inquisitorial nature of the McCarthy era. In 1950, Lattimore was fingered by Senator McCarthy as a "top" Soviet agent—possibly the head of the ring that included Alger Hiss; McCarthy later backed away from his espionage allegation but contended that Lattimore was the chief architect for the government's Far East policy. Although McCarthy could never produce concrete evidence to back up his claim, Lattimore nevertheless appeared before a Senate committee chaired by Maryland Democrat Millard Tydings to answer McCarthy's charges.

Shortly before appearing before the Tydings Committee, Lattimore's wife secured the services of Arnold, Fortas & Porter to represent her husband. Abe Fortas, occasionally relieved by Arnold, represented Lattimore before the Tydings Committee and, later, the McCarran Committee. Lattimore's first committee appearance went well, and as Lattimore's testimony before the committee (which, in marked contrast to the later McCarran Committee hearings, were fairly restrained, even cordial) concluded, all concerned believed the matter to be closed. The chairman, Senator Tydings, even announced that the senators' examinations of summaries of Lattimore's FBI files found no evidence that Lattimore was a spy or even a communist (Kutler 1982, 192–194).

The invasion of South Korea by the North in 1950, and the subsequent involvement of the Chinese, gave new life to the "Who Lost China" controversy. In 1952, Lattimore was summoned to appear before the Senate's Internal Security Subcommittee, chaired by Nevada Senator Pat McCarran, who was also the chair of the Senate Judiciary Committee. For twelve days, the committee harangued Lattimore, who, though he had counsel present (Fortas and, occasionally, Arnold), was unable to consult with them during questioning. His lawyers were, according to Lattimore's biographer, "treated . . . like dirt" (Newman 1992, 366).

The original charge—that Lattimore was the head of a Soviet espionage ring—was all but forgotten as the McCarran Committee concentrated on catching Lattimore in a misstatement that could later form the basis for a perjury indictment. As Arnold himself described it to former Yale law school dean Robert Maynard Hutchins, "The policy of the McCarran Committee is first to have the witness in secret session, get him to testify to the best of his recollection as to events from five to ten years ago, then bring him on at a public hearing, ask him if he did not so testify at the secret session and then give him some letter to which he has not previously been given access which shows he is wrong." It was all calculated, wrote Arnold, to "give the impression that he is an evasive and untruthful witness" (Kalman 1990, 149–150). After bringing significant public pressure to bear first on Truman's, then on Eisenhower's, attorney general, McCarran convinced the government to prosecute Lattimore for perjury (Arnold 1965, 217; Kutler 1982, 205–206).

Although it was Fortas who had squired Lattimore through his appearances before the committees, once the indictment was handed up, Arnold took over. In his memoirs, Arnold describes Lattimore's indictment as "one of the most curious documents in the history of criminal law" (Arnold 1965, 217). It alleged, among other things, that Lattimore was a "communist sympathizer" and a "follower of the communist line" who had lied to the committee when he testified to the contrary. In addition, wrote Arnold, "there were six other counts of so frivolous a nature that they were later dismissed without going to trial" (Arnold 1965, 217).

Luckily for Lattimore and Arnold, the case was assigned to a federal district court judge named Luther Youngdahl, a former Republican governor from Minnesota, who refused to bow to either government pressure or public opinion. Youngdahl immediately dismissed the count alleging that Lattimore lied about being a "communist sympathizer"; the judge agreed with Arnold that the charge was so vague as to preclude preparation of any defense. The count, the judge wrote, was "so nebulous and indefinite that a jury would have to indulge in speculation in order to arrive at a verdict" (Kutler 1982, 207). Other counts were also dismissed as being similarly vague (Arnold 1965, 218; Kutler 1982, 207). The court of appeals upheld Youngdahl's decision on the first and seventh counts by a vote of 8 to 1 (Kutler 1982, 208); however, the judge was reversed on counts related to Lattimore's testimony about the publication of articles by communists in a journal of which he had been editor (Kutler 1982, 208).

Undeterred, the government sought, and received, a second perjury indictment against Lattimore. Arnold drolly noted later that the difference between the two counts of the second perjury indictment—in which Lattimore was accused of lying about being a "follower of the Communist line" and a "promoter of Communist interests"—"was never clear to me as counsel for the defense" (Arnold 1965, 222). Furthermore, the government filed a motion requesting that Judge Youngdahl recuse himself from the case (Arnold 1965, 218; Kutler 1982, 208). Later, Arnold would excoriate the prosecutor and the attorney general, Herbert Brownell, for this filing. Except for the adverse ruling of the judge in dismissing the first indictment, the prosecution could not point to any action of the judge that evinced bias or prejudice. During arguments regarding the motion, Arnold later recalled that the U.S. attorney "was positively insulting to the Judge; indeed, his argument was not addressed to the Judge, but, rather, to a crowded courtroom with the press present" (Arnold 1965, 224). When he was finished, reports Lattimore's biographer, Arnold rose to deliver an "impassioned defense of the original . . . ruling, and of the court of appeals that had upheld the vital part of it" that "is a model for students of judicial pleading" (Newman 1992, 478).

The government's attempt to intimidate Judge Youngdahl and perhaps replace him with a less independent judge failed. Not only did Youngdahl refuse to step aside, he dismissed the second indictment in January 1955. "To require defendant to go to trial for perjury under charges so formless and obscure as those before the Court," he wrote, "would be unprecedented and would make a sham of the Sixth Amendment and the Federal Rule [of Criminal Procedure] requiring specificity of charges" (Newman 1992, 484). That June, the court of appeals upheld the dismissal on a 4–4 vote. The close vote troubled Arnold, who later wrote: "I have often wondered on what grounds half the judges of the Court of Appeals could have sustained the second indictment, which seems to me even worse than the first. Could it possibly be that the affidavit attacking Judge Youngdahl for ruling against the government made these four judges . . . hesitate?" (Arnold 1965, 226). Lattimore's ordeal—which began with explosive charges of espionage—closed with a whimper as the solicitor general and the attorney general decided not to appeal the decision to the U.S. Supreme Court. Arnold, Fortas & Porter charged Lattimore nothing for its services, even though his defense was estimated to have cost $2.5 million in 1950 dollars (Kutler 1982, 212). Little wonder, then, that Lattimore's biographer dedicated his story to Thurman Arnold, Abe Fortas, and the lawyers of Arnold, Fortas & Porter, as well as to Judge Luther Youngdahl (Newman 1992, v).

"Voltaire and the Cowboy"

Although he considered himself an ardent civil libertarian, Arnold became increasingly disillusioned with the radicalism of the 1960s—even privately resigning from the American Civil Liberties Union over its advocacy, as Arnold saw it, of civil disobedience (Gressley 1977, 476). Late in life, Arnold also publicly defended both President Johnson's policies in Vietnam and his former law partner Abe Fortas, who was eventually forced to resign from the U.S. Supreme Court because of financial improprieties.

After Arnold's death in 1969, remembrances were studded with tributes to his "inner gaiety" (Levi 1970, 983), his intense dislike of "pomp" (Rostow 1970, 985), and his "generosity as a human being," which "prevailed over his sardonic awareness of the importance of stupidity and nonsense in our affairs" (Rostow 1970, 986–987). Despite his trenchant wit and his impatience with affectation, writers noted that he had none of the "meanness" that can make a wit seem boorish and rude (Levi 1970, 984; Rostow 1970, 987). Yale Law School dean Eugene Rostow claimed that Arnold "asked fundamental questions, beyond the reach of more pedestrian professors. And he posed bold solutions for them" (Rostow 1970, 987). That quality, his wit, and the fact that "in gait, cigar and style" Thurman Arnold looked as if he had stepped from a Remington painting (Rostow 1970, 985) are the reasons why a contemporary could describe Arnold's character as a combination of "Voltaire and the cowboy" (Gressley 1977, xiv).

—*Brannon P. Denning*

Arnold, Thurman. *Fair Fights and Foul*. New York: Harcourt, Brace and World, 1965.

Duxbury, Neil. "Some Radicalism About Realism? Thurman Arnold and the Politics of Modern Jurisprudence." *Oxford Journal of Legal Studies* 10 (Spring 1990): 11–41.

Fortas, Abe. "Thurman Arnold and the Theatre of the Law." *Yale Law Journal* 79 (May 1970): 988–1004.

Gressley, Gene M., ed. *Voltaire and the Cowboy: The Letters of Thurman Arnold*. Boulder: Colorado Associated University Press, 1977.

Hawley, Ellis W. "Thurman Wesley Arnold." In *Dictionary of American Biography*, edited by John A. Garraty and Mark C. Carnes. Suppl. 8. New York: Scribner, 1977.

Kalman, Laura. *Abe Fortas: A Biography*. New Haven: Yale University Press, 1990.

Kearny, Edward N. *Thurman Arnold, Social Critic: The Satirical Challenge to Orthodoxy*. Albuquerque: University of New Mexico Press, 1970.

Kutler, Stanley I. *The American Inquisition: Justice and Injustice in the Cold War*. New York: Hill & Wang, 1982.

Levi, Edward H. "Thurman Arnold." *Yale Law Journal* 79 (May 1970): 983–984.

Newman, Robert K. *Owen Lattimore and the "Loss" of China*. Berkeley: University of California Press, 1992.

Rostow, Eugene V. "Thurman Arnold." *Yale Law Journal* 79 (May 1970): 985–987.

BAILEY, F. LEE

(1933–)

F. LEE BAILEY

O. J. Simpson and his defense attorney F. Lee Bailey (left) consult with each other during the Simpson double murder trial in Los Angeles, 30 June 1995. (AP Photo/Reed Saxon, Pool)

DURING HIS FORTY-YEAR legal career, F. Lee Bailey epitomized the role of the criminal defense attorney. Equally lauded and criticized for his brash, aggressive style, Bailey was involved in nearly all of the most noteworthy American criminal cases of the late twentieth century, winning most of them. Because of his preeminent legal skills and mastery of the art of cross-examination, Bailey has contributed numerous stylistic and strategic innovations to the practice of American criminal law. Many of Bailey's innovations—most notably the use of cutting-edge scientific evidence and technology in mounting a defense and the use of the mass media in the hopes of "educating" the general public to develop a sympathetic jury pool for his clients—have become so ingrained in the public's perception of lawyers that few realize that he was the first lawyer to use such tactics. For these reasons, Bailey remains among the most influential, and controversial, American lawyers of the twentieth century.

The eldest of three children, Francis Lee Bailey was born in 1933 in Waltham, Massachusetts, to middle-class parents. His father was a newspaper salesman who was forced to work for the Works Progress Administration during the Great Depression, and his mother ran a nursery school. From a young age, Bailey showed great academic promise, graduating from private school at age sixteen, then attending Harvard with the intention of becoming a writer. Bailey's youth, however, served as a disadvantage at Harvard, and, after two years of mediocre scholastic achievement, he dropped out to enlist in the Navy flight corps.

It was while in the Navy that Bailey, on reading Lloyd Paul Stryker's *The Art of Advocacy*—a book that argued that the defense lawyer was an honorable profession but also a dying species—became interested in practicing law. After joining the Marine Corps, Bailey, without the benefit of either an undergraduate or a law degree, served as a defense counsel in court-martials, participating in more than two hundred cases. At the same time, Bailey taught himself a practical form of criminal law by working as a private investigator for a North Carolina defense attorney named Harvey Hamilton. Hamilton became Bailey's first legal mentor, repeatedly stressing to him the value of courtroom experience over book learning in mastering the skills needed for criminal litigation.

Based on his experience as a military lawyer, Bailey received the equivalent of a bachelor's degree, and in 1957, he enrolled in law school at Boston University. While attending law school, Bailey supported himself by starting his own private investigative service, thus continuing his extra-classroom education in courtroom law. Despite the considerable time demands of his investigative service, Bailey still graduated first in his class at Boston University in 1960. Bailey's dual careers served him well shortly after graduation when he was asked to join the legal defense team of George Edgerly, who was accused of murdering his wife in the sensationalized "torso murder," so named because the victim's head was never found. In that case, Bailey's proficiency from his detective experience with the use of the newly developed polygraph (better known as the lie detector) served him well as he cross-examined the man who administered an incriminating polygraph to Edgerly. Bailey's first cross-examination as a member of the Massachusetts bar established his preeminent credentials in this indispensable legal skill as he forced the test administrator to concede that although the accuracy of the polygraph required that the subject be in perfect health, Edgerly had been tested while still hung over from the previous night's drinking, thus casting doubts on the results of the test. After this auspicious performance, Bailey became a permanent member of Edgerly's legal team, initially supplementing the efforts of lead counsel John Tobin, who was seventy-two years old and hindered by poor health, and later taking over the case. Because of the strength of Bailey's witness examination and summation, Edgerly was found not guilty, leading Bailey to become involved in several more cases dealing with the polygraph. Because of this experience, Bailey advocated that the polygraph become a permanent tool in the U.S. criminal system.

Bailey's profile took on national dimensions when he battled to free from prison Sam Sheppard, a Cleveland osteopath who had been convicted in a sensational trial in 1954 for the murder of his pregnant wife. Sheppard's argument that he had tried to fight off the real murderer, a "bushy-haired intruder," became the basis for the popular television series and movie *The Fugitive*. Years later, DNA testing (a scientific technique that did not exist at the time of the trial) conducted on blood drops preserved from the Sheppard home raised the prospect that this might well have been true, with the murderer being an itinerant window washer who was later convicted of a similar murder (although a jury in a civil trial on this case did not agree).

Shortly after Sheppard's brother Steven brought Bailey onto the case in November 1961, the attorney sought permission to give the defendant a polygraph examination in jail. With no obvious legal avenues for appeal on this issue, Bailey invented a new tactic for defense lawyers by waging a public campaign for Sheppard's lie-detector test with the press on television shows such as the *Mike Douglas Show* and the *Tonight Show*. Although the Ohio Supreme Court refused Bailey's request, the media campaign was effective in renewing public interest in the case.

Bailey then filed a writ of habeas corpus with the U.S. Supreme Court in April 1963, claiming that the judge's inability to control the media and protect the jury from outside influence in Sheppard's trial had prevented him from receiving justice. The Supreme Court's ruling in Sheppard's favor in this case became a legal landmark for the establishment of a fair trial.

Freed from jail, Sheppard faced a second trial in October 1966, with Bailey serving as lead defense counsel. At this trial, Bailey developed and pursued several highly risky strategic maneuvers. Knowing that his client had effectively incriminated himself in more than three days of testimony in the first trial, Bailey chose not to call Sheppard as a witness. Then, relying on his use of cutting-edge technology, he called to the stand an expert in "blood spatter" arrays, arguing that a man of Sheppard's strength could not have left the murder scene as it was found. Finally, Bailey argued that by immediately assuming Sheppard to be the killer, the police missed other obvious suspects, such as a married couple in the neighborhood who were rumored to be having affairs with one or both of the Sheppards. By putting them on trial, rather than Sheppard, Bailey was able to prove enough "reasonable doubt" for the jury to find his client not guilty. At age thirty-three, F. Lee Bailey was universally acknowledged by the American people as the nation's preeminent defense attorney.

In the midst of his five-year struggle to exonerate Sam Sheppard, Bailey was involved in several other high-profile cases. First, he defended those accused of the "Great Plymouth Mail Robbery," the robbery of $1.5 million from a Federal Reserve truck—the largest such robbery of its time—which took place in August 1962 and set off the largest manhunt in the history of New England. Although the money was never found, Bailey protested against the undue harassment of his clients by U.S. postal inspectors assigned to investigate the case. Postal officials tore apart one man's house looking for the stolen money and agreed to pay another of the accused men $100,000 to testify falsely against his cohorts. This case marked the first of many times that Bailey would butt heads with government officials, as he filed several ultimately unsuccessful harassment claims against the postal inspectors. After two of the four defendants had disappeared, in August 1967 the federal government indicted the remaining two suspects just before the expiration of the statute of limitations on the crime. In the trial, Bailey's withering cross-examination persuaded the jury that none of the eyewitness testimony was reliable, and his two clients were cleared of the crime.

During this period, F. Lee Bailey also defended the notorious "Boston Strangler," Albert DeSalvo, who was charged with the rape and murder of eleven women between June 1962 and January 1964 even though there never was any evidence of forced entry into their homes. After meeting De-Salvo in March 1965 through another of his clients, George Nassar, Bailey's defense of the accused murderer was complicated by the fact that he wanted to confess to the crimes in exchange for access to psychiatric help and permission to write a book about his killing spree, with the royalties going to his wife and child. Once more Bailey clashed with government authorities who wanted to charge DeSalvo with first-degree murder and seek the death penalty. After arranging for DeSalvo to be examined by psychiatrists, who concluded that he was a schizophrenic with uncontrollable sexual urges, Bailey arranged for his client to be questioned only to persuade the Massachusetts authorities that he was indeed the killer, but not for the purposes of admitting his statement into a trial. As a result of this agreement, De-Salvo pleaded innocent by reason of insanity in the trial, and the district attorney agreed not to seek the death penalty.

In the trial, which began in January 1967, Bailey argued that DeSalvo's schizophrenia rendered him unable to contain his sexual desires and thus called for a "not guilty" verdict. Despite the testimony of several psychologists who confirmed Bailey's position, prosecutors argued that the kind of skill and forethought that the defendant would have had to use to talk his way into the victims' homes to commit the crimes was evidence of his clear premeditation. In addition, the prosecutors were aided by the archaic standard for determining insanity at the time, the nineteenth-century McNaughten Rule, which claimed that a person could be insane only if he or she did not know the nature or quality of his or her act. With the legal cards stacked against him, DeSalvo was found guilty of the crime and sentenced to life in prison, marking Bailey's first defeat in a major case.

Ralph Nader: Public Interest Lawyer No. 1?

Few lawyers are better known to most contemporary Americans than Ralph Nader. Nader has made his reputation primarily as a consumer advocate and public interest lawyer rather than as a litigator. The son of immigrants from Lebanon who earned an undergraduate degree at Yale and a law degree at Harvard, Nader first came into public prominence with the publication of a book entitled *Unsafe at Any Speed* (1965), which took on the General Motors Corporation for what Nader alleged to be safety lapses in the production of the Corvair. When Nader testified about these defects before a congressional committee, General Motors hired an undercover investigator to threaten Nader and to come up with negative information about him. Nader subsequently was awarded $425,000 for invasion of privacy, money that he used to fund a number of public interest groups.

As his use of his legal settlement funds suggests, Nader is known for his spartan lifestyle, as a speaker recognized for his candor in addressing college students and other groups, and for his fervency in advocating his ideas. Numerous attorneys work in some of the many public interest groups that he has founded and that he oversees, including a litigation group that works under the auspices of Public Citizen. He has run for president as a candidate of the Green Party, advocating environmental and reform issues.

REFERENCE

Litwak, Mark. *Courtroom Crusaders: American Lawyers Who Refuse to Fit the Mold*. New York: William Morrow, 1989.

In terms of his legal ideology in these cases, F. Lee Bailey would be best described as a realist. In his later book, *The Defense Never Rests*, published in 1971, Bailey acknowledged that innocence or guilt has little bearing on the decision that a jury makes in criminal cases. Rather, Bailey believes that the chance that a person accused of a crime has of being acquitted is directly related to the competency of the person's lawyer, which in turn is directly related to the amount of money that the person has to spend on mounting a defense. Another aspect of Bailey's legal ideology is the belief that justice simply means that a person is granted a fair trial, not that absolute innocence or guilt is found. Bailey extends this belief to mean that all persons accused of a crime—no matter how despicable or how certain their guilt— are entitled to adequate legal representation. Consistent with this belief, throughout his career, Bailey unapologetically represented many clients who were accused of heinous crimes with a great presumption of guilt.

After the Boston Strangler case setback, Bailey faced the vengeful wrath of an angry organized bar and government for his defense tactics in the first of several professional condemnations. In 1970, a Massachusetts judge censured Bailey for breaching legal ethics by criticizing the conviction of one of his clients on the *Tonight Show with Johnny Carson*. A year later, Bailey's license to practice law in New Jersey was suspended for one year after he accused a prosecutor of pressuring and attempting to bribe witnesses. Finally, in 1973, Bailey, along with a client, was indicted for mail fraud in Florida, although charges were never brought to trial. After ten years of aggressively challenging governmental authority, it seemed as if the legal establishment was seeking to punish F. Lee Bailey to make him an example of the dangers of such behavior.

In the early 1970s, Bailey took on a series of high-profile legal cases that were demonstrative of the U.S. political environment at the time. In 1971, he defended Captain Ernest Medina in a court-martial over his alleged role in leading troops in the 1968 massacre of civilians at My Lai, an infamous event in the Vietnam War. Here Bailey again effectively used the media during the pretrial stages, persuading the public that the army was putting Medina on trial to create a scapegoat for public relations purposes. During the court-martial at Fort Benning, Georgia, Bailey used positive lie detector results to claim that rather than ordering his troops to kill innocent civilians, Medina was unable to stop the killing when he became aware of it. In September 1971, Medina was acquitted of all charges, a result that Bailey later cited as being among his proudest achievements.

After Medina's trial, Bailey took on a client with political overtones by representing James McCord, the former security chief of President Richard Nixon's reelection campaign, who was one of five men arrested while breaking into the Democratic party headquarters at the Watergate complex in Washington, D.C. Bailey's defense was unsuccessful, as McCord was convicted for burglary and subsequently served nearly a year in prison. After his conviction, McCord spurred the Watergate political investigation by informing Judge John Sirica of the White House's involvement in the burglary in the hopes of reducing his sentence. In 1974, McCord filed a $10 million lawsuit against Bailey, claiming that he had provided inadequate legal counsel at the trial by conspiring with John Mitchell and other White House officials to prevent McCord from disclosing his knowledge of high-level involvement in the burglary at his trial. Eventually, in 1983, Bailey settled McCord's lawsuit out of court for an undisclosed amount of money.

In his third high-profile case in the early 1970s, Bailey once again entered the world of the "trial of the century" by agreeing to defend Patricia Hearst, the heir to the Hearst publishing empire. In 1974, when she was a student at the University of California at Berkeley, Hearst had been abducted by members of a terrorist organization known as the Symbionese Liberation Army and subsequently participated in several bank robberies. Bailey's defense was that Hearst had been brainwashed and participated in the crimes only out of fear for her life. The "brainwashing" defense was considered to be an innovative legal strategy at the time in that Bailey was not claiming insanity for his client, but rather that the weeks of mental torture had rendered Hearst unable effectively to resist her abductors. Once more, Bailey supplemented his legal moves by seeking to persuade the media, and through them public opinion, that his client was the victimized daughter of wealthy parents rather than the transformed "urban guerilla" as the authorities claimed. After Hearst was found guilty of all charges in March 1976, for which she served seven years in jail before being released by President Jimmy Carter, the case ended in legal squabbling between Bailey and his client.

The negative fallout associated with Hearst's conviction seemed to take Bailey out of the public limelight. Younger, slicker lawyers, all following the defense-lawyer model that Bailey had developed in his fifteen-year run of trying high-profile cases, began to come to the forefront. In fact, though, between 1976 and 1994, Bailey maintained a busy legal career, albeit at a much lower profile. Partly due to his interest in aviation stemming from his days as a pilot in the Marine Corps, Bailey made a lucrative living by representing family members of those who perished in commercial plane crashes. Among Bailey's clients were the families of victims of Korean Air flight 007, which was shot down by the Russian military, and Pan Am flight 103, which exploded over Lockerbie, Scotland, as a result of a bomb placed on board by Libyan terrorists.

Bailey also became involved in a series of cases challenging the legal practices of the U.S. government. For example, in 1992, during the drug trial of deposed Panamanian dictator Manuel Noriega, Bailey compared the government's policy of granting immunity to witnesses to bribery, claiming that a former client, drug dealer Gabriel Taboada, lied about Noriega's connection to Colombian drug cartels to get a reduced sentence. Bailey was highly critical of the federal government's decision to seize his fees for defending convicted drug trafficker Mario Lloyd, claiming that the government's policy of seizing lawyer fees was having the effect of pushing better lawyers out of criminal defense. Finally, in 1991, Bailey served as defense counsel in an American Bar Association mock war crimes trial of Saddam Hussein, and he took the opportunity to point out the hypocrisy of U.S. politicians seeking a war crimes indictment for Hussein, considering the U.S. disregard for international law in pursuit of foreign policy objectives. Because of all of his legal successes, in a 1993 poll of its readers the *National Law Journal* found that F. Lee Bailey was the most admired lawyer in the United States.

Just one year later, Bailey was center stage in his third "trial of the century," introducing his unique legal style to a new generation of Americans as part of the "Dream Team" defending ex–football star O. J. Simpson on charges that he murdered his ex-wife and her friend Ronald Goldman. Bailey's main contribution to Simpson's defense was his cross-examination of Los Angeles detective Mark Fuhrman, who had discovered a bloody glove on Simpson's property, the piece of evidence that for many most strongly tied Simpson to the crime. Under Bailey's withering cross-examination, Fuhrman denied that he had ever uttered a particular racial epithet in the previous ten years. Some months later, however, an author who had interviewed Fuhrman came forward with audio tapes of him using that precise epithet, thus discrediting his entire testimony to the mostly African-American jury and leading to Simpson's eventual acquittal. Bailey's involvement in the case was not without cost. In the years that followed, he had a serious falling out with the friend who had brought him into the case, attorney Robert Shapiro, and faced ethics charges in Florida over his management of some government-seized stock in a case involving a French drug trafficker he had been defending, named Claude Duboc. The result was a forty-four-day jail term on a contempt-of-court charge and legal hearings as to whether his license to practice law in the state should be lifted.

These problems notwithstanding, F. Lee Bailey's career has been nothing short of remarkable, making him the virtual prototype of the modern criminal defense lawyer.

—Bruce Murphy and Scott Featherman

Sources and Suggestions for Further Reading

Bailey, F. Lee, and Harvey Aronson. *The Defense Never Rests*. New York: Stein and Day, 1971.

Bailey, F. Lee, with John Greenya. *For the Defense*. New York: Signet, 1975.

Bradlee, Ben, Jr. "The Great Defender." *Boston Globe Magazine*, 25 August 1996, 16.

Linn, Edward. "F. Lee Bailey: Renegade in the Courtroom." *Saturday Evening Post*, 5 November 1966, 80–93.

Silverman, Ira, and Fredric Dannen. "A Complicated Life." *New Yorker*, 22 March 1996, 44–53.

BATES, EDWARD

(1793–1869)

EDWARD BATES
Library of Congress

ABRAHAM LINCOLN'S FIRST attorney general, Edward Bates, born on September 4, 1793, was one of twelve children born to Thomas Fleming Bates, a Virginia planter and merchant, and Caroline Matilda Woodson. Educated by his father and a cousin, Benjamin Bates, Edward Bates attended Charlotte Hall Academy in St. Mary's County, Maryland. In February 1813, he joined a volunteer militia company to assist in protecting Norfolk from a threatened attack by the British. He served until October, rising to the rank of sergeant.

His brother, Frederick Bates, then secretary of Missouri Territory, persuaded Edward to move to Missouri, where he studied law under Rufus Easton, the most prominent lawyer in the territory. Bates was licensed to practice law in 1816 and in 1818 formed a partnership with Joshua Barton, a relationship that lasted until 1823. That same year, Bates married Julia Davenport Coalter. She bore them seventeen children.

Bates was elected to the U.S. House of Representatives in 1826 and completed a single term. Previously, he had served as a member of the State Constitutional Convention in 1820, as state attorney general, and as a member of the state legislature. He was the choice of the Whig Party for the U.S. Senate, but he lost to the followers of Thomas Hart Benton and the Jacksonian Democrats.

After his defeat for a second term in Congress in 1828, Bates resumed his thriving law practice. In 1830, he was elected to the state senate, where he served for four years, and in 1834 he was again elected to the Missouri House of Representatives.

In 1847, as president of the River and Harbor Improvement Convention, which met in Chicago, he delivered an eloquent speech that attracted national attention. Just three years later, Bates's reputation growing, President Millard Fillmore nominated him secretary of state, but for personal reasons Bates declined the appointment.

Nonetheless, by this time his views on social, political, and constitutional questions were frequently sought. In speeches and newspaper articles, he expressed opposition to the repeal of the Missouri Compromise, thereby aligning himself with the "Free Labor" party in Missouri, although he still considered himself a Whig. In 1856, he acted as president of the Whig national convention at its meeting in Baltimore. Simultaneously, he grew close to the newly formed Republican Party after his opposition to the admission of Kansas under the Lecompton Constitution.

In 1860, supporters in Missouri launched a Bates-for-President movement, arguing that a Free-Soil Whig, from a border state, if elected on the Republican ticket, could avert secession. He won early support from many Republicans in the border states, but the decision of the national Republican committee to hold the convention in Chicago instead of St. Louis proved a fatal setback to the Bates boom by adding strength to the candidacy of ABRAHAM LINCOLN. On the first ballot, Bates received only forty-eight votes, and by the time the balloting was over on the third ballot, his number had shrunk to twenty-two, and Lincoln was the nominee.

After the Republican victory that November, the relatively unknown and inexperienced Lincoln decided to offer Bates a cabinet position in deference to the latter's national support. Some urged that Bates be appointed secretary of state, but the president-elect believed that this position was more appropriate for the better-known William H. Seward, who had been his chief rival at the convention. Instead, Bates was offered his choice of any other cabinet position. He wisely opted to become the twenty-sixth attorney general and become the first cabinet officer chosen from west of the Mississippi River.

Although he was regarded as a political conservative, Bates initially exerted considerable influence in the cabinet. He suggested, for example, that the federal navy equip a fleet on the Mississippi River, an idea that proved decisive in the coming civil war. During the *Trent* affair (ignited when the navy seized two Confederate diplomats on the high seas), he sought to avert war with Great Britain, arguing that the question of legal rights should be waived. Later, he differed with Lincoln on the admission of West Virginia to the Union, asserting that such a move would endorse secession by one section of a state, thus validating the whole notion of secession. He declared the movement for separate statehood "a mere abuse, nothing less than attempted secession, hardly veiled under the flimsy forms of law" (*Opinions* 1868, 431–432). But Lincoln ignored this advice.

In response to *Ex parte Merryman* (1861), he defended Lincoln's suspension of the privilege of the writ of habeas corpus on the grounds that the three branches of government were coequal and that Chief Justice Roger B. Taney could not order Lincoln to act. Bates disliked the suspension but thought it preferable to martial law. The Confiscation Acts, applying to the property of rebels, ran counter to Bates's sense of property rights, and his office rarely supported them. Even Lincoln claimed that no slave was ever freed by the Second Confiscation Act.

Bates believed that free blacks could be U.S. citizens because he narrowly construed *Dred Scott v. Sandford* (1857) to apply only to blacks "of African descent" suing in Missouri. He affirmed that every free person born in the United States was "at the moment of birth *prima facie* a citizen." Thus, the attorney general proclaimed the *Dred Scott* decision unconstitutional.

Bates went on strongly to support the Emancipation Proclamation, as long as it remained limited to areas still under rebel control and those freed were colonized or repatriated to Africa. His support was linked to his hope that Lincoln was more likely than Congress to provide for colonization of freed blacks. Bates always opposed policies that might lead to equality of blacks with whites in the United States and particularly disliked the employment of blacks as soldiers. Despite his prejudices, Bates also delivered an opinion to the president that suggested that black soldiers merited equal pay with whites. For a while, Lincoln ignored the opinion.

In May 1864, when the administration learned of the Fort Pillow massacre, in which hundreds of black Union soldiers were slaughtered by Confederates, Bates reminded the president of his early warnings of "the great probability of such horrid results" (*Opinions* 1869, 43). Nevertheless, Bates saw no choice but to order anyone involved in the massacre executed unless the Confederate government disavowed the act and surrendered the commanding officers.

As the "president's lawyer," Bates disagreed with many of the administration's military policies, worrying that as the war progressed constitutional rights were giving way to military authority. Resenting the interference of the secretary of state in matters that he thought belonged to the attorney general's office, Bates repeatedly questioned the actions of Seward, Secretary of War Edwin M. Stanton, and Secretary of the Treasury Salmon P. Chase. He felt that Lincoln lacked the will power to end what Bates considered constitutional abuses by the cabinet departments.

Yet, Bates's conception of the presidency was broad. He thought the president should undertake the big acts of national leadership, while scrupulously avoiding wasted time on small problems. Repeatedly, he urged Lincoln to act as commander in chief of the army, the actual director of events. "The *General-in-Chief* or *Chief General—is your only lieutenant* . . . to command under you," he told Lincoln (Bates 1933, 200). He considered the president the officer who should give general directions and dismiss the unsuccessful and the disobedient. He never doubted Lincoln's character or purposes, but he did voice concern over whether Lincoln demonstrated "the *power to command*" (Bates 1933, 20). This view of presidential authority contrasted sharply with that of Roger B. Taney, a former U.S. attorney general who, as chief justice of the U.S. Supreme Court, evinced growing disloyalty to both the chief executive and the Union.

Bates held a Hamiltonian conception of the presidency, arguing that the president needed to lead the nation energetically. He often advised what Lincoln could do constitutionally, but told the president no more often than yes. This aspect of the relationship between the attorney general and the president was quickly reflected in Bates's first opinion on April 18, 1861. He advised the president that he could not, without legislation, reorganize the War Department to set up a separate division of militia with Lincoln's young friend E. E. Ellsworth in charge. Although he often acted as a naysayer to Lincoln on such minor matters, his opinions upholding the habeas corpus suspension, supporting the naval blockade of the South, and endorsing the Emancipation Proclamation were among the most important issues confronting the administration and represented confirmation of major administration policy. Bates's enduring legacy is primarily based on those opinions. He remained a conservative loyalist to the president and the Union.

During the Bates era, the role of attorney general was not yet considered a major job, even if it was one of the four oldest cabinet positions, dating back to the Washington administration. A department of justice with a professional staff was still ten years in the future. The attorney general possessed a staff of only six, including clerks and messengers. His functions were to deliver opinions requested by the president and department heads and to handle government litigation in the Supreme Court. He had no real authority over the U.S. attorneys; they were responsible only to the president. The pay and perquisites of the judiciary and the government law offices were largely in the hands of the Interior Department. Government claims were for the most part handled by the Treasury.

In these circumstances, no attorney general had made much of the office, in contrast to JOHN MARSHALL's creative behavior on the Supreme Court. Of the famous men who had served as attorney general, few had enhanced their reputation by service in that office. Most attorneys general before Bates have been utterly lost to history. The few great advocates, like REVERDY JOHNSON and JEREMIAH S. BLACK, made a mark, but unlike them, Bates was no courtroom lawyer, and he farmed out most of his Supreme Court work. Yet the attorney general always provided two crucial functions for the president: He was an important political adviser and he could legitimize the actions of the president.

Unfortunately, Bates's legacy was limited by his functionary role and small portfolio within the Lincoln cabinet. He remained something of a minister without a department, and he drifted gradually into disaffection with most of his cabinet colleagues. William Seward, Edwin Stanton, and Postmaster General Montgomery Blair at times seemed outright enemies.

Nonetheless, Bates performed a specialized and occasionally important legal job in the Lincoln administration. His 154 opinions, published in two volumes of the *Opinions of the Attorneys General*, amount to a public diary of his intellectual and professional life. The product is a measure of the man. Although the opinions may be classified in a variety of ways, since the categories overlap, the following table suggests the broad scope of Bates's official work:

Opinions of Attorney General Bates, 1861–1864

Routine administration	77
Claims	30
Scope and general powers of the president	14
Blockade, prize, international	10
Procurement duties	9
Scope of attorney general's office	8
Citizenship and slavery	5
Other	1
Total	154

Like any opinion giver, the attorney general determines his own jurisdiction. Ironically, Bates did not consider himself a court of last resort, since other cabinet members might choose to overrule him. As he told Gideon Welles, when the navy secretary asked for his "decision": "Pardon my criticism of the last word in your letter. You refer the matter for my 'decision.' I beg to state that the Attorney General has no power to *decide* a question of law. He can only give his *opinions,* to aid, as far as he can, the judgment of his coordinate departments" (*Opinions* 1868, 48). Unfortunately, Bates never understood the need to win over other members of the president's administration.

The complex relationship between the president and the attorney general also embraced the issue of mercy. Bates and the president collaborated often on the matter of pardons. Whereas Bates firmly believed that, for political reasons, the president must not pardon convicted slave traders, he and the president frequently found reason to avoid death penalties. In deference to his own leniency in this regard, Lincoln sometimes joked about his "chicken-hearted" attorney general. Bates was a firm, but not a bloodthirsty, man, and his prudent temperament made him a valuable counselor.

Bates finally decided to leave office in November 1864. For a while he was under consideration for appointment as chief justice of the United States, but the president instead chose the more politically astute and politically progressive Salmon P. Chase to succeed Roger B. Taney.

Bates resigned effective November 30, 1864. The president's private secretaries, John Nicolay and John Hay, believed that Lincoln would have retained Bates as attorney general if Bates had not suggested or expressed a desire to resign.

On January 6, 1865, a Radical constitutional convention assembled in St. Louis to draw up a new state constitution for Missouri. It also passed an ordinance emancipating the slaves in an ouster ordinance, which was intended to place the state judiciary in the hands of the Radicals. Back at home, Bates fought the Radicals by publishing a series of newspaper articles in which he pleaded for a government of law instead of a government of force. This struggle against the Missouri Radicals proved to be Edward Bates's final political contest. Soon thereafter, his health began to deteriorate. Bates died on March 25, 1869. The one-time lawyer, politician, and former attorney general ended his public life battling extremists in his adopted state, just as his mentor Abraham Lincoln had fought both Northern and Southern extremists nationally.

—*Frank J. Williams*

SOURCES AND SUGGESTIONS FOR FURTHER READING

Bates, Edward. *The Diary of Edward Bates 1859–1866*. Edited by Howard K. Beale. Vol. 4. Washington: U.S. Government Printing Office, 1933.

Cain, Marvin E. *Lincoln's Attorney General: Edward Bates of Missouri*. Columbia: University of Missouri Press, 1965.

Opinions of the Attorneys General of the United States. Vol. 10, *March 5, 1861 to October 9, 1863*. Washington: U.S. Government Printing Office, 1868.

Opinions of the Attorneys General of the United States. Vol. 11, *November 6, 1863 to July 14, 1866*. Washington: U.S. Government Printing Office, 1869.

Williams, Frank J. "'Institutions Are Not Made, They Grow': Attorney General Bates and Attorney President Lincoln." R. Gerald McMurtry Lecture. Fort Wayne, Indiana: The Lincoln Museum, 2001.

BELLI, MELVIN MOURON, SR.

(1907–1996)

MELVIN MOURON BELLI SR.

Jack Ruby (center), the man who shot Lee Harvey Oswald, confers with his attorneys Marvin Belli (right) and Joe Tonnehill (left) in district court in Dallas, 20 January 1964. (AP Photo)

MELVIN M. BELLI FOREVER changed the landscape of the modern courtroom with the introduction and refinement of many trial techniques. He has been called both "the King of Torts" and "the Father of Demonstrative Evidence." He was a brash and flamboyant maverick who turned accepted notions of corporate and professional liability on their heads. Belli was born on July 29, 1907, in Sonora, California, to Leonie Mouron Belli and Caesar Arthur Belli. His family included early California bankers and educators. His grandfather had been a headmaster at some of California's first schools. Anna Mouron, his grandmother, was an early California pharmacist. His father was a prominent California banker.

Belli attended the University of California at Berkeley and was described as a mediocre student and a carouser. After a short time serving as a seaman, he enrolled at the University of California Boalt School of Law. He graduated from there in 1933, thirteenth in his class. One of his first jobs was to write a report on the Depression's effect on the vagrant population of the United States for the National Recovery Administration of the federal government. He assumed the role of an indigent and traveled by boxcar across the United States. His report was part of the basis for transient relief programs for the nation.

He was admitted to the California bar in 1933. Belli began his legal career as counsel for the Catholic priest of San Quentin prison. He defended death-row inmates, filing appeals for those already condemned to die. He once remarked that the execution of two prisoners wiped out his entire practice. His interest and success in the area of torts began early in his career. In one of his early courtroom victories, he represented Chester Bryant, an injured cable car gripman. In a rare but not unheard of move, and over objections by the defendant insurance company's lawyers, he brought into the courtroom a large model of a cable car intersection and the gearbox and chain involved in the accident. The jurors awarded his client thirty-two thousand dollars, a large verdict for the time.

Belli is remembered for his involvement with a long list of famous clients and important cases. Celebrity clients of Belli's over the years included Mae West, Errol Flynn, Tony Curtis, Martha Mitchell, Lana Turner, Muhammad Ali, Lenny Bruce, Jim and Tammy Faye Baker, Zsa Zsa Gabor, and the Rolling Stones. He represented Jack Ruby in 1954 for the murder of Lee Harvey Oswald. The Korean jetliner disaster, the MGM Grand Hotel fire in Las Vegas, the collapse of the Kansas City Hyatt walkway, the Bendectin birth defect cases, the Bhopal Union Carbide isocyanate gas disaster, the Dow Corning breast implant cases, computer piracy, and cable television rights are among the headline-grabbing cases he became involved with during his career, which spanned six decades.

Melvin M. Belli headed the law firm of Melvin M. Belli, Sr., which operated offices in San Francisco, Los Angeles, Stockton, San Diego, Pacific Grove, Santa Cruz, Santa Ana, and Sacramento, California, and Rockville, Maryland. He was a founder and former president of the Association of Trial Lawyers of America, which served to unite plaintiff's lawyers in a way the American Bar Association never had. In addition, he was the founder and dean of the International Academy of Trial Lawyers, served on the board of directors of the Barrister's Club, and was provost of the Belli Society.

Melvin Belli was a prolific writer and speaker. He authored or coauthored some sixty books, mainly dealing with civil and criminal trial procedure. His five-volume *Modern Trials*, first published in 1954 and later revised, discusses the law, trial techniques, demonstrative evidence, cross-examination, the merits of factual disclosure, the value of just and early settlements, the employment of medicolegal information, and the necessity of a just and proportionate (adequate) award for the dead and injured, among many other topics. It is said to have forever changed the face of the American courtroom and has been called the plaintiff lawyer's bible. Although most of Belli's scholarship deals with techniques for success in the courtroom, he also wrote books about the significant trials in which he was involved, such as three books about the defense of Jack Ruby. As a result of his interest in the legal systems of other countries, he wrote books comparing the legal systems of Japan and Russia to that of the United States. Belli was a popular speaker and is credited with training scores of lawyers, judges, and the public about the evolution of tort law. In his article "The Adequate Award," information from plaintiff's lawyers across the country was used to illustrate the point that tort verdicts were substantially less than cost-of-living indicia. It was the first meaningful study of actual damage awards and their relationship to plaintiffs' lives.

Belli's flamboyant nature found outlets in artistic pursuits other than writing. He played the role of an evil superbeing disguised as "Friendly Angel" in episode 60 of the television program *Star Trek*, "And the Children Shall Lead," which first aired on October 11, 1968. He appeared as himself in the 1968 film *Wild in the Streets*. He lived a life of extravagance and was arguably the most flamboyant lawyer of his generation. His San Francisco office has been described as resembling a bordello more than a lawyer's office, with its heavy Victorian interior and outer walls constructed of glass so that passers-by could glimpse in. When Belli won a case, he would hoist a Jolly Roger flag and fire a small cannon from the top of his office building. His courtroom attire often drew criticism, with leanings toward snakeskin boots, suits lined with red silk, and heavy gold chains across his considerable girth.

Belli died July 9, 1996, in his San Francisco home of complications resulting from pancreatic cancer. The autopsy reported hypertension and cardiovascular disease as the cause. His monument, in his hometown of Sonora, California, bears his likeness and the title "the King of Torts." He was survived by six children and a widow, his fifth wife, Nancy Ho Belli, whom he had married on March 29 of the year of his death. Each of his previous four marriages had ended in an acrimonious divorce. Almost immediately upon his death, clashes broke out among his heirs regarding his estate and even the cause of his death. The last years of his life were embroiled in financial, professional, and health problems. He had declared personal bankruptcy in December 1995, and a federal judge had ordered that his practice be taken over by an independent examiner one week before his death. He fought with former partners and employees and had been the target of malpractice and tax evasion charges in the years preceding his death.

Throughout the beginnings of his career in the 1940s, Belli took on all kinds of personal injury cases involving such diverse matters as medical malpractice and product liability. The awards he won for his clients continually grew as a result of his innovative and often controversial techniques. He did not gain national notoriety, however, until the 1950s. He started writing then and lecturing across the country about torts and trial practice. Belli was given the title "King of Torts" by *Life* magazine in 1954, the same year that his *Modern Trials* was first published. He is pictured on the cover of the magazine in a convertible automobile with "Elmer," a skeleton he used for jury demonstrations during trials. Elmer, one of his favorite props, even became the subject of a dispute among his heirs shortly after his death.

Belli became the scourge of the medical profession because of his aggressive pursuit of medical malpractice claims. In 1949, in one of his early and more controversial cases, a beautiful English woman claimed that a plastic surgeon who had operated on her breasts had replaced several of the parts unevenly. During the trial of her case, Belli asked the trial judge if his client could display her breasts to the judge and jury. She was permitted to do so, and the jury returned a substantial award. When asked later by a reporter what he had been thinking when his client had her head bowed and the tears dropped on her scars, Belli replied, " I could hear the angels sing and the cash register ring."

The 1944 case of *Escola v. Coca-Cola* helped to expand corporate liability for defective products. The case involved an exploding Coke bottle. In it, Belli established the idea that Coke was responsible even if it could not be proved what was wrong with that particular bottle. *Res ipsa loquitor,* "the thing speaks for itself," became a legal theory frequently applied in many product liability cases. It helped set the stage for later consumer product litigation. Consumer advocate extraordinaire Ralph Nader has called Belli "the Babe Ruth of Torts."

Belli was part of the legal team that represented Jack Ruby, a Dallas nightclub owner, in his murder trial. Other members of the team included Joe Tonahill and Phil Burleson, both Texas lawyers. President John F. Kennedy had been killed by an assassin's bullet in Dallas, Texas, on Friday, November 22, 1963. On the following Sunday, the nation was riveted to television screens as the alleged assassin, Lee Harvey Oswald, was transferred between jails. Ruby darted from the crowd and fired a single fatal bullet into the torso of the handcuffed Oswald. Bail was denied in the case, as was a defense team motion for a change of venue. Jack Ruby's Dallas trial opened three months later. Eleven of the twelve jurors had seen the shooting on television. The issue was not whether Jack Ruby had done it, but why. Ruby's defense was brain damage. Belli's psychiatric experts testified that Ruby's uncontrollable explosiveness was a symptom of psychomotor epilepsy. Prosecutors presented Ruby as a glory seeker who was simply in the right place at the right time. The jury took two hours and nineteen minutes to find Ruby guilty of murder. His sentence was death in the electric chair. In 1966, Ruby's conviction was reversed by an appeals court, which ruled that the motion requesting a change of venue should have been granted and that some statements made by Ruby to police should not have been admitted into evidence. Ruby had fired Belli, and a new defense team was set to retry the case in February 1967 in Wichita Falls, Texas. The trial never

Fanny Holtzmann

Known as "the Greta Garbo of the bar" (Berkman 1976, x), Brooklyn-born Fanny Holtzmann (1902–1980) established herself as a counselor to celebrities and royal families in New York, Hollywood, and England. Even before she graduated from night classes at the Fordham Law School, Holtzmann had gained an entrée into the entertainment world after persuading the firm for which she was working to contact performers who had failed to pay their advertising bills to the *Morning Telegraph*.

Rather than focusing on the bills, Holtzmann found ways that she could help authors and performers with negotiating contracts, putting their financial houses in order, and taking care of other legal problems. She proved so adept that many began treating her as their attorney even before she passed the bar. Holtzmann, who set up practice in New York with her brother Jack, was better known for her behind-the-scenes negotiations than for her courtroom advocacy. She developed a good grasp of the entertainment industry (as well as a good feel for lucrative plays and movies) and was often able to find common ground between her clients and those with whom they were in disagreement rather than going to court.

Holtzmann's biggest victory, which was actually argued by English barristers, was a suit that she brought on behalf of the Romanov family against MGM Studios for false portrayals of the Russian royal family in a movie about Rasputin. The English lawyers obtained the highest libel award to that date, and Holtzmann settled other claims outside of court for an undisclosed sum.

Deeply influenced by her grandfather, Rabbi Hirsch Bornfeld, who had lived with her family in Brooklyn, Holtzmann was strongly committed to the Jewish people. Holtzmann did her best to save fellow Jews—especially relatives—from Hitler's holocaust, and as a friend of Winston Churchill and members of the English royal family, she tried to foster support for Britain prior to the entry of the United States into World War II. During this time, she also helped transport English children to the United States, where they would not have to endure the fear of bombings.

After the war, Holtzman served as counsel to the Chinese delegates at the United Nations. Like her grandfather, she was also a strong Zionist who supported the establishment of Israel. In addition to her friendships with entertainment and literary figures as diverse as Eddie Goulding, Fred Astaire, and George Bernard Shaw, she knew Eleanor Roosevelt, Adlai Stevenson, Golda Meir, Dwight D. Eisenhower, and John F. Kennedy. Holtzmann also impressed U.S. Supreme Court justices Benjamin Cardozo and Felix Frankfurter.

Although she could be shy, Holtzmann made friendships easily (especially when she could find individuals familiar with Yiddish phrases), and she carved out a unique legal niche at a time when few if any American women were as prominent in the profession of law as she was.

Reference

Berkman, Ted. *The Lady and the Law: The Remarkable Life of Fanny Holtzmann*. Boston: Little, Brown, 1976.

occurred. Jack Ruby died of cancer on January 3, 1967, in Parkland Memorial Hospital, where four years earlier John F. Kennedy had died.

Belli was dubbed "the Father of Demonstrative Evidence." Demonstrative evidence is defined as the depiction or representation of something. It has always been a part of trial practice. However, Belli's often controversial use of this technique took it to new heights. He turned the courtroom into theater with the use of props, wardrobe, and his stentorian oratory. His sometimes graphic technique of demonstratively presenting evidence to a jury became one of his trademarks. In his 1976 autobiography, *My Life on Trial,* Belli states, "Jurors learn through all their senses, and if you can tell them and show them, too, let them feel and even taste or smell the evidence, then you can reach the jury." Belli claims he literally stumbled on to the value of demonstrative evidence early in his legal career. He tripped and dumped dozens of prison-made knives in front of a jury trying Ernie Smith, a San Quentin inmate, for murder. The panel, convinced of self-defense, came back with an acquittal.

In a 1941 case, Katherine Jeffers's leg had been severed by a San Francisco streetcar. During the trial, an oblong object wrapped in butcher's paper lay on the plaintiff's table. The courtroom was horrified when, during closing arguments, Belli unwrapped the object and tossed it into the lap of a juror. "Ladies and gentlemen of the jury, this is what my pretty young client will wear for the rest of her life. Take it. Feel the warmth of life in the soft tissue of its flesh, feel the pulse of the blood as it flows through the veins, feel the marvelous smooth articulation of the joint and touch the rippling muscles of the calf," he exhorted, as the jury passed around the woman's new artificial leg. The award of $120,000 was ten times the usual amount for similar injuries of that era.

Belli has been called a pioneer, a pacesetter, a legend in his time; brilliant at law, spellbinding in court, and voracious in his appetites. He led a life of passionate enjoyment and fierce combat, both in and out of court. Most of his battles were fought on behalf of individuals against establishment powers, the insurance industry, the medical profession, or great corporations. His inventiveness in the courtroom, his imaginative use of demonstrative evidence, and his successful quest to raise the levels of personal injury awards have made him arguably the most imitated trial lawyer in the world.

—*Sarah Bartholomew*

Sources and Suggestions for Further Reading

Belli, Melvin M. "The Adequate Award." *California Law Review* 39 (1954): 1.

Belli, Melvin M. *Dallas Justice: The Real Story of Jack Ruby and His Trial*. New York: McKay, 1964.

_____. *Modern Trials*. Indianapolis: Bobbs-Merrill, 1954.

Belli, Melvin M., with Robert Blair Kaiser. *Melvin Belli, My Life on Trial*. New York: William Morrow, 1976.

BENJAMIN, JUDAH P.

(1811–1884)

JUDAH P. BENJAMIN, BEST KNOWN for serving as Confederate president Jefferson Davis's right-hand man during the American Civil War, had previously distinguished himself as an outstanding Louisiana attorney and politician. After fleeing the South, Benjamin went on to become a prominent member of the bar in Great Britain.

Of Sephardic Jewish ancestry, Judah Benjamin was born to Philip Benjamin and Rebecca de Mendes in Christiansted, St. Croix, in the West Indies. His parents later settled in Charleston, South Carolina, where his father proved relatively unsuccessful in business but his mother managed to provide for the family through a shop where she sold dried fruit. She also secured aid from relatives to educate her son, the oldest living male of seven children. Judah's education included two years at Yale University, where he left under still-disputed circumstances.

JUDAH P. BENJAMIN
National Archives

After a brief return to Charleston, Benjamin went to New Orleans, where he was apprenticed to Greenburg R. Stringer, a notary with a commercial law firm. Benjamin was admitted to the bar in 1832 and shortly thereafter married Natalie St. Martin, a young Catholic Creole girl whom he had tutored in English. Natalie's religion and primary language were but two of the many differences between them (Benjamin does not appear to have been an observant Jew, but, although he was given Catholic last rites at his wife's request, he does not appear to have affiliated with any other church either). They spent much of their married life apart after Natalie moved to Paris, where she raised their only child, a daughter named Ninette, born ten years into the marriage.

Two years after being admitted to the bar, Benjamin wrote, with Thomas Slidell, an influential digest of the twenty-five volumes of Louisiana cases, and thereafter his business and reputation grew rapidly. Benjamin focused primarily on civil and commercial law. He subsequently built a massive plantation house, Bellechasse, with 140 slaves, where he experimented with raising sugar cane and even wrote a book on the subject. Faced with financial difficulties, Benjamin would later sell the farm.

Unlike many Southerners of the day, Benjamin did not appear to believe that slaves were inherently inferior or that their slavery could be justified through the Bible. Although his arguments were undoubtedly tailored to the case he was arguing, Benjamin, in one of his most famous cases involving a revolt aboard the *Creole*, argued that slaves were human beings and that, as in institution, slavery was against the law of nations. In language subsequently published as an abolitionist brochure, Benjamin asked, "What is a slave?" and responded:

> He is a human being. He has feeling and passion and intellect. His heart, like the heart of the white man, swells with love, burns with jealousy, aches with sorrow, pines under restraint and discomfort, boils with revenge and ever cherishes the desire for liberty. (Evans 1988, 38)

Slaves who found themselves on free British soil after a mutiny aboard ship were therefore free, and the insurance company Benjamin was representing should not be responsible for paying damages to their masters. Benjamin's argument against Louisiana's use of the three-fifths ratio for slave representation appears to have been more designed to favor New Orleans (where slaves were less plentiful than in more rural parts of the state) than to reflect concerns over the morality of slavery, and, indeed, Benjamin appears to have later switched sides on this issue.

Benjamin did sometimes take unpopular stances. Although pubic opinion was reflected in a number of hung juries that refused to convict, Benjamin aided the government in prosecuting prominent New Orleans citizens who had attempted to foment trouble in Cuba, a practice then known as filibustering. In this case, Benjamin painted a picture portraying Cubans as a contented people who did not care for outside interference.

After service as a delegate to the Louisiana Constitutional Convention of 1842, as a Whig presidential elector in 1848 (he would later become a

Democrat), and as a Louisiana legislator, Benjamin was chosen in 1852, with the help of Slidell's New Orleans machine, to the U.S. Senate. Benjamin was the first person to so serve who did not hide his Jewish ancestry (the one prior Jewish senator, Florida's David Yulee, had claimed to be a descendant of a Moroccan prince). Had Benjamin accepted the appointment to the U.S. Supreme Court that was first offered to him, and later to two of his law partners by Millard Fillmore in 1853, he might have become the first Jewish justice as well, but, at the time, he was more interested in his political career.

Benjamin pushed hard for Southern railroads and tried to spearhead efforts to develop a rail line that would go from the South through a Mexican isthmus to the Pacific Ocean. Benjamin did not find his service in the Senate to be incompatible with continuing legal work. In 1854, Benjamin argued on behalf of relatives of a bachelor seeking to have his bequest to educate poor children reversed in *Murdoch v. McDonough*. Although succeeding in the Louisiana circuit court, Benjamin lost before the U.S. Supreme Court in a decision generally attributed to the weakness of his case rather than to his own presentation. Thus, a newspaper reporter observed that "whoever was not in the Supreme Courtroom this morning missed hearing one of the finest forensic speakers in the United States." He noted that Benjamin's address was "refined, his language pure, chaste and elegant; his learning and reading evidently great; his power of analysis and synthesis *very* great" (Meade 1943, 70). Maryland attorney REVERDY JOHNSON observed that "Benjamin had a power of argument rarely, if ever, surpassed" (Evans 1988, 103). Benjamin spent four days arguing *United States v. Castillero* (1860), a case involving a California silver mine, and, although he lost, he collected a fee of twenty-five thousand dollars.

Benjamin's argumentation and speaking skills were manifested in the Senate, where the official reporter of forty years identified Benjamin as the ablest and best-equipped senator he had known (Evans 1988, 103). Although he supported the Southern cause, Benjamin was recognized as a moderate. The orations Benjamin made in departing from that body after Louisiana's secession from the Union were widely praised and reprinted. Although Benjamin and Mississippi's senator Jefferson Davis had once had a personal dispute in the Senate that very nearly led to a duel, they had subsequently become friends, and Davis, as president of the Confederacy, chose Benjamin to sit on his cabinet, first as attorney general, and later as secretary of war and secretary of state. Benjamin established close relations with both Davis and his wife, Varina, and appears to have been one of Davis's closest advisors, even his alter ego, during the war. Benjamin rarely spoke out in public, and he sometimes took the blame for crises that might otherwise have been pinned on Davis or explained by circumstances that were better not publicized. Unlike most cabinet members, Benjamin believed from the beginning that the war would be long, and he tried unsuccessfully to get the South to sell large amounts of cotton to foreign governments at the beginning of the war to enlist their support.

Benjamin's pragmatic approach contrasted with Davis's more rigid ideology. Among Benjamin's most daring plans was one for the emancipation of either all Southern slaves or those who agreed to take up arms on behalf of the Confederacy; on this occasion, Benjamin advocated and ably defended his views before a public audience in a display of oratorical talents that had undoubtedly been polished in the courtroom. As one who spent much of the war trying, usually without success, to secure help from foreign governments, Benjamin was motivated largely by his belief that such a policy could prove effective in securing such support. Not surprisingly, Benjamin was often targeted for criticism, especially in the South, not only for his willingness to advocate emancipation (for which he escaped censure by the Confederate Congress) but also because of his Jewish ancestry. Andrew Johnson was among those who had negatively focused on the fact that Benjamin was a Jew; another congressman called him "Judas Iscariot Benjamin" (Evans 1988, 235). In *John Brown's Body*, poet Stephen Vincent Benét would refer to Benjamin as "the dapper Jew," "a dark prince" (Evans 1988, vii).

After the fall of the Confederate capital at Richmond, Virginia, Davis and Benjamin headed south and later separated. Although Davis was captured, Benjamin escaped. He successfully disguised himself as a Frenchman and, after a series of harrowing escapes and brushes with death, which brought him south to Florida and through a number of Caribbean islands, he arrived in England, where he was a citizen because of his birthplace. One of the agents that Benjamin had commissioned for sabotage during the war had some links to one or more of Lincoln's assassins, and, with rumors abounding, Benjamin's life was probably even at greater risk than Davis's at a time when children were singing, "We'll hang Jeff Davis from a sour apple tree."

Although Davis would spend much of the rest of his own life reliving and seeking to justify the past, Benjamin preferred to look to the future. After arriving in England, Benjamin displayed the remarkable resiliency and cheer that is often reflected by his slightly upturned smile in pictures and reiterated in Stephen Vincent Benét's description of him in *John Brown's Body*. Benjamin took up the study of English law at Lincoln's Inn and served an apprenticeship to Charles Pollock.

Benjamin was admitted to the English bar in six months, and, much as he had done in Louisiana, in 1868 he used his extensive knowledge of French, Spanish, English, and American laws to publish *Treatise on the Law of Sale of Personal Property, with Reference to the American Decisions, to the French*

Code and Civil Law (usually called *Benjamin on Sales*) that was a standard text for thirty years (Evans 1988, 344). In 1868, Benjamin successfully argued a case on behalf of a former Confederate agent in London in *United States v. McRae*.

By 1872, Benjamin had been appointed as queen's counsel. From 1872 to 1882, he participated in more than 136 cases before the House of Lords and the Judicial Committee of the Privy Council (Evans 1988, 375). These included *Queen v. Keyn* (1876), also called the *Franconia* case, in which he successfully denied British jurisdiction in defending a German captain who had run down an English vessel. When after several days of intense questioning, the judges inquired how much longer he would take, Benjamin responded that it depended on how many more questions they asked! Acknowledging Benjamin's great command of international law, Lord Chief Baron commented, "You might pertinently ask us the questions" (Evans 1988, 376).

Although he arrived in Britain, as he had once come to New Orleans, virtually penniless, Benjamin was soon earning a substantial income, with which he continued to support his wife in Paris and other family members in America. Benjamin's high reputation at the English bar was similar to that which he acquired in America, and a number of stories circulated about his legal prowess. On one much-reported occasion, after hearing the lord chancellor mutter "Nonsense!" in response to an audacious opening proposition, Benjamin immediately folded his papers and left the courtroom, eliciting a subsequent apology from the chancellor and impressing all observers with Benjamin's own sense of dignity. Baron Pollack reported that Benjamin "thoroughly knew the rules of the game [and] presented his client's case with great force to a jury" (Evans 1988, 373). British observers sometimes commented negatively on Benjamin's American accent, and there are some indications that, as he aged, his voice was not quite as sonorous as it had once been, but British observers were just as impressed with his legal skills as Americans had been earlier. Despite his knowledge of languages, Benjamin does not appear to have used foreign words either in written or spoken speech for effect, but he was quite skillful in painting pictures with words. A fellow barrister noted that "he makes you see the very bale of cotton that he is describing as it lies upon the wharf in New Orleans" (Evans 1988, 377). Benjamin may have profited in part from the fact that, as a Louisiana lawyer, he had not only become familiar with Continental law, but he had also exercised functions that were divided in England between English barristers and solicitors. In England, as in America, his reputation had been given a boost by his writing skills.

The short and portly, but generally spry, Benjamin was injured when jumping off a trolley car in 1880, and he retired in 1882 after suffering a heart attack, apparently brought on by diabetes. In an extraordinary display of respect, Benjamin was feted to a banquet at the Inner Temple in his honor by more than two hundred lawyers and judges, including most notables of the British bar and bench. Benjamin moved to Paris, where he had recently constructed a magnificent new house. He died on May 6, 1884, at age seventy-three, and was buried in Paris under the name Philippe Benjamin.

Benjamin, who kept an uncluttered desk, made it a practice to destroy personal papers, and little survives outside of official orders issued as a cabinet member during the Civil War and reports of cases in which he served as counsel. Benjamin published no memoirs, and, curiously, Jefferson Davis's own fifteen-hundred-page memoir (*The Rise and Fall of the Confederacy*, 1881) made only a single reference to Benjamin: "Mr. Benjamin of Louisiana had a very high reputation as a lawyer, and my acquaintance with him in the Senate had impressed me with the lucidity of his systematic habits and capacity for labor. He was therefore invited to the post of Attorney General" (Evans 1988, 386). In addition to achieving several firsts as an American Jew and serving in the Confederate cabinet, Benjamin will long be remembered for rising to the top of the bar in two countries.

—John R. Vile

Sources and Suggestions for Further Reading

Butler, Pierce. *Judah P. Benjamin*. New York: Chelsea House, 1980.

Evans, Eli N. *Judah P. Benjamin: The Jewish Confederate*. New York: Free Press, 1988.

Goodhart, Arthur L. *Five Jewish Lawyers of the Common Law*. Freeport, N.Y.: Books for Libraries Press, 1971.

Meade, Robert D. *Judah P. Benjamin: Confederate Statesman*. New York: Oxford University Press, 1943.

Neiman, S. I. *Judah Benjamin*. Indianapolis: Bobbs-Merrill, 1963.

BIDDLE, FRANCIS BEVERLY

(1886–1968)

FRANCIS BEVERLY BIDDLE WAS a successful Philadelphia corporate attorney, but it was his performance as a public attorney that distinguished him from other lawyers. During his professional life, Biddle served as an assistant U.S. attorney, a federal appellate judge, solicitor general, and attorney general of the United States. He was born in Paris, France, on May 9, 1886, while his parents, Algernon Sydney Biddle and Frances Robinson Biddle, were living abroad. The Biddles were a prominent Philadelphia family and had roots in the legal profession going back several generations, which prompted an observer to suggest that "Philadelphia plus law equals Biddle, and always has." One of the Biddle family ancestors was Edmund Randolph, who played a highly significant role at the Constitutional Convention in Philadelphia and was the country's first attorney general. Biddle's father built a very successful private practice and later became a member of the law faculty at the University of Pennsylvania. Biddle attended Groton Academy from 1899 to 1905, received his B.A. cum laude from Harvard University in 1909, and earned his LL.D. cum laude from Harvard Law School two years later.

FRANCIS BEVERLY BIDDLE
Former U.S. Attorney General Francis Biddle, tribunal judge for the Nuremberg trials, photographed in Paris, 19 November 1945. (AP Photo)

Biddle served a year as secretary to Supreme Court justice Oliver Wendell Holmes. He would later say that the experience "roused and stimulated" him more than anything "since the first exciting plunge into common law" at Harvard. Biddle, admitted to the Pennsylvania bar following his year in Washington, accepted a position with the Philadelphia law firm of Biddle, Paul, and Jayne. This was the firm founded by his father, and Biddle admitted the "weight of his father's achievements at times became hard to bear" (Biddle 1961, 293). He knew the firm was "antiquated if not moribund" but was determined to "change all that." He was soon to learn that his new associates "had not asked me to join them with the idea of my reorganizing their firm" (Biddle 1961, 293). Coming from Harvard and his year with Holmes, he was "pretty well pleased with the daydream of my future, and blithely unconscious of my shortcomings." The time with the firm his father had founded was a "sheer waste"; he had "no hard work to do" and received "no criticism and no encouragement" (Biddle 1961, 294). Two years later, he joined the practice of Barnes, Biddle, and Myers, also in Philadelphia. In 1918, he married Katherine Garrison Chapin, who became a well-known poet. The Biddles had two sons.

Biddle specialized in corporate law throughout his private practice. Almost immediately after joining Barnes, Biddle, and Myers, he was defending the Pennsylvania Railroad in accident claims cases. The opposing lawyers sought to get accident claims to sympathetic juries, while the "railroad solicitor—as we were officially designated" sought to keep cases away from juries (Biddle 1961, 336–337). Nonetheless, Biddle was a highly skilled and effective trial attorney and was particularly adept in the use of cross-examination. The secret of successful cross-examination, he suggested, was to know where to stop. Knowing where to stop, in turn, was a product of preparing the opponent's case as carefully as one's own in order to know exactly what questions to ask witnesses (Biddle 1961, 338).

Biddle came from a conservative background, but he eventually subscribed to a more progressive life view. In 1912, he supported the Bull Moose Party candidacy of Theodore Roosevelt and unsuccessfully sought election to the Pennsylvania state senate. Biddle interrupted his private practice in 1922 to serve as assistant U.S. attorney for the eastern district of Pennsylvania for three years, and gained "invaluable experience, particularly in trying cases" (Biddle 1961, 344). After several years in private practice and three years as a government attorney, Biddle "got to know the active bar well." He said there was "no pleasanter feeling for a lawyer than the sense of being at home in his profession, of handling the techniques of practice with confidence, and knowing the bar's traditions and talking shop" (Biddle 1961, 349). As his court practice became more extensive, Biddle became more active with the state and local bar associations. He found this experience "deeply satisfying," giving him a "sense of escaping from the loneliness of forever living with my own egotism." He served on the board

Francis L. Wellman and the Art of Cross-Examination

Few attorneys have done more to promote thinking about cross-examination than Francis L. Wellman (1854–1942). Wellman's *The Art of Cross-Examination* was published in four editions from 1903 to 1936 and continues to be reprinted and to have an impact on the legal profession. The book's trademark is Wellman's deft use of examples, many drawn from his own practice as an assistant corporation counsel and an assistant district attorney in New York (and later in full-time private practice), to illustrate appropriate and inappropriate cross-examination strategies.

Although Wellman put primary emphasis on thorough preparation and knowledge, some of his most striking examples involve subtle trickery. The author's favorite involves a laborer injured in an electric car collision who alleged that a dislocated shoulder had permanently impaired his ability to raise his arm above his shoulder. When Wellman asked the witness to illustrate his current condition, he reported that "the plaintiff slowly and with considerable difficulty raised his arm to the parallel of his shoulder."

Wellman then requested, "Now, using the same arm, show the jury how high you could get it up before the accident."

Before he realized what he was doing, the plaintiff responded by extending the arm above his head, bringing the entire court to laughter, and presumably helping Wellman win the case (Wellman 1962, 64).

Reference

Wellman, Francis L. *The Art of Cross-Examination*. New York: Collier, 1962.

of governors of the Philadelphia Bar Association and the County Board of Examiners (Biddle 1961, 349–350).

Biddle was deeply affected by the plight of the poor and unemployed during the Great Depression. He had a "singular noblesse oblige" that took him into reform politics and ultimately Roosevelt's New Deal agenda (Whitman 1968). He switched his affiliation from the Republican to the Democratic party, and in 1932 became an enthusiastic supporter of Franklin D. Roosevelt, with whom he had attended Groton and Harvard. In February 1934, Biddle accepted appointment to a commission created to investigate coal and iron policies and learned much of the "intolerable conditions" under which the miners and steelworkers of Pennsylvania were living (Biddle 1961, 353). "I saw the dark and dismal conditions under which the miners lived; and the brutality that was dealt them if they tried to improve things" (Whitman 1968). His work on this committee was "my first affront" to two of his law firm's most important clients, the Berwynd-White Coal Company and the Pennsylvania Railroad (Biddle 1961, 353).

Several months later, Biddle was appointed chair of the newly created National Labor Relations Board (NLRB). Since Biddle came from a corporate law background and had little experience in labor relations, some of Roosevelt's advisers were skeptical of his capacity to deal effectively with such "militant labor leaders" as John L. Lewis and "hard-boiled, recalcitrant industrialists." Biddle proved equal to the task, however. He brought to the position a "lively sense" of the legal difficulties involved in investigating and adjusting controversies arising under the code-making section of the National Industrial Recovery Act between employers and employees. He also took on the Roosevelt Justice Department about its inaction on NLRB cases, testifying before the Senate Labor Committee in support of the Wagner Act provision that allowed NLRB attorneys to appear in court instead of the Justice Department attorneys. Biddle reminded the committee that in the NLRB's two years of operation, the Justice Department had brought suit in fewer than ten percent of the cases in which he had sought litigation. Biddle suggested that this failure to advance NLRB cases amounted to a "complete nullification of the law" (Irons 1982, 221).

Under Biddle's leadership, workers secured the right to decide if they wanted to be represented by a union and the right to collective bargaining between the designated employee unions and employers. The NLRB under Biddle's leadership was not administratively strong, but it was successful in defining federal labor laws to the benefit of workers. The NLRB wrote a number of thoughtful decisions, which became invaluable for the second NLRB created by the Wagner Act. Within a year, however, the Supreme Court declared the National Industrial Recovery Act unconstitutional, and Biddle resigned his position on the NLRB to return to private practice. His work as chair of the NLRB increased the "extent and variety" of his practice, but when he returned to Philadelphia to resume his private practice and become a director of a Federal Reserve Bank, he missed the "sense of freedom, the feeling of power, and the experience of the enlarging horizons of public work" (Biddle 1961, 366). During this period, Biddle served as chief counsel for the congressional investigation of the Tennessee Valley Authority. In 1939, Biddle gave up his partnership in his Philadelphia law firm and became a judge of the U.S. Court of Appeals for the Third Circuit.

Biddle found the judicial position unrewarding, and the following year he left the life-tenure judgeship to become U.S. solicitor general. The solicitor general represents the United States in cases reviewed by the Supreme Court—the United States is "his only client." Biddle wrote that the work "combines the best of private practice and of government service." The solicitor general determines what cases to appeal but is "responsible neither to the man who appointed him nor to his immediate superior in the hierarchy of administration" (Biddle 1962, 97). Furthermore, there are none of the "drawbacks that usually go with public work, no political compromises, no shifts and substitutes, no cunning deviations, no considerations of expediency." In short, the solicitor general "has no master to serve except his country" (Biddle 1962, 97–98). Biddle averaged a case before the Supreme Court every two weeks and spoke of the many long evenings he worked "to be ready to answer Justice Frankfurter's questions, [and Frankfurter] had the ability to swallow records like oysters" (Biddle 1962, 98). As was the custom for newly appointed solicitors general, Biddle called on the members of the Supreme Court. Chief Justice Stone, he recalled, "could not understand why I resigned from the Circuit Court." On the other hand, Justice McReynolds, who was not without a "certain cunning insight," did understand. He suggested to Biddle that "lawyers, not judges, make the law" (Biddle 1962, 96).

Most of the cases testing the constitutionality of New Deal legislation had already been argued before the Court before Biddle's appointment, but there were still a "few undetermined issues," which he presented. He felt a "certain historical pride in winning" the argument in *United States v. Darby Lumber Co.*, 312 U.S. 100 (1941). *Darby* determined that federal commerce power could reach manufacturing that precedes actual transport and extended the reach of federal regulatory power. Similarly, in *United States v. Appalachian Electric Power Co.*, 311 U.S. 377 (1940), the Court gave the government "sweeping control over water power, expanding the former test that the particular stream must in fact be navigable to include waters that could be made so" (Biddle 1962, 102). Biddle also helped write Roosevelt's statement approving the Smith Act, under which leaders of the Communist party were later prosecuted. He later expressed regret over his endorsement of this law. During his brief tenure as solicitor general, Biddle won fifteen of the sixteen cases he argued before the Supreme Court.

When ROBERT H. JACKSON was appointed to the Supreme Court in 1941, Roosevelt nominated Biddle to replace Jackson as attorney general. Biddle served as attorney general until Roosevelt's death. World War II largely defined his priorities. For example, he was in charge of the registration of aliens during the war and defended this measure as protecting loyal aliens. Furthermore, far fewer people were prosecuted for sedition by Biddle's Justice Department than had been the case during World War I, in part because "local United States attorneys were not permitted to bring charges without Biddle's personal approval" (Polenberg 1972, 47). Criminal acts of enemy aliens were an altogether different matter. Biddle was the chief prosecutor of eight German spies and saboteurs who landed from submarines on the coasts of Florida and Long Island and were caught by federal agents. He was also responsible for structuring the military commission before which they were tried. The commission could impose the death penalty on a two-thirds vote of the judges, and the president "alone had power of review" (Polenberg 1972, 44). Six of the eight were ultimately executed following their convictions.

Biddle was very critical of the effort by Congress to deport radical labor leader Harry Bridges, an action subsequently blocked by the Supreme Court in *Bridges v. Wixon*, 326 U.S. 135 (1945). Biddle's views earned him the praise of some laborites and the distrust of conservatives. His attempt to enforce an order of the War Labor Board against Montgomery Ward, the giant mail-order and retailing corporation, reinforced this perception of Biddle. Sewell L. Avery, the vehemently antiunion president of Wards, refused to deal with a Congress of Industrial Organizations (CIO) union, arguing that a majority of the work force no longer favored it. In April 1944, the union went on strike. The president, under terms of the Smith-Connally (War Labor Disputes) Act, had the power to take over a strikebound plant if it was "useful" to the war effort. Secretary of War Henry Stimson argued that because Wards was not doing "war business," federal intervention was inappropriate. Biddle disagreed. Wards supplied the army and millions of farmers, and it seemed to Biddle to fall clearly within the scope of Smith-Connally. Roosevelt agreed with him and ordered troops to execute the seizure of the company (Goodwin 1994, 498). When Avery refused to leave his office, Biddle ordered the military police forcibly to remove him from the premises. As Avery was carried out, he turned to Biddle and shouted, "You New Dealer," the harshest words he could summon at the moment. Media coverage of this incident generated much sympathy for Avery and unleashed a torrent of anti–New Deal rhetoric. Biddle's assertion of federal power, however, had "potently demonstrated to labor the indispensable importance of its wartime partnership with government" (Kennedy 1999, 642).

Three months after Biddle's elevation to attorney general, the Japanese attacked Pearl Harbor. Biddle immediately began to intern enemy Japanese aliens. This process was extended to German and Italian enemy aliens three days later when these nations declared war against the United States. Biddle was determined, however, to avoid "mass internment, and the persecution of aliens that had characterized the First World War." He issued an appeal to state governors urging them to join him against any "molestation of peaceful and law-abiding aliens, whether Japanese, German, or Italian." His request was "backed almost universally" (Biddle 1962, 209–210). He later commenced a program to naturalize aliens who were loyal to the United States who were citizens of the countries against whom the United States was at war.

Biddle sought to intern aliens on a selective basis, but there was a great deal of sentiment in favor of moving the West Coast Japanese on an "immense scale" and holding them in relocation camps. The necessity for mass evacuation was, in Biddle's view, based primarily on public and political pressures rather than on evidence of criminal conduct. Public hysteria and, in some instances, the comments of the media brought tremendous pressure on government officials and military authorities. Biddle told Secretary of War Henry Stimson, an advocate of mass evacuation, that the Justice Department would have nothing to do with interfering with the rights of U.S. citizens, including those of Japanese ancestry. Roosevelt was predisposed toward unlimited evacuation and had Stimson prepare a plan to that end, which was later contained in Executive Order 9066. This order required the forced removal of all Japanese from designated military areas on the West Coast. Biddle had urged Stimson not to engage in mass internment of the Japanese but wrote that "I was new to the Cabinet, and disinclined to insist on my view to an elder statesmen whose wisdom and integrity I greatly respected" (Biddle 1962, 226). In late 1943, Biddle requested that Roosevelt institute a liberal release and return program that would have examined the loyalty of all interned and released those found to be loyal. This request was rejected, but Biddle continued to press for "accelerated releases" for internees certified to be loyal by the Justice Department. Anything else, he argued, "is dangerous and repugnant to the principles of our government" (Kennedy 1999, 755). Roosevelt agreed. Biddle later regretted that he had not opposed mass evacuation more forcefully.

When Harry S Truman became president in April 1945, he asked Biddle to resign so that he could replace him with Tom Clark. Soon thereafter, Biddle served as a member of the International Military Tribunal, which tried former Nazi leaders at Nuremberg. As a private citizen in the last two decades of his life, Biddle maintained his commitment to liberal causes. From 1950 until 1953, Biddle was head of Americans for Democratic Action, a liberal organization, and he served as an advisor to the American Civil Liberties Union. He also served as chair of the Franklin Delano Roosevelt Memorial Commission for ten years. During this period, he authored a number of books, including *In Brief Authority* (1962), *The Fear of Freedom* (1951), *Democratic Thinking and the War* (1944), *The World's Best Hope* (1949), and *Justice Holmes, Natural Law and the Supreme Court* (1961). In *The Fear of Freedom*, Biddle strongly argued against guilt by association, the House Un-American Activities Committee, censorship of textbooks, banishment of nonconformist teachers, the federal loyalty programs, and the vilification of those who stood up to the so-called subversive inquiries. Biddle was vocal in his condemnation of the way Senator Joseph McCarthy treated witnesses testifying before his Senate committee.

Biddle became a practicing liberal and a legal pragmatist. Biddle believed that the duty of the law is to "draw the line between the individual's rights and the protection of society." That line must "necessarily vary as the needs of the one or the other seem at any particular time to be more imperative." His national political life spanned twelve years. Biddle died at his summer home on Cape Cod on October 4, 1968. He was survived by his wife of fifty years, Katherine Garrison Chapin Biddle.

—*Peter G. Renstrom*

Sources and Suggestions for Further Reading

Biddle, Francis B. *A Casual Past*. Garden City, NY: Doubleday, 1961.

_____. *In Brief Authority*. Garden City, NY: Doubleday, 1962.

Goodwin, Doris Kearns. *No Ordinary Time: Franklin and Eleanor Roosevelt: The Home Front in World War II*. New York: Simon & Schuster, 1994.

Irons, Peter H. *The New Deal Lawyers*. Princeton: Princeton University Press, 1982.

Kennedy, David M. *Freedom from Fear: The American People in Depression and War, 1929–1945*. New York: Oxford University Press, 1999.

Morgan, Ted. *FDR: A Biography*. New York: Simon & Schuster, 1985.

Polenberg, Richard. *War and Society: The United States 1941–45*. Philadelphia: J. B. Lippincott, 1972.

Whitman, Alden. "Noblesse Oblige." *New York Times*, 5 October 1968, 5.

BLACK, JEREMIAH SULLIVAN

(1810–1893)

JEREMIAH SULLIVAN BLACK served as chief justice of the Pennsylvania Supreme Court, as U.S. attorney general and secretary of state, and as reporter for the U.S. Supreme Court. However, his chief fame was as a litigator and Supreme Court advocate who brought fiery rhetoric and reasoned arguments against Reconstruction policies.

Jeremiah Sullivan Black, oldest of the three children of Henry Black and Mary Sullivan, was born January 10, 1810, on his family's farm near Stony Creek, Pennsylvania. Henry Black served in the Pennsylvania legislature, as a lay judge of Somerset County for more than twenty years, and in the U.S. Congress. Patrick Sullivan, Jeremiah's maternal grandfather, had achieved the rank of captain during the American Revolution and was a Federalist member of the Pennsylvania legislature.

JEREMIAH SULLIVAN BLACK
Library of Congress

As a youngster, Black attended village schools until he transferred to a classical academy in Bridgeport. He later indicated that, although he had hated school and being confined, he loved books. By age fifteen, he had memorized the works of Horace and translated them first into English prose and then to verse from the original Latin. He also devoured the works of Shakespeare and the Bible and later frequently quoted the three in courtroom oratory. On leaving the Bridgeport school at age seventeen, Black wished to establish a career in medicine; however, Henry Black had different plans for his son—a career in law.

Black duly began his legal studies under the guidance of Chauncey Forward, a renowned lawyer and Democratic member of Congress. Three years later at age twenty, Black was sufficiently proficient to take and pass the bar examination. The congressman then departed for Washington, leaving his practice to his former student. Forward etched indelible imprints on Black's life as his teacher, his political mentor, his religious guide, and as his father-in-law. Mary Forward and Black were married on March 23, 1826. The couple had five children: Rebecca, Chauncey Forward, Henry, Mary, and Anna.

Black's thriving legal practice was further bolstered by his appointment as deputy attorney general for the county of Somerset. Between his own practice and that appointment, Black appeared frequently in court, often against such nationally known opponents as Charles Ogle and Joseph Williams, later a federal judge and chief justice of Iowa. In addition, Black served as deputy sheriff for the county.

The son and father differed not only about Black's career but also in political viewpoints. Henry Black was an active Whig, but his son established his Democratic credentials as early as 1828 through his support of Andrew Jackson. This political participation led both to acquaintances with prominent activists such as James Buchanan and to Black's appointment at age thirty-two as president judge of the Sixteenth Judicial District.

In 1851, Black was elected to the Supreme Court of Pennsylvania, chosen as chief justice, and reelected in 1854 as the sole statewide winner in the Democratic party. Of the 1,200 opinions issued during his tenure on the bench, Black wrote more than 250 of them. His opinions were couched in distinguished, distinct, and sometimes stinging language. One of his satirical dissents almost caused him to be cited for contempt of the court. His chief contribution as a justice was the formulation of jurisprudence relating to corporate charters, powers of corporations, and the authority of the government to regulate them.

Black was serving on the Pennsylvania Supreme Court when he was chosen as attorney general of the United States by his friend President James Buchanan. Black was unaware of his nomination or appointment until he was advised by the president in a letter that his commission as attorney general had been signed on March 6, 1857.

The new attorney general's initial argument before the Supreme Court was in *United States v. Cambuston* on January 7, 1858—Black's first appearance as an advocate in fifteen years. The United States had obligated itself to recognize valid Mexican land grants in California, but there were a number of forged deeds and fraudulent claims that had been ratified by the U.S. District Court in California. Under Black's guidance, seventeen grants were rejected by the Supreme Court, and more than one thousand square miles of land were restored to the public domain or to the rightful owners. *Cambuston* was merely the first of the "California land title" cases that Black would be involved with as attorney general and later in private practice.

As attorney general, Black enforced controversial and locally unpopular laws dealing with the slave trade and fugitive slaves. Slavery was accepted under the Constitution, in the statutes, and in the Bible. Aspects of slavery, especially the separation of families, personally troubled Black, but, for him, the law was the law and should be enforced.

On another volatile issue, secession, Black was every bit as steadfast. "The Union is necessarily perpetual. No state could lawfully withdraw or be expelled from it." Anticipating events, President Buchanan formally asked the attorney general for an opinion of the powers of the president to protect property of the United States in case of rebellion. As the president's constitutional legal advisor, Black responded on November 20, 1860, that "The right of the Central Government to preserve itself . . . by repelling a direct and positive aggression upon its property or its officers, cannot be denied. But this is a totally different thing from an offensive war, to punish the people for the political misdeeds of their State Government." Black viewed the question as a constitutional and legal issue rather than a political one, but his was the minority stance. The opinion created a storm of controversy, and clearly it was a political issue, especially in light of Abraham Lincoln's election two weeks earlier.

Despite the disagreement between Buchanan and Black about the president's failure to strengthen certain garrisons, Black was appointed as the new secretary of state when Lewis Cass resigned. He took office on December 17, 1860, the same day that the South Carolina convention met to consider the Ordinance of Secession.

This was not the office that Black and others had anticipated him assuming. There had been a vacancy on the Supreme Court since May with the death of Justice Peter V. Daniel, and there was a widespread belief that the retirement of eighty-four-year-old Chief Justice Roger B. Taney was imminent. Buchanan had withheld Black's nomination to the Court in expectation of Taney's retirement, but finally, on February 5, 1861, Buchanan forwarded the nomination of Black as associate justice to the Senate. The delay was most unfortunate because twelve Southern senators who might have supported Black had withdrawn from that body, and both the Douglas Democrats and the Republicans strongly opposed the nomination. In the end, the Senate decided by a stormy vote of 26 to 25 to decline consideration of the appointment, effectively killing the nomination.

At age fifty-one, Black returned to private life, suffering both from poor health and financial woes because of unwise investments. To support his family, Black became the reporter to the Supreme Court, a position of much lower prestige than he had expected at the Court. Black published two volumes of reports before he resigned to meet the pressures of his very large and substantial practice.

Black's initial appearance as attorney general before the Supreme Court involved land titles in California, and his return to the Court as a private lawyer replicated that. During the next four years, he appeared sixteen times as counsel for either the claimants or the government as special counsel in suits about California land titles; he was totally victorious in thirteen of the cases and partially successful in another. Black's extensive knowledge and expertise about the titles stemming from his term as attorney general allowed him to reestablish his fortune and his reputation as a successful litigator.

That reputation led to his selection, along with J. E. McDonald, DAVID DUDLEY FIELD, and James A. Garfield (arguing his first case at any level), for the defense in *Ex parte Milligan*. James Speed, Henry Stanbery, and Benjamin F. Butler presented the government's case. The arguments lasted a week, from March 16 to March 23, 1866, against a background of tumultuous public discussions and congressional debate over continuing military control beyond the close of the war.

The writ of habeas corpus had been suspended during the Civil War, first by presidential proclamation and then by congressional act in 1863. The 1863 legislation mandated that a list of detained prisoners was to be provided to federal judges, who were authorized to discharge all unindicted prisoners within twenty days after the next session of the grand jury, but the procedure was often ignored.

Lambdin P. Milligan, a resident and citizen of Indiana and a U.S. citizen, was arrested at his home on October 5, 1864, by order of a military commander and placed in military prison although the civil courts were open, no state of rebellion existed in Indiana, and no enemy troops were within the borders. On October 21, Milligan and two others, Boles and Horsey, were tried and convicted by a military commission of conspiracy, inciting insurrection, giving aid and comfort to the enemy, engaging in disloyal conduct, and violating the laws of war. All three were sentenced to death by hanging.

In Milligan's appeal, he invoked the 1863 law and demanded his rights under the Constitution and the congressional acts rather than focusing on the military trial. Black's two-hour concluding argument, given without notes, focused on the right to jury from the Magna Carta to the Constitution, drawing extensively on history, the writings of great legal commentators, and precedent; he concluded by reminding the Court that the civil courts were open and military tribunals were therefore powerless over civilians in areas that had not been the scene of hostile actions. The Court agreed.

Black's fight against Reconstruction continued on two fronts. First, he acted as advisor to President Andrew Johnson and assisted in drafting Johnson's veto message of the Reconstruction Acts that would establish martial law in the South, but the measures were passed over the veto. He also counseled the president in the initial proceedings over impeachment. Second, just as *Milligan* ended military control in the North, Black sought in *Ex parte McCardle* to end it in the South.

In Vicksburg, Mississippi, William McCardle offended the military commander by the opinions he expressed in his newspaper. On November 13, 1867, military troops arrested McCardle and placed him in a military prison. A military tribunal tried and convicted McCardle; he appealed to the circuit court for a writ of habeas corpus, which was denied on the basis that the Reconstruction Acts were constitutional. Under a statute permitting appeal of all habeas corpus proceedings, Black invoked the jurisdiction of the Supreme Court.

The initial proceeding before the Court involved the question of the Court's jurisdiction. The attorney general refused to act for the government, and Senator Lyman Trumbull, James Hughes, and Matt A. Carpenter presented the argument that the Court lacked jurisdiction. Black and William L. Sharkey persuaded the justices otherwise, and the case proceeded to hearing on the issues on March 2, 1868. Black's arguments, resounding with the same fervor that produced *Milligan*, averred that the rebellion did not permit government to govern contrary to the law any more than it could have previously. After oral arguments but before the Court released its decision, Congress passed a law withdrawing the jurisdiction of the Court to hear proceedings involving the writ of habeas corpus—even those already made, thereby mooting Milligan's appeal.

Black's opposition to Reconstruction continued in *Bylew v. United States* and the *Slaughterhouse Cases*, both dealing with states' rights during Reconstruction. The *Bylew* case arose from an assault and murder in Kentucky involving African-American victims and witnesses and white perpetrators. The surviving members of the attack were statutorily prohibited from testifying as witnesses in trials against whites because of their race; therefore, the federal court assumed jurisdiction under the Civil Rights Act of 1866, even though criminal proceedings had begun in state court. Kentucky perceived this as usurpation of its traditional powers, and the governor retained Black and Isaac Caldwell for the Supreme Court appeal. Representing the United States was the first solicitor general, Benjamin H. Bristow, and the attorney general, Amos T. Akerman. A year later, the Supreme Court announced its decision, essentially agreeing with Black that the national government had deprived Kentucky of one of its basic attributes of sovereignty and that federal jurisdiction did not accrue solely because of the race of the witnesses. The decision greatly impaired the potency of federal protections and remedies under the Civil Rights Act, a key piece of Reconstruction legislation.

In the *Slaughterhouse Cases*, Black, Matt A. Carpenter, and Thomas Jefferson Durant were chosen to represent the state of Louisiana. The state had passed a regulatory statute requiring that all butchering of animals in New Orleans occur at a particular slaughterhouse; the effect was to create a monopoly. Former Supreme Court justice JOHN A. CAMPBELL and J. Q. A. Fellows, representing the butchers, unsuccessfully sought an injunction in state court claiming that the butchers had been deprived of their property in violation of the Fourteenth Amendment's privileges and immunities clause. On appeal, the U.S. Supreme Court rejected that position and effectively nullified the privileges and immunities clause of the Fourteenth Amendment, again weakening one of the centerpieces of Reconstruction legislation.

Black's practice was truly a general one involving patents, fraud, land titles, will contests, and other matters. It was usually a solo practice, although at various times he entered into partnerships with his son-in-law, James F. Shunk, and with Ward H. Lemon, Lincoln's former law partner. From the time of *Milligan*, Black frequently practiced with James A. Garfield, although there was no formal partnership agreement. For example, the two appeared together in the will contest of Alexander Campbell, one of the founders of the Disciples of Christ Church. Black's father-in-law had been a staunch adherent of the denomination, and Black himself had been baptized by Campbell. Another prominent client was Cornelius Vanderbilt, who was seeking to overturn the will of his father, Commodore Vanderbilt. Settlement of the case resulted in a substantial payment to the son.

Black also engaged in business litigation. Railroads were frequent clients and adversaries. He won the right of railroad companies to consolidate in Pennsylvania and then caused the railroads to lose land grants in Kansas to the settlers already homesteaded there. Black represented the Providence Rubber Company in its losing battle against the Goodyear Rubber Company's allegations of patent infringement. Joining him were CALEB CUSHING, Garfield, J. H. Parsons, Abraham Payne, and W. W. Boyce; W. E. Curtis, W. M. Evarts, E. W. Stoughan, and J. H. Ackerman represented Goodyear. The printed arguments before the Supreme Court covered more than seven hundred pages. Another business client was H. S. McComb, who claimed to have purchased corporate stock that was never delivered to him. The subsequent investigations and resulting evidence at trial led to the revelation of congressional corruption (and the ensuing taint on Garfield's reputation), because the corporation was none other than the infamous Credit Mobilier Company.

Black frequently traveled across the nation to meet his speaking commitments and for various trials. He was also a prolific writer of articles and editorials, ever willing to challenge those with whom he disagreed, often using strong invective. At the time of his death on August 19, 1893, at his Pennsylvania home, he was fashioning a rebuttal to an editorial by Jefferson Davis and had completed preparations and briefs for another Supreme Court case involving the disenfranchisement of former polygamists in Utah.

Although he held high public offices and advised presidents, Black's chief legacy was that of a litigator who shaped the constitutional and legal history of the nation.

—*Susan Coleman*

Sources and Suggestions for Further Reading

Black, Chauncey F. *Essays and Speeches of Jeremiah S. Black.* New York: Appleton, 1886.

Brigance, William N. *Jeremiah Sullivan Black.* Philadelphia: University of Pennsylvania Press, 1934.

Clayton, Mary Black. *Reminiscences of Jeremiah Sullivan Black.* St. Louis: Christian Publishing, 1887.

Goldstein, Robert D. "Bylew: Variations on a Jurisdictional Theme." *Stanford Law Review* 14 (1989): 469.

Klingelsmith, Margaret Center. "Jeremiah Sullivan Black." In *Great American Lawyers,* edited by William Draper Lewis. Vol. 6. Philadelphia: John C. Winston, 1908.

Thorpe, Francis Newton. "Jeremiah S. Black." *Pennsylvania Magazine of History and Biography* 50 (1926):117–133; 273–286.

BOIES, DAVID

(1941–)

David Boies
Reuters NewMedia Inc./Corbis

AS GEORGE BUSH AND AL Gore contested the electoral votes for Florida in November 2000, attorney David Boies emerged as a point man for Gore. Not only did he argue successfully for Gore in the Florida Supreme Court that the state's secretary of state could not certify the ballots for Bush until an additional week of recounting (a decision later called into question by the U.S. Supreme Court), but he also led the trial court team before Judge N. Sanders Sauls in the Leon County Circuit Court petitioning for additional voting hand counts. In addition, Boies appeared frequently on television to explain Gore's case to the nation (Harvard law professor LAURENCE TRIBE, another lawyer described in these volumes, argued the first of two historic appeals of the Florida Supreme Court decision before the U.S. Supreme Court). Although the fifty-nine-year-old Boies was not as initially recognizable as Warren Christopher and James Baker (also spokesmen for Gore and Bush, respectively), he was well known among fellow lawyers and was hardly a stranger to the limelight.

Noting his "steel-trap mind, a laser-sharp memory, a head for chess and a skill with words," the *National Law Journal* had during the previous December named Boies as its Lawyer of the Year ("Boies Wonder" 1999, A8). Similarly, Boies had been featured in publications like *People Magazine* and *Van-*

ity Fair that are better known for highlighting celebrities than lawyers. Stephen Gillers, a New York University law professor, observed that "David Boies is on the cusp of becoming one of those lawyers who has achieved legendary status, like WEBSTER or DARROW" (Bryant 2000, 50). Making another celebrity connection, the *National Law Journal* has likened Boies to the "Michael Jordan of the courtroom" ("Boies Wonder" 1999, A8).

Boies was born on March 11, 1941, in Sycamore, Illinois, the oldest of five children born to parents who were both school teachers. The family moved to Fullerton, California, during Boies's youth, and one of his early jobs was delivering newspapers in the Watts section of Los Angeles. Hindered by dyslexia, Boies did not start out as a particularly good student; indeed, he did not learn to read until he was in the third grade. Boies decided to marry Caryl Elwell shortly after graduating from high school, and he worked in construction and as a bookkeeper before gaining admission to the University of Redlands, Redlands, California, and later to Northwestern University in Chicago. Subsequently entering the graduate program in economics at Yale University (education that has served him well in subsequent antitrust cases), Boies transferred to the law school, earning his LL.B. degree in 1966 and graduating magna cum laude and second in his class.

At one time interested in becoming a full-time law professor (Boies has taught at New York University and the Benjamin Cardozo School of Law in New York City), Boies instead took his first job with the prestigious New York firm of Cravath, Swaine & Moore, and was, by his second year, involved with partner Tom Barr in the firm's mammoth 13-year defense of IBM against antitrust charges (Barr is described in Vinson 1994, 7–10). Promoted ahead of schedule to a partnership in 1972, by 1976 Boies was handling IBM cases on his own and won a stunning victory against California Computer Products and its attorney, Maxwell Blecher, who has been described as "one of California's savviest and most experienced litigators" (Reich 1986).

In 1977, Boies left Cravath to spend two years working for the Senate Antitrust Subcommittee and the Senate Judiciary Committee, for which he became chief counsel before returning to Cravath. In 1984, Boies was involved in the defense of CBS News against libel in a $120 million case brought by General William Westmoreland alleging inaccuracies and malice in a story that CBS did about him alleging that he had underreported enemy troop strength in Vietnam. Even though Boies had not previously handled a First Amendment case (Responding to the question, "What does David know about libel? About the First Amendment?" his wife replied, "Well, it's a very short amendment" [Vinson 1994, 24]), his meticulous reconstruction of the research that had gone into the CBS report, as well as his skillful cross-examination of General Westmoreland, resulted in Westmoreland's dropping his case. Boies's cross-examination was so effective that members of the press corps reportedly began humming the theme of *Jaws* during his examinations (Vinson 1994, 26). In 1986, Boies successfully negotiated a settlement for Texaco against a $10.6 billion suit by Pennzoil for interfering with its purchase of Getty. (For the impressive work on Pennzoil's behalf by attorney Joseph D. Jamail, see Vinson 1994, 43–46).

In 1997, although reportedly making close to $2 million a year ("Boies Wonder" 1999, A9), Boies decided to strike out on his own after refusing to drop George Steinbrenner, owner of the New York Yankees, as a client (Perine 2000). Boies founded Boies, Schiller & Flexner in Armonk, New York, in Westchester County—a firm that has now grown to 55 to 60 attorneys and is earning kudos for its corporate and litigation work that match or exceed the reputation of Cravath.

The same year that he founded his new firm, Boies accepted an offer from Joel Klein, the deputy attorney general for antitrust matters in the U.S. Department of Justice, to lead its case against Microsoft. Boies, who can command as much as $600 to $700 an hour in other cases, agreed to work on the IBM case for a mere $50 per hour in what has been described by one government official as "the bargain of the century" ("Hang 'em High" 1999, 100). To date, Boies's leadership in the Microsoft case (the government's first monopolization case since its failure in the IBM case) has been credited with his team's success in leading to a trial court decision that might eventually result in the breakup of the huge corporation. Boies, who followed massive cramming sessions digesting the case by delivering an impressive three-hour opening without notes, also distinguished himself as one who was able to put an appropriate spin on developments for the local media and as one who could use the media to test the credibility of some of his legal theories. In addition, he showed himself to be a canny cross-examiner able to impeach the credibility of witnesses, including Bill Gates the founder and owner, with statements and concessions that he gained from them during extensive depositions. The *New York Law Journal* likened Boies's performance to putting on a "legal clinic" (Donovan 1999).

In 1999, Boies helped win an antitrust settlement of more than $1 billion from the vitamin industry (the largest such antitrust award in history); he successfully represented the state of Alaska in an antitrust case against BP Amoco; and he took on suits against health maintenance organizations Humana and Aetna-US Healthcare as well as a price-fixing suit against Sotheby's and Christie's prestigious auction houses in New York (Kahn 2000, 75). In 1999, Boies also helped a real estate magnate, Sheldon Solow, win an $11.5 million claim for asbestos damage against W. R. Grace & Company, and, apparently largely at the urging of his children, he chose to represent the Napster music service in its controversy with the Recording Industry of America over violations of copyrights.

Olson, Theodore B.
(1940-   )

Few who knew him were surprised when President George W. Bush nominated Theodore Bevry Olson in February 2001 to serve as solicitor general—the government's lead lawyer responsible for arguing cases before the U.S. Supreme Court—under newly appointed Attorney General John Ashcroft. Olson already had plenty of experience as an appellate lawyer, including the two oral arguments he made before the U.S. Supreme Court in *Bush v. Gore* (2000), which ultimately brought the Florida presidential election recount to an end, giving a slim state voting majority, Florida's electoral votes, and a majority of the national electoral college vote to Bush.

Olson was born in Chicago on September 11, 1940. He graduated from the University of the Pacific and attended law school at the University of California. He was employed with Gibson, Dunn & Crutcher in Los Angeles, and when firm partner William French Smith was appointed by Ronald Reagan to be attorney general, Olson was appointed as head of the Office of Legal Counsel. Accused of misleading Congress during its investigation of the Iran-Contra controversy (a charge that was later dropped), Olson was one of the named parties in the historic Supreme Court decision in *Morrison v. Olson* (1988) that upheld the constitutionality of the federal Independent Counsel Statute—a law that has since lapsed—against Olson's challenge.

Primarily responsible for appellate litigation in the Washington office of Gibson, Dunn & Crutcher after he rejoined the firm in 1984, Olson appeared before the U.S. Supreme Court eight times before successfully arguing *Bush v. Gore*. Olson unsuccessfully defended the Virginia Military Institute before the Supreme Court in the 1996 case that resulted in the admission of women to that institution, but he succeeded in a 1999 Hawaii case in convincing the Court to void a law restricting voting of trustees of a social welfare agency to original islanders (Schmidt 2000).

Olson unsuccessfully argued to reduce the sentence of Jonathan Pollard, who was convicted of passing secrets to the Israelis (Lane 2001). He also helped prep Paula Jones's lawyers for their appearance before the U.S. Supreme Court. In 1994, Olson successfully argued the pathbreaking case of *Hopwood v. Texas*, which led a U.S. Circuit Court to strike down an affirmative-action program

(*continues*)

As of November 1999, Boies was credited with losing only one case—defending Continental Airlines for predatory pricing against American Airlines—of the 45 major cases he had taken (Taft 1999). This record may, however, be overstated, since another observer noted that Boies lost a case in August of that year when a jury awarded $18.5 million against the Florida Power & Light Co. whom Boies had defended against breach of contract ("Boies Wonder" 1999, A9). Then too the verdicts in many cases are compromises rather than all-or-nothing victories or defeats.

(continued)

operated by the University of Texas. In a case that may come before the Court during his tenure, Olson recently filed a suit arguing that a section of the Endangered Species Act prohibiting landowners from killing wolves who come on their property is unconstitutional (Lewis 2001).

Long associated with conservative Republican causes, Olson serves on the board of directors of, and writes columns for, the *American Spectator* magazine, which has been particularly critical of President Clinton. Olson has jokingly told the Federalist Society that he is "at the heart" of "the vast right-wing conspiracy" (Tapper 2000). Olson is a friend of former prosecutor Kenneth Starr and of Justices Antonin Scalia and Clarence Thomas. Olson's wife Barbara Bracher, a one-time federal prosecutor, wrote a book critical of Hillary Rodham Clinton entitled *Hell to Pay*.

As assistant attorney general and head of Reagan's Office of Legal Counsel from 1981 to 1984, Olson authored numerous decisions, some of which did not always support the President's policies. This has led some observers, among them Walter Dellinger, who served as an acting solicitor general under Clinton, to predict that, as solicitor, Olson will be independent and might be willing to uphold some laws that are not to his own personal liking (Lane

2001). As a specialist in appellate cases, Olson is said to have "a clear, direct speaking style, devoid of rhetorical flourishes" ("At the Podium" 2000). Reflecting on his experience in arguing cases before the U.S. Supreme Court, Olson has said that:

> Before the Supreme Court, it doesn't work to have the emotional content that lawyers get away with at the trial level. There's no lack of passion about the case, but the justices want to have a conversation with you. You have to meet and discuss their questions, and they don't want you to bob and weave. ("At the Podium" 2000)

REFERENCES

"At the Podium with the Presidency on the Line." *Legal Times*, 4 December 2000, 16.

Lane, Charles. "Olson Nominated as Solicitor General: Lawyer Argued Bush Case in Disputed Election." *Washington Post*, 14 February 2001, A21.

Lewis, Neal A. "Man in the News: Prize Job for a Bush Rescuer." *New York Times*, 15 February 2001, A26, col. 3.

Mauro, Tony, and Jonathan Ringel. "Olson Expected Pick for Solicitor General." *The Legal Intelligencer*, 5 February 2001, 4.

Schmidt, Susan. "The Lawyers: Friends on Opposite Sides of a Landmark Fight." *Washington Post*, 2 December 2000, A15.

Tapper, Jake. "Boies vs. Olson." Found on the web at the address: <http://www.salon.com/-politics/feature/2000/11/19/lawyers/>.

Perhaps in partial compensation for his early problems with dyslexia, Boies has the reputation of working only from a bare outline and for drawing from what *People Weekly* somewhat hyperbolically described as "a memory that could be measured in megabytes" ("Making His Case" 1999, 88). Partner Jonathan D. Schiller has joked about Boies's extraordinary concentration and memory by noting that, "He blinks a couple of times and he's got a new cassette in place" ("Boies Wonder" 1999, A9).

Observers have noted that Boies's courtroom demeanor is calm and methodical rather than blustery and that transcripts of his trials do not necessarily make for riveting reading. Former partner Tom Barr of Cravath, Swaine & Moore notes that "the one talent of David's that stands out is his ability to lay out a course of action that would take into account any sort of complicated facts and develop a far-reaching scenario. It's a chess player's sense: if I do this, the following 15 things are going to happen, and if step 11 goes so, I'll do this rather than that. It's a fantastic game-playing ability" (Reich 1986, 74).

Boies is also credited with his "ability to take calculated risks" (Reich 1986, 74), as when, in the Westmoreland libel case, he chose to attempt to demonstrate the truth of the CBS commentary rather than simply defending CBS against charges that it had maliciously aimed at destroying the reputation of the general (Reich 1986, 74).

Boies is also known for emphasizing major points on cross-examination rather than nit-picking. Speaking of his role in the IBM case, Boies observed that "I want to get to the handful of central points that are at issue, while pausing to hit items that illustrate problems with the testimony. I don't want to nibble at the edges" ("'Hang 'em-High' Boies" 1999, 101). Although Boies is quoted as saying that, "I never want people to say, 'That's a great lawyer,' I want them to say, 'He sure has a great case,'" an observer has noted that Boies is "too much the showman to let his audience get bored" ("'Hang 'em-High' Boies" 1999, 101).

It has been said that Boies's casual cross-examinations are conducted without notes, as though he were "casually following the natural course of interrogation as if rafting down some lazy river" (Bryant 2000, 50). Boies has an uncanny way of using innocuous early admissions gathered during the first hour or so of such examinations to fashion a verbal noose that will successfully impeach a witness. One observer has said that Boies has "the understated canniness of a courtroom Columbo" (Sandberg 1999, 56), while another has likened his skill at cross-examination to a taste for blood ("Boies Wonder" 1999, A9).

Boies has had two children by each of three successive wives; his current wife, Mary, is herself an antitrust attorney, and of his four grown children, all of whom are attorneys, three work in the New York firm that he founded. A prodigious worker who told a colleague that he would rather win cases than sleep, Boies owns a wine cellar and an 86-foot sailboat (Thomas 2000, 43). He is known for enjoying good food and wine, for his skill at bridge, and for his gambling trips to Las Vegas. In contrast to many other high-paid lawyers, Boies typically dresses in black sneakers and suits bought off the rack at Sears or from a Land's End catalog; he also wears a Timex watch.

Responding to a critic who observed that, "He's got the whole Jimmy Stewart thing going on that makes him seem very normal and one of us when he's really a New York millionaire," one of Boies's associates responded that, "It's not a false image. David has the ability to know what's going to be important and then focus on just that. Everything else doesn't matter. Clothes don't matter" (Taft 1999). Comedian Garry Shandling, who hired Boies for a case that was later settled without trial, noted that he was "taken" by Boies's "earthiness and his authenticity" ("Boies Wonder" 1999, A9). Pointing to his mastery of the courtroom, Boies's attorney wife points instead to his artistry and likens watching him in action to seeing "Baryshnikov at the ballet" (Thomas 2000, 43).

—*John R. Vile*

Sources and Suggestions for Further Reading

"Boies Wonder." *The National Law Journal*, 27 December 1999, A8–A9.

Bryant, Adam. "A David (Boies) vs. Goliaths: Microsoft is just one of his high-profile cases." *Newsweek*, 12 June 2000, 50.

Donovan, Karen. "Boies Puts on a Legal Clinic at Microsoft Trial." *New York Law Journal*, 4 February 1999.

Grimaldi, James V., and Ceci Connolly. "Gore's Legal Eagle Has Daunting Task." *The Washington Post*, 4 December 2000, AO1.

"'Hang 'em High' Boies." *Fortune*, 15 February 1999, 101.

Kahn, Jeremy. "Why HMOs and Auction Houses Should Fear This Law Firm." *Fortune*, 15 May 2000, 74–75.

"Making His Case: Champ Litigator David Boies Takes a Bite Out of Bill Gates and His Software Giant." *People Weekly*, 22 November 1999, 87–88.

Perine, Keith. "Busting Bill Gates." *The Standard: Intelligence for the Internet Economy*, 24 April 2000.

Reich, Cary. "David Boies, the Wall Street Lawyer Everyone Wants." *The New York Times Magazine*, 1 June 1986, 18–24, 48, 50, 70, 74–76, 84.

Sandberg, Jared. "Microsoft's Tormentor: How an Affable Trial Lawyer with an Understated Canniness Is Driving Gates & Co. to the Wall." *Newsweek*, 1 March 1999, 56.

Taft, Daryl K. "The Legal Eagle." *Computer Reseller News*, 15 November 1999.

Thomas, Cathy Booth. "Master of the Impossible: The Lawyer Who Would Save Gore." *Time*, 27 November 2000, 42–43.

Vinson, Donald E. *America's Top Trial Lawyers: Who They Are & Why They Win*. Englewood Cliffs, NJ: Prentice-Hall Law & Business, 1994.

BRANDEIS, LOUIS DEMBITZ

(1856–1941)

Louis Dembitz Brandeis was a lawyer, social activist and reformer, and associate justice of the U.S. Supreme Court. Brandeis was born in Louisville, Kentucky, the youngest of four children of Adolph Brandeis and Frederika Dembitz, both first-generation immigrants from Prague. Adolph established a successful wholesale grain business and oversaw a household in which lively conversation about current events was common. The senior Brandeis was also a prudent businessperson and correctly anticipated the economic depression of 1873. Shortly before it hit, he sold his business and moved the family to Europe for three years. There Louis received some education, although he failed to gain admission to the highly competitive Vienna Gymnasium. After months of travel with his father, Louis enrolled in the An-

Louis Dembitz Brandeis
Bettmann/Corbis

nen-Realschule in Dresden, Germany, studying there from 1873 to 1875. In later years, Brandeis attributed much of his skill at legal analysis to the demanding education he received in Dresden. He returned to the United States in 1875 to begin study at Harvard Law School. His decision to do so was influenced by his uncle, Lewis Dembitz, a noted Louisville attorney. So strong was Dembitz's influence on the young Brandeis that he changed the middle name given him at birth (David) to Dembitz.

Brandeis arrived at Harvard just as one of the great changes in legal education was taking place. Christopher Columbus Langdell, the new dean, had introduced the case-study method. This new technique replaced the traditional practice of professors lecturing from legal treatises; instead Langdell emphasized the analysis of selected cases in depth in an effort to isolate key legal principles. This scientific approach to the law suited Brandeis particularly well given his German education, and he excelled. He finished his legal studies and did an additional year of graduate work, graduating in 1877 as the class valedictorian.

Brandeis was initially uncertain about where to begin his law practice. He decided to move to St. Louis to join the firm of his brother-in-law, James Taussig. The arrangement lasted only a year; Brandeis returned, lonely and unhappy, to Boston. There he opened a practice with Samuel Warren, a law school classmate and a prominent Boston socialite. Their firm quickly prospered, both in stature and income; within a decade it was one of the largest in the city. Brandeis also found Warren intellectually compatible, and together they published in the *Harvard Law Review* a path-breaking essay on the law of privacy.

Brandeis specialized in commercial law, and the firm, which ultimately became known as Brandeis, Dunbar & Nutter, built a reputation for knowing more about the business of its clients than they did. Much of Brandeis's time as a lawyer was spent consulting with clients about business strategies to pursue rather than mounting defenses once action had already been taken. At the same time, Brandeis was uniformly recognized as one of the toughest, smartest, and most knowledgeable lawyers in the city, a position that fueled his reputation as a litigator to be feared in the courtroom. That reputation served Brandeis well; by the 1890s he was hailed as one of the nation's most accomplished lawyers. The average salary of a lawyer during these years was five thousand dollars a year; Brandeis regularly earned ten times that much.

A stream of moral commitment also ran throughout Brandeis's career. He summed up his views about the relationship of law to public service in an article originally given as a speech to the Harvard Ethical Society in 1905. Entitled "The Opportunity in the Law," the essay exhorted his colleagues to develop careers that would place them in an independent position between the people and the huge industrial corporations then forming. The lawyer, according to Brandeis, was responsible for curing the excesses of either. This role meant that the lawyer had to use the law as an active instrument to shape the nation's social, economic, and political future. Recognizing these responsibilities, Brandeis reminded his peers to confront two realities. First, that the individual was the key force in society; second, that individuals, no matter how talented, all had limited capabilities. That meant that government in general and lawyers in particular had a strongly paternalistic role, one in which the state, operating through the law, had a responsibility to help people make the best of themselves. Brandeis's paternalism did not require that government coddle the individual; to the contrary, it meant that government had to foster regulated competition that would allow all persons to realize their full potential. Brandeis also reminded his fellow lawyers that individuals were most likely to realize their potential through small rather than large communities and that democracy itself was threatened by the development of giant corporations.

These themes of individual commitment and the value of small communities in control of their own destinies made Brandeis one of the nation's most influential Progressive lawyers. With his practice secure, Brandeis took the then-unorthodox step of providing his services for free to reform causes he supported. His role as a public advocate began in Boston. For example, with Edward Filene in 1900 he formed the Public Franchise League, which ultimately reached a compromise over the consolidation of all of the city's public utilities, including the subway. He was instrumental as well in developing the savings bank life insurance program for workers. Brandeis believed that large insurance companies sapped the average person of an inefficiently high proportion of their income with little real protection in the case of disaster. Instead, he proposed the establishment of savings banks that offered similar services at lower cost and with a guaranteed rate of return. The new arrangement was adopted not only in Boston but in other parts of the nation. So proud was he of this new scheme that close to the end of his life he remarked the savings bank life insurance program was his most important achievement.

Brandeis's fame quickly spread beyond Boston as he became known nationally as "the People's Attorney." In 1908, for example, Brandeis successfully argued the case of *Muller v. Oregon* before the U.S. Supreme Court. *Muller* involved an Oregon statute that limited women to ten hours of work per day in laundries and other industries. Curt Muller, the owner of the Grand Laundry in Portland, Oregon, required one of his female workers to stay on the job for a longer period. He was subsequently tried and fined ten dollars, and the Oregon Supreme Court upheld his conviction on appeal. Muller then turned to the U.S. Supreme Court, claiming that the Oregon law violated the principle of freedom to contract that the justices had recently proclaimed in *Lochner v. New York* (1905). Brandeis was brought into the case at the request of the Oregon attorney general and through the aegis of Josephine Goldmark, his sister-in-law and the head of the National Consumer's League.

Brandeis recognized that, given the precedent in *Lochner*, he had little chance of winning by demanding a strict application of precedent. Instead, he pioneered a new kind of legal brief that had long-term consequences for legal analysis and Supreme Court litigation. Brandeis's brief devoted a mere two pages to the discussion of the legal issues; the remaining 110 pages addressed the consequences of having women work overly long hours. Brandeis argued that the health, safety, and general welfare of working women would suffer if they were forced to toil too long. To buttress this position, he turned to a wide array of evidence, much of it drawn from studies of the impact of the industrial revolution in England and Europe. This evidence was taken from medical reports, psychological treatises, statistical compilations, and legislative studies. Brandeis mustered this broad range of social scientific evidence to demonstrate the importance of taking account of the impact rather than the strict letter of the law.

From these materials Brandeis persuaded a unanimous Supreme Court that the Oregon legislature had acted reasonably in passing the ten-hour law. He also asserted that legislative bodies were more appropriate forums for determining reasonable social needs than were courts. Judges were required, as a result, to take account of the evidence used by state legislatures in drafting laws to deal with the impact of the industrial revolution. A court might well conclude that legislators had used faulty data to draw unreasonable conclusions about social conditions, but at least judges had a duty to weigh such information. Lawyers, at the same time, had a duty to assess for the courts what the impact of a particular piece of legislation might be on the social fabric. This new approach opened the evaluation of any law to its policy implications rather than just its inherent legal logic.

The Brandeis brief became one of the central features of the new sociological jurisprudence. This new approach quickly gained a following among lawyers, such as Brandeis, who were eager to support a wide range of economic and other reform legislation. Not surprisingly, even Brandeis's staunchest conservative critics decided that the best way to fight this new approach was to adopt it. Over the longer term, the technique of using social scientific evidence to frame legal arguments was adopted by practitioners in contexts far removed from economic regulation, such as abortion and the death penalty.

Brandeis's national reputation also grew as a result of his leadership against the proposed merger by wealthy financier J. P. Morgan of the New Haven and Hartford Railroad Company with the Boston & Maine Railroad. Brandeis's objection to the proposed merger was based on his assessment that the combined railroads would concentrate too much power in the hands of one person. What concerned Brandeis most, however, was his growing realization that bigness in and of itself was antithetical to democracy. His solution was to regulate competition, so that all businesses could play on a level field. This position put Brandeis at odds with the other great trustbuster of the Progressive era, Theodore Roosevelt, who believed that the best approach was to regulate particular monopolies.

Brandeis became a leading opponent of industrial concentration in the years leading up to World War I. His opposition to bigness was rooted in what he viewed as a sound approach to business practices and not just a philosophical disagreement about the best way to promote democracy. For example, he sharply criticized large railroad companies because they increased shipping rates without explanation. Brandeis charged that the managers of these companies owed their shareholders the best possible return on their investments. Borrowing from the writing of Frederick Taylor and other advocates of greater industrial efficiency, Brandeis developed the concept of scientific management. By this idea he meant that the managers of any business should precisely determine the resources and time necessary to complete any task. If they did so, then the use of capital would be maximized, thereby benefiting shareholders, and costs would be kept in check, thereby benefiting consumers. What Brandeis wanted from business was a reduction in waste, a softening of the struggle between capital and labor, and a commitment to a new gospel of efficiency.

Brandeis stirred national attention in other ways. During the administration of President William Howard Taft, for example, Secretary of the Interior Richard A. Ballinger came under attack for his stewardship of the nation's natural resources. Much as he had criticized J. P. Morgan for corruption in cooking the books of the railroad companies he sought to merge, so Brandeis turned his lethal legal gaze on charges of corruption by Ballinger. Brandeis led a team of lawyers who successfully demonstrated that Ballinger's decision to open certain lands to public entry had been motivated, at least in part, by a desire to serve major corporate interests. Even though a congressional investigation exonerated Ballinger, Brandeis had so successfully focused public attention on the matter that the secretary of the interior resigned in March 1911.

As a result of these actions, Woodrow Wilson, the Democratic candidate for president in 1912, eagerly sought Brandeis's counsel on a host of economic and social reform matters. That relationship grew even stronger after the former New Jersey governor entered the White House. The new president had originally wanted to offer Brandeis the position of solicitor general, but that idea faded when the business wing of the party raised objections. Ever the realist, Brandeis refused to let this opposition color his attitude, and he continued to interact regularly with Wilson. As Brandeis explained to his brother, the "future has many good things in store for those who can wait, . . . have patience and exercise good judgment" (Paper 1986, 144).

Wilson ultimately rewarded Brandeis for his loyalty by nominating him to the Supreme Court in January 1916 to replace Justice Joseph R. Lamar.

A combination of conservative forces drawn from corporations, a bar resentful of Brandeis's public advocacy, and anti-Semites coalesced in opposition to the nomination. The result was one of the most bruising confirmation processes in U.S. history that was notable for being the first one to be fought through open rather than closed hearings. President Wilson remained steadfast in support of his nominee, as did the major reform groups. Finally, in June 1916 the full Senate confirmed him by a vote of 46 to 22, making Brandeis the first Jew to sit on the high court.

On the bench, Brandeis exercised fidelity to the same causes and methods that guided his law practice for more than three decades. Brandeis was a consummate legal craftsman, perhaps the finest to sit on the high court in the twentieth century, and he was also the Court's greatest authority on commercial law. He also recognized that justices could not act as legislators and, as a result, he became one of the leading exponents of judicial restraint. He also remained mindful of the need to weigh the facts in a particular case, much as he had done as a lawyer. Through much of his judicial career, however, such a stance often placed him at odds with his colleagues and promoted regular dissents. As a justice, Brandeis wrote 528 opinions, 454 on behalf of the Court, and the rest in concurrence or dissent. Brandeis's dissents were invariably longer, and crammed with detail reminiscent of his earlier work on *Muller*, than his opinions for the Court.

Although Brandeis believed that the justices should defer to the legislature in matters of economic policy, he often took a different stance in cases involving civil liberties and civil rights. In *Whitney v. California* (1927), for example, he eloquently defended free expression rights against intrusion by the government. In *Olmstead v. United States* (1928), he objected to the Supreme Court's finding that wiretapping did not constitute a violation of the Fourth Amendment. Through his dissent he instructed his fellow justices on the right of privacy, about which he and Warren had written years earlier. "The makers of our Constitution," Brandeis wrote, "conferred, as against the government, the right to be let alone—the most comprehensive of rights and the right most valued by civilized man" (277 U.S. 438, 478). Much of Brandeis's thinking on the subject of privacy as a constitutional matter was adopted by the Court in *Griswold v. Connecticut* (1965). Brandeis believed strongly in the value of dissent generally, because he saw it as a way to speak to future generations about what might be done with the law when social circumstances had changed. As he once told Felix Frankfurter, "My faith in time is great" (Urofsky 1992, 85).

Brandeis's most important contribution on the bench was his majority opinion in *Erie Railroad Co. v. Tompkins* (1938). He believed that the federal judiciary should have only limited jurisdiction and that it should apply only to matters that went beyond the concerns of any one state. As both a commercial lawyer and later a justice, he repeatedly argued that the historical rule in *Swift v. Tyson* (1842), that allowed federal courts to ignore state law in favor of a federal common law of commercial relations, was wrong because it confused the law and prompted litigants to engage in wasteful forum shopping. In *Erie* he finally carried the day in a decision that required lower federal courts to follow state rules.

Brandeis continued his political contacts even while a justice, a practice that has stirred recent criticism from students of the Court. On the one hand, Brandeis set a strict standard for his behavior, refusing to comment publicly on the work of the Court or even to accept an honorary degree. On the other hand, Brandeis repeatedly consulted directly with President Franklin D. Roosevelt and other members of the administration and used his good friend and Roosevelt confidant, Professor Felix Frankfurter of the Harvard Law School, to serve on other occasions as an intermediary.

Few American lawyers have had the impact that Brandeis did, either in practice or on the bench. He not only redefined the nature of legal argument through the adoption of the Brandeis brief, but he also demonstrated both on and off the bench the value of social scientific information as a way of adapting the law to meet social change. Perhaps the greatest testament to Brandeis's influence is that much of what he urged as a Progressive reformer and later as a justice in dissent has become commonplace today.

—*Kermit L. Hall*

Sources and Suggestions for Further Reading

Mason, Alpheus T. *Brandeis, A Free Man's Life*. New York: Viking Press, 1946.

McGraw, Thomas K. *Prophets of Regulation: Charles Francis Adams, Louis D. Brandeis, James M. Landis, Alfred E. Kahn*. Cambridge: Belknap Press of Harvard University Press, 1984.

Murphy, Bruce A. *The Brandeis/Frankfurter Connection*. New York: Oxford University Press, 1982.

Paper, Lewis J. "Louis D. Brandeis." In *Encyclopedia of the American Constitution*, edited by Leonard Levy. New York: Macmillan, 1986, 1:140–144.

Strum, Phillipa. *Louis D. Brandeis: Justice for the People*. Cambridge: Harvard University Press, 1984.

Urofsky, Melvin. "Louis Dembitz Brandeis." In *The Oxford Companion to the Supreme Court of the United States*, edited by Kermit L. Hall. New York: Oxford University Press, 1992, 83–85.

BUGLIOSI, VINCENT T., JR.

(1934–)

VINCENT T. BUGLIOSI JR.

A crowd of reporters surround Los Angeles prosecutor Vincent Bugliosi as he leaves the courtroom during the trial of Charles Manson, 3 August 1971. (Bettmann/Corbis)

VINCENT T. BUGLIOSI JR. SPENT EIGHT YEARS AS A PROSECUTOR with the Los Angeles County District Attorney's Office, trying nearly 1,000 cases, and winning 105 out of 106 felony jury trials. Bugliosi achieved his greatest fame as lead prosecutor in the early 1970s trial of Charles Manson and four members of his "family" for the brutal 1969 murders of seven people. Bugliosi won convictions in those trials, as he did in all of the twenty-one murder trials he prosecuted. Since 1972, Bugliosi has been in private practice and has continued to achieve a string of courtroom victories. He has also established a very successful career as a writer of several best-selling books based on his own career as a prosecutor and defense attorney, as well as two novels and several works on contemporary legal issues.

Bugliosi was born in Hibbing, Minnesota, on August 18, 1934, the son of Vincent and Ida Bugliosi. Bugliosi senior was an Italian immigrant and the owner of a grocery store in Hibbing before he began working as a conductor for the Great Northern Railroad. Vincent Bugliosi Jr. moved to Los Angeles for his last year of high school and then attended college at the University of Miami, Florida, where he received a B.A. degree in 1956. He achieved the rank of captain in the U.S. Army in 1957. Bugliosi then entered law school, graduating with an LL.B. degree in 1964 from the University of California at Los Angeles, where he was the president of his class. After graduation, he was admitted to the California bar and joined the Los Angeles district attorney's office, where he remained for eight years before becoming a partner in the Beverly Hills law firm of Steinberg & Bugliosi. From 1968 to 1974, he was a professor of criminal law at the Beverly Hills School of Law. Bugliosi twice ran for elective office, losing both times, first in 1972 when he sought to become the Los Angeles district attorney (DA), and then in 1974 in an election for the California attorney general. He has been married since 1956 to his wife Gail (Talluto), and they have two children, Wendy and Vincent.

Bugliosi's success as both a prosecutor and defense attorney has made him one of the most well-known authorities on trial practice in the United States. In addition to giving numerous lectures and appearing in seminars, he has written several essays explaining his techniques in preparing for and handling criminal trials. According to Bugliosi, preparation is the most essential factor in success at trial. He credits his achievement as a trial lawyer to detailed preparation. Most important, he advocates that lawyers write down everything they know about a particular case, and then write down the way they intend to proceed at trial. Accounts of his most famous cases include numerous references to his detailed note-taking on all phases of the trial, from the initial investigation and discovery phases, to questions for witnesses, to the final arguments. He has said that he determines the evidence and testimony he will need to win a lawsuit, and then, based on what he has found, he carefully plans the best way to present his case to a jury, having much of his final argument drafted even before jury selection begins. Even as a prosecutor, Bugliosi joined in the investigation of the crime, working with the police to seek out evidence and witness testimony himself. Bugliosi believes that such intense preparation allows attorneys more control over the events that follow, even allowing for unexpected developments. He describes the trial as "the acting out of the scenario or script you have already written."

Bugliosi achieved national prominence through his investigation and successful prosecution of Charles Manson, Susan Atkins, Patricia Krenwinkle, and Leslie Van Houten in the brutal 1969 Tate-LaBianca murders. The trial was complicated by the brutal nature of the murders, the presence of multiple defendants and their attorneys, and the DA's removal of Bugliosi's co-prosecutor shortly after the beginning of the trial. Adding to the confusion was the often disruptive behavior of Manson and his followers throughout the nine-and-a-half-month trial, and the fact that all of this took place under the glare of the media spotlight. Nonetheless, Bugliosi and the prosecution team convinced the jury of Manson's guilt despite the fact that he had not been present during the murders. The prosecution focused on Manson's part in the conspiracy to commit each atrocity, with Bugliosi skillfully establishing Manson's motive and his control over his followers while still proving Atkins, Krenwinkle, and Van Houten's own culpability in committing the crimes.

Given the seemingly random nature of the Tate-LaBianca killings, as well as Manson's nonparticipation at the murder scenes, Bugliosi has described his search for a motive as one of the key elements he sought to uncover during his investigation of the case. After interviewing the many people who had interacted with the Family in prior months and years, Bugliosi eventually began to focus upon Manson's belief in "helter skelter," a complex philosophy created from, among other things, the book of Revelation and lyrics by the Beatles. Although he had difficulty at first convincing his co-prosecutor to accept this theory, Bugliosi eventually presented evidence and arguments to the jury showing that Manson hoped to spark an apocalyptic race war by implicating African-Americans in the Tate-LaBianca murders. During "helter skelter," the African-American race would murder all of the white population except for the Manson Family, who would be hidden away in Death Valley. At that point, according to Manson, the victors would turn to him for leadership. After months of testimony, argument, and courtroom disruption, the jury convicted Manson and the three women on all charges. Later in 1971, Bugliosi successfully prosecuted the fifth member of the Manson family accused in the Tate-LaBianca murders, Charles Watson, who was convicted of seven counts of murder and one count of conspiracy to commit murder, and, like the other four defendants, sentenced to death (although the California Supreme Court subsequently overruled the state capital punishment law).

Although the Manson trial established Bugliosi's national reputation, he had already won a large number of high-profile courtroom victories and had been recognized for his determination, courtroom skill, and flair for publicity in his previous four years with the Los Angeles DA's office. One of Bugliosi's earlier murder trials became the basis of a 1978 book. In a scenario that has been compared to the film *Double Indemnity*, Alan Palliko, a former Los Angeles police officer turned automobile insurance investigator, and his girlfriend, Sandra Stockton, were charged with murdering her husband for insurance money. Palliko was also charged with murdering his wife for the same reason. No physical evidence tied Palliko or Stockton to the crimes, yet prosecutor Bugliosi successfully built a case on circumstantial evidence, including Palliko's and Stockton's extravagant expenditures after the death of Mr. Stockton, and Palliko's dogged search for a wife—one that he quickly insured—in the months that followed. In his jury summation, Bugliosi compared circumstantial evidence to different strands of rope that when bound together create enough strength to establish guilt. The jury accepted the prosecution's case and convicted both defendants.

Although Bugliosi has said that he is happiest in a courtroom and has spoken of his wish to become a leading criminal defense attorney, he has only sporadically taken cases since he entered private practice in 1972. His courtroom success, however, has continued in the cases he has handled, as he has won acquittal for his clients in each of the three murder trials he has handled for the defense. Despite this, he has perhaps failed in his stated ambition to find a case that would do for his defense career what the Manson trial did for his reputation as a prosecutor. His representation of accused murderer Jennifer Jenkins has received the most attention because of his subsequent book on the case and the movie that followed. A great deal of circumstantial evidence tied Jenkins to the 1974 murder of a woman on an island in the South Seas, including the fact that she and her ex-lover had shown up in Hawaii in a boat owned by the victim and her husband, who had both disappeared. The prosecution also focused on the vicious nature of the murder, arguing that this made it unlikely that Jenkins's lover could have committed the crime without her knowledge. Furthermore, Jenkins was a troublesome client, with both a criminal record and a seeming reluctance to aid her attorneys in her defense. Still, after speaking with her and investigating the case, Bugliosi believed in her innocence. During the trial, he successfully refuted the circumstantial evidence presented against his client, and through his examination of Jenkins convinced the jury to distinguish between her and the ex-lover who had already been convicted of the crime, despite Jenkins's insistence that he also was innocent. Bugliosi took Jenkins's actions, including her lies and her sometimes less-than-savory actions, and created a convincing argument that, rather than supporting her guilt, substantiated her lack of culpability in the murder.

Nonetheless, Bugliosi's participation in criminal defense work has been limited by his unwillingness to represent persons charged with murder or other violent crimes unless he is convinced of their innocence or finds substantially mitigating circumstances. For example, he investigated and turned down the opportunity to represent Dr. Jeffrey MacDonald, accused of murdering his wife and children. Later he refused to defend Dan White, who was charged in the San Francisco Moscone-Milk murders. When asked whether his reluctance to take on certain defendants denies them the right of counsel, Bugliosi has said that if a situation arose where he was indeed

Defending the Innocent

Lawyers throughout the Anglo-American world are often confronted with the ethical dilemma of defending those accused of heinous crimes. Canadian defense attorney Edward L. Greenspan was confronted by his eight-year-old daughter Julie after he agreed to represent a man accused of raping and killing a six-year-old girl named Lizzie Tomlinson.

When Julie asked, "Dad, why are you defending the man who killed Lizzie?" Greenspan first considered a legal explanation.

He settled instead for the following:

"I'm not defending the man who killed Lizzie. Do you understand, Julie? I'm defending the man who didn't kill her" (Greenspan and Jonas 1987, 128).

At trial, Greenspan succeeded in showing that the accused killer had been mistakenly identified and was not guilty of the crime of which he was accused.

REFERENCE

Greenspan, Edward L., and George Jonas. *Greenspan: The Case for the Defence.* Toronto: Macmillan of Canada, 1987.

the only attorney available, he would willingly take on the representation of such a client. Apart from that, he does not believe that the canons of ethics require him to represent every client who asks for his help, and he has said he believes his conscience would not allow him to help a guilty murderer win an acquittal.

Nonetheless, Bugliosi's reputation as an attorney has grown over the years, in large part because publishers and the entertainment world also recognized Bugliosi's fame in and out of the courtroom. Even before the Manson trial, he had served as the inspiration for two television movies and then a short-lived television series called *The D.A.*, starring Robert Conrad. Bugliosi was the show's technical advisor, and he edited scripts for the two movies that aired in 1969 and 1971. The series debuted in September 1971, but it ended the following January. *The D.A.* followed young deputy district attorney Paul Ryan as he investigated a crime and then prosecuted the accused.

Although the television series lasted only three months, Bugliosi himself achieved much greater success as the author of three books detailing his role in three of his most notable trials. All three were later turned into well-received television movies. Three years after the Manson trial, Bugliosi and coauthor Curt Gentry penned the bestseller *Helter Skelter: The True Story of the Manson Murders*. *Till Death Us Do Part: A True Murder Mystery*, cowritten by Ken Hurwitz, was published in 1978 and received the Edgar Award from the Mystery Writers of America the next year. Two novels followed: *Shadow of Cain* (with Hurwitz) in 1981, and *Lullaby and Good Night: A Novel Inspired by the True Story of Vivian Gordon* in 1987. Bugliosi returned to his own legal exploits in 1991's *And the Sea Will Tell,* coauthored by Bruce B. Henderson. The movie *Helter Skelter* aired in 1976, *And the Sea Will Tell* in 1991, and *Till Death Us Do Part* in 1992. As in the three books, Bugliosi was a central character in the movies, and he was portrayed in the films by George DiCenzo, Richard Crenna, and Arliss Howard, respectively.

Invariably in the last twenty years, Bugliosi has been called upon as a leading authority and commentator on trial advocacy and other legal issues, including some of the most controversial of the last forty years. In one rather unique instance, Bugliosi successfully "prosecuted" accused assassin Lee Harvey Oswald in an unscripted 1985 televised docudrama, which was played out before a real judge and jury and involved real witnesses to the 1963 shooting. He and defense attorney GERRY SPENCE—who had not lost a jury trial in seventeen years—participated in a three-day trial, with Bugliosi spending almost five months engaged in his usual pretrial preparation. In recent years, with the explosion of television legal commentary, Bugliosi has often been seen on various news programs discussing issues ranging from the parole requests of the Manson defendants to the O. J. Simpson case. He has been an outspoken critic of the parties involved in the Simpson trial and has published a book on the trial and a twelve-hour videotape pointing out where he thinks the prosecution went wrong and how he would have tried the case. He has also penned works discussing the nation's drug problem and criticizing the Supreme Court's ruling in the Paula Jones case. He remains an outspoken advocate for the rights of both the people and the accused and one of the most respected trial attorneys in the United States.

—*Ruth Anne Thompson*

Sources and Suggestions for Further Reading

Bugliosi, Vincent T. "A Case for Not Defending the Guilty." In *Criminal Justice: Opposing Viewpoints,* edited by Jill Karson. San Diego: Greenhaven Press, 1998, 172–176.

_____. *Outrage: The Five Reasons O. J. Simpson Got Away with Murder.* New York: W. W. Norton, 1996.

_____. "Tactics and Techniques for Handling Each Phase of a Criminal Trial." In *The Trial Masters: A Handbook of Strategies and Techniques That Win Cases,* edited by Bertram G. Warshaw. Englewood Cliffs, N.J.: Prentice-Hall, 1984, 12–34.

Bugliosi, Vincent T., and Curt Gentry. *Helter Skelter: The True Story of the Manson Murders.* New York: W. W. Norton, 1974.

Bugliosi, Vincent T., and Bruce B. Henderson. *And the Sea Will Tell.* New York: Ballantine, 1991.

Bugliosi, Vincent T., and Ken Hurwitz. *Till Death Us Do Part.* New York: W. W. Norton, 1978.

Lief, Michael S., H. Mitchell Caldwell, and Benjamin Bycel. *Ladies and Gentlemen of the Jury: Greatest Closing Arguments in Modern Law.* New York: Scribner, 1998.

CAMPBELL, JOHN ARCHIBALD

(1811–1889)

JOHN ARCHIBALD CAMPBELL
Collection of the Supreme Court of the United States

BORN IN WASHINGTON, GEORgia, to lawyer and state legislator Duncan Green Campbell and his wife, Mary Williamson, in 1811, John Archibald Campbell was recognized as a prodigy. He enrolled in what is today the University of Georgia at age eleven, graduated with honors, and subsequently enrolled in the U.S. Military Academy at West Point. After his father died the day before he hoped to be elected governor, John left West Point for a one-year teaching job in Florida and subsequently returned to Georgia, where by special act he was admitted to the bar at age eighteen in 1829, a year before he moved to Alabama and found similar acceptance there.

In Alabama, Campbell married Anna Esther Goldthwaite, by whom he would father a son and four daughters. In 1836, Campbell was elected to the state legislature and moved from Montgomery to Mobile, where he began his study of civil law. Although he twice refused nominations to the state supreme court (the first offer coming when he was but twenty-four years of age), in 1850 Campbell served as a delegate to the Nashville Convention, where he represented Southern views. In 1852, he opposed DANIEL WEBSTER in arguments in an inheritance case, *Gaines v. Relf*, before the U.S. Supreme Court, one of six cases that he argued that term (Connor 1971, 11). The next year, after failing to replace Justice John McKinley, who had died, with Senator George Badger, President Franklin Pierce appointed Campbell to the U.S. Supreme Court, then headed by Chief Justice Roger Taney, after Justices James Catron and Benjamin Robbins Curtis wrote a letter urging the President to do so. Commenting at the time on Campbell's "learning," "industry," "analytical" mind, and "temperate" and "just" character, *The New York Times* ranked him with former Supreme Court justice JOSEPH STORY (Connor 1971, 17).

On the Court, Campbell established a reputation as a moderate Southerner whose best-known decision, apart from his concurrence in *Dred Scott v. Sandford* (1857), was his dissent in *Dodge v. Woolsey* (1856). In that case, Campbell argued, somewhat contrary to MARSHALL's decision in the *Dartmouth College Case*, for state legislative discretion over state-chartered corporations.

Campbell, who had freed his own household slaves, worked both on the Supreme Court and while riding circuit to moderate the growing conflict between the North and South. He ruled that the slave trade was illegal, and he prosecuted those engaged in filibusters (military expeditions) designed to foment revolution in Cuba and other Latin American nations to add them to the Union. Campbell believed that slavery was a transitory institution, but in an article in the *Southern Quarterly Review*, he did argue for changes in the law of slavery designed to protect slave families (Connor 1971, 105–107).

As war approached, Campbell was sometimes suggested as a compromise Democratic candidate for president. He counseled his state against secession and tried to avert war by attempting to convince Abraham Lincoln not to reinforce Fort Sumter, but, when war came, he joined Alabama when it seceded and resigned from the Court shortly after the start of the Civil War. In 1862, he became assistant secretary of war for the Confederacy, a position in which he chiefly exercised his legal and administrative skills. He resigned in 1865, thereafter meeting with ABRAHAM LINCOLN in Richmond in an unsuccessful attempt to reconvene the Virginia legislature to end the war. He was imprisoned for four months at the end of the war but was released by President Andrew Johnson, after which he moved to New Orleans and resumed legal practice in partnership with his son, Duncan (who preceded him in death), and with Judge Henry M. Spofford.

Campbell's postbellum career was every bit the equal of his previous work, and, like fellow former justice BENJAMIN CURTIS, to whom he is often compared, Campbell appeared frequently before the U.S. Supreme Court. Campbell continued to be known for his wide reading in, and knowledge of, both common and civil law and for his thorough preparation of cases.

When confronting a difficult case, his fellow citizens were known to say, "Turn it over to God and Mr. Campbell" (Twiss 1962, 43).

A fellow New Orleans attorney, Carleton Hunt, said that "he threw himself into the contests in which he became engaged, with a degree of intensity which it is difficult to express." Hunt continued:

> He became absorbed in his professional undertakings. He would sit for hours in his great library lost in thought, without turning the leaves of the volume before him. At other times, he would walk in the streets gesticulating, as he went, to the surprise of all who passed him. He spoke in Court customarily from the many books spread out before him. His language seemed to be borrowed from the books and was apt to be technical and quaint, as the authorities themselves. His style, for the most part, was measured and grave, as became his years and standing at the Bar. From time to time, however, as he caught fire from the concussion of debate, he became inflamed and fierce in his assaults upon his adversary's side. (Connor 1971, 207)

Cases that Campbell argued before the U.S. Supreme Court included *Waring v. The Mayor* (1869), involving the validity of city taxes on imported goods, and the *Tonnage Cases,* in which he succeeded in helping to invalidate state taxes on steamboats (Connor 1971, 208).

It is generally recognized that Campbell's finest hour as a lawyer came in a case that he lost. After the Civil War, the nation had adopted three constitutional amendments. These were the Thirteenth Amendment, which eliminated involuntary servitude, the Fourteenth Amendment, which defined who citizens were and what rights they exercised, and the Fifteenth Amendment, which prohibited race from being used to deprive individuals of their right to vote.

The *Slaughterhouse Cases* (1873) were the first in which the U.S. Supreme Court was asked to interpret the first two of these amendments. Opposing attorneys Matthew Hale Carpenter and JEREMIAH S. BLACK, Campbell used these amendments to argue against the state's granting of monopoly privileges to a slaughterhouse operation in New Orleans. In so doing, Campbell argued for an expansive interpretation of these amendments. Far from being limited to protecting the rights of former slaves, he contended that the Thirteenth and Fourteenth Amendments were designed to guarantee rights to everyone, including those in this case who could no longer operate out of their own abattoirs. In this case, Campbell mustered his considerable knowledge of law in both England and France to argue that limitations on economic freedoms amounted to "servitude" as outlawed by the Thirteenth Amendment and to a denial of the "privileges and immunities" guaranteed to all citizens under the Fourteenth Amendment. Campbell, the former Confederate, now argued for broad federal protection of individual rights:

> The tie between the United States and every citizen in every part of its jurisdiction has been made intimate and to the same extent the Confederate features of the Government have been obliterated. The States, with their connection with the citizen, are placed under the oversight and enforcing hand of Congress. The purpose is manifest to establish, through the whole jurisdiction of the United States, one people, and that every member of the empire shall understand and appreciate the constitutional fact that his Privileges and immunities cannot be abridged by State authority. (Connor 1971, 215)

Further evoking the importance of the economic rights to run one's business that he was defending, Campbell contended that "the rights of a man, in his person, to the employment of his faculties and to the product of those faculties, do not come to him by any concession of the State. They are his inviolable prerogative" (Connor 1971, 216).

Although the Court voted 5 to 4 against this broad interpretation of the privileges and immunities clause (which continues to this day to be narrowly interpreted), within a decade or so the Court increasingly began to interpret the due process clause of the Fourteenth Amendment as providing just this sort of protection for economic rights, so it could be argued that Campbell lost this legal battle only to win the larger legal war.

In any event, even though he lost, the *Slaughterhouse Cases* undoubtedly enhanced Campbell's own reputation as a lawyer, and he continued to argue about six cases per year before the U.S. Supreme Court. Campbell's most notable advocacy centered in *New York v. Louisiana* and *New Hampshire v. Louisiana* (1883), in which he successfully established the immunity of states under the Eleventh Amendment to suits to which they did not consent. Again, Campbell's arguments were distinguished both by their logic and by their many references to history. Campbell also argued a number of cases on behalf of railroads seeking to avoid state regulations (Connor 1971, 250–251). In a case, that Campbell won before the U.S. Supreme Court after a loss before the Louisiana Supreme Court, *New Orleans Gas Light Co. v. Louisiana Light Co.* (1885), Campbell defended the continuing legitimacy of a state grant to an original light company against a grant to a new company sought by the state's attorney general. Showing his ability to use rhetoric to evoke emotions, Campbell argued that

> in the stock of this "defendant" corporation is reposed the property of the widow and the orphan. Brothers have given it to unprovided sisters. Mothers

and fathers have bought it for the support of their young daughters. The object of this suit is to make these deposits a spoil and booty for the greedy. (Connor 1971, 256)

Similarly, in arguing a case before Justice Joseph Bradley in Circuit Court, Campbell referred to the Eighth Circle of Dante's Inferno as the place most appropriate "for those people who traffic in the public interest for their own private advantage" (Connor 1971, 266). He further argued that

this open, flagrant, public, shameless traffic, in acts of legislation, in corporate rights obtaining monopolies and exclusive grants of the public domain of various kinds, infringing the personal rights, the individual rights of men, by bribes and corruption, is the most frightful of all the circumstances that attend the present condition of society. (Connor 1971, 267)

Those who knew Campbell as a lawyer frequently commented on his wide knowledge, his love of books, and his hard work. A reporter for the *Philadelphia Record* who heard him argue *New Hampshire v. Louisiana* noted that

Mr. Campbell is absorbed in his work. He has no eyes or ears for anything or anybody not immediately concerned in the case in hand. He lives quietly in New Orleans, surrounded by one of the finest law libraries, in all languages, in the world. He is a profound civil lawyer, with Justinian at his tongue's end, and, at the same time, a common-law lawyer, competent to battle with the best of that class. His memory is as wonderful as [the historian] George Bancroft's. He apparently remembers every scrap of law he ever saw or heard, and he has his resources so classified and catalogued that he can bring them forth at will. . . . Once retained in a case, he becomes a recluse. When he emerges from his books, he has absorbed that case with all its bearings, either his own side or the other. (Connor 1971, 261)

Lawyer George Tichnor Curtis further said of Campbell that

he ranks with the greatest advocates of our time, not for eloquence, not for brilliancy, nor for the arts of the rhetorician, but for those solid accomplishments, for that lucid and weighty argumentation, by which a court is instructed and aided to a right conclusion. The day of mere eloquence has passed away from this forum. What is effectual here now is clearness of statement, closeness and accuracy of reasoning, and the power to making learning useful in the attainment of judicial truth. These accomplishments were possessed by Judge Campbell in a very uncommon degree. He has lived to a great age, and in the whole of his long life there has never been a public act or utterance that is to be regretted. (Connor 1971, 284–285)

Campbell retired from general practice in 1884 after the death of his wife and moved to Baltimore to be near two of his daughters, but he continued to argue select cases before the U.S. Supreme Court. Campbell died in Baltimore in 1889 before being able to attend the centennial celebrations of the U.S. Supreme Court, to which the Court had invited him. In answering his invitation, the man who had once resigned from that body wrote, "Tell the Court that I join daily in the prayer, 'God save the United States and [its] honorable Court'" (Connor 1971, 280).

—*John R. Vile*

Sources and Suggestions for Further Reading

Connor, Henry G. *John Archibald Campbell: Associate Justice of the United States Supreme Court, 1853–1861.* Boston: Houghton Mifflin, 1920. Reprint, New York: Da Capo Press, 1971.

Paddock, Lisa. *Facts About the Supreme Court of the United States.* New York: H. W. Wilson, 1996.

Twiss, Benjamin R. *Lawyers and the Constitution: How Laissez Faire Came to the Supreme Court.* New York: Russell & Russell, 1962.

Ward, Artemus E. "Campbell, John Archibald." In *American National Biography,* edited by John A. Garrarty and Mark C. Carnes. New York: Oxford University Press, 1999, 4:285–286.

CHASE, SALMON P.

(1808–1873)

SALMON P. CHASE
Library of Congress

A MAJOR FIGURE DURING the middle third of nineteenth-century America, Salmon Portland Chase pioneered use of the courtroom as a forum and litigation as a force for change on the most pressing moral and social issue of that day: slavery. He did more than fight for the freedom of fugitive slaves and the acquittals of those who abetted them. He formulated and articulated a theory for antislavery activists that was a respectable alternative to extreme abolitionism. He was convinced that a centrist position, which he abandoned only after the Civil War began, would lead to slavery's extinction. The antislavery part of Chase's law practice in turn rewarded him with the visibility, the contacts, and a base that led to a career in public office spanning a quarter century. Without his antislavery practice, Chase might well have had no political career; like other talented and prosperous attorneys from that era, he would today rest among the ranks of the long forgotten.

The eighth child of Ithamar and Janette Ralston Chase, Salmon was born on January 13, 1808, in Cornish, New Hampshire, a town founded by his grandfather. Ithamar was a successful farmer with an extended family that was also prosperous and precocious. Most of Salmon's uncles were educated professionals, including Philander Chase, an Episcopal minister, and Dudley Chase, later U.S. senator from Vermont. His pretentious name, which he came to dislike, derived from Salmon Chase, another uncle who had been the leading lawyer in Portland in what is now the state of Maine. Young Salmon's comfortable childhood and promising future were placed in jeopardy in 1817, however, when his father suffered a fatal stroke. After struggling to provide education for her children, Janette arranged for Salmon to travel to Ohio in 1820 to live with his uncle Philander, who was by that time Episcopal bishop of the state and director of an academy for boys. With a regimen of discipline, hard work, religiosity, and instruction, Bishop Chase had a profound impact on Salmon's upbringing in emphasizing the importance of accomplishment. Briefly studying at Cincinnati College after his uncle became its president, Salmon returned to New Hampshire in 1823 and in 1824 enrolled at Dartmouth College, where he was graduated as a member of Phi Beta Kappa in 1826.

Although he considered entering the Christian ministry in New England, Chase shortly moved to the District of Columbia and found a position as schoolmaster. Among his pupils were two sons of WILLIAM WIRT, the distinguished lawyer, friend of Thomas Jefferson and James Madison, and President JOHN QUINCY ADAMS's attorney general. Wirt gave Chase access to the upper levels of Washington society, where he learned, if he had not known before, that his overly refined sense of humor and large, muscular build made him enormously attractive to women and that he could write puppy-love poetry. Chase also nurtured the useful habit of making friends with those who might later serve him well.

In the estimate of more than one biographer, Wirt became a role model, even a father figure, and, with Uncle Philander, was the second of the two men most influential in shaping Chase's future. If his uncle had stressed achievement, Wirt imparted humanitarian concerns (although he was also a slave owner) and demonstrated the rewards and stature that a well-lived public career could bring. Both men contributed to the complex personality that Chase developed: piety alongside pomposity; demanding standards for himself and others that made him a difficult person with whom to work; and ambition, vanity, and pride coupled with caring for, and generosity toward, others.

Chase's relationship with Wirt and his family led very soon to a realization that he could more easily achieve the life he wanted to lead as a lawyer than as a teacher. Chase therefore asked Wirt to tutor him in law. Entering into an informal apprentice-type relationship with an established attorney was the route almost everyone took into the legal profession in Chase's day. One "read law" under another's tutelage—typically for three years in Washington—and learned by asking, by doing, and by observing. Education in law schools would not become the preferred preparation for practice until the twentieth century. But given the demands on Wirt's time, it seems likely that Chase was mainly self-taught.

But for Andrew Jackson's victory (and Adams's defeat) in the presidential election in 1828, Chase might never have left Washington. Not only did Chase detest Jackson, but Jackson's ascendancy sharply curtailed Wirt's influence in Washington. Chase decided to seek his legal fortune elsewhere, but he first needed to be admitted to the bar. So on December 7, 1829, Chase appeared before an examining panel in Washington headed by the noted jurist William Cranch. Although he answered questions competently, he admitted that he had not studied the full three years. When Cranch (a fellow New Englander and a friend of Chase's uncle Dudley) advised him that he would have to prepare for yet one more year, Chase replied, "Please your honors. I have made all my arrangements to go to the Western country and practice law" (Hart 1969, 13). After a brief discussion with the panel, Judge Cranch decreed, "Swear in Mr. Chase" (Niven 1995, 27).

The "Western country" proved to be Cincinnati, where Chase arrived on March 13, 1830. With its population and wealth on the increase, this Ohio city of nearly twenty-five thousand was already an important Ohio River port just opposite the slave state of Kentucky. Because of its economic ties to the South, Cincinnati was also the most proslavery city in Ohio.

As a fledgling practice developed, Chase quickly displayed both public spirit and intellectual energy. In October, he organized the Cincinnati Lyceum, comparable to a community enrichment program that a university might sponsor today. Two of his four lectures at the lyceum were published in the *North American Review,* a major periodical that circulated widely, especially in the East. One of the two lectures approvingly portrayed British statesman Henry Brougham's fight against the slave trade and was Chase's first recorded public comment on slavery. Within five years, he was known throughout the Ohio bar after he published a three-volume set that for the first time compiled the laws of Ohio and of the Northwest Territory (prior to statehood). His commentary praised the Northwest Ordinance of 1787 for its ban on slavery, yet it reported (without condemning) later legislation and customs that excluded African-American males from the franchise, jury duty, and public education.

Connections he nurtured with notable Cincinnatians paid off professionally and personally. By 1832, his clients included the local branch of the Bank of the United States, and in 1834 he was elected solicitor and a director of Cincinnati's Lafayette Bank. Beginning about 1834, Chase had a succession of young men studying law in his office, as he had done in Wirt's. Several, like future Supreme Court justice Stanley Matthews, achieved positions of prominence. The *Ohio Reports* indicate that Chase was in demand chiefly for commercial law, land law, and chancery but also on other matters ranging from murder to patent law. After three short-lived partnerships, Chase acquired a new partner in 1838 who possessed the improbable name of Flamen Ball. Chase & Ball did business until 1858; after 1849 most of the firm's litigation tended to be in the federal courts, as illustrated by *O'Reilly v. Morse* (1854), a landmark telegraph case.

O'Reilly was a newspaper editor turned telegraph entrepreneur. After erecting telegraph lines for Samuel F. B. Morse, O'Reilly strung his own lines to offer a competing service. When a court concluded that O'Reilly had infringed on Morse's patents and enjoined construction of his lines in Kentucky, Chase was one of several counsel who took over the case and argued it before the U.S. Supreme Court in December 1852. Their principal contention was that Morse had used his patents not only to shield particular telegraphic devices but to control all use of electromagnetism for communication. Although the Court found that O'Reilly's equipment had infringed on the Morse patents, the justices narrowed the scope of those patents to exclude the technology from which they were derived. The decision thus left open the option for competing companies to construct devices not covered by Morse's patents.

Chase was far less fortunate familially than professionally. True, his marriage to Catharine Jane ("Kitty") Garniss in 1834 linked him to one of the city's leading families, but she died a year later. His marriage to Eliza Ann ("Lizzie") Smith in 1839 was cut short by her death in 1845. He married Sarah Bella ("Belle") Dunlop Ludlow the following year but was left a widower for the third time in 1852. Chase's three unions yielded six daughters, yet only two survived infancy or early childhood: Catharine Jane ("Kate") Chase (1840–1899) and Janet Ralston ("Nettie") Chase (1847–1925). Such mortality was appalling even by the standards of the nineteenth century, when medicine lagged well behind the progress of other sciences. It may be that the antislavery side of his law practice, involving as it did the anguish of others, provided a healthful diversion from the calamities of his own life.

"When a moral conviction was once established in Chase's mind," declared one biographer, "it never could be removed" (Hart 1969, 54). Yet Chase's antislavery views had less to do with the evils of slavery than with the harm it did to white society. The galvanizing event occurred in July 1836, when a mob of five thousand, including city officials, sacked the editorial office and smashed the press of James G. Birney's *Philanthropist*, an abolitionist newspaper, and then went on a rampage through the black quarter. Although he did not share Birney's extreme views, Chase was outraged by the lawlessness and brought a successful suit for damages on Birney's behalf against some of the ringleaders.

Their paths soon crossed again in the first of a series of career-altering cases that earned Chase the epithet "Attorney General for Runaway Slaves." In 1836, a light-skinned slave named Matilda escaped from a boat moored at a Cincinnati wharf. Birney (who would be the Liberty Party's candidate for president in 1840 and 1844) took her into his household as a servant. Matilda's owner (and father) hired a detective, who found and seized her under the terms of the Fugitive Slave Act, passed by Congress in 1793. Chase intervened on her behalf in a state court, claiming that she was neither a slave nor a fugitive. Freedom, not slavery, was the natural or default status for all Americans. Slavery was therefore unique as a species of property in that it could exist only by the positive law of a state (hence its designation as the "peculiar institution"). On this point the law of a state was final. Ohio, where slavery was forbidden, was as sovereign as Maryland, where slavery was allowed and from which Matilda had come. Thus, the national government was as powerless to interfere with the status of slavery within a state that recognized or prohibited it as that state's recognition of slavery was to determine a person's status outside its borders. Arriving on free soil, Matilda became free, and having been freely brought there by her owner, she was not a fugitive. Moreover, Matilda's recapture violated at least two provisions of the Bill of Rights: the Fourth Amendment guaranty against unreasonable searches and the due process clause of the Fifth Amendment. For Chase, the significance of his reasoning went well beyond Matilda's freedom. Without protection elsewhere, slavery as an economic institution could not survive.

His elaborate argument was to no avail. Before an appeal could be taken against an adverse court ruling, Matilda was returned to her captors, ferried to the opposite shore, and literally "sold down the river." Birney's opponents then sued him for sheltering a fugitive. Pressing arguments similar to those he had advanced in Matilda's case, Chase appealed Birney's conviction to the state supreme court, which, bypassing Chase's fundamental argument, held for Birney on the technical ground that he lacked knowledge ("scienter") that Matilda was a fugitive. Nonetheless, the court took the unusual step of ordering that Chase's argument be published, presumably believing it to be sufficiently meritorious to bring it to the attention of the bar (*Birney v. State*, 1837).

Chase's most extended antislavery case began in 1842. Ex-slaveholder John Van Zandt was an abolitionist and a member of the underground railroad who inspired the character John Van Trompe in Harriet Beecher Stowe's *Uncle Tom's Cabin*. On April 22, as Van Zandt hauled a load of vegetables to market in his wagon, he met a band of fugitives. He agreed to carry them to a destination north of Cincinnati, but slave catchers soon overtook the party and whisked all but one of the fugitives back to Kentucky. Their owner, Wharton Jones, sued Van Zandt to recover the value of the one who had escaped recapture and the cost of recovering the others. A federal marshal charged Van Zandt with harboring fugitives in violation of the 1793 act. Waiving his fees as he usually did in such cases, Chase defended Van Zandt in a three-hour argument before Supreme Court justice John McLean (with whom Chase had been friends since he lived in Washington and who would become his uncle-in-law in 1846) and the district judge who sat together as the U.S. Circuit Court. After the jury returned a damage assessment against Van Zandt of twelve hundred dollars and the court imposed a penalty on him of five hundred dollars for violating the law, Chase asked William H. Seward of New York to join him in presenting the case to the Supreme Court.

Chase's 108-page brief to the Supreme Court (*Jones v. Van Zandt*, 1847) expanded on his Matilda arguments by forthrightly attacking the Fugitive Slave Act of 1793. Among other claims, he argued that Article IV of the U.S. Constitution was not, as commonly considered, sufficient authority for the Fugitive Slave Act. Slavery was entirely a matter for each state to decide. If the Constitution did not recognize slavery, Congress could not support it. The point was bold but risky. Chase was assailing the Court's own recent decision in *Prigg v. Pennsylvania* (1842), which had upheld the statute.

The unanimous bench that ruled against Van Zandt underscored a reality of Chase's pro bono practice: Inventive arguments and tireless efforts for runaways and those who aided them made him a hero among antislavery activists and a sought-after speaker in Ohio and elsewhere, but only occasionally did those arguments prevail. True, his thinking rejected the one theme shared by both abolitionists (who loathed it) and slave owners (who celebrated it): that the Constitution and the judges who interpreted it both recognized and condoned slavery. Yet, ironically, his courtroom defeats seemed to validate precisely what he denied, that the Constitution and the courts were at one with the slave interests.

Perhaps the failure of courtroom remedies pushed him to pursue political ones. His early political identity in Washington had been with the National Republicans. In Ohio, he was first aligned with the Whigs and then with the Liberty, Free Soil, and Democratic parties before helping to found the Republican party. Despite this partisan pilgrimage, Chase remained close to the Democrats on most issues except their opposition to central banking and their acceptance of slavery. And as much as any politician before or since, he craved the presidency, unsuccessfully courting the Republican nomination in 1856, 1860, and 1864 and the Democratic nomination in 1868.

His first election to major political office came in 1849 when a coalition among Democrats and Free Soilers in the state legislature sent him to the U.S. Senate. There he opposed both the Compromise of 1850 (that combined a more aggressive fugitive slave act with some extension of slavery westward and a cessation of the slave trade in the District of Columbia) and the Kansas-Nebraska Act of 1854 (that repealed the Missouri Compromise of 1820 and allowed slavery to be decided on by the settlers in those territories). In 1855, he won the governorship as a Republican by a statewide plurality of sixteen thousand votes (while finishing third in his home county with only 19 percent of the vote) and was reelected in 1857.

The state legislature favored him with election again to the Senate in 1860, service that was cut short by his appointment in 1861 as President Abraham Lincoln's secretary of the treasury. His finance policies equipped an army of one million and a navy that, briefly, was second only to Great Britain's. Upon Roger B. Taney's death in 1864, LINCOLN picked Chase as the sixth chief justice of the United States, at a time when the Supreme Court's prestige still languished because of the *Dred Scott* decision (1857). The meticulous fairness he displayed when presiding over the Senate's impeachment trial of President Andrew Johnson doomed whatever hopes he may have had for the Republican nomination in 1868. A stroke in 1870 damaged his health so severely that he could neither lead the Court effectively nor pursue the Democratic nomination in 1872. A second massive stroke in 1873 ended his life on May 7. He was buried in Oak Hill Cemetery in Washington, but in 1886 Ohio officials arranged for his remains to be moved to Cincinnati, where he was re-interred alongside his daughter Kate.

—*Donald Grier Stephenson Jr.*

Sources and Suggestions for Further Reading

Birney v. State, 8 Ohio 230 (1837).

Blue, Frederick J. *Salmon P. Chase: A Life in Politics.* Kent, Ohio: Kent State University Press, 1987.

Diary and Correspondence of Salmon P. Chase. Washington: American Historical Association, 1903. Reprint, New York: Da Capo Press, 1971.

Hart, Albert Bushnell. *Salmon Portland Chase.* 1899. Reprint, New York: Greenwood Press, 1969.

Hughes, David Franklin. "Salmon P. Chase: Chief Justice." Ph.D. dissertation, Princeton University, 1963.

Hyman, Harold M. *The Reconstruction Justice of Salmon P. Chase:* In Re Turner *and* Texas v. White. Lawrence: University Press of Kansas, 1997.

Jones v. Van Zandt, 46 U.S. (5 Howard) 215 (1847).

Middleton, Stephen. *Ohio and the Antislavery Activities of Attorney Salmon Portland Chase, 1830–1849.* New York: Garland, 1990.

Niven, John. *Salmon P. Chase: A Biography.* New York: Oxford University Press, 1995.

———, ed. *The Salmon P. Chase Papers.* 5 vols. to date. Kent, Ohio: Kent State University Press, 1993.

O'Reilly v. Morse, 56 U.S. (15 Howard) 62 (1854).

Phelps, Mary Merwin. *Kate Chase, Dominant Daughter: The Life Story of a Brilliant Woman and Her Famous Father.* New York: Thomas Y. Crowell, 1935.

Prigg v. Pennsylvania, 41 U.S. (16 Peters) 539 (1842).

Schuckers, J. W. *The Life and Public Services of Salmon Portland Chase.* New York: D. Appleton, 1874.

Scott v. Sandford, 60 U.S. (19 Howard) 393 (1857).

Wambaugh, Eugene. "Salmon Portland Chase." In *Great American Lawyers*, edited by William Draper Lewis. Philadelphia: John C. Winston, 1908, 5:329–371.

Warden, Robert B. *An Account of the Life and Public Services of Salmon Portland Chase.* Cincinnati: Wilstach, Baldwin, 1874.

CHOATE, JOSEPH H.

(1832–1917)

JOSEPH H. CHOATE
Library of Congress

JOSEPH HODGES CHOATE earned a reputation as an exceptional orator and advocate due to his mastery of language and ability to argue eloquently. His most famous achievement was his successful argument in the historic *Pollock* case, in which he convinced the Supreme Court to invalidate the income tax of 1894 as unconstitutional. But even more notable than any one case he argued is the fact that Choate served as counsel in so many difficult and prominent cases, winning a large number of them. Choate was often described as the greatest jury lawyer of his time.

Choate was born in Salem, Massachusetts, on January 24, 1832, to George and Margaret Manning Hodges Choate. His father was a native of Salem and a well-known physician. The Choate family's presence in Massachusetts dated back to the early seventeenth century, with the first American ancestor emigrating from England in 1643. George Choate sent all four of his sons to Harvard, and all became successful professionals.

One of Choate's brothers was president of the Old Colony Railroad, another brother was a physician, and the third was a U.S. district judge for the Southern District of New York. Perhaps the most notable of Choate's relatives was his father's first cousin, RUFUS CHOATE, a congressman who was recognized for his skill as a lawyer and as an orator.

Receiving his primary education in the public schools of Salem, Choate then attended Harvard College, from which he graduated fourth in his class in 1852. His brother William gave the valedictory address, and Joseph delivered the salutatory address, being the first brothers at Harvard to give both speeches for the same class. Choate attended Harvard Law School, earning a living tutoring boys preparing to enter college, and graduated in 1854. He studied an additional year in the Boston office of Hodges and Saltonstall and was admitted to the Massachusetts bar in 1855.

Although he began the practice of law in Massachusetts, Choate did not remain in his native state long. He soon relocated to New York City, where he practiced for most of his career. He first joined the firm of Scudder & Carter in 1855 and afterwards was invited to join the firm of WILLIAM M. EVARTS in 1856 as an apprentice. In 1858, he became partners with William H. L. Barnes, and he briefly practiced in this partnership until 1859, when he returned to the Evarts firm as a partner. The firm then became Evarts, Southmayd & Choate, and Choate remained a partner in the firm for the rest of his career.

The majority of Choate's cases were heard in New York, but he also argued at least sixty-five cases before the U.S. Supreme Court. His record as a litigator includes cases spanning a wide range of substantive law, including wills, trusts and estates, patent law, contract law, tort law, fraud, securities law, international law, admiralty law, and interstate commerce. This broad assortment of substantive law, together with his roles as advisor, trial counsel, and appellate advocate, underscored Choate's versatility and skill.

Choate was an industrious man who thought of success as always having enough work to do, and he had the highest regard for the law, which he considered to be a science. He had an independent nature and would not allow himself to be bullied by a judge. Choate was unafraid politely to point out when a judge was acting improperly, but at the same time he never treated a judge with disrespect. Choate was calm and relaxed in the courtroom, and he spoke to the jury in this manner, having a conversation with its members rather than giving a performance. His courtroom appearances gave the impression that he had not given the case much thought, but this was only part of his mastery of the art of litigation. Each case received careful preparation, and this allowed Choate to conduct himself at trial with such apparent ease. He did not harass hostile witnesses but rather used seemingly benign questions to draw out just the testimony he wanted without the witness even being aware of the trap into which he was being led. Technical arguments were not part of Choate's style, which was based on simple language and targeted the listener's sense of reason and justice.

Choate was a founder of the New York City Bar Association and was president of this association from 1888 to 1889. He served as president of the American Bar Association from 1898 to 1899, and he also served as president of the New York State Bar Association, of the New York County Lawyers' Association, and of the Harvard Law School Association. He was a founder of the American Museum of Natural History, and he served as one of its trustees from 1869 to 1917. Choate was also an incorporator of the Metropolitan Museum of Art and served as a trustee for forty-seven years. He was elected a Bencher, or partner of the governing body, of the Middle Temple (one of four that train and admit members of the British bar), London, in 1905. A life-long Republican, the only political office Choate ever held was as president of the New York State Constitutional Convention of 1894. In January 1899, President William McKinley appointed Choate as ambassador to Great Britain, and he served in this capacity from 1899 to 1905. He also served as ambassador and first delegate of the United States to the Hague Peace Conference of 1907.

Choate donated a considerable amount of his time to public causes or to individuals who were not able to pay for his services. One example was his pro bono representation of Union general Fitz-John Porter, who had been stripped of his rank and command, court-martialed, and convicted of treason in 1863. General Porter continued to profess his innocence, and in 1878 President Rutherford B. Hayes appointed an advisory board of officers to reexamine the charge. Choate, fifteen years after the underlying events and the original conviction had transpired, convinced this board to reverse the general's conviction. Consequently, Congress reinstated Porter's rank and he regained at least part of his honorable reputation. Choate considered this case to be his greatest victory.

On at least one occasion, Choate cited the Bible during a trial. He was representing his client, Mr. Laidlaw, against the defendant, Mr. Sage, for damages in tort. Sage was a wealthy older man, and Laidlaw had come to his office to discuss business. During this visit, a man entered the office with a bag containing a bomb and demanded money from Sage upon the threat of dropping the bag and exploding the bomb. Just before the man dropped the bag, Sage grabbed Laidlaw and used him as a human shield against the explosion. Laidlaw sued Sage for injuries caused by the explosion. After reading the story in Luke of the rich man and the beggar, Choate then turned to the defendant and said, "There comes the rich man, and here is the poor man still bearing sores he suffered in protecting him" (Strong 1917, 220). This tactic won his client a considerable damages award.

An example of his trademark use of humor as a weapon was demonstrated in the case in which Choate represented the architect Richard M. Hunt against Mrs. Paran Stevens for payment relating to construction of a hotel. The contract had been made between Hunt and Mr. Stevens, but Mr. Stevens had died before he could make the final payment to Hunt. Mrs. Stevens had not been born wealthy but had gained a considerable fortune and was determined not to relinquish any of it to Hunt. Choate described her rise in social status to the jury: "And at least the arm of royalty was bent to receive her gloved hand, and how, gentlemen of the jury, did she reach this imposing eminence? [pronounced pause] Upon a mountain of unpaid bills" (Strong 1917, 187). In his final bit of humor, he incorporated the facts of the case into the nursery rhyme "The House that Jack Built."

Until he was forty-four, Choate was largely in the shadow of Evarts. He was known as an outstanding jury lawyer but had played only a junior role in appellate cases. When Evarts joined President Hayes's administration, Choate had the opportunity to display his ability as an appellate advocate. His simple style of calm explanation, making his side of the case seem natural, served him just as well before appellate benches as with juries and trial courts. His extensive knowledge in various areas of law was especially imposing with respect to constitutional law. During the 1880s and 1890s, Choate often appeared before the Supreme Court and many state courts in cases involving constitutional questions.

The most important case argued by Choate before the Supreme Court was *Pollock v. Farmers' Loan & Trust Co.* (1894). The income tax of 1894 levied a 2 percent tax on personal income in excess of four thousand dollars and on all corporate net profits. Taxable income included interest on state and municipal bonds, rents from real estate, and income from personal property. Claiming that the income tax was unconstitutional, Charles Pollock brought a stockholder's suit to prevent the Farmers' Loan & Trust Company of New York from filing a tax return and paying the levy. Attorney General Richard Olney represented the government. Choate and his legal team offered three arguments against the income tax act: a tax on income from land was effectively a tax on the land itself, a direct tax, and so required to be apportioned among states based on population under Article I, Section 2 of the Constitution; a tax on income from other property was either a direct tax and likewise unconstitutional or, if not a direct tax, unconstitutional for lack of uniformity required by Article I, Section 8 [due to its four-thousand-dollar exemption]; Congress could not tax income from state and municipal bond interest.

Choate's oral argument revealed his strong belief in individual private property rights and in government's fundamental duty to protect these rights. He characterized the tax as "communistic in its purposes and tendencies" and pictured the measure as an invasion of fundamental property rights (*Pollock*, 157 U.S. 532 [1894]). Choate also stressed the regional implications of the levy. The four-thousand-dollar exemption for personal income, with no exemptions for corporate income, was simply a confiscation of property of the residents of a few high-income states by the other states. Because 90 percent of the tax collected would come from just four states, Chaote stressed that the tax law purposely divested the wealthy individuals in these states of their property and redistributed it to the less wealthy in other states. He characterized the attorney general's argument in support of the law as an argument that men who were affected by the tax were too rich—hence, his reference to communism. He also stressed that allowing Congress to enact this type of law would render the Court powerless against future tax laws that could be much more confiscatory. Choate appealed to the Court as the guardian of minority rights against majoritarian tyranny; his strategy avoided focusing on the technical constitutional requirements on which the holding was ultimately based, but rather centered on sensitive social and political ideas of the time.

In an opinion by Chief Justice Melville W. Fuller, the majority held that taxes on income from land were direct taxes, which were unconstitutional because not apportioned, and that Congress could not tax income from state and municipal bonds. The eight sitting justices were evenly divided on the issue of an income tax from other sources, and the entire case was reargued before all nine justices. As a result of this rehearing, Fuller declared that the entire act was unconstitutional because taxation of income from personal property was a direct tax, requiring apportionment among the states according to population.

It is revealing that Choate credited his retired senior partner, Charles F. Southmayd, with his victory in the *Pollock* cases. Southmayd had a strong sense of private property rights, and when he learned that Choate was representing Pollock, he offered to prepare a brief. This brief, according to Choate, was the foundation of his entire argument to the Supreme Court.

Even in defeat, Choate's gift of persuasion was not without positive effect. In *Mugler v. Kansas* (1887), another leading case, the Supreme Court ruled against Choate's client, a brewer, by upholding Iowa's prohibition act. However, in response to Choate's argument that the statute deprived Mugler of property without due process of law required by the Constitution, the Court emphasized that it had the authority to scrutinize state regulations to determine whether the means they employed actually related to the given purpose behind the regulation. This was a major step toward the Supreme Court's eventual use of substantive due process to preserve private property rights.

Although frequently representing propertied interests, Choate sometimes appeared before the Supreme Court on behalf of underdogs. In *Fong Yue Ting v. United States* (1893), for example, he unsuccessfully defended a Chinese alien in an attack on Chinese exclusion legislation.

Choate's legal skills and persuasive abilities served him well in other areas besides the courtroom. When he arrived in England as ambassador, the Joint High Commission of 1898 for the settlement of disputes between the United States and Canada was at a deadlock concerning the Alaskan boundary. The setting of this boundary had financial implications, because it would determine which country owned gold-producing land. Choate secured the agreement of all involved to a treaty that created a tribunal of an equal number of members from each country that would hear the evidence and render a decision. The tribunal sat in London in 1903 and decided the Alaska boundary dispute, as well as all of the other issues between America and Canada that the Joint High Commission had been unable to resolve.

Choate was also instrumental in the construction of the Panama Canal. At the time when the United States had recognized the need for a canal across Central America, the Clayton-Bulwer Treaty of 1850 was in effect. The treaty required that a canal in this location would be under joint control of the United States and Great Britain. The United States desired to maintain exclusive control over the Panama Canal that it was to build, so Choate secured the substitution of this treaty with an agreement that any canal under exclusive American control would be equally open to commercial and military ships of every nation.

Toward the end of his life, Choate actively urged U.S. intervention in World War I. He died in New York City on May 14, 1917.

—*James W. Ely Jr.*

Sources and Suggestions for Further Reading

Ely, James W., Jr. *The Chief Justiceship of Melville W. Fuller, 1888–1910.* Columbia: University of South Carolina Press, 1995.

Garraty, John A., and Mark C. Carnes, eds. *American National Biography.* Vol. 4. New York: Oxford University Press, 1999.

Hicks, Frederick C., ed. *Arguments and Addresses of Joseph Hodges Choate.* St. Paul: West, 1926.

Johnson, Allen, and Dumas Malone, eds. *Dictionary of American Biography.* Vol. 4. New York: Scribner, 1930.

Martin, Edward S. *The Life of Joseph Hodges Choate.* New York: Scribner, 1927.

The National Cyclopedia of American Biography. Vol. 9. New York: James T. White, 1899.

Strong, Theron G. *Joseph H. Choate.* New York: Dodd, Mead, 1917.

Who Was Who, 1916–1928. Vol. 2. London: Adam & Charles Black, 1967.

CHOATE, RUFUS

(1799–1859)

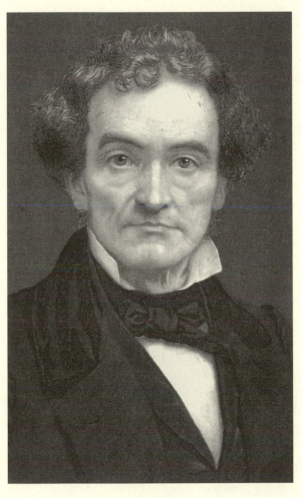

RUFUS CHOATE
Archive Photos

RUFUS CHOATE WAS NEW England's premier trial lawyer of the antebellum period and was America's first celebrity defense attorney. Controversial in his day, Choate pioneered many of the techniques modern lawyers use. He was expert in front of juries. His powerful oratory and ability to win cases packed courtrooms and brought him unusual notoriety. Choate's reputation did not develop from his involvement with landmark legal cases; rather, it stemmed from his spectacular victories in a number of widely covered trials. Choate's theatrical style and his extravagant oratory created the American taste for courtroom drama.

Born in Essex County, Massachusetts, on October 1, 1799, Choate was the fourth of Miriam Foster and David Choate's six children. Choate entered Dartmouth in 1815 during the college's famous legal controversy with the state legislature of New Hampshire (*Trustees of Dartmouth College v. Woodward*, 4 Wheaton 518). The case and the college's attorney, DANIEL WEBSTER, captivated Choate, who decided to become a lawyer. After giving the valedictory oration at his graduation in 1919, Choate entered Harvard Law School. He left Harvard in 1821 to study law at the office of William Wirt, the attorney general of the United States, but he left after less than a year because of his brother's death. He then completed his legal studies with Judge Cummins of Salem, Massachusetts, and was admitted to the bar as an attorney in September 1823. He opened an office in South Danvers and practiced there for about five years. During this time he married Helen Olcott, with whom he had seven children (Brown 1879, 11–33; Matthews 1980, 5–20).

Choate moved his law office to Salem in 1828. There his fame as an orator and courtroom dramatist spread. Large crowds began attending his trials. When his growing reputation enlarged his practice, Choate moved his offices to Boston in 1834. During these early stages of his legal career, Choate was involved in Whig politics on the local and national level. After election to the state house and senate, Choate served in the U.S. House of Representatives from 1831 to 1834. In 1841, Massachusetts selected Choate to replace Daniel Webster as senator when Webster became secretary of state. Choate left the Senate in 1845. Although he remained an active leader of the Whig party until his death, Choate did not have either the temperament or the inclination for a political career (Brown 1879, 41–67, 173; Matthews 1980, 38). After his resignation from the Senate, Choate devoted his time to building his practice, first in partnership with William Crowninshield, then with his nephew and son-in-law Joseph M. Bell. Bell proved a good partner for Choate, whose skills as a businessman did not equal his skills as a lawyer. Bell was the partnership's financial manager, balancing Choate's careless and forgetful money practices. Choate relished his successful private practice and never found fulfillment outside the courtroom. His brief stint as attorney general of Massachusetts in 1853 ended his legal career as anything other than a trial lawyer (Brown 1879, 215, 260, 287; Matthews 1980, 147, 152, 160).

Choate built his reputation as New England's premier trial lawyer on his power in front of a jury. Choate's successes with juries stemmed from a carefully cultivated strategy. He analyzed the background and position of each individual juror picked for his cases. He then focused his attention and arguments on those jurors whom he thought would be hostile to his view of the case. Often Choate directly confronted hostile jurors and tried to intimidate irresolute jurors by speaking to them individually. As Choate's fame spread, jurors in his cases were aware of his reputation in manipulating a jury and came into the case determined to resist him. This made his successes even more impressive.

Choate relied heavily on his powers as an orator in swaying a jury and convincing them of his view of the case. He was a master of rhetoric and of organization. Believing the first fifteen minutes made the critical impression with a jury, he always began his remarks in a conversational tone and slipped unobtrusively into his arguments. He presented the jury with a rapid and comprehensive view of the whole trial. He grouped together and emphasized the circumstances of the case that would make the strongest impression in his client's favor. Then he took the jury through a detailed analysis of the case. He centered his argument on a theory of the case and led jurors to an easily understood conception of it.

Observers credited Choate's power over a jury in part to his mastery of rhetoric. A scholar and compulsive reader, Choate worked on his rhetorical skills daily. He read aloud, practiced expression, and cultivated the ability to feel emotion. Choate thought that an orator achieved effect through choice and arrangement of words. He used long, descriptive sentences designed to steer an audience to his desired conclusion. Believing that jurors needed repetition mixed with variety to capture their attention, he alternated his notoriously flowery language with popular slang, anecdotes, and common illustrations. His dominant style was theatrical and took advantage of his exotic persona. Working himself into passions, Choate overwhelmed his audience with excited emotions, torrents of words, and exaggerated mannerisms. At first many ridiculed his style, but Choate created a taste for his dramatics that changed the American courtroom.

His two most famous cases of the 1840s amply illustrate his talent. The first was the 1843 case of William Wyman, who was indicted for embezzlement as president of the Phoenix Bank of Charleston. Choate was part of an all-star defense team that consisted of Daniel Webster, Ebenezer Hoar, and Franklin Dexter. After a hung jury and a conviction, Choate bore the major responsibility for the defense on appeal. Here Choate displayed his abilities in cross-examination. On the stand he forced each of the bank directors, all witnesses for the government, to deny that he had given Wyman the right to dispose of the bank's funds. Choate then argued that since the funds had never been under Wyman's control or in his possession, he could not be convicted of embezzlement. The court agreed and directed an acquittal (Feuss 1928, 147).

By far Choate's most famous trial was his 1846 defense of Albert J. Tirrell. This celebrity case demonstrated many of the tactics that built Choate's reputation. Tirrell, a well-connected young man, was accused of murdering his mistress, Maria Bickford, in a brothel where the two lived together. The government's case against Tirrell seemed compelling, but it was circumstantial. Early one morning, residents of the brothel heard a cry coming from Bickford's room and the sound of someone going down the stairs; they found her in a blazing room with her throat cut. Later that morning, Tirrell, apparently in a great hurry and claiming that someone had tried to murder him in his room, appeared at a livery stable asking for a vehicle and driver to take him out of town. Tirrell was later arrested in New Orleans and brought to trial. The case drew great public attention and universal assumptions of Tirrell's guilt.

Choate, in defending Tirrell, relied on the fact that the burden of proof lay with the prosecution. His favorite technique in defense cases was to present the jury with alternative hypotheses that fit the evidence yet showed his client to be innocent. He appealed to the jury's imagination through creating new motives and new explanations for the evidence.

Basing his case on the circumstantial nature of the government's evidence against Tirrell, Choate offered the jury two theories that he claimed were as compatible with the evidence as the government's case. Maria Bickford might have committed suicide. Claiming this was the natural end of a prostitute, Choate offered witness who testified to Bickford's emotional problems and her propensity to threaten suicide. Reputable physicians testified that her wounds could have been self-inflicted. Another possibility was that Tirrell had been sleep walking. Choate presented indisputable evidence that Tirrell was a life-long somnambulist. Along with these two alternate theories, Choate emphasized that there was no motive for this murder and no evidence that ruled out a third party.

In Tirrell's defense Choate relied heavily on the testimony of witnesses. Choate always tried to impress on juries the worthiness of his clients and the contrasting dubious character of people on the other side. He ruthlessly destroyed the character of hostile witnesses to undermine their credibility and thus dispose of their evidence. He used sarcastic humor to make elements of an opposing witness's testimony seem ridiculous. Choate rarely asked many questions of a witness; he discovered a witness's weak points and aimed a choice few questions in that direction.

The jury acquitted Tirrell. The trial caused a public sensation and propelled Choate to fame. Although some questioned his tactics in the case, most lawyers of the day respected the verdict as a sound reflection of the government's circumstantial case (Brown 1879, 174–183; Parker 1860, 219–225; Matthews 1980, 157).

Choate was now the most famous trial lawyer in the country. His rival for celebrity was Daniel Webster, known as much for his oratorical and political skills as for his legal cases. New England's two great lawyers often shared a courtroom in the late 1840s and 1850s—as partners and as opponents. After serving as co-counsel in *Rhode Island v. Massachusetts*, 45 U.S. 591 (1838), a boundary dispute before the Supreme Court, Choate and Webster teamed again for the landmark legal case *Norris v. Boston*, 48 U.S. 283; 45 Mass (4 Met.) 282 (1842), decided in the Supreme Court as the *Passenger Cases*. Acting for the plaintiff, Choate and Webster challenged the legality of a Massachusetts law that taxed aliens entering the state. In a 5–4 decision, the Supreme Court ruled the law unconstitutional as an infringement on Congress's exclusive power to regulate foreign commerce, even in the absence of congressional legislation.

Choate and Webster were on opposite sides in one of New England's local-interest trials, the 1847 Oliver Smith Will Case. Rather than trying to match Choate's oratory, Webster used simple statements to undo his opponent's use of rhetoric to weave a spell over a jury. This strategy won Webster the case (Fuess 1928, 149–150). The two great attorneys faced off in *Goodyear v. Day*, 10 F. Cas. 678 (No. 5569) (C.C.D.N.J. 1852), an important 1852 patent dispute before the Supreme Court. Choate, acting for the defendant, tried to impugn the plaintiff's patent on vulcanized rubber. His strategy failed. Choate later remarked that the successful way to handle the defense in a patent dispute would be "to insist on the non-infringement, and not to rely too much on the non-novelty of the plaintiff's invention." This is now the commonly accepted position. This case also involved an important point of law. Choate wanted a trial by jury, but Webster argued that the court had authority on grounds of equity. This case thus established the possibility of removing a technical class of cases from the purview of a jury (Matthews 1980, 165).

Choate worked on a staggering number of cases—by the 1850s he averaged seventy cases a year. Choate was not a specialist; his cases covered nearly every aspect of law. A large number, however, were criminal cases, a fact that was unusual for a lawyer with Choate's reputation in the 1850s. Choate prepared by researching every conceivably relevant legal point for each case. He believed in marshaling as much evidence as possible on points of law. To hone his skills, Choate read each volume of the *Massachusetts Reports* and made a full brief for opposing sides on every question in every case.

Choate's final celebrated trial cases both occurred in 1857. In *Shaw v. Boston and Worcester Railroad*, 74 Mass (8 Gray) 45 (1857), Choate was counsel for the plaintiff, a woman who had been crippled when a train crashed into her horse and buggy at a crossroads. The accident killed her husband, who was driving the buggy. Both parties alleged negligence. Choate argued that the train did not give sufficient notice of its approach; the railroad claimed the plaintiff's husband had been drinking. Choate won the case, largely through his use of exaggerated rhetoric and humor to discredit opposing witnesses and the claims of the railroad company: "This witness swears he stood by the dying man in his last moments. . . . Was it to administer those assiduities which are ordinarily proffered at the bedside of dying men? Was it to extend to him the consolations of that religion which for eighteen hundred years has comforted the world? No, gentlemen, no! He leans over the departing sufferer; he bends his face nearer and nearer to him—and what does he do! What does he do? *Smells gin and brandy!*" The jury found for the plaintiff, and Choate won both appeals (Matthews 1980, 166).

One of his most celebrated defenses was the 1857 Dalton divorce trial. As usual for Choate's cases, the courtroom was packed with observers and news coverage was extensive. Mr. Dalton, counseled by R. H. Dana Jr., accused his wife of adultery and sued for divorce. Choate, acting for Mrs. Dalton, used ridicule to expose improbabilities in the testimony of two witnesses who swore that Mrs. Dalton confessed. In his famous closing argument, Choate, as he did in the Tirrell case, claimed the burden of proof had not been met. The evidence, Choate argued, showed indiscretion, but indiscretion consistent with innocence. He asked the jury to draw a line between Mrs. Dalton's erring and imprudent behavior and her innocence of adultery. Choate charged the jury with the responsibility for the future happiness of the couple. He told jurors that their verdict of innocence would assure Mr. Dalton that he could take his wife back without dishonor. Choate won the case (Brown 1879, 335; Parker 1860, 477).

Choate died on July 13, 1859, two years after the Dalton case. Ending his career as New England's foremost trial lawyer, he enjoyed equal fame as an orator at the time of his death. In an age when Americans held orators in the highest esteem, his contemporaries considered him in the top echelon. Antebellum Americans judged his eulogy for Daniel Webster one of the great pieces of rhetoric produced in the period. Some of Choate's well-known orations and addresses are collected in *The Works of Rufus Choate*

(1862) and *Addresses and Orations of Rufus Choate* (1878), but the texts of his arguments in his most famous jury trials have been lost.

—**Lorien Foote**

Sources and Suggestions for Further Reading

Brown, Samuel Gilman. *The Life of Rufus Choate*. 3d ed. Boston: Little, Brown, 1879.

Choate, Rufus. *The Works of Rufus Choate, with a Memoir of His Life. By Samuel Gilman Brown*. Boston: Little, Brown, 1862.

_____. *Addresses and Orations of Rufus Choate*. Boston: Little, Brown, 1878.

Fuess, Claude M. *Rufus Choate: The Wizard of the Law*. New York: Minton, Balch, 1928.

Matthews, Jean V. *Rufus Choate: The Law and Civic Virtue*. Philadelphia: Temple University Press, 1980.

McWhirter, Darien A. *The Legal 100: A Ranking of the Individuals Who Have Most Influenced the Law*. Secaucus, N.J.: Carol Publishing Group, 1998.

Parker, Edward G. *Reminiscences of Rufus Choate, the Great American Advocate*. New York: Mason Brothers, 1860.

CLAY, HENRY

(1777–1852)

HENRY CLAY MADE HIS MARK on American history as Speaker of the House, U.S. senator, secretary of state, and presidential candidate. He earned the titles the "Great Compromiser" and the "Great Pacificator" for his service to the Union in times of sectional crisis. The Henry Clay of the history books would never have existed, however, if it had not been for Clay's earlier successes as a trial lawyer in Kentucky. Clay's stature as one of the leading lights of the Kentucky bar opened the way first for state office and then for Congress. Once in Congress, Clay displayed many of the same talents and abilities that made him an outstanding attorney. Clay continued the practice of law while in Congress, even while serving as Speaker of the House. He argued a number of cases before the U.S. Supreme Court, in-

HENRY CLAY
Library of Congress

cluding such important cases as *Osborn v. Bank of the United States* (1824) and *Groves v. Slaughter* (1841). Like his contemporary Daniel Webster, Clay was one of the nation's most accomplished attorneys as well as one of its leading statesmen.

Henry Clay was born on April 12, 1777, in Hanover County, Virginia. His father, the Reverend John Clay, was a tobacco planter and Baptist preacher known for his eloquence. After Clay's father died in 1781, his mother, Elizabeth Hudson Clay, soon married Captain Henry Watkins. Although in later years Clay described his background in modest terms, his parents and stepfather were solidly middle-class. Clay's formal education as a child consisted of three years in the Old Field School under Peter Deacon, an English schoolmaster with a colorful reputation. In 1791, Watkins and Clay's mother decided to move to Kentucky. Before leaving, however, Watkins was able, through connections, to secure a place for his stepson in the office of the clerk of the Virginia High Court of Chancery, Peter Tinsley.

While working in the clerk's office, Clay favorably impressed Chancellor GEORGE WYTHE. A signer of the Declaration of Independence and law professor to Thomas Jefferson and John Marshall, Wythe was Virginia's most eminent jurist at the time. Because his trembling hands made it virtually impossible for him to write, Wythe needed a private secretary and amanuensis, and he selected Clay for that position. Clay spent four years as Wythe's personal secretary, during which time he studied law, history, classics, and literature under Wythe's supervision. This amounted to an "irregular" education at best, as Wythe was "an old and busy man," and Clay was dividing his time between Wythe and his duties in the clerk's office (Van Deusen 1937, 13–14). Clay's association with Wythe also had an added benefit—during this time, he was introduced to Richmond society and developed the social graces and manners that were lacking from his upbringing.

With Wythe's assistance, Clay acquired a place in the office of Virginia's attorney general, former governor Robert Brooke, in 1796. According to Van Deusen (1937, 14), Clay's time with Brooke was "the one period of systematic training in his whole life." After a year with Brooke, Clay, then twenty years old, presented himself to the Virginia Court of Appeals for admission to the Virginia bar on November 6, 1797. After being examined by the panel, which included Spencer Roane, Clay was licensed to practice law in Virginia.

At this point, Clay decided to leave Richmond and follow his mother and stepfather to Kentucky. Although family connections certainly played some role in this decision, it also made sense given Clay's ambitions. After all, there were many lawyers in Richmond, and it would have been difficult for a young attorney to make a name for himself there. Kentucky, on the other hand, was the frontier, where a bright young man could distinguish himself much more quickly. Kentucky was also "a paradise for lawyers" given the chaotic condition of land titles in the newly admitted state (Van Deusen 1937, 15). At times, as many as six grants covered the same parcel of land, much of which had never been surveyed, and some parcels were identified by such warrants as "two white oaks and a sugar-tree" (Clay 1910, 25). This confusion of titles provided a fertile field for litigation.

Clay arrived in Lexington, the "Athens of the West," in late November 1796. Rather than setting out immediately in the practice of law, Clay took a few months to familiarize himself with Kentucky law and politics. The Fayette County Court of Quarter Sessions admitted Clay to the Kentucky bar on March 20, 1798.

Clay quickly became a leading member of the Kentucky bar. Although he divided his practice between civil and criminal cases, his handling of criminal cases established his reputation. According to local legend, no client of Clay's ever received capital punishment. Although this is not quite accurate—Remini (1991, 22) points to at least two of Clay's clients who were sentenced to death—Clay was a great criminal defense attorney. In one of his first cases, Clay defended an ordinary, respectable woman, Mrs. Doshey Phelps, who had killed her sister-in-law in "a moment of 'temporary delirium'" (Mayo 1937, 99). The crime had been committed in front of several witnesses, and thus the only question was whether the crime was murder or manslaughter. As one admirer of Clay's summed up the outcome of the case: "Mr. Clay not only succeeded in saving the life of his client, but excited in her behalf such intense pity and compassion, by his moving eloquence, that her punishment was mitigated to the lowest degree permitted by law" (Prentice 1831, 13).

Writers have attributed much of Clay's success as a trial lawyer to "his knowledge of human nature, intuitive sense of what affected men, an instinctive dramatic flair, and his gift of speech" (Mayo 1937, 88). This ability to play to and move an audience made him particularly effective with juries composed of rough Kentucky frontiersmen, but Clay was also able on occasion to overwhelm the bench as well as the jury. There can be little doubt that Clay's legal training, as irregular as it was, was much superior to that of most of the frontier judges before whom he appeared, and Clay was not above using his quick wits to bluff these judges while zealously representing his clients.

This point is well illustrated by Clay's defense of another accused murderer, Willis. Despite the weight of evidence against Willis, Clay was able to divide the jury. The prosecutor then requested a second trial, to which Clay did not object. At the outset of this second trial, however, Clay argued to the new jury that, "whatever opinion the Jury might have of the guilt or innocence of the prisoner, it was too late to convict him, for he had been *once tried*, and the law required, that no man should be put twice in jeopardy for the same offense" (Prentice 1831, 15). The court immediately ordered Clay to desist from making this specious argument, given that the protection against double jeopardy was clearly inapplicable. With a dramatic flair, Clay stated that, "if he was not to be allowed to argue the whole case to the Jury, he could have nothing more to say" (Prentice 1831, 15). Then he gathered his papers and left the courtroom. A messenger from the court soon arrived to inform him that, if he would return to court, he would

John C. Calhoun, Congressman and Political Theorist

Few attorneys have achieved the public reputations of three attorneys—DANIEL WEBSTER, HENRY CLAY, and John C. Calhoun—who served in Congress in the first half of the nineteenth century. Each represented a different section of the nation (the North, the West, and the South), articulated a different political philosophy, and unsuccessfully sought the presidency. Each grappled with the problem that slavery posed for the Union, and each, in his own way, attempted without success to prevent the breach that ultimately resulted in the Civil War.

This book includes full essays on Webster and Clay but not on Calhoun (1782–1850). Although no less brilliant than his colleagues, Calhoun's courtroom reputation was not on a level with theirs. Calhoun was educated in TAPPING REEVE's law school at Litchfield, Connecticut. Although Calhoun established a successful practice on his return to his native South Carolina, he detested riding the frontier circuit and preferred to appeal to the intellect of his audience rather than to their emotions or sense of humor. A historian notes that Calhoun regarded much of contemporary legal practice as a distasteful form of "pettifoggery" (Peterson 1987, 24). Soon after returning to South Carolina, Calhoun was elected to public office, eventually serving as vice-president under Andrew Jackson (a position from which he resigned) and as a South Carolina senator. Calhoun preferred this service, and farming, to legal practice and thus, despite his legal abilities, did not participate in as many important cases as his two colleagues.

Calhoun was a strong apologist for the institution of slavery and an advocate of the doctrine of nullification. Despite Calhoun's defense of these discredited doctrines, his *Disquisition on Government* and *Discourse on the Constitution and Government of the United States* (1851) are still highly regarded works of political theory.

REFERENCES

Calhoun, John C. A *Disquisition on Government and Selections from the Discourse.* Indianapolis: Bobbs-Merrill, 1953.

Peterson, Merrill D. *The Great Triumvirate: Webster, Clay, and Calhoun.* New York: Oxford University Press, 1987.

---

be allowed to proceed with the case as he saw fit. The jury in this second trial acquitted Willis based on Clay's double jeopardy defense, despite the weight of the evidence against him.

In civil cases, Clay's work in title suits brought him prosperity as well as fame. By 1805, he owned more than six thousand acres of land. Clay represented prominent Kentuckians in land suits, including John Breckinridge, a fellow lawyer who went on to become a U.S. senator and later U.S. attorney general. Within a few years, Clay was representing merchants from the eastern states in Kentucky, and in 1806 he became Noah Webster's legal representative in the West.

Although Clay represented a number of prominent individuals during his years as a trial attorney, his most famous client was none other than Aaron Burr. In 1806, the federal prosecutor in Kentucky, Joseph Hamilton Daveiss, an ardent Federalist, sought to indict Burr for conspiring against the Union and planning to attack Mexico. Burr approached Clay, who agreed to represent him. Clay clearly believed at the time that the charges were a Federalist attempt to discredit Burr, an extremely popular figure in the West. In his first attempt to indict Burr, however, Daveiss did not have enough evidence against Burr to proceed and the grand jury was dismissed. Before Daveiss could try to indict Burr again, the state legislature elected Clay to the U.S. Senate to fill out the remaining term of John Adair, who had resigned after being defeated for reelection. Clay was reluctant to continue representing Burr, worrying that it was inappropriate for a senator to represent a man accused of conspiring against the laws of the United States. Apparently, Clay had started to doubt Burr. Burr assured Clay in writing, however, that the charges were completely unfounded and that he had no designs against the Union. Clay continued as Burr's attorney, and, once again, the hapless Daveiss was unable to indict Burr. After arriving in Washington, D.C., however, Clay met with President Jefferson, who showed him conclusive evidence of Burr's treachery.

Clay's political career began in 1803, when he was first elected to the Kentucky state legislature. He quickly became a leader in the general assembly and was selected to fill out remaining terms in the U.S. Senate in 1807 and 1809. In 1810, Clay was elected to the U.S. House of Representatives; in 1811, he was selected as Speaker of the House, a position he held for most of his House career, which spanned the years 1811 to 1814, 1815 to 1821, and 1823 to 1825. In 1814 and 1815, he served as a delegate to the peace conference that resulted in the Treaty of Ghent, which ended the War of 1812. After Clay's unsuccessful bid for the presidency in 1824, President JOHN QUINCY ADAMS appointed him secretary of state in 1825, a position he held until 1829. He then served in the Senate from 1831 until 1842, and again from 1849 until his death in 1852. During his congressional career, he was a principal architect of the Missouri Compromise and the Compromise of 1850 and a key player in the Nullification Crisis of the 1830s. Clay also sought the presidency, but despite repeated attempts the office eluded him. He ran unsuccessfully for president in 1824 and was the Whig candidate for president in 1832 and 1844.

The skills that had made him a great trial lawyer—especially his oratorical skills and his intuitive sense for human nature—contributed greatly to Clay's success on the national political stage. Clay's eloquence and debating skills served him as well on the floors of the House and Senate as they had in court. This is not to say, however, that Clay gave up the practice of law when he embarked on his political career. To the contrary, during this period Clay argued many cases before the Supreme Court and established himself as one of the most prominent attorneys in the nation. Much of Clay's energy as an attorney during these years was dedicated to representing banking interests, including the second Bank of the United States. Clay served as counsel for the Bank of the United States in Ohio and Kentucky from 1820 until he became secretary of state in 1825. During this period, he, with others, including Webster, represented the bank in the important case of *Osborn v. Bank of the United States* (1824), dealing with the jurisdiction of the federal courts, among other issues.

In the first half of the nineteenth century, oral argument before the Supreme Court was as much a social as a legal event. When prominent lawyer-statesmen like Clay appeared before the Court, Washington society would pack the courtroom, then located in the Capitol, for days at a time. In February 1841, for example, Clay appeared before the Supreme Court in the case of *Groves v. Slaughter*, the first case involving state laws regulating the introduction of slaves into a state. As such, the case involved the commerce clause and states' powers to regulate interstate commerce. The Mississippi Constitution of 1832 prohibited the introduction of slaves into the state as merchandise. In violation of this constitutional provision, Slaughter had entered the state with slaves in 1836 and sold them, on credit. When the note came due, however, the purchasers claimed that it was void because it violated the state constitution. Representing Slaughter, Clay was again paired with Webster; the two great lawyers were described as "the Ajax and Achilles of the Bar" by their co-counsel in the case, Walter Jones (Warren 1922, 342). During the seven days of oral arguments in this case, every seat in the courtroom was occupied, many of them by Clay's admirers. One reporter described Clay's performance in *Groves* in the following manner: "Mr. Clay spoke for some three hours, and with a patient audience to the end. With a jury, he would be irresistible. With grave Judges, to address, of course he is less successful; but many who heard him today pronounced his argument to be a very able one" (Warren 1922, 342). As was often the case, Clay's client prevailed before the Supreme Court in *Groves*.

Clay's last noteworthy appearance before the Supreme Court was in the case of *Houston v. City Bank of New Orleans*, argued in 1848. As Swisher (1974, 145) notes, "it seemed as if the population of Washington went en masse to the Courtroom to hear him," despite the fact that the case dealt with a highly technical issue under a statute that had been repealed five years earlier. Of his performance on this occasion, one reporter remarked: "It has been often said . . . that [Clay] never was and never could be, reported successfully. His magic manner, the captivating tones of his voice, and a natural grace, singular in its influence, and peculiarly his own, can never be transferred to paper" (Warren 1922, 440). Another reporter noted that, even at the age of seventy-one, Clay "exhibited as much vigor of intellect, clearness of elucidation, power of logic and legal analysis, as he ever did in his palmiest day" (Warren 1922, 441). The Court was unanimous in holding in favor of Clay's client.

After *Houston v. City Bank of New Orleans*, two notable events mark the last chapters in Clay's political career. In 1848, he was passed over for the Whig nomination in favor of General Zachary Taylor. In the Senate, he was one of the principal architects of the Compromise of 1850, which proved to be his last important service to the Union. Clay fell ill while returning to the capital from Lexington in late 1851 and resigned his seat in the Senate. He spent his last days largely confined to his rooms in the National Hotel, in Washington, D.C., where he died on June 19, 1852.

—Emery G. Lee III

SOURCES AND SUGGESTIONS FOR FURTHER READING

Clay, Thomas Hart. *Henry Clay*. Philadelphia: George W. Jacobs, 1910.

Mayo, Bernard. *Henry Clay: Spokesman for the New West*. Boston: Houghton Mifflin, 1937.

Prentice, George D. *Biography of Henry Clay*. 2d rev. ed. New York: John Jay Phelps, 1831.

Remini, Robert V. *Henry Clay: Statesman for the Union*. New York: W. W. Norton, 1991.

Swisher, Carl B. *History of the Supreme Court of the United States*. Vol. 5, *The Taney Period 1836–64*. New York: Macmillan, 1974.

Van Deusen, Glyndon G. *The Life of Henry Clay*. Boston: Little, Brown, 1937.

Warren, Charles. *The Supreme Court in United States History*. Vol. 2, *1821–55*. Boston: Little, Brown, 1922.

COCHRAN, JOHNNIE L., JR.

(1937–   )

JOHNNIE L. COCHRAN JR.
Defense attorney Johnnie Cochran puts on a pair of gloves to remind the jury in the O. J. Simpson double murder trial that the gloves Simpson tried on did not fit, 27 September 1995. (AP Photo/Vince Bucci/Pool)

JOHNNIE L. COCHRAN JR., the Shreveport, Louisiana, native who became a prominent defense counsel, civil rights advocate, and television presence, is the grandson of a Louisiana sharecropper, Alonzo Crockrum, who changed his surname. Crockrum's death in 1935 as the result of faulty medical procedures forced his articulate son, John Cochran Sr., to forgo a college education. Nonetheless, John Cochran Sr. went on to flourish in the insurance business. In 1943, he joined the massive African-American migration to the San Francisco Bay area that enabled the nation to build its arsenal for victory over Germany and Japan when he decided to move his young family to Oakland, California, to secure lucrative work in the Alameda Shipyards.

After V-J day and its concomitant reduction in the war industries workforce, Cochran moved the family to San Diego, and by 1949 he returned to work in the insurance industry, this time with Golden State Mutual in Los Angeles. His office was located next to what still remains the city's leading African-American newspaper, the *Los Angeles Sentinel* (Cochran and Rutten 1996, 37).

In the early 1950s, Johnnie Cochran Jr. matriculated in Los Angeles High, which not only had an outstanding academic reputation but had a student body considered "the best dressed in the city" (Cochran and Rutten 1996, 51). Receiving tutorials on fashion from parents of Jewish friends in the garment business, Cochran began to develop his fashion sense, which, like his cross-examination techniques, became one of his trademarks. Cochran continues to cut a dashing figure sartorially and verbally, whether appearing on national media outlets or presenting himself to a high school assembly in Oklahoma. "Johnnie Cochranisms" such as "If it doesn't fit, you must acquit," used in closing arguments in reference to the infamous glove introduced by prosecutor Chris Darden in the O. J. Simpson case, have become part of the national consciousness.

After high school graduation, Cochran entered the University of California at Los Angeles (UCLA), where as a freshman he pledged to Kappa Alpha Psi, the leading African-American fraternity on majority-white college campuses. Initially chartered at the University of Indiana at Bloomington early in the twentieth century, Kappa Alpha Psi has had other prominent members, including the late Thomas Bradley, former mayor of Los Angeles (Crump 1991, 635). Bradley, also a native southerner who had migrated to California, was Cochran's fraternity big brother and remained close to Cochran for the remainder of his life.

Cochran earned his B.S. degree at UCLA in 1959. Loyola University of Los Angeles awarded him a law degree in 1962. About the same time that he matriculated at UCLA, Cochran also passed the state licensing examination for selling insurance and went to work with his father, from whom he absorbed his qualities of optimism and empathy as they served clients, many of whom were fellow African-American migrants from the South. Service to the African-American community and a commitment to civil rights continue to be emblematic of Cochran's endeavors. These were views nurtured by his and his family's strong lifelong involvement with the Baptist Church.

Inadvertently, Mayor Bradley had a profound influence on Cochran's family life. Bradley, who had served as a member of the Los Angeles Police Department and concurrently attended Southwestern Law School at night, had been elected to the city council and subsequently won the mayor's office after an initial loss to Sam Yorty. Bradley appointed Cochran to the Los Angeles International Airport Commission, where he served from 1981 until 1994, including three terms as its president. On a commission business trip to Portland, Oregon, Cochran met and, after a whirlwind courtship,

The Case of the Gloves that Didn't Fit: Déjà vu All Over Again?

Few observers of the O. J. Simpson murder trial can forget the dramatic moment when it appeared that Simpson's hands did not fit into the gloves that the prosecution had accused him of wearing when he allegedly murdered his wife and a friend. There was a similarly dramatic incident in an earlier California case. Attorney Jerry Giesler, who had established a reputation for defending celebrities, was defending Paul Wright for the murder of his wife and his best friend, whom he had discovered at night engaged in a sexual act on a piano bench in his house.

Far from denying the crime, Wright immediately called the police to confess. At trial, he testified that his mind had become a "white flame" when he saw his wife cheating on him and that he had snapped. However, he also reported that he had fired two sets of shots, two from the door where he had first observed them and three when he had come closer to the bodies. A neighbor seemingly called Wrights's credibility into question by reporting that she had heard all five shots had been fired

sequentially one after the other, and Giesler had done his best to ask her a minimum of questions so as not to reinforce her testimony.

The prosecution, who had been taught to use audio and visual displays to reinforce the effect of such testimony, proceeded on redirect examination to ask the woman to use a pencil to tap out what she had heard. Instead of tapping out five even shots as her testimony had seemed to require, she instead made two taps, then paused and followed with three others.

Giesler quickly stipulated that this demonstration indicated "that there was a noticeable interruption between the second and third shots" (Giesler and Martin 1960, 169). Although the jury found his client guilty of manslaughter, it subsequently decided that he had not been sane at the time of the act.

REFERENCE

Giesler, Jerry, with Pete Martin. *The Jerry Giesler Story*. New York: Simon & Schuster, 1960.

---

married Sylvia Dale, a New Orleans native. (Cochran divorced his first wife, Barbara Jean Berry—who, in a book, *Life after Johnnie Cochran* (1995), accused him of abuse—and was sued for palimony in 1995 by his mistress, Patricia.) The couple traveled to New Orleans to secure the blessing of her parents before marrying, and they currently reside with his surviving parent, Johnnie L. "The Chief" Cochran Sr.

One of Cochran's civil cases paralleled an unfortunate experience of his own. While driving with his children in his Rolls-Royce bedecked with "JCJR" license plates in 1979, Cochran was stopped by police officers with drawn guns. Although they later apologized when Cochran showed them his badge from the district attorney's office, Cochran recognized the role that race had played in his being stopped. A far greater tragedy befell the family of college athlete Ron Settles, who was stopped in 1981 while driving his Triumph TR-7 by police of the Los Angeles–area municipality of Signal Hill, taken into custody, and later found hanged in his cell. After an autopsy of his exhumed body showed that Settles had been strangled rather than hanged, Cochran was able to secure an out-of-court settlement in a civil case for the young man's grief-stricken parents. The settlement was announced on Martin Luther King's birthday (Cochran and Rutten 1996, 224).

Questions of racial justice have usually intertwined with most of Cochran's civil and criminal litigation efforts; by 1995, Cochran was estimated to have secured over $45 million against California police departments (Creager 1997, 100). For nearly thirty years he worked to overturn the murder conviction of former Los Angeles Black Panther Party leader Geronimo Pratt. Cochran's persistence paid off, as Pratt's murder conviction was overturned in the spring of 2000, and the former Black Panther received a $4.5 million settlement ("Winners" 2000). Cochran also brought Reginald Denny's suit against the police department for failing to come to his aid after Denny, a white man, was severely beaten in riots that occurred after police were acquitted for the beating of Rodney King.

Cochran is especially known for his debonair courtroom manner, which the *New York Times* has called "disarmingly smooth, confident, and captivating," and which a Los Angeles Superior Court judge has characterized as being persuasive and charming. An attorney told a newspaper reporter that "if Johnnie tells jurors that a turkey can pull a freight train, they'll look for a rope" (Creager 1997, 99). Cochran's life and legal work have been influenced both by the automobile culture of Los Angeles and by Hollywood celebrity. Cochran worked to win an acquittal for attempted murder for actor Todd Bridges of the *Different Strokes* television series. Similarly, Elizabeth Taylor turned to Cochran when her friend Michael Jackson was accused of child molestation. He negotiated an out-of-court settlement for Jackson shortly before the fateful day of June 13, 1994, when he learned through news reports of the stabbing deaths of Nicole Brown Simpson and Ronald Goldman (Creager 1997, 226).

The notoriety wrought by his involvement with *California v. Simpson* (1995) brought Cochran fame as a fixture on cable television during the trial. He was also featured on his own program, as well as on *Both Sides with Jesse Jackson* and *Larry King Live*. Cochran emerged as the lawyer most emblematic of the television age. He was the obvious role model for the character of Cosmo Kramer's attorney on the television comedy *Seinfeld*. Before being retained as lead counsel for the defense of O. J. Simpson, Cochran had been contacted about being a legal commentator on the case for NBC. Instead, Cochran led the defense for the well-liked and widely admired former professional football player, Heisman trophy winner, Hertz rental car spokesman, and costar of several *Naked Gun* films. Cochran was hardly the first member of the bar to become a household name through his association with a television-saturated criminal trial. That distinction went to F. LEE BAILEY, who had defended Dr. Sam Sheppard in the mid-1950s in a case that inspired the *Fugitive* television series of the 1960s and the film of the same name of the 1990s. Appropriately enough, F. Lee Bailey played a pivotal role as a member of the legal team that Cochran led in defense of O. J. Simpson. The *Simpson* case marked the first time the two lawyers worked together. As they did, Cochran's respect for Bailey grew (Cochran and Ruttan 1996, 265). Bailey's cross-examination of Mark Fuhrman elicited the statement that he had not said the word "nigger" in the previous ten years. This statement strained Fuhrman's credibility with the jury, which included eight African-American members, and was impeached months later by Fuhrman's own tape-recorded words in an interview that had previously been conducted by screenwriter Laura Hart McKinney (Cochran and Ruttan 1996, 294). Bailey's major task in the case was to undermine the prosecution's credibility by casting reasonable doubt on its timeline for Simpson's alleged commission of the murders.

The attorney who was pivotal in questioning DNA evidence put forth by the prosecution was Brooklyn-born Barry Scheck. Cochran describes Barry Scheck and Scheck's coworker Peter Neufeld as "America's leading authorities on the forensic application of DNA." Although such evidence can be quite reliable, Scheck argued effectively that the "anarchic crime scene" undermined the credibility of the prosecution's DNA evidence. While the court proceedings generated controversy—three hundred complaints were filed with the state bar against the attorneys involved in the case (Chemerinsky 1997, 1)—Scheck was one of the few lawyers to be reproved by the California Bar Association. He participated in the case even though his California law license had lapsed. Nancy McCarthy has written the following:

> After an exhaustive investigation of ten attorneys involved on both sides of the O. J. Simpson murder trial, one of the former football star's defense lawyers was disciplined by the State Bar last month and another was negotiating a settlement with the bar at press time. Carl Douglas, an associate of lead attorney Johnnie Cochran, was publicly reproved for misusing his subpoena powers. The bar was attempting to negotiate a public reproval for New York–based

Barry Scheck, who is a member of the California bar but participated in part of the trial while on inactive status. (McCarthy 1997, 3)

Although Cochran had assembled what came to be popularly known as the "Dream Team," the resources of the prosecution were ample. More than forty-two deputy district attorneys and dozens of clerks were assigned to *California v. Simpson*. Although the prosecution had the same access to the scientific jury selection techniques used by the "Dream Team," strangely they did not avail themselves of them.

In his opening statement, Cochran went through what he described as a "laundry list" of defense witnesses and the anticipated significance of their testimony (Cochran and Rutten 1996, 285). He believed his efforts were hindered by the failure of co-counsel Robert Shapiro to comply with California's reciprocal discovery statutes and provide the statements of defense witnesses to the prosecution. Shapiro, another celebrity lawyer who had once successfully defended F. Lee Bailey in a case in which he was accused of driving under the influence of alcohol, was one member of the "Dream Team" in whom Cochran lost confidence as the case progressed.

As one who had held the third-highest position in the Los Angeles prosecutor's office (Cochran had been the first African-American law clerk to work there), Cochran was sympathetic to the plight of prosecutor Marcia Clark and to that of fellow African-American Chris Darden, with whom he came into conflict in court. Cochran had raised funds for the initial election of Clark and Darden's boss, District Attorney Gil Garcetti, and had introduced Darden to the Second Baptist and African Methodist Episcopal churches in Los Angeles, both prominent in the realm of political activism. Clark brought a wealth of experience to the *Simpson* case, having won nineteen homicide convictions, including one in 1991 that had featured DNA evidence ("Clark" 1998, 15).

Cochran is generally credited with—and blamed for—"playing the race card" in the *Simpson* case by suggesting to the jury that Simpson had been framed for the murders because of his race. Questions about the character of police investigator Mark Fuhrman, as well as the complexity of the state's DNA evidence, both aided Cochran's case. The acquittal that resulted was generally applauded by African-Americans but disdained by whites. In a subsequent civil trial, in which Simpson could no longer invoke his Fifth Amendment right to silence and in which the burden of proof was lower, Simpson was ordered to pay restitution to the families of the two victims.

After his victory in the *Simpson* case—which began in January and lasted until October 1995—Cochran continued his activism. He traveled to Bogalusa, Louisiana, in October 1995 to assist the Gulf Coast Tenants Association in its efforts to assist citizens endangered by a chemical leak in a case of environmental injustice. He has spoken extensively on high school and college campuses. Cochran considers promoting conversations about race to be one of his major goals. He also continues his fight against police brutality.

Cochran is well known for being outspoken about his opinions. He criticized the "erratic behavior" of Mayor Rudolph Giuliani of New York in responding to the police killings of Amadou Diallo and Patrick Dorisman, maintaining that these incidents were provoked by "stereotypical thinking" (*Both Sides* 2000). Cochran continues to decry that "people are being targeted by the color of their skin" and treated brutally for "breathing while black" (*Both Sides* 2000). He provided legal advice to the Diallo family and provided the following observation concerning the notable absence of the topic of race in the trial that led to the acquittal of the officers who killed Amadou Diallo: "It was like there was a big pink elephant in the room and everyone acted like it wasn't there" (White 2000, 28). Cochran praises cities such as San Diego and Boston that have reduced crime and minimized or eliminated police brutality by promoting police-community relations.

Cochran has been honored by Kappa Alpha Psi by being chosen as their Man of the Year. He was also chosen as Man of the Year by the Brotherhood Association of Los Angeles in 1994. Cochran's activism has involved not only fraternal and community associations, but professional associations as well, including the California Assembly of Black Lawyers, on whose twentieth-century anniversary program he served as a moderator. In 1984, when the Democratic National Convention was convened in San Francisco, Cochran served as special counsel to the chairman of its rules committee (*Marquis* 1999, 824).

In April 2000, Cochran traveled to Nigeria in an effort to reconcile Islamic law with civilian law. There he met with that nation's minister of justice and attorney general and with representatives of Amnesty International. In March 2001, Cochran was on the team that successfully defended rapper Sean "Puffy" Combs against charges of weapons possession and bribery in connection with a shooting in a Manhattan dance club. That same month, Cochran agreed to join a team handling the appeal of Lionel Tate, a 14-year-old Florida youth who was given a life sentence for the murder two years earlier of a six-year-old girl (CNN 2001).

—*Henry B. Sirgo*

Sources and Suggestions for Further Reading

Both Sides with Jesse Jackson. Cable News Network broadcast, 2 April 2000.
Chemerinsky, Erwin. "An Outside Voice: Kudos to the Bar for Impartiality." *California Bar Journal* (July 1997). Available at <http://www.calbar.org/2cbj/97jul/-art01.htm>.

"Clark, Marcia Rachel." In *West's Encyclopedia of American Law*. St. Paul: West Group, 1998, 3:15–17.

"Cochran, Johnnie L., Jr." In *West's Encyclopedia of American Law*. St. Paul: West Group, 1998. 3:51–53.

Cochran, Johnnie L., Jr., with Tim Rutten. *Journey to Justice*. New York: One World, 1996.

CNN Live Today. Cable News Network Broadcast, 23 March 2001, Transcript #01032304V75.

Creager, Allen. "Johnnie Cochran." In *Newsmakers, 1996*. Detroit: Gale, 1997, 98–101.

Crump, William L. *The Story of Kappa Alpha Psi: A History of the Beginning and Development of a College Greek Letter Organization 1911–1991*. Philadelphia: Kappa Alpha Psi Fraternity, 1991.

Marquis Who's Who in America 1999. New Providence, N.J.: Reed Elsevier, 1999.

McCarthy, Nancy. "Bar Reproves 2 Simpson Attorneys." *California Bar Journal* (July 1997). Available at <http://www.calbar.org/2cbj/97jul/caljnl.htm>.

White, Jack E. "Big Al's Finest Hour." *Time*, 6 March 2000, 28.

"Winners & Losers." *Time*, 8 May 2000, 25.

CONKLING, ROSCOE

(1829–1888)

ROSCOE CONKLING
Library of Congress

WITHOUT DOUBT ROSCOE Conkling of New York is much better known today as an influential nineteenth-century politician, whose patronage system rankled many a political opponent and rewarded friendly allies, than as an attorney. Nonetheless, during his lifetime he was equally well known for his trial skills. He was an eagerly sought-after advocate in cases ranging from simple assault and battery to momentous arguments before the U.S. Supreme Court. In fact, it was Conkling's oratorical skill, alongside a dogged fidelity to preparation and use of aggressive cross-examination techniques, that propelled him to a preeminent position in both law and politics. These attributes led U.S. Supreme Court justice Samuel F. Miller to say of him, "For the discussion of the law and the facts of the case Mr. Conkling is the best lawyer who comes into our court" (Jordan 1971, 417).

Conkling's family originally came from Nottinghamshire, England. Elizabeth (Allseabrook) and John Conklin moved to Salem, Massachusetts, in 1635. Roscoe Conkling was the seventh in direct descent from Elizabeth and John. His father, Alfred Conkling, the first in his family to receive a college degree (Union College at Schenectady), moved first to Albany,

127

then to Utica, later serving in the U.S. Congress and for twenty-seven years as U.S. district judge in the Northern District of New York. Alfred married Eliza Cockburn; they had three daughters and four sons. They named Roscoe, the youngest son, after William Roscoe, the English historian, poet, and barrister, whom Alfred extremely admired. Although Roscoe Conkling had no formal education beyond high school, he was considerably well read. It was during his formative years that he read *The Art of Speaking,* by James Burgh, a book first published in the early eighteenth century, that was to have a significant influence on his career as an orator.

Fresh from the Auburn Academy in New York, which he attended while living with his brother Frederick, Conkling began to read law under two of New York's foremost attorneys, Joshua A. Spencer and Francis Kernan. Spencer was a Whig, and Kernan a Democrat whom Conkling opposed again and again at trial and as contestants for the congressional seats in 1862 and 1864. Kernan and Conkling eventually become colleagues in the U.S. Senate. Conkling was barely twenty years old when he was admitted to the New York bar in 1850 and tried his first case before his father (which he won). That same year, as he entered a five-year partnership with the city's former mayor, Thomas R. Walker, Governor Hamilton Fish appointed the young Conkling to be district attorney for Oneida County. From that time, although he had some partnership relationships, he remained for the most part a loner at the bar.

Conkling's long and illustrious careers spanning nearly four decades shifted so much between law and politics it is impossible to say which were sojourns and which was his dwelling. His political career was prodigious: he was elected mayor of Utica, New York, in 1857, served for nearly a decade in the U.S. House of Representatives (serving on the historic Joint Committee on Reconstruction, the principal architect of postwar reconstruction, and casting weighty votes on the Civil War amendments and the impeachment of President Andrew Johnson), and as a member of the Senate, where he cast a "vigorous" vote to convict President Johnson in his Senate trial.

In summarizing Conkling's illustrious legal career, many cases can illuminate his oratorical skills, tenacious propensity for preparation, and pugnacious cross-examination style. An early case, *Doe v. Roe,* established his reputation as a fierce cross-examiner. Conkling represented the plaintiff, who was resisting repayment of a loan on the grounds that the interest rate was usurious. The defendant's counsel produced several sworn documents executed by the plaintiff in which he had expressly affirmed the lack of any "fraud and usury." Despite the fact that Conkling's associate had recommended dismissing the case, Conkling remained undaunted, insisting that the defense be required to plead. Conkling's cross-examination of the defendant was so effective that the audience on two occasions applauded, and the jury returned a very quick verdict for the plaintiff (Conkling 1889, 43–44).

Conkling's insistence on thorough and meticulous pretrial preparation and his aggressive cross-examination of witnesses were continually rewarded, but never more so than in a notable 1861 murder trial in which he represented the Reverend Henry Burdge. Burdge's wife was found dead with her throat slashed from ear to ear in the family's home. The initial coroner's report ruled that the death was a suicide. Later, when Burdge accepted a position with a church at Port Leyden, some disgruntled congregants, who were displeased with his hiring, began to circulate a poem that accused him of murdering his wife. When Burdge sued one of the congregants for libel, the disgruntled group managed to have Mrs. Burdge's body exhumed by a highly reputed physician, Dr. Swinburne, who was one of Burdge's church enemies. Swinburne instigated Burdge's indictment for murder and became the main witness against him at the trial. Since Dr. Swinburne claimed that Mrs. Burdge's assailant first suffocated her and then cut her neck, Conkling conducted a studious examination of the effects on lungs by suffocation. In fact, so thorough was his preparation that he obtained a cadaver and had it dissected to study pertinent anatomical parts of the human body. A local physician, Dr. Alonzo Clark, who spent an entire night just before the trial coaching Conkling, stated, "Mr. Conkling learned in a few days what it took me thirty years to find out" (Conkling 1889, 131).

Conkling used the services of a noted physician from New York City to prove that a struggle always accompanied suffocation—a fact that was noticeably absent in this incident. He went on to show that even small, weak women were capable of tremendous struggles while being suffocated by strong men, a most significant point, since Burdge was barely larger than his wife. Moreover, Conkling effectively used demonstrative aids to refute the prosecution's claim that suicide victims could not make an ear-to-ear incision. Even so, Conkling's most effective maneuver was his cross-examination of Dr. Swinburne's direct testimony that claimed the postmortem examination unequivocally showed suffocation to be the cause of death. Conkling disproved this account by getting the physician to admit that one side of the lungs was not congested—an absolute necessity when suffocation occurs—and also that he had negligently performed several forensic procedures during his postmortem examination.

A very interesting case, and one that illustrates Conkling's oratorical skill, was an 1864 case involving another clergy member—but this time Conkling was on the opposite side. The cleric, Reverend Sawyer, sued Conkling's client for comments the latter had made about the plaintiff's book, entitled *Reconstruction of Biblical Theories: Or, Biblical Science Improved*. The defendant, Mr. Van Wyck, the proprietor of a New York periodical, the *Christian Intelligencer*, had penned a scathing critique of Sawyer's book, saying, among other things, that "the author [should] go without delay, to Natal [a British colony in South Africa], and assist the bewildered bishop of that enlightened colony, or else remove to England and take orders in the Established Church" (Conkling, 1889, 209).

Conkling's summation in *Sawyer v. Van Wyck* contained a quintessential example of his elocution:

> The temple has till now been open since free government began, but the hinges so long rusted must creak again, and the doors be closed, if this action stands before an American jury. . . . The plaintiff chooses to become a theological pugilist . . . he takes refuge in court and asks damages against a man who has scratched him with a pen—a pen! the very weapon he himself has wielded to destroy tranquility, to unsettle faith, to darken hope, to put out the only light which burns unquenched amid the deadly vapors of the tomb. (Conkling 1889, 209–210)

This appeal to the jury is all the more impressive because it accuses a member of the clergy, who claims himself to be attacking the profane, of profanity.

We can read more of Conkling's eloquence in a summation to the jury in an 1853 murder trial:

> Dark and dreary as is the day, it is far too bright for such a deed. "Hung be the heavens with black" and let the courthouse and all Herkimer County be hung in mourning on the day when twelve of her sons will take from their fellowman his life or his liberty on such testimony as this. . . . The day is too bright and too beautiful for such a deed. Nature and man should shudder! Heaven and earth should give note of horror; the skies should be weeping; the winds should be sighing; the bells should be tolling; the court-house should be hung in mourning; the jury-box should be covered with crape on the day when a father, a husband and a citizen of Herkimer County is sent to a prison or a gallows upon such testimony as this. (Conkling 1889, 379)

One final instance of his oratory—regarding espousal of unpopular causes—comes from a closing argument made in an 1874 railroad tax case while he was still a member of the U.S. Senate:

> In this country the *morale* of the profession in this respect has not yet reached the standard which has long been maintained in Westminster Hall; but I would hold myself unworthy a place on the rolls if, on being asked to argue a

case involving a great sum of money, the reputations of many and the interest of many more, and involving also grave questions of law, I should shrink from standing at the bar of the country and vindicating as best I could the Constitution, the law and the right, even for an unpopular or hated client, because political opponents or slanderers might defame me for doing it. I give my gage that if the time shall ever come, politics or no politics, when I am afraid to brave such dangers—afraid to hew to the line of professional integrity and fidelity, let the chips fly where they may, I will confess myself unworthy membership of the Bar, unworthy the association of men who place truth and honor above the passionate discords, the groveling resentments, or the acclamations of the hour. (Conkling 1889, 390)

Just as Conkling's closing in the railroad tax case involved both his legal and political careers, so did his involvement with the passage and implementation of the Fourteenth Amendment to the U.S. Constitution. This venture also places his laudatory self-image in stark contrast with reality. It begins in 1865 with service on the Joint Committee on Reconstruction, whose most notable progeny was the Fourteenth Amendment. Ostensibly, the Fourteenth Amendment attempted to thwart the so-called Black Codes enacted by Southern states in their efforts to continue the subjugation of African-Americans. A narrow construction of the amendment was that it related only to matters affecting freed slaves, a point of view initially adopted by the Supreme Court in the *Slaughterhouse Cases*, 83 U.S. 36 (1873). A more radical view, the one shared by Conkling, was that the amendment should guarantee and protect the rights of all people equally. Indeed, some, Conkling included, went so far as to claim that "people" should be defined so as to even include juridical entities such as corporations as well.

Conkling's legislative role shifted to legal advocacy with his involvement in *County of San Mateo v. Southern Pacific Railroad Co.*, 116 U.S. 138 (1885), which, along with a companion case, *County of Santa Clara v. Southern Pacific Railroad Co.*, 118 U.S. 394 (1886), represent some of the earliest opportunities seized by the Court to enunciate (albeit as *obiter dicta*) the notion that corporations were entitled to protection under the Fourteenth Amendment. These cases involved a tax levied by county governments in California on real property. Although the law permitted taxpayers to deduct the amount of any mortgage from the taxable basis, railway companies were specifically prohibited from doing so. Railway companies filed a multitude of cases that contested the distinction on various grounds, including the claim that it violated the equal protection clause of the Fourteenth Amendment of the U.S. Constitution. Mr. Justice Field, sitting on circuit in both cases, 13 Fed. 722 (C.C.D. Cal. 1882) and 18 Fed. 385

(C.C.D. Cal. 1883), ruled in favor of the railway companies, holding that private corporations are persons within the meaning of the Fourteenth Amendment and entitled to its protection, in this case the equal protection clause. When the California governments petitioned the U.S. Supreme Court for writs of error, the railway companies retained the noted California attorney John Norton Pomeroy to write the brief of law, and Conkling to present the oral argument before the Supreme Court in the *San Mateo* case, which he did on December 19–20, 1882.

While legal scholars have generally credited the *Santa Clara* case with establishing corporate protection under the Fourteenth Amendment, it is nonetheless tenable that Conkling's argument in the *San Mateo* case was instrumental in the Court's general movement toward that position. In fact, the Court decided neither *San Mateo* nor *Santa Clara* on the basis of a Fourteenth Amendment claim. Agreement of the parties dismissed the former; the latter was decided on the basis of state law. Nevertheless, they structured the dismissal of *San Mateo* on the assumption that the Fourteenth Amendment was applicable, and the *Santa Clara* opinion, which was written on the heels of Conkling's *San Mateo* argument, contained a matter-of-fact, almost incurious, footnote, declaring, "The court does not wish to hear argument on the question whether . . . the Fourteenth Amendment . . . applies to these corporations. We are all of the opinion that it does" (118 U.S. 394, 396). Indeed, one noted legal historian goes so far as to give Conkling's argument direct credit for persuading the Supreme Court to adopt the natural entity theory of corporate existence along with protection under the Fourteenth Amendment (Twiss 1962, 61).

Although Conkling's presentation of the law and facts may have duly impressed Justice Miller, the great orator was apparently at times capable of a bit too much factual innovation if not downright factual invention—before the Supreme Court, no less. This was evident during his *San Mateo* argument when he exhibited what he represented as a copy of an unpublished journal of the 1865 proceedings of the Joint Committee on Reconstruction. Conkling quoted a portion that clearly suggested the committee's understanding that corporations were to be beneficiaries of the Fourteenth Amendment's protection. Historians have roundly discounted the authenticity of Conkling's claim, and to this day no such journal has apparently been found (Jordan 1971, 418).

In any event, whatever may have been Conkling's ethical shortcomings in this one situation, his reputation as an aggressive and talented advocate certainly does not include a general propensity unethically to exaggerate, much less fabricate, facts. On the contrary, his skills repudiate the necessity. Indeed, Conkling's meritorious reputation as a premier trial advocate can only be appreciated today, particularly as we witness ever more emphasis on logical presentations by retinues of narrowly focused experts.

—*Clyde Willis*

Sources and Suggestions for Further Reading

Bassett, John Spencer. *Makers of a New Nation*. Vol. 9 of *The Pageant of America: A Pictorial History of the United States*, edited by Ralph Henry Gabriel. New Haven: Yale University Press, 1928.

Chidsey, Donald Barr. *The Gentleman from New York: Roscoe Conkling*. New Haven: Yale University Press, 1935.

"Conkling." In *Oxford Companion to the Supreme Court of the United States*, edited by Kermit L. Hall. New York: Oxford University Press, 1992.

Conkling, Alfred R. *The Life and Letters of Roscoe Conkling: Orator, Statesman, Advocate*. New York: Charles L. Webster, 1889.

"Conkling, Roscoe." In *Encyclopædia Britannica Online*. <http://www.britannica.com/bcom/eb/article/4/0,5716,26294+1+25883,00.html?query=roscoe%20-conkling>.

Horwitz, Morton J. *The Transformation of American Law: 1870–1960*. New York: Oxford University Press, 1992.

Jordan, David M. *Roscoe Conkling of New York: Voice in the Senate*. Ithaca: Cornell University Press, 1971.

Schumacher, Paul. "Conkling Could Have Been Chief Justice." *Stamps* 251, no. 12 (17 June 1995).

Twiss, Benjamin R. *Lawyers and the Constitution: How Laissez Faire Came to the Supreme Court*. New York: Russell & Russell, 1962.

COVINGTON, HAYDEN C.

(1911–1978)

HAYDEN C. COVINGTON

Cassius Clay (Muhammad Ali) laughing with attorney Hayden Covington (right). (Bettmann/Corbis)

HAYDEN C. COVINGTON WAS LEAD COUNSEL FOR THE JEHOVAH'S Witnesses at a time during which the exercise of their beliefs resulted in an extraordinary number of appearances before the courts. Often defeated at the local level, where prejudices were strong, Covington succeeded in winning numerous victories at the U.S. Supreme Court for the Witnesses on First and Fourteenth Amendment grounds, including at least two dramatic reversals (Abraham 1994, 235; Martin 1993; Harrison 1978, 13). Covington is said to have presented 111 petitions and appeals to the Supreme Court (*Jehovah's Witnesses* 1993, 697) and to have won 85 percent of the 44 cases he brought before the Court (Quackenbush n.d.). Covington was assisted in the United States by Louisiana's Victor V. Blackwell (see Blackwell 1976), another gifted attorney, and Covington sometimes assisted W. Glen How, who successfully represented the Witnesses' legal interests in Canada. Covington is also known for helping boxer Muhammad Ali get a ministerial draft exemption as a Muslim.

Standard biographical sources contain little information about Covington, whose life was largely dominated by his services to the Witnesses. Born in Hopkins County, Texas, in 1911, Covington reported in an interview with two fellow Witnesses that his father was a Texas Ranger who hoped that his son would go into politics. Indeed, Covington reported that, when he became interested in the Witnesses, he was working in a political job in a Texas county clerk's office, apparently at the same time he was pursuing a law degree at the San Antonio Bar Association's School of Law (now St. Mary's). Covington further reported that he passed the Texas bar a year before completing his law degree and joined a law firm. After moving to another law office defending suits for the Maryland Casualty Company in San Antonio, Covington became involved in defending a few Witnesses who had been arrested for conducting a meeting as well as for helping Witnesses in San Antonio, who, like Witnesses elsewhere, carried signs affirming their leaders' beliefs that religion was a "snare" and a "racket." In addition to their intolerance of religion in general, Witnesses often specifically identified the Catholic Church as the "whore of Babylon" described in the Biblical book of Revelation.

Covington was invited by the Witness leadership to attend their convention at Madison Square Garden in New York, where anti-Witness rioting, largely led by the followers of Roman Catholic radio personality Father Charles Coughlin, erupted. Covington's testimony proved helpful in exonerating the Witnesses who had physically defended themselves, and group leaders invited Covington to come to the Jehovah's Witnesses' "Bethel" headquarters in Brooklyn in 1939, where he served until 1963. Initially, J. F. Rutherford was arguing most Witness cases, but Covington took an increasingly leading role as the primary Witness attorney, and he was a member of the board of directors and vice-president of the Watchtower Bible and Tract Society at the time of Rutherford's death.

Few roles could have done more to immerse a modern lawyer in the intricacies of constitutional law than such service. The Jehovah's Witnesses (who did not formally adopt this name until 1914) grew out of the millennial movements in nineteenth-century America when Charles Taze Russell, a former Pittsburgh merchant, began a series of Bible studies in which he began to predict the imminent second coming of Christ. Although several dates for this physical coming proved false, these dates were subsequently reinterpreted and spiritualized, and the movement continued under the leadership of "Judge" J. F. Rutherford, a one-time Missouri circuit judge, who increasingly proclaimed the Witnesses to be the exclusive means of salvation and other religious leaders to be frauds. The authoritarian Rutherford—who, with most other American Witness leaders, was jailed under the Espionage Act of 1917 during World War I but released after the war—was also responsible for centralizing increasing power in the Witness headquarters in Bethel, Brooklyn, where the Watchtower Society's major printing operation—the publisher of *The Watchtower* and *Awake!* magazines—was also located. Jehovah's Witnesses developed a number of unique doctrines related to the end times, including the belief that 144,000 Witnesses would rule in heaven while others would live in an eternal earthly paradise. Witnesses also developed distinctive views of the relation of their members to governmental authorities and popular culture (members do not give gifts on Christmas or other holidays or celebrate birthdays), and they rejected a number of tenets of Christian orthodoxy, including belief in the physical resurrection of Christ, the trinity, the equality of Jesus with God, and the existence of hell.

Expecting the imminent return of Christ, who was to usher in his millennial rule in a new earthly Eden, the Witnesses under Rutherford and his successor, Nathan Homer Knorr—a less educated leader with whom Covington was a rival for power and for whom he had little esteem (Bergman 1999, 9)—became increasingly evangelistic and helped expand the Witness presence to other countries, where they were often treated much more harshly than in the United States. In addition to street preaching, their members engaged in aggressive door-to-door solicitations and sales of materials published by the Watchtower Bible and Tract Society, sometimes descending en masse on a town to finish their solicitations before local authorities had an opportunity to try to enforce antisolicitation laws and licensing requirements against them. Members often played phonograph records of recordings by their leaders denouncing other religions, especially Roman Catholicism, and not surprisingly raising the hackles of those of other faiths.

Although this belief has since been somewhat modified to acknowledge the legitimate role of governments in keeping order, the Witnesses believe that governments, like established churches, are largely under the influence of Satanic powers. The Witnesses accordingly oppose participation in wars; they also view all Witnesses as full-time ministers whose kingdom activities preclude such service. In addition, Jehovah's Witnesses regard saluting the flag as a form of idolatry forbidden by the Ten Commandments and prohibited their children from participating, despite a host of laws making flag saluting compulsory in public schools.

Judge Rutherford took the lead in the first flag-salute case to appear before the Supreme Court in *Minersville School District v. Gobitis* (1940). The dramatic reversal of this decision in *West Virginia Board of Education v. Bar-*

nette (1943) was probably as attributable to the widespread acts of violence against the Witnesses that this decision sparked and to the change in the world situation brought about by U.S. entry into World War II as to the efforts of Hayden Covington in the latter case (Rutherford died in 1942). Covington noted that "the reason that [the *Minersville* case] was lost was not because of Brother Rutherford, but because of the times we were in" ("Interview" 1978, 4).

During this same period, Covington represented Witnesses who were denied permits to solicit from door to door (see *Cantwell v. Connecticut* [1940] and *Jones v. Opelika [II]* [1943], overturning an earlier negative ruling against the Witnesses in *Jones v. Opelika [I]* [1942]), or to solicit in company towns (*Marsh v. Alabama* [1943]) or to preach on street corners; who were accused of using "fighting words"; who were denied the right to demonstrate, to use public gathering places, or to use sound trucks; who were accused of violating child labor laws for using their children to sell Witness literature (one of the rare instances in which the Jehovah's Witnesses lost; see *Prince v. Massachusetts* [1944]); who were accused of sedition; who were denied draft exemptions; who had been victims of mob violence, etc. In the period when Covington was most active in arguing cases before the Supreme Court, that body was paying increasing attention to the defense of civil rights and liberties against both state and federal action, so many of its decisions might have been the same no matter who argued the cases, but Covington undoubtedly highlighted the legal issues involved, and he took the lead in arguing that the Bill of Rights should apply equally to state and national governments (Newton 1995, 133–135).

Covington, a tall, handsome man described in a *Newsweek* article as a "Texas tornado with sea-green eyes," was known as a dapper dresser who engaged in animated arguments. A Supreme Court clerk noted that, "He may not have done more talking than anyone I've heard here, but he did more calisthenics" ("Witness's Angle" 1943, 70; for a similar view, see Manwaring 1962, 224). Like many of his Witness counterparts going door to door, at least in his early years as an advocate, Covington apparently valued forthrightness more than tact. The *Newsweek* article noted that Covington thought that the dignity of the Supreme Court was "irrelevant to the legal process" and observed that Covington glowered directly at Catholic Supreme Court justice Frank Murphy when noting that "They [the Witnesses] don't preach in a dead language" ("Witness's Angle" 1943, 68).

The reference to Murphy is fascinating, because, in an interview he gave two days before his death, Covington noted that Murphy "got a good name among us because he was always dissenting in cases in our favor." Covington observed that an unnamed law review article had noted that, "if Justice Murphy is ever sainted, it will be by the Jehovah's Witnesses, not the

Catholic Church. He was a notorious Catholic" ("Interview" 1978, 6). Covington also referred favorably to General Louis B. Hershey, head of the selective service system, whom Covington described as "honorable and fair in his dealing with Jehovah's Witnesses" ("Interview" 1978, 8; see also Macmillan 1957, 186; and Blackwell 1976, 122, 133). By contrast, Covington identified Justice Felix Frankfurter—a Jewish justice who wrote the opinion in *Gobitis*, was the lone dissenter in *Barnette*, and who generally advocated a doctrine of judicial restraint that led to deference to legislative judgments—as "adverse," "hostile," "vicious," "a hypocrite," "an enemy," and "a pawn in the hands of the devil" ("Interview" 1978, 7, 14).

Covington reported one meeting in which he and Knorr met with President Harry Truman about a pardon for a Witness who had been convicted of evading the draft. Covington claimed that Truman cursed and claimed to have no use "for that SOB who didn't want to die for his country in time of war." Apparently, Truman softened this view under the influence of Attorney General Tom Clark, whom Truman later appointed to the Supreme Court and whom Covington also regarded as a fair justice ("Interview" 1978, 11).

In 1950, Covington authored a pamphlet for the Watchtower Bible and Tract Society entitled *Defending and Legally Establishing the Good News*. The pamphlet, designed to help Witnesses who encountered legal problems, is fascinating both for the range of issues it deals with and for its numerous references to opinions throughout state court systems as well as in the U.S. Supreme Court and foreign courts. In advice that may well have reflected his own strategy in arguing before the courts, Covington urged Witnesses who read his pamphlet to "be respectful and courteous" while showing no "fear of men" (Covington 1950, 18). Indeed, Covington likened such appearances to successful "back-calls" on prospective converts and advised that Witnesses were permitted to rise when the judge entered the room and to take an oath to testify to the truth (Covington 1950, 19). Covington further noted that, "In democratic lands we have found, as a refuge from tyranny, the courts of the land. The foremost court to render aid by extending the constitutional shield of protection to Jehovah's witnesses is the Supreme Court of the United States" (Covington 1950, 30; for similar sentiments, see Blackwell 1976, 102). Moreover, although Witnesses did not believe in military service or in such acts of civic participation as voting, serving on juries, or saluting the flag, Covington noted that they "respect the flag and the things for which it stands." In arguments he apparently used in his own appearances before the Supreme Court, Covington tied the legal defenses of the Witnesses to a larger public good: "They have valiantly fought on the [home front] in many lands for liberty for which the flag stands, namely, freedom of speech, press, conscience, and worship of

Almighty God, and they push these fights through the courts so as to maintain these liberties for all" (Covington 1950, 61; for an author who cites similar arguments of Covington, which she views as somewhat "disingenuous" in view of the Witnesses' negative attitude toward secular governments—a way of "using the Devil's weapons against the children of darkness"—see Harrison 1978, 205–206; for similar arguments, see Blackwell 1976, 171).

Although Covington dealt in his pamphlet with many issues, he inexplicably did not address the emotional cases involving blood transfusions, which most Witnesses reject as part of the Biblical prohibition against "eating" blood.

While acknowledging that such teachings had sometimes proved false in the past, Covington believed that, for the sake of unity, Witnesses were obligated to accept and obey Witness doctrines and policies until they were changed (Franz 1991, 24–25). The irony of an intolerant and authoritarian religious group grounding its arguments in the Bill of Rights has not been lost on some scholars (McAninch 1987), but, given that Puritan settlers in America valued their own religious freedom while denying it to others, Witnesses are hardly unique in this respect.

The hard-driving Covington's flamboyant style, and an alcohol problem, possibly exacerbated by intense headaches (Quackenbush n.d.) or an inner ear disease (Penton 1985, 324, n. 7), apparently brought him into increasing conflict with Nathan Knorr, to whom Covington had conceded the presidency of the Witnesses after Judge Rutherford's death. In the early 1960s Covington left the Watchtower headquarters, moved to Cincinnati, Ohio, with his wife and children and was for a time disfellowshipped, or excommunicated, before later being reinstated into the Witnesses. An interview with Covington posted on the Internet is said to have taken place on November 19, 1978, two days before his death ("Interview" 1978, 1); Covington's memorial service at Bethel was not preached until the spring of 1980 (Penton 1986, 324, n. 7).

—*John R. Vile*

Sources and Suggestions for Further Reading

Abraham, Henry J., and Barbara A. Perry. *Freedom & the Court: Civil Rights & Liberties in the United States*. 6th ed. New York: Oxford University Press, 1994.

Bergman, Jerry. *Jehovah's Witnesses: A Comprehensive and Selectively Annotated Bibliography*. Westport, Conn: Greenwood Press, 1999.

Bergman, Jerry. Telephone interview with the author, 1999.

Blackwell, Victor V. *O'er the Ramparts They Watched*. New York: Carlton Press, 1976.

Cantwell v. Connecticut, 310 U.S. 296 (1940).

Covington, Hayden C. *Defending and Legally Establishing the Good News*. Brooklyn, New York: Watchtower Bible and Tract Society, 1950.

Franz, Raymond. *In Search of Christian Freedom*. Atlanta: Commentary Press, 1991.

Harrison, Barbara G. *Visions of Glory: A History and a Memory of Jehovah's Witnesses*. New York: Simon & Schuster, 1978.

"Interview with Watchtower Attorney Hayden Covington." 1978. <http://www.freeminds.org/history/covington.htm>.

Jehovah's Witnesses—Proclaimers of God's Kingdom. Brooklyn, New York: Watchtower Bible and Tract Society of Pennsylvania, 1993.

Jones v. Opelika [I], 316 U.S. 584 (1942).

Jones v. Opelika [II], 319 U.S. 103 (1943).

Macmillan, A. H. *Faith on the March*. Englewood Cliffs, N.J.: Prentice-Hall, 1957.

Manwaring, David R. *Render unto Caesar: The Flag-Salute Controversy*. Chicago: University of Chicago Press, 1962.

Marsh v. Alabama, 326 U.S. 501 (1946).

Martin, William D. "Jehovah's Witnesses, the Supreme Court and the Press: Expanding First Amendment Freedoms from 1938 to 1948." M.A. thesis, University of North Carolina, 1993.

McAninch, William S. "A Catalyst for the Evolution of Constitutional Law: Jehovah's Witnesses in the Supreme Court." *University of Cincinnati Law Review* 55 (1987): 997–1077.

Minersville School District v. Gobitis, 310 U.S. 586 (1940).

Newton, Merlin Owen. *Armed with the Constitution: Jehovah's Witnesses in Alabama and the U.S. Supreme Court, 1939–1946*. Tuscaloosa: University of Alabama Press, 1995.

Penton, M. James. *Apocalypse Delayed: The Story of Jehovah's Witnesses*. Toronto: University of Toronto Press, 1985.

Peters, Shawn Francis. *Judging Jehovah's Witnesses: Religious Persecution and the Dawn of the Rights Revolution*. Lawrence: University Press of Kansas, 2000.

Prince v. Massachusetts, 321 U.S. 158 (1944).

Quackenbush, Colin. *Hayden Covington Memorial*. Manhattan Beach, Calif.: Free Minds, n.d. Audio tape.

West Virginia State Board of Education v. Barnette, 319 U.S. 624 (1943).

"Witness's Angle." *Newsweek*, 22 March 1943, 68, 70.

COX, ARCHIBALD

(1912–)

ARCHIBALD COX
AP Photo

ARCHIBALD COX IS CONSID-ered one of the great Supreme Court lawyers of the twentieth century. He earned that reputa-tion as President Kennedy's highly principled solicitor gen-eral, arguing dozens of landmark cases in the nation's highest court. In the 1970s, Cox achieved even greater national fame as the first Watergate special prosecutor. His trademarks were his bristly crewcut, his stiff New England bearing, his bow ties, and his ab-solute integrity. Cox stood up to President Richard M. Nixon in demanding the release of tape recordings that ultimately proved Nixon's complicity in the Water-gate scandal. He took the posi-tion that no man (not even the President) was above the law, and convinced the courts to adhere to that principle. Cox came to rep-resent, during a particularly trou-bled time in U.S. government, the embodiment of honesty and integrity in public service.

Archibald Cox was born in Plainfield, New Jersey, on May 17, 1912. From both sides of his family, Cox inherited a reverence for law and public service. His father, Archibald Cox Sr., was a well-respected copyright and patent lawyer in New York City who helped to establish the "red cross" symbol as the trademark for Johnson & Johnson. On his mother's side, Cox was a direct descendant of Roger Sherman, signer of the Articles of Confederation, the Declaration of Independence, and the Constitution. (Sherman forged the "Connecticut Compromise," which broke the deadlock in the Constitutional Convention.) Cox's mother (née Frances Perkins) was the granddaughter of WILLIAM M. EVARTS, famous nineteenth-century lawyer and public servant from New York, who served as U.S. attorney general, secretary of state, and U.S. senator from New York. Ironically, Evarts represented President Andrew Johnson during his infamous impeachment trial in 1868 (see entry for William M. Evarts, below). The Evarts tradition of public service would have a major impact on Cox throughout his life.

Archibald Cox grew up in the affluent town of Plainfield, New Jersey. However, there was a decidedly New England component to his character. His family spent summers in Windsor, Vermont, living in the old Evarts homestead, a portion of which his mother had inherited. After attending St. Paul's preparatory school in Concord, New Hampshire (his great-grandfather Perkins had helped establish that school), Cox attended Harvard College. He did not excel academically, at least initially, satisfying himself with "gentlemanly C's" (Gormley 1997, 21). Yet Cox slowly resolved to become a lawyer, and doubled that resolve when his father (at age fifty-six) died unexpectedly during Archibald's sophomore year.

At Harvard Law School, which he entered in 1934, Cox found his niche. He earned the Sears Prize for achieving the highest grade average in the first-year class. Cox also developed a great admiration for Professor Felix Frankfurter, who later became a Supreme Court justice. Frankfurter emphasized the importance of government service and instilled in Cox a respect for "great figures in the law" (Gormley 1997, 35). During Cox's third year, Frankfurter recommended Cox for a clerkship with the famous Judge Learned Hand of New York, who had known Cox's father in New York. The clerkship with Judge Hand, in the federal district court in New York City, became a turning point in Cox's life.

Hand taught "not by precept, but by example" (Gormley 1997, 46). He admonished his young clerk to revere the law, to respect legal precedent, and to remain true "to these books about us" (Gormley 1997, 46). Although his clerkship with Learned Hand lasted only a year, it influenced Cox for the rest of his career.

In 1937, the same year he clerked for Judge Hand and was admitted to the Massachusetts bar, Archibald Cox married Phyllis Ames, whom he had met after a Harvard football game. Professor Felix Frankfurter sent a note, which read, "My God, what a powerful legal combination!" (Gormley 1997,

33). On one side, Phyllis Ames was the granddaughter of James Barr Ames, noted dean of Harvard Law School in the 1890s. On the other side, her grandfather was Nathan Abbott, founder of Stanford Law School.

After a brief stint at the prestigious Ropes Gray firm in Boston, with World War II escalating, Cox took a series of government jobs in Washington as his own way of contributing to the war effort. In 1941, he was hired as an assistant solicitor general under Charles Fahy. Professor Felix Frankfurter had referred to this office as the "Celestial General"—it provided an opportunity to represent the government in the nation's highest court. Cox viewed it as the ultimate honor for a lawyer in government service.

In Cox's first case before the Supreme Court, *Weber v. United States*, 315 U.S. 787 (1942)—a California case involving the denial of old-age pensions to resident aliens—Cox was directed to "confess error" on behalf of the U.S. government. This was tantamount to the government admitting it had erred in the court below, and requesting the Supreme Court to reverse its victory. Confessing error was considered an easy "win." Cox presented the *Weber* argument in the Supreme Court, and, as he later recalled, "eight justices jumped down my throat. . . . It must have verged on being a very pathetic scene if you were at all sympathetic to the young man" (Gormley 1997, 52). The Court refused to accept the government's "confession" of error. Cox lost the case. But it would be one of Archibald Cox's few defeats in the Supreme Court over the next forty years.

After World War II, Cox returned briefly to the firm of Ropes Gray in Boston, thinking it would be for life. Within five weeks, he was invited to join the faculty at Harvard Law School, where he would teach for a half century. Cox became (initially) a leading labor law expert in the country, authoring the first modern labor law textbook in print—*Cases on Labor Law* (1948)—and handling labor arbitrations across the country. But he gradually merged his academic work with assignments in the public sphere.

Based on this growing reputation, in 1952 President Harry Truman named Cox chairman of the Wage Stabilization Board, which was designed to impose wage and price controls on defense-related industries and prevent the country from slipping into economic chaos during the Korean War. Cox remained chairman for only six months: When President Truman overturned Cox's board on a critical decision involving John L. Lewis of the United Mineworkers, Cox resigned in protest, informing the president that he could not in good conscience abide by the decision. In December 1952, Cox returned to Harvard, believing that his excursions into public service were over for good.

But Cox attracted the attention of a young senator from Massachusetts, John F. Kennedy, who turned to Cox for labor advice. Between 1957 and 1959, Cox traveled to Washington (in between teaching classes) to help

Perry Mason in Novels and Films

When many Americans think of a trial attorney, they may be most likely to think of Perry Mason, the fictional invention of novelist Erle Stanley Gardner (1889–1970). Gardner was born in Massachusetts but grew up in Oregon and California, where he "read law" and was admitted to the bar in 1911.

Gardner practiced law in Oxnard, California, until 1918, worked as a salesman for Consolidated Sales Company until 1921, and then practiced in Ventura, California, where he began writing for pulp magazines, eventually abandoning his practice in order to write full-time. Gardner enjoyed traveling and could speak Chinese fluently. When defending Chinese clients for gambling, Gardner, who knew police could rarely distinguish one Chinese person from another, asked his clients to move. Police who arrived at the house of one of his clients named Wong Duck ended up arresting someone else, leading to a headline that read, "Wong Duck May Be Wrong Duck," and causing an embarrassed district attorney to drop charges (McWhirter 1998, 382).

Gardner's first Perry Mason stories appeared in 1933. By the time of his last novel, published in 1973, Gardner had published more than eighty. The popular television series, in which Raymond Burr starred as Perry Mason, began in 1957.

Much of the action in Gardner's stories takes place in the courtroom, with Mason often dramatically eliciting unexpected confessions from the guilty and almost always using the skills of his secretary Della Street and private detective Paul Drake to foil District Attorney Hamilton Burger. Although modern trials, with their extensive discovery rules, rarely embody such high drama, Mason as embodied by Raymond Burr has still become something of a folk hero, presenting a positive view of a lawyer with personal integrity who believes in, and fights for, his clients.

References

"Erle Stanley Gardner." <http://www.kirjasto.sci.fi/gardner.htm>.

McWhirter, Darien A. *The Legal 100: A Ranking of the Individuals Who Have Most Influenced the Law.* Secaucus, N.J.: Carol, 1998.

Kennedy draft labor legislation and shepherd it through Congress. This effort culminated in the Landrum-Griffin Act, one of the landmark pieces of labor legislation of the twentieth century. It turned out to be John F. Kennedy's only major legislative accomplishment before running for president in 1960.

During the 1960 campaign, Kennedy appointed Cox to head a group of academic advisors known as the "Brain Trust." This group of "academic eggheads"—led by Cox—produced hundreds of speeches and position papers on behalf of the candidate. Cox was dispatched by Kennedy to sit with his pregnant wife, Jackie, during the first televised debate with Richard Nixon, as a symbol of the trust Kennedy reposed in his academic advisors.

When Kennedy was elected president in the fall of 1960, he named Cox to serve as his solicitor general—one of the top appointments in the Kennedy administration.

It was as solicitor general that Cox left an indelible print as one of the great Supreme Court lawyers of the twentieth century. Although Cox was initially skeptical of the appointment of the president's brother, Robert F. Kennedy, as attorney general, Cox soon developed a warm relationship with Robert Kennedy. Working in tandem with Robert Kennedy's Justice Department, Cox argued and won a host of landmark constitutional decisions, many of them furthering the civil rights movement of the 1960s.

Cox made his debut as solicitor general in *Burton v. Wilmington Parking Authority*, 365 U.S. 715 (1961). In that case, he convinced the Court that the Fourteenth Amendment equal protection clause was broad enough to outlaw racial discrimination by a privately owned coffee shop, located in a state-owned parking garage in Wilmington, Delaware. Nervous at the prospect of his first appearance as solicitor general, Cox drove to the parking garage and noticed the flag of the United States and that of Delaware flying above it. When Cox stood before the Supreme Court, he highlighted this fact—although it appeared nowhere in the record. "Anyone who was the victim of discrimination in this coffee shop," Cox told the Court, "could not escape the fact that the discrimination took place in a public building and, literally, here, under the flag of the United States and of Delaware" (Gormley 1997, 150).

When the Supreme Court handed down its decision in *Burton*, it noted the existence of the flags flying over the roof. "The State has so far insinuated itself into a position of interdependence with (the coffee shop)," wrote Justice Tom Clarke, "that it must be recognized as a joint participant in the challenged activity" (Gormley 1997, 151).

Cox quickly earned a reputation as one of the great solicitors general of all time, the "Willie Mays" of Supreme Court lawyers (Gormley 1997, 181). He argued more cases in the Court than any other lawyer of his era, more than anyone since JOHN W. DAVIS in the 1920s. Dressed in striped pants and swallow-tail coat (the same formal attire that he had been married in), Cox cut an impressive figure at the wooden Supreme Court lectern. He prevailed in 80 percent of the cases he argued, and won 87.7 percent of the cases in which government was amicus curiae, many of them important civil rights victories (Gormley 1997, 191). Law clerks were known to line up along the sides of the courtroom to watch him argue. He was often known to lecture the Court in a professorial style. But his complete mastery of the facts, his powerful brief-writing ability, his deep respect for legal precedent, and his absolute honesty in presenting cases to the Court combined to make him a rock-like figure in the well of the Supreme Court.

A vacancy occurred on the Supreme Court in 1962, after Felix Frankfurter suffered a devastating stroke. Robert Kennedy suggested Cox for the vacancy. President Kennedy instead selected Arthur Goldberg, his secretary of labor—stating that he had made a commitment to Goldberg. It was understood, however, that Cox would be next in line. Explained Kennedy confidant Arthur Schlesinger Jr., "Had Kennedy lived, he would have appointed [Cox] to the Supreme Court. He had it on his mind" (Gormley 1997, 181).

In a series of "sit-in" cases—involving protests at Southern lunch counters that had refused to serve African-Americans—Cox initially found himself at odds with Attorney General Robert Kennedy. Kennedy was sympathetic with the sit-in protestors and wanted to take swift action to support them. Cox, however, was troubled by the *Civil Rights Cases* of the 1880s, which held that the Fourteenth Amendment did not reach purely private conduct (which included discrimination by private lunch counters). Cox felt uncomfortable telling the Court to ignore one hundred years of precedent, however distasteful. Instead he proceeded to win each of the sit-in cases on narrower grounds, waiting for Congress to enact comprehensive civil rights legislation to moot the issue. He accomplished his goal in *Bell v. Maryland*, 378 U.S. 226 (1964), and *Griffin v. Maryland*, 378 U.S. 130 (1964), persuading a slim majority of the Court to sidestep the nettlesome *Civil Rights Cases* and rule on behalf of African-American demonstrators on narrower grounds.

In the landmark reapportionment cases, Cox once again clashed with the Kennedy Justice Department and the White House that had appointed him. Cox had convinced the Supreme Court in *Baker v. Carr* (1962) that the Fourteenth Amendment was broad enough to allow the Court to hear challenges to state reapportionment plans, many of which had become greatly skewed in terms of population. But Cox was haunted by Justice Frankfurter's vehement dissent in *Baker*, arguing that the federal government should stay out of state "political questions."

The Kennedy administration favored an aggressive stand in the reapportionment cases. In many states, legislative districts had not been redrawn for decades, disadvantaging urban populations that were predominantly Democratic turf.

Yet Cox proceeded cautiously. For two centuries, the Supreme Court had stayed out of state reapportionment matters. He refused to advocate abrupt change, which might jeopardize the Supreme Court as an institution. In his view, it was up to the Court to decide if (and when) to break with precedent in the reapportionment cases. Attorney General Robert Kennedy declined to second-guess Cox—he knew that Cox was viewed as "integrity incarnate"; he had enormous credibility within the Court. Robert Kennedy thus allowed the solicitor general to argue on narrow grounds and remain true to his convictions.

In the historic case of *Reynolds v. Sims,* 377 U.S. 533 (1964), the Court struck down a particularly skewed Alabama legislative apportionment scheme, easily endorsing the "one person, one vote" principle—which required that all legislative districts be roughly equal in population. Cox had stuck to his principles. And the Court had made its own break with precedent.

Throughout the truncated Kennedy administration, Archibald Cox maintained a close working relationship with the president. When Kennedy was faced with a particularly thorny legal issue, he would jokingly instruct his brother the attorney general, "Bobby, ask Archie" (Gormley 1997, 163).

The last telephone call that President John F. Kennedy ever made from the White House was to his solicitor general, Archibald Cox, on November 21, 1963, at 6:45 P.M. The next day the president left for Houston, and then Dallas (Gormley 1997, 182).

After President Kennedy's assassination, Cox won a pair of major victories in the Supreme Court—in *Heart of Atlanta Motel,* 379 U.S. 241 (1964), and *Katzenbach v. McClung,* 379 U.S. 294 (1964)—upholding the landmark Civil Rights Act of 1964. Cox took the unusual step of defending the Civil Rights Act under the commerce clause, to avoid the "state action" issue that had plagued him in the sit-in cases. He argued that Congress had broad authority under its commerce power to enact sweeping prohibitions against racial discrimination by hotels, restaurants, and other places of public accommodation. Cox won these cases unanimously, paving the way for implementation of the greatest civil rights legislation in American history.

In 1965, Cox assisted Attorney General Nicholas Katzenbach in drafting the Voting Rights Act, then successfully defended that piece of civil rights legislation in *South Carolina v. Katzenbach,* 383 U.S. 301 (1966). He argued that case even after tendering his resignation and leaving behind the office that he loved, believing that President Lyndon Johnson should be permitted to name his own solicitor general.

Shortly after his return to Harvard, Cox found himself heading a commission to examine the sources of campus unrest and violence at Columbia University in New York, writing a report entitled "Crisis at Columbia." From 1969 through 1972, Cox became de facto president and troubleshooter at Harvard, as protests over the Vietnam War and student riots swept across his own university.

By 1973, student disruptions had subsided; Cox was looking forward to returning to quiet teaching duties. On the day before his sixty-first birthday, Cox received a telephone call from Elliot Richardson—a former student who had become President Richard M. Nixon's newest attorney general—asking him to serve as special prosecutor in the case involving the Watergate scandal. Seven prominent lawyers and judges had already turned Richardson down. Cox told his wife, Phyllis, "Somebody clearly has to do it . . . maybe there's no one better to do it than a sixty-year-old tenured law professor who isn't going anywhere (in public life) anyway" (Gormley 1997, 240).

Cox was appointed with bipartisan support in the Senate. As Watergate special prosecutor, he worked doggedly to unravel the mystery of the Watergate break-in and determine if President Nixon (and other top administration officials) had participated in a criminal cover-up. After the existence of a White House taping system was revealed, Cox subpoenaed nine critical tape recordings that he believed were essential to prove (or disprove) the president's complicity in the Watergate cover-up.

President Nixon's attorneys refused to turn over the tapes, citing executive privilege. Cox appeared in front of Judge John J. Sirica, in the sixth-floor ceremonial courtroom of the federal district court in Washington, arguing forcefully that no citizen—not even the president of the United States—should be above the law.

"This is a grave and dramatic case," Cox told the hushed courtroom. Under the U.S. legal system, "judges apply the same law whether the case is great or small." Cox quoted from the great English jurist Bracton, "*Non sub homine sed sub Deo et lege*" ("Not under man, but under God and the law").

Judge Sirica sided with Cox, directing the president to turn over the tapes. The U.S. Court of Appeals affirmed. On the eve of the deadline for President Nixon's lawyers to file an appeal in the Supreme Court—October 20, 1973—Nixon ordered Attorney General Elliot Richardson to fire Cox. Richardson refused and resigned, as did his deputy, William Ruckelshaus. Solicitor General Robert Bork executed the order to fire Cox, in what came to be known as the "Saturday Night Massacre." This action unleashed a firestorm of public protest, which led to the appointment of a new special prosecutor (Leon Jaworski), the release of dozens of damning White House tapes, and the ultimate unraveling of the Nixon presidency.

Archibald Cox, who had stuck to his principles, became a national hero.

After Watergate, Cox continued to argue important cases before the Supreme Court, often appearing pro bono. He represented the citizens' group Common Cause in defending the Federal Election Reform Act of 1974, culminating in a partial victory in *Buckley v. Valeo*, 424 U.S. 1 (1976). He represented the University of California in the celebrated *Bakke* case, 438 U.S. 265 (1978), establishing that affirmative action programs in higher education were constitutional, under appropriate circumstances.

Cox served as chairman of Common Cause for twelve years, urging the passage of comprehensive campaign finance reform. In 1987, Cox published *The Court and the Constitution*, which received glowing reviews. He continued to teach at Harvard Law School and Boston University School of Law until age eighty-five. Although he was passed up for federal judgeships several times and was never appointed to a seat on the Supreme Court, Cox was widely regarded as one of the great Supreme Court lawyers in U.S. history. His absolute integrity and his adherence to the rule of law gave him a powerful credibility that was unmatched in the history of the highest court.

Like his great-grandfather, William M. Evarts, Archibald Cox was the rare public servant "who did not seek office, but let it seek him." He did not promote himself for career advancements or federal appointments. Yet when called upon (during the Kennedy years and Watergate) to protect the institutions of government, he did so forcefully and masterfully. Having risen to the challenge, on each brilliant occasion, he indelibly shaped the future of U.S. history.

— *Ken Gormley*

Sources and Suggestions for Further Reading

Ben-Veniste, Richard, and George Frampton Jr. *Stonewall: The Real Story of the Watergate Prosecution*. New York: Simon & Schuster, 1977.

Caplan, Lincoln. *The Tenth Justice: The Solicitor General and the Rule of Law*. New York: Vintage Books, 1988.

Cox, Archibald. *The Court and the Constitution*. Boston: Houghton Mifflin, 1987.

Doyle, James. *Not Above the Law: The Battles of Watergate Prosecutors Cox and Jaworski*. New York: William Morrow, 1977.

Gormley, Ken. *Archibald Cox: Conscience of a Nation*. Boston: Addison-Wesley, 1997.

Kutler, Stanley I. *The Wars of Watergate: The Last Crisis of Richard Nixon*. New York: Alfred A. Knopf, 1990.

Navasky, Victor S. *Kennedy Justice*. New York: Atheneum, 1971.

Schlesinger, Arthur M., Jr. *A Thousand Days: John F. Kennedy in the White House*. Boston: Houghton Mifflin, 1965.

CUMMINGS, HOMER STILLE

(1870–1956)

HOMER STILLE CUMMINGS, who would serve as U.S. attorney general during the introduction of the New Deal, was born in Chicago, Illinois, on April 30, 1870. He received his Ph.B. from Yale University in 1891 and an LL.B. in 1893. He was admitted to the Connecticut bar in 1893 and practiced in Stamford, Connecticut, where he also served as mayor from 1900 to 1902 and from 1904 to 1908. He was state's attorney for Fairfield County, Connecticut, from 1914 to 1924 and was a corporation counsel from 1908 to 1912 and from 1925 to 1932. He was chair of the Democratic National Committee from 1919 to 1925 and a delegate to the Democratic National Conventions of 1900, 1904, 1924, 1932, 1936, 1940, and 1944. He was appointed attorney general of the United States by President Franklin Roosevelt on March 4, 1933, and served until January 2, 1939. He died on September 10, 1956.

Homer Cummings was the only child of Uriah Cummings and Audie Stillé Cummings. His mother traced her ancestry back

HOMER STILLE CUMMINGS
Library of Congress

150

to Emma Smith (Van) Ostrom and the famous Knickerbocker Dutch Van Nostrom family of New York. His father's family had come to Massachusetts in 1627 and traced their lineage back to "Red" Comyn, a rival of Robert Bruce's for the crown of Scotland in the early fourteenth century. Uriah Cummings was an unusually talented individual. An industrialist, writer, historian, successful inventor, leading scientific expert on cement, he was also an avid supporter of the American labor movement and one of the most prominent Indian specialists in the United States. Uriah Cummings's versatile accomplishments, his civic awareness, and his humanitarian qualities profoundly influenced his son (Mazza 1978, 1–10).

Cummings received his early education at Heathcote School in Buffalo, New York. As a student at Yale, Cummings began to struggle with the questions of law and politics that would later dominate his life and career. Influenced by his father's championship of labor, Cummings focused his studies on the history of American capitalism. He was concerned that large trusts and monopolies posed a threat to the free-enterprise system and exploited workers. Not only should corporations be required to adhere to fair business codes and market regulations, Cummings concluded, but American prosperity ultimately rested on protection of the working classes and a more equitable distribution of the wealth generated by capitalist enterprise (Mazza 1978, 12–13). He would later champion these causes in his politics and his legal advocacy.

After completing his legal studies at Yale in 1893, Cummings was admitted to the Connecticut State Bar Association and began practice as an associate in the law offices of the state's attorneys, Samuel Fessenden and Galen Carter. Two years later, Cummings was named partner in the firm of Fessenden, Carter, and Cummings. On June 27, 1897, he married Helen Woodruff Smith, the daughter of a talented New York financier and leading reform Republican, and the couple had a son, Dickinson Schuyler Cummings, born June 17, 1898.

Inasmuch as his partners spent a large part of their time as prosecutors for the city and state, Cummings handled a high percentage of the firm's cases. The firm was regarded as one of the elite appellate firms in the state, and Homer Cummings gained a reputation as a brilliant litigator, handling many of the most important cases in the state (Swisher 1972, xv). In one early, well-publicized case in 1896, Cummings successfully represented the town of Darien, Connecticut, in a suit against its own town selectmen, who refused to hold a town meeting to elect a new tax collector as required by the city charter. In another case, involving his defense of a woman who was the victim of an assault, Cummings's eloquent closing led to an ovation from courtroom spectators (Mazza 1978, 20).

In 1900, Cummings left his partners and began a solo practice. He had become a prominent silver Democrat and an avid supporter of William Jennings Bryan, a position that was at odds with the Republican views of his former partners. That same year, he was elected mayor of Stamford, a position that he held for three terms. At the time of his election he was thirty years old, the youngest individual to ever hold the office of mayor. Joining other major urban progressives of the era, Cummings championed government reform and challenged corporate structures when necessary to protect public interests. He broke the local utility's monopoly, secured safety regulations for public transportation, professionalized and modernized the city's fire and police departments, established public swimming facilities and parks, and reorganized the municipal government. In addition, he initiated investigations into meat slaughterhouses and butcher shops in the city, urged the city to pass legislation regulating the humane treatment of animals, and argued for food inspectors to ensure that products sold in the city were safe (Mazza 1978, 73). In July 1902, Cummings proposed that the city acquire land for a public park, but the Common Council split on a 4–4 vote over whether to purchase the land. Cummings broke the tie with his own vote. As a tribute to Cummings's progressive reforms as city mayor, the park was named in his honor in 1927.

Despite Cummings's growing political and professional prominence, his marriage to Helen Smith ended in divorce in March 1907. Two years later, on December 16, 1909, Cummings married Marguerite T. Owings, an heir to a silk manufacturing fortune. Continuing his private practice while serving as mayor, in 1909, Cummings also organized the law firm of Cummings & Lockwood with his close friend, Charles D. Lockwood.

On July 1, 1914, Cummings was appointed state's attorney for Fairfield County, a position he held until he resigned in 1924. Cummings gained national notoriety as a prosecutor for entering a nolle prosequi in the 1924 case of *State v. Israel*. Harold Israel was accused of shooting a priest. The evidence against him was staggering. He had been identified by witnesses, he was in the area of the murder at the time it occurred, he was found with the gun used in the crime, and, after extensive interrogation, he confessed to committing the murder, although he later recanted and professed his innocence. In the face of what appeared to be an open-and-shut case, Cummings conducted his own exhaustive investigation and eventually decided not to prosecute. In a lengthy statement to the court explaining his decision, Cummings meticulously rebutted the circumstantial evidence against Israel and discounted his confession as the product of a coercive interrogation of a defendant with diminished mental capacity. Cummings argued to the judge that "it is just as important for a state's attorney to use the great powers of his office to protect the innocent as it is to convict the guilty." The dramatic case and Cumming's courtroom performance was later dramatized in a 1947 movie, entitled *Boomerang!*, starring Dana Andrews and Arthur Kennedy.

Cummings's growing reputation as a brilliant litigator, a progressive mayor, and later an effective state's attorney eventually catapulted him into national politics. In 1900, he was elected as chair of the Connecticut Democratic party and the state's national committeeman, where he was an avid supporter and important advisor to Democratic presidential candidate William Jennings Bryan. In 1902, he ran for an at-large Connecticut seat in the U.S. House of Representatives and successfully molded the state party platform around the progressive ideals he had come to accept: direct election of senators, direct primaries, the secret ballot, condemnation of special interest groups, stronger antitrust enforcement, and a forty-hour workweek. Following a national trend, however, Republicans swept Connecticut in 1902, and Cummings was defeated. During the next fourteen years, Cummings served in various capacities in the national Democratic party. He was elected vice-chair of the party in 1913 and head of the Democratic Speakers Bureau in 1916; he served as an important campaign advisor to Alton Parker during the 1904 presidential election, to Bryan again in 1908, and to Woodrow Wilson in the 1912 and 1916 elections. He ran for the U.S. Senate in 1916 but was again narrowly defeated in a state that went solidly Republican. Despite this, his close ties to Wilson led to his selection as chair of the Democratic National Committee in 1919. In that capacity, he delivered the keynote address to the 1920 Democratic Convention in San Francisco, a speech that won him national acclaim as a gifted orator and prominent figure in Democratic politics. He continued to chair the party until 1925, when he decided to rededicate himself to his private law practice.

After a seven-year absence from politics, in which Cummings concentrated on corporate law and litigation, he returned to the national political arena in 1932 as an advisor to the campaign of Franklin D. Roosevelt. Cummings and Roosevelt had been close friends and political allies in Democratic party politics since they first met during the Wilson campaign in 1912. On March 28, 1933, Cummings resigned from Cummings & Lockwood, and Roosevelt appointed him to become the fifty-fifth attorney general of the United States. During his six years as attorney general, Cummings transformed the Department of Justice and was the crucial figure in the battle between the Court and the Roosevelt administration over the constitutionality of New Deal programs and policies.

Cummings reorganized the Justice Department and modernized its operations. He abolished or merged several of its divisions, reorganized and strengthened the Federal Bureau of Investigation, and created the Office of Legal Counsel, a new division that was given responsibility for drafting the formal legal opinions of the attorney general and rendering legal advice to executive department officials. These responsibilities were transferred from the solicitor general's office, and the latter was given exclusive control over the federal government's appellate litigation. By centralizing control over appellate litigation, Cummings transformed the solicitor general's office into a strategic resource for controlling agency policymaking and a powerful force in shaping federal judicial policy. Cummings also began a comprehensive review and update of the federal rules for practice and procedure in federal courts and reformed the federal prison system, establishing the Alcatraz Island prison in San Francisco Bay in 1934 as a model prison for hardened criminals.

As attorney general, Cummings personally argued few cases before the Supreme Court, but he was closely involved in overseeing the government's most important litigations. During his first three years as attorney general, the Supreme Court invalidated more than thirteen major pieces of legislation at the heart of the administration's New Deal agenda. Indeed, the Court's opposition to the New Deal was so broad based that between 1934 and 1936 the Justice Department, for the only time in history, lost more cases than it won before the Court. Undeterred, Cummings hoped to convince the Court to reverse its *Lochner*-era jurisprudence, which had supported laissez-faire individualism, and uphold key elements of the New Deal, or, short of that, to see resignations from the Court so as to allow change through appointments. But after the Court struck down three more major pieces of New Deal legislation in early 1936, Cummings agreed to lead a more overt assault on the Court. He and Assistant Attorney General ROBERT H. JACKSON advanced the administration's infamous Court-packing bill, aimed at expanding the size of the Court from nine to fifteen members. Although Cummings defended the plan as a measure to promote efficiency on the Court, it was a clear attempt to mute Court resistance to the administration's policy agenda. Cummings admitted in Senate testimony to the Senate: "We are facing not a constitutional but a judicial crisis . . . (in which) the deciding vote of one or two judges has nullified the will of Congress, has overruled the approval of the President . . . and has run counter to the sentiment of the country" (Clayton 1992, 124).

Cummings also delivered a series of public addresses attacking the Court and its *Lochner*-era jurisprudence. In a 1935 address to the American Bar Association, Cummings argued that the Court "does not operate in a legalistic vacuum," that it is only one of several interpreters of the Constitution in the U.S. system (Cummings 1936). Later, in a 1937 radio address defending the Court-packing bill, he argued that the Court was "but a coordinate branch of Government. It is entitled to no higher position than either the legislative or the executive. If the Constitution is to remain a living document and the law is to serve the needs of a vital and growing nation, it is essential that new blood be infused into our judiciary" (Cummings 1937).

The administration's efforts to expand the size of the Court proved unnecessary in the end; the Court began upholding key elements of the New Deal in spring of 1937. Cummings's litigation and public-relations strategies, however, were crucial for pressuring the Court and forcing its eventual reversal. Cummings's tenure as attorney general also ushered in a new era in the relationship of that office to the White House. Previous attorneys general had been more removed from White House policymaking. Cummings's close personal relationship with the president, his unabashed advocacy of New Deal programs, and his creation of the Office of Legal Counsel as an institutional mechanism for harmonizing White House policy with Justice Department legal positions became the model for a more partisan style of attorney general in contemporary U.S. politics (Clayton 1992). Many of Cummings's accomplishments as attorney general are recounted in a 1937 book, coauthored by Cummings while he was attorney general with historian Carl McFarland, entitled *Federal Justice*. The book was at that time the most extensive history of the office of attorney general and the Department of Justice and has been an important resource for subsequent scholars and historians.

Homer Cummings resigned as attorney general on November 15, 1939. Thereafter he reorganized the firm of Cummings & Lockwood in Washington, D.C., and continued as counsel until the time of his death in 1956. The firm of Cummings & Lockwood is still thriving in Connecticut.

—*Cornell W. Clayton*

Sources and Suggestions for Further Reading

Clayton, Cornell. *The Politics of Justice: The Attorney General and the Making of Legal Policy.* Armonk, N.Y.: M. E. Sharpe, 1992.

Cummings, Homer S. "Address of Homer S. Cummings, Attorney General of the United States." *American Bar Association Journal* 22 (1936): 24.

———. "Radio Address of the Attorney General." *Congressional Record*, 15 February 1937, A217.

Cummings, Homer S., and Carl McFarland. *Federal Justice.* New York: Macmillan, 1937.

Mazza, David L. "Homer S. Cummings and Progressive Politics from Bryan through Wilson, 1896–1925." Ph.D. dissertation, St. Johns University, New York, 1978.

———. "Mayor Homer S. Cummings, the Dawn of a Reformer." Manuscript. Gimsford Historical Society Library, Stamford Connecticut, 1972.

Swisher, Carl Brent. *Selected Papers of Homer Cummings.* New York: Da Capo Press, 1972.

CURTIS, BENJAMIN ROBBINS

(1809–1874)

BENJAMIN ROBBINS CURTIS, best known for his dissenting opinion in *Dred Scott v. Sandford* (1857), practiced law in Boston both before and after his six-year tenure on the U.S. Supreme Court. His contemporaries considered him to be the foremost attorney in Boston, in Massachusetts, and perhaps in the United States. The Curtis family was descended from William and Sarah Curtis, who emigrated from England in 1632 on the ship *Lyon* and settled in Massachusetts in 1639. They were an old family, respected, and of solid Puritan stock.

Benjamin Robbins Curtis was born November 4, 1809, in Watertown, Massachusetts. He was the son of Benjamin Curtis III and Lois Robbins. He had one brother, George Ticknor Curtis, who was born November 28, 1812. His father was a ship captain whose ship was lost at sea

BENJAMIN ROBBINS CURTIS
Collection of the Supreme Court of the United States

when Benjamin was five years old. His mother, the daughter of a manufacturer and storekeeper in Watertown, supported the family by operating a dry goods store and a small circulating library.

As a boy, Benjamin took full advantage of his mother's circulating library. He read widely and demonstrated from a young age superior intellect and reasoning ability. He first attended a school run by Samuel Worcester in

Newton, Massachusetts, then Mr. Angier's school in Medford. There, he was a classmate of John James Gilchrist, who became the chief justice of the Superior Court of New Hampshire and then chief justice of the U.S. Court of Claims. One of Benjamin's teachers was John Appleton, who became chief justice of Maine.

His early years were spent reading and engaging in the usual activities and pursuits of boys at that time. He was a well-rounded young man, but his voracious appetite for books, both fiction and nonfiction, set him apart from his peers. It was obvious that he had extraordinary potential. He was destined for Harvard College and a legal career.

Curtis entered Harvard in 1825, when he was sixteen years old. His mother could not afford the tuition, so she moved to Cambridge and ran a boarding house for Harvard undergraduates. She also received financial assistance from Benjamin's uncle, George Ticknor. Ticknor was Benjamin's father's half brother and a professor of belles lettres at Harvard. Benjamin had a close, lifelong relationship with his uncle. They corresponded regularly until George Ticknor's death in 1870. While at Harvard, Curtis was a member of several clubs, and he won the Bowdoin essay competition prize in his third year. He graduated second in his class in August 1829 and entered the law school at Harvard the following month. He won a second Bowdoin award in 1830, while studying law.

Curtis entered the law school the same month JOSEPH STORY began lecturing there. Story was instrumental in strengthening the law curriculum and instituted the practice of holding moot courts. Curtis excelled in the moot courts. In 1831, about a year and a half before completing his degree, Curtis left Harvard to practice law in the small country town of Northfield, Massachusetts. He assumed the law practice of John Nevers, who became sheriff. Since he was not yet admitted to the bar, he practiced in the offices of Wells & Alvord in Greenfield. He and James C. Alvord became close, life-long friends. His motive for leaving Harvard stemmed in part from his desire to court Eliza Marie Woodward, of Hanover, New Hampshire. She was the youngest daughter of Curtis's paternal aunt, who was the wife of William H. Woodward, treasurer of Dartmouth College during the famous legal dispute *Dartmouth College v. Woodward* (1819). He and Eliza were married May 8, 1833. They were married for eleven years and had five children. Eliza died in 1844. Two years later, Curtis married Anna Wroe Curtis, a distant relative. They were married for sixteen years and had three children. Anna died in 1860, and the following year Curtis married Maria Malleville Allen, grandniece of the Reverend Eleazar Wheelock, D.D., founder of Dartmouth College. The couple had four children.

As was his family, Curtis was a member of the Unitarian faith. In the 1860s, he joined the Episcopal church. Curtis studied religion as he studied law—seriously and with dedication. Once, when he was practicing law in Northfield, a visitor noticed an open Bible in his office and commented (in jest) that it was a strange book for a lawyer to read. Curtis replied, "Then I pity the lawyers; for those who are ignorant of the principles inculcated in that book cannot be thoroughly furnished for the duties of the profession" (Curtis 1879, 1:326). Throughout his life he always offered a silent prayer for wisdom and guidance before taking his seat on the bench or charging a jury (Curtis 1879, 1:326).

While at Northfield, Curtis developed a diverse practice. He also read widely in the law. He attended the spring and summer 1831 terms at Harvard, then returned to Northfield, where he continued his studies while practicing law. He completed his legal studies, graduated from Harvard, and in September 1834 was admitted to the bar at Northampton. Shortly thereafter he moved his family to Boston, where he practiced law with Charles Pelham Curtis, a distant relative and the father of his second wife, Anna. In 1836, he was admitted as a counsellor before the Supreme Judicial Court of Massachusetts.

Curtis excelled at the bar and quickly became known as one of Boston's finest attorneys. He practiced law in Boston from 1834 to 1851, when he became a U.S. Supreme Court justice, then again from 1857 until his death in 1874. In a letter to a friend in 1831 he described the law as a "noble science," which he loved "unaffectedly" and which he "studied closely" (Leach 1955, 255). He also became one of the leading members of Boston society. He was elected a fellow of the Harvard Corporation and, along with Joseph Story, was a founding member, officer, and trustee of the Mt. Auburn Cemetery Corporation.

Although he was not active in party politics, he became embroiled in the politics of the times. He was a fervent supporter of the Union and defender of the Constitution when abolitionism and secessionism threatened both. He firmly and unyieldingly defended the rule of law embodied in the Constitution throughout his legal career. Whenever possible, he sought to prevent sectional strife and to keep the Union intact.

In 1836, when he had been in Boston for only two years, he argued the case *Commonwealth v. Aves* before the Massachusetts Supreme Court, presided over by Chief Justice Lemuel Shaw. In this case he defended the right of a slaveholder from Louisiana to hold a slave while visiting Massachusetts, a free state, and to take the slave (a six-year-old girl named Med) back to New Orleans against her will. He argued that the rule of comity among nations gives the right of private property in a slave that Massachusetts must recognize. Although he personally believed that slavery violated natural rights and could be enforced only by positive law, he also believed that since Article IV of the Constitution embodied the concept, it was his duty to support it. The Massachusetts Supreme Court ruled against him. Chief Justice Shaw asserted that the concept of property following the owner applies only to commodities that are considered everywhere to be property. This did not apply to slaves.

Curtis may have lost the case, but his eloquence, lucid arguments, careful analysis, and comprehensive discussion of the issue were impressive and reinforced his reputation as a first-rate attorney. Throughout his professional life he always prepared thoroughly, exhaustively researched his topics, carefully developed his arguments, and delivered clear, reasoned presentations from premise to conclusion, all without a superfluous word. His dignified demeanor and the force of his arguments captivated his audiences. He was a legal craftsman and orator of consummate skill. DANIEL WEBSTER wrote of him in 1849: "His great mental characteristic is clearness; and the power of clear statement is the great power at the bar" (Curtis 1879, 1:83).

Curtis continued to hone his legal skills and master new legal fields. He built a comprehensive law practice that included commercial law in the state courts, and maritime, insurance, bankruptcy, and patent law in the federal courts. He represented primarily large private corporations that were engaged in trade and manufacturing and were concerned about government regulation of commerce. His legal practice helped foster the development of marine insurance corporate law. Between 1836 and 1851, he argued many cases before the Circuit Court of the United States for the First Circuit, with Justice Joseph Story presiding, many cases before the U.S. District Court, and 138 cases before the Supreme Court of Massachusetts

He was elected to the lower chamber of the Massachusetts legislature in 1851 and served on the judiciary and conference committees. He drew up a plan to revise the state's judicial proceedings and chaired the commission that implemented it. His commission framed a new code of court procedure, the Massachusetts Practice Act of 1851, which put the state, along with New York, in the forefront of state legal reform efforts.

As a conservative Whig, he supported Daniel Webster's 1840 presidential election bid. In 1844, he wrote a treatise for the *North American Review* supporting Webster's argument that states could not repudiate their public debt. He also gave public addresses supporting Daniel Webster's position in favor of the Compromise Acts of 1850, including the controversial Fugitive Slave Act of 1850.

When U.S. Supreme Court justice Levi Woodbury died in 1851, President Millard Fillmore, with the wholehearted concurrence of Secretary of State Daniel Webster, nominated Curtis to fill the seat. Their first choice was Curtis's friend and fellow attorney RUFUS CHOATE, but Fillmore and Webster knew Choate would not accept the position. Curtis was nominated to the Court on September 22, 1851, as an interim appointment, was formally nominated on December 11, and was confirmed by the Senate on December 20, 1851. He served six terms on the Court, from September 1851 to September 1857. He left a lucrative law practice to sit on the Court, and very early in his tenure he realized that the salary would be insufficient to support his large and growing family. Although he was popular in Washington society, he did not particularly enjoy his life there, and he missed his family and his newly purchased farm. In addition, his temperament was more suited to the practice of law than to the work of the Court.

Justice Curtis began his tenure as a U.S. Supreme Court justice riding circuit. He was assigned to the First Circuit, Justice Story's former circuit, which comprised Maine, New Hampshire, Rhode Island, and Massachusetts. His belief in the supremacy of the Constitution and national law, including the Fugitive Slave Act of 1850, earned him the nickname "the slave-catcher judge."

Judicial and legal scholars agree that, had he remained on the bench, Benjamin Curtis would have become one of the great justices. His opinion of the Court in *Cooley v. Board of Wardens of the Port of Philadelphia* (1851), in which he articulated the doctrine of selective inclusion when interpreting the commerce clause of the Constitution, is a fine example of his legal craftsmanship. In that opinion, he asserted that the commerce clause does not exclude states from exercising authority over minor, local commerce, such as pilotage. States have the authority to regulate pilotage into bays, rivers, and harbors, until Congress decides to regulate it. In other words, local problems should be addressed locally and national problems should be addressed in Congress.

He considered serving on the Court much less taxing and time-consuming than practicing law. Thus, he had the opportunity to pursue other interests. He edited *Reports of Cases in the Circuit Courts of the United States* (1854), and one of the earliest compilations of condensed Supreme Court decisions, the 22-volume *Decisions of the Supreme Court of the United States* (1856). He is best remembered, however, for his dissent in *Scott v. Sandford* (1857), the case in which Chief Justice Roger Taney ruled that blacks were not citizens, that Congress did not have the authority to regulate slavery in the territories, and that Dred Scott's status as a slave did not change by his residence in a free state.

In his dissent, Curtis refuted each point in Chief Justice Taney's opinion. He demonstrated that blacks had been citizens under the Articles of Confederation and also under the Constitution. He concluded that Congress had the power to regulate slavery in the territories, and Dred Scott's freedom should be established. This is a reversal of his argument for the defendant in *Commonwealth v. Aves* in 1836. In that case he asserted that the rule of comity among nations gave the right of private property in a slave that Massachusetts must recognize. In his *Scott* dissent, he argued essentially Chief Justice Lemuel Shaw's opinion in the 1836 case—that the concept of property following the owner applies only to commodities that are considered everywhere to be property, and this does not apply to slaves. Slavery can only be enforced through positive law, and should a slave owner remove his slaves to a locality in which slavery is not sanctioned by law, the relationship of master and slave no longer applies. The laws of the local jurisdiction apply. These conflicting positions can be reconciled by viewing them in the light of Curtis's firm belief in the supremacy of the Constitution and his staunch defense of the Union. In each case he believed that his argument was the appropriate one to achieve his goal of preserving the Union from secessionist threats.

After the *Dred Scott* decision was announced and all of the opinions read in open court, Curtis gave a copy of his dissent to a reporter. Unbeknownst to him, the other opinions were not immediately made public. This created a furor in the press. When he discovered that his was the only opinion made public, he wrote to Chief Justice Taney requesting a copy of Taney's opinion. Taney refused. The resulting conflict made him lose confidence in the Court and cemented his decision to resign.

Upon his resignation from the Court in 1857, Curtis again practiced law in Boston. By now his legal reputation was affirmed, and his practice thrived. The majority of his work was as a consulting attorney. His sterling reputation and sound advice earned him large fees. Between 1857 and his death in 1874, he argued fifty-four cases before the U.S. Supreme Court, seventy-nine before the Supreme Court of Massachusetts, and many in the lower courts. Three of his most significant arguments before the U.S. Supreme Court were in *Paul v. Virginia* (1868), *Hepburn v. Griswold* (1869), the most noted of the legal tender cases, and *Virginia v. West Virginia* (1870).

During the Civil War he firmly adhered to the Nationalist Whig philosophy, although by that time the Whig party was in disarray and he had become a Democrat. He strongly supported the Union, although in 1862 he published a pamphlet, *Executive Power*, in which he criticized President Lincoln's Emancipation Proclamation and his suspension of the writ of habeas corpus. He argued that no emergency justified such a loss of liberty or sanctioned such an increase of the president's war powers.

In 1869, President Andrew Johnson was impeached for, among other charges, violating the Tenure of Office Act of 1867 by firing Secretary of War Edwin M. Stanton. WILLIAM EVARTS, Thomas Nelson, Henry Stanbery, and Benjamin Robbins Curtis were Johnson's attorneys. Curtis presented the opening arguments in defense of Johnson's actions, speaking for five hours on April 9 and 10, 1869, before the Senate and Chief Justice

Salmon P. Chase. He argued that impeachment was not a political process but a judicial one under Article III, Section 4, of the Constitution. President Johnson did not violate the Tenure of Office Act of 1867 when he fired Stanton, because Stanton was a Lincoln appointee and the Act did not cover that specific situation. He also asserted that Andrew Johnson became president in his own right when Abraham Lincoln died; as president, he had the right to fire political appointees; and the Tenure of Office Act would be declared unconstitutional were it to be challenged in court.

History records the result of the trial. After Johnson was acquitted, he offered Curtis the position of attorney general, but Curtis declined. Five years later he also declined to be an attorney in the Geneva Arbitration. Instead, he continued to practice law. In 1872 and 1873, he gave a series of lectures at the law school at Harvard on the jurisdiction and practice of the federal courts. His health failed, and he died at his residence in Newport, Rhode Island, of a brain hemorrhage on September 15, 1874. He is buried in Mt. Auburn Cemetery in Cambridge, along with members of his family, his friends, including Joseph Story, and other luminaries of the bench and bar. His papers are at the Library of Congress, the American Antiquarian Society, and the Harvard Law School Library.

—*Judith Haydel*

Sources and Suggestions for Further Reading

Curtis, Benjamin R., ed. A *Memoir of Benjamin Robbins Curtis, LL.D., with Some of his Professional and Miscellaneous Writings.* 2 vols. Boston: Little, Brown, 1879.

Leach, Richard H. "Benjamin Robbins Curtis: A Model for a Successful Legal Career." *American Bar Association Journal* 41 (1955): 225.

_____. "Benjamin Robbins Curtis: Case Study of a Supreme Court Justice." Ph.D. dissertation, Princeton University, 1951.

CUSHING, CALEB

(1800–1879)

CALEB CUSHING
Corbis

CALEB CUSHING WAS KNOWN throughout his life as much for his controversial views on slavery as for the role he played as a statesman and political leader. Cushing negotiated important international treaties and served in the legislature of his home state of Massachusetts and in the U.S. Congress. He organized and led a force in the Mexican-American War, served as the attorney general of the United States, and acted as legal advisor to four presidents.

Cushing's family could trace its lineage directly back to Matthew Cushing, who came to the colonies in 1638 from Hardingham, England. His grandson, the second Caleb in the line, was a delegate at the Constitutional Convention of 1778. This Caleb was John Newmarch Cushing's grandfather. John Newmarch was drawn to the seas early in his life, leaving formal education to pursue trading in Europe and the West Indies. He met and married Lydia Dow, and their firstborn and only surviving son was the third Caleb in the family, born on January 17, 1800.

In 1802, John Cushing moved the family from Salisbury, where the family had lived since coming to the colonies, to Newburyport, where Caleb would spend much of his life. Caleb began studies at Harvard College in

1813 at age thirteen, and four years later he matriculated as one of Harvard Law School's first students. After his first year of law school, Caleb decided that what interested him about the law were the applied elements of its practice. So, in September 1818, he entered an apprenticeship with Ebenezer Mozeley, a distinguished attorney and statesman. After three years of study and work, Cushing was admitted to the Massachusetts bar.

By 1821, Cushing was a regular contributor to the influential *North American Review* in addition to publishing several volumes, both original and translated, on contracts and maritime law, most notably his translation of Robert Pothier's *A Treatise on Maritime Contracts of Letting to Hire* (1821). In 1821, on his return to Newburyport, he met his future wife, Caroline Elizabeth Wilde, daughter of Judge Samuel Sumner Wilde (a Federalist who presided over the Supreme Court of Massachusetts and would later take issue with his son-in-law's version of democracy), although the couple did not marry until three years later.

In 1824, the same year as his wedding, Cushing was selected to the Massachusetts General Court as a representative from Newburyport, where he was known for his sharp wit and powerful debating skills. In the fall of 1825, Cushing was elected to the state senate, where he served on the judiciary committee and was recognized for his "knowledge of the law, soundness of judgment, and effective presentation of a case" (Fuess 1923, 65). However, in his early career, Cushing was not always successful in his litigation, due in part to his inability to connect with those in the jury.

After two failed attempts at gaining a seat in Congress, Cushing again took a seat in the General Court in 1828. The following year, Cushing and his wife took leave for a year, traveling throughout Europe. He returned to the United States in 1830 with renewed vigor and energy, but within two years he had again lost a campaign for Congress and had also lost his young wife. Cushing remained a widower until his own death in 1879.

In 1834, on his third attempt, Cushing was finally elected to Congress as a member of the new Whig party. It was around this time that Cushing began to write and speak on the issue of black servitude. Although Cushing was not in favor of slavery, he denounced the abolitionist movement because of its potential ill effects on the Union. He argued that it was not the place of the North to interfere with the South's interpretation of the still rather new Constitution. As the new opposition Whig party entered the government, Cushing—as a strong political player in this new opposition—was sure that at age thirty-four he had secured his place on the national political scene. Having acquired his seat in the House of Representatives, he remained at the Capitol for four terms, from 1834 to 1842. During his terms in the House, Cushing was chair of the Committee on Foreign Affairs. He was known to participate in virtually every debate that went to the legisla-

Splitting Hairs

Philadelphia lawyer George Wharton Pepper, one-time law professor at the University of Pennsylvania and a Pennsylvania senator, married the daughter of Dr. George Park Fisher, a Yale history professor who enjoyed telling stories about old New England attorneys. One of his favorites centered on Roger Sherman, who told the court that his adversary was no more able to make an attempted distinction than to split a hair with a penknife.

After his opponent plucked a hair from his beard, split it with his pocketknife, and held it up for the court to observe, Sherman retorted, "I said a *hair*, sir—not a bristle" (Pepper 1944, 37).

REFERENCE

Pepper, George Wharton. *Philadelphia Lawyer: An Autobiography*. Philadelphia: J. B. Lippincott, 1944.

---

tive floor and was considered a persuasive and influential orator and a leader of his party.

In 1842, Cushing found himself twice acting as counsel to President John Tyler before the House. The first of these occasions resulted from a debate over a tariff increase. When the president's secretary, John Tyler Jr., appeared in front of the House to summarize the chief executive's objections to the bill, Cushing rose to his defense both in the chamber and in subsequent writings. Fuess writes that Cushing, "who was now recognized as Tyler's spokesman in the House, rose to justify the President, quoting extensively from *The Federalist* to prove that the President's course was in full accord with the plan of the founders of the republic" (Fuess 1923, 1:350).

The second incident arose from a resolution "requiring the Secretary of War to communicate certain reports relative to the affairs of the Cherokee Indians" (Fuess 1923, 350). When the secretary stated that such disclosure would not be in the best interest of the public, Tyler's political opponents in the House took issue with this withholding of information. Cushing once more defended the executive's decision, acting in his capacity as an attorney. In a debate that clearly outlined the Whig's political views of the day in regard to the proper balance of the executive and the legislative branches, Cushing argued that the secretary of war was fully within his rights to withhold information of national import and that the House had neither the right nor the means to compel disclosure.

In 1843, President Tyler sent Cushing's name before the Senate three times for confirmation as secretary of state. Each time, the Senate strongly defeated the nomination. After this series of failures, Cushing was relieved to receive an appointment as minister to China. He left the United States, spending seventeen months traveling through the Far East and securing several treaties that opened important Chinese ports to American trading vessels. On his return, Cushing took an extended trip through the Northwest Territories to settle boundary disputes and secure protection for traders. Not long after he returned from this expedition, Cushing, at age forty-five, raised a regiment and headed south to fight in the Mexican-American War. Before leaving on this venture, he was again chosen as a representative to the General Court of Massachusetts and took his seat that autumn before leaving for the war. He left for the war in 1847, but by the time he and his troops reached Mexico City, the fighting had come to an end.

In May 1851, Cushing helped to pass a bill in the Massachusetts legislature incorporating Newburyport as a city, at which point Cushing was elected its first mayor. In 1852, Cushing was appointed associate justice to the Supreme Court of Massachusetts. In preparation for taking his seat on the bench, Cushing read the entire series of the *Massachusetts Reports* in only six weeks. Those who sat on the bench with Cushing commented on his extensive knowledge of the law and his ability to recall obscure parts of the legal code. He often eagerly took on written opinions that the other justices viewed as tedious and dull. That same year, he took part in the successful presidential campaign of Democratic candidate Franklin Pierce. On February 25, 1853, Cushing was rewarded for his work in the Pierce campaign, receiving an appointment as the attorney general of the United States.

Cushing made several important changes to the office of attorney general. He was the first attorney general to give up his private practice on entering his new office and the first to be paid the same salary as other cabinet officers (Baker 1992, 57). In addition, he expanded the duties of the office. Although he did so partly at the request of the secretary of state, the *New York Evening Mirror* noted that he was referred to as "Richelieu" for aggrandizing his power (Baker 1992, 73). At Secretary Marcy's behest, pardons, legal and judicial appointments, and extraditions were relocated to the office of the attorney general. He also wrote voluminously on issues of political import during this time. Unlike his predecessors, who often offered brief opinions on political and legal questions, Cushing went beyond a brief statement of the facts. At the end of his four years in office, his writings filled three full volumes (about 760 pages each) in the *Official Opinions of the Attorneys General of the United States*, more than any other attorney general before or since.

Among these opinions were suggestions on how to expand the federal judiciary. He argued that the then-current circuit court structure, in which the Supreme Court judges literally rode circuit around the states to hear cases with two district court judges, was ineffective. The justices found the additional task of riding circuit arduous and often could not make it to all the necessary venues, forcing the district court judges to hold court themselves. Cushing suggested a modification to the system, with nine judges appointed to sit permanently at the head of each circuit, leaving the Supreme Court justices on the bench in Washington, D.C. Although the politics of the time held up the reformation of the circuit court system, when the circuits were reformed in 1869, the system mirrored the suggestions put forth by Cushing a decade earlier.

Of particular significance during his time in office (1853–1857) was the question of slavery. Cushing argued that, although slavery was not necessarily a "positive good," he viewed the servitude of blacks as "an economic system which the southern plantation owner should be allowed to maintain if he so desired" (Fuess 1923, 2:153). More important, Cushing argued that radical abolitionists were as much a threat to the union as were the slave owners. He chose to frame the issue in terms of states' rights and economics, avoiding the morality of servitude altogether. At the president's request, Cushing authored an opinion addressing the issues that would later be addressed in the *Dred Scott v. Sandford* case of 1857. In addition to his writing on the slavery issue, Cushing also wrote and published opinions on whether an aggressive force can "rightfully make use of the territory of a neutral state for military purposes, without the specific consent of the neutral government" (Fuess 1923, 2:168). This published opinion, entitled *Concerning British Recruitment in the United States*, is considered to display his "legal knowledge and argumentative powers at their best" (Fuess 1923, 2:167).

During this period, Cushing was considered one of the most powerful cabinet members of Pierce's administration. In his first year, he prepared and argued seventeen cases on behalf of the United States involving claims to the gross amount of $45 million against the United States. On completing his term as attorney general in 1857, Cushing had single-handedly taken what had previously been considered a rather unimportant cabinet position and transformed it into a powerful tool for political change. It was said that "his training as a lawyer and judge, his long experience in legislation, his intimate association with great men, had all provided him with a background which was incalculable value to the government" (Fuess 1923, 2:186).

On his return to New England in 1858, Cushing entered into private practice with Sidney Webster. Not long after, he again found himself in the lower chamber of the Massachusetts legislature. Meanwhile, the slavery question was coming to a climax nationwide. After the Supreme Court issued its decision in *Dred Scott*, Cushing felt confident that his approach to this debate would become the law of the land. However, ABRAHAM LINcoln's victory in the presidential election of 1860 changed his mind, and he became convinced that there would be no way to save the Union, which was at the core of his antiabolitionist position. In the time between the November election and Lincoln's inauguration, Cushing was sent to the South by President Buchanan to request a delay in the passing of the secession ordinance. By the time he arrived on December 20, the Southern states had signed the order. The act of secession hit at the very heart of Cushing's pro-Union sentiments and signaled his official break with Southern sympathizers.

As the Civil War progressed, Cushing acted as legal assistant to Lincoln, consulting in various affairs of war. Throughout the war, in addition to his role as legal advisor to the president, Cushing was called in to act as counsel and issue written opinions for various members of the cabinet.

Between 1861 and 1865, Cushing also argued several interesting and important cases before the Supreme Court. Most important among these was *McGuire v. Massachusetts* (1865). Cushing argued this case before the Supreme Court in December 1865 and reargued it the following February. McGuire was accused of keeping a dwelling exclusively for the storage and sale of liquor, and under a Massachusetts statute he had been convicted and severely fined. It was Cushing's contention that the Massachusetts statute under which McGuire had been convicted was unconstitutional, as it was contrary to the notion of contracts established by the Constitution. He argued that the prohibition of intoxicating liquors would be both impossible and inadvisable, causing greater harm than good. Although Cushing's argument was vigorous and caught the attention of the public, his claim was denied and the conviction was upheld. The Court argued that, although the provision may have seemed outdated, it was properly enacted and violated no provision of the federal Constitution.

Having reentered private practice, Cushing came to be called "the representative public lawyer in the country." At this stage he accepted few retainers and confined his practice almost exclusively to arguing before the Supreme Court. He had reached a level in private practice that had rivaled the work he had done in public service. Even as his private career flourished, Cushing still took on even the most menial of public service tasks.

In 1866, Cushing argued *DeHaro's Heirs v. United States*. The case involved a claim for a large tract of land in the city of San Francisco. The legal talent drawn into this case included two U.S. senators, the attorney general, and two ex-cabinet members. The case, which was argued over the course of 1866 and 1867, dealt with legal documents that had been drawn up in Spanish by the claimant's father. Cushing's command of the Spanish language dominated the courtroom argument and ultimately helped his clients win their case.

In *Goodyear v. Providence* (1868), Cushing acted as counsel for the defendants, protesting that the hard rubber patents held by Goodyear resulted in a practical monopoly. This suit was an outgrowth of an earlier dispute in which DANIEL WEBSTER, who was attorney for Goodyear, secured a favorable verdict that gave his client control over the production and use of vulcanized rubber. Again, Cushing was successful in securing a victory for his clients.

Probably the most famous case of Cushing's career was *Gaines v. New Orleans* (1868). Cushing argued this case, forty years in the making, before the Supreme Court in 1861 for the sixth time. Mrs. Myra Gaines was the daughter of wealthy Southern landowners. Her father abandoned her and her mother not long after she was born, although he returned a few years later and placed his daughter in the care of a friend. On his death, there was a question as to whether Mrs. Gaines could properly claim the lands her father had left behind. Her husband, General Gaines, pursued the matter, and although she lost much of her wealth in pursuing this real estate, she eventually won title and recovered her lost assets. The length and notoriety of the case held the public interest for years, although it was ultimately Cushing's ease and grace in the courtroom that secured the favorable verdict.

In 1871, at age seventy-one, Cushing was once again called into service by the government. President Ulysses S. Grant asked Cushing to issue an opinion on the claims made against the *Alabama*, the *Florida*, and other vessels that had been built under British registry and later flew under the Confederate flag. On issuing his opinion in this matter, Cushing was appointed senior counsel for the United States and attended an international conference in Geneva, where he brokered a compromise that enabled both the United States and Great Britain to come away from the hearings without loss of dignity.

In December 1873, President Grant nominated Cushing to be chief justice of the Supreme Court. The nomination was offered to two individuals before it fell to Cushing. However, Cushing's earlier antiabolitionist writings and the grudges of old political enemies quickly rose to the surface, so Cushing asked Grant to withdraw his name from the confirmation process. According to one source, this is the "most notable instance in our history of a rejection for high office on purely partisan grounds" (Hough 1964, 628). Soon thereafter, Cushing took leave to Spain, where he had been appointed ambassador. He retired from this post in 1877 and died of a prolonged illness two years later, on January 2, 1879.

Cushing's command of the law was unparalleled in his day. Although his courtroom appearances tended to be matters of civil litigation and claims, his work as an attorney went far beyond the courtroom. His role as political and legal advisor to four presidents, his work in foreign countries as negotiator and treaty maker, and his voluminous writings and legal opinions all combine to make a remarkable lawyer and statesman.

—*Elizabeth Mazzara*

Sources and Suggestions for Further Reading

Baker, Nancy V. *Conflicting Loyalties: Law & Politics in the Attorney General's Office, 1789–1990*. Lawrence: University Press of Kansas, 1992.

Fuess, Claude M. *Caleb Cushing*. Vols. 1 and 2. New York: Harcourt, Brace, 1923.

Hough, Walter. "Cushing, Caleb." In *Dictionary of American Biography*, edited by Allen Johnson and Dumas Malone. Vol. 2. New York: Scribner, 1964, 623–630.

DANA, RICHARD HENRY, JR.

(1815–1882)

RICHARD HENRY DANA JR.
Corbis

BETTER KNOWN TODAY FOR HIS literary accomplishments, Richard Henry Dana Jr. was also one of the most prominent American trial lawyers of the middle years of the nineteenth century, specializing in international law.

Dana was born on August 1, 1815, in Cambridge, Massachusetts, the oldest of four children of Richard Henry Dana Sr., a poet and essayist and founder of the *North American Review,* and Ruth Charlotte Smith Dana, formerly of Taunton. His grandfather, Francis Dana, had been a delegate to the Continental Congress, the first U.S. minister to Russia, and chief justice of the Massachusetts Supreme Court.

After the death of his mother in 1822, the young Dana endured the strict and sometimes cruel discipline of a succession of local private grammar schools until, in July 1831, he entered Harvard College. During his junior year, the shy, sensitive youth suffered an attack of measles, which so weakened his eyesight that he could not read. Restless, he enlisted in August 1834 as a common sailor on the brig *Pilgrim,* a sailing vessel bound around Cape Horn for California. Returning home two years later much matured, a hardened and healthy young man of twenty-one resumed his undergraduate studies and graduated from Harvard College in June 1835, taking prizes in English prose composition and elocution.

Long-haired, bronzed, and broad-shouldered, the short, stocky Dana was at this stage of his life robust, both physically and intellectually, and radiated charm and sincerity. He enrolled in the law school presided over by Supreme Court justice JOSEPH STORY and simultaneously assisted Professor Edward T. Channing in teaching elocution to Harvard undergraduates. In February 1840, he entered the Boston law office of Charles G. Loring, who later became a prolific publicist in the field of international law. Utilizing extensive notes kept during his time at sea, he took time from his continuing legal studies to author a manuscript published by Harper Brothers later that year as *Two Years before the Mast,* an unconventional account of maritime life from the perspective of an ordinary sailor, a work that soon brought the twenty-five-year-old Dana considerable fame, even more in England than in the United States.

A year later, in 1841, Little, Brown of Boston published Dana's 225-page treatise, *The Seaman's Friend,* which at once became a standard reference work on maritime law, both in the United States and in England. Meanwhile, Dana opened his own law office, specializing in admiralty cases. Success was almost immediate, and the young author-lawyer soon felt prosperous enough to marry. Sarah Watson of Hartford, Connecticut, became Mrs. Dana on August 25, 1841, and in time they had six children.

During the first two decades of his adult life, Dana, in keeping with his family's Federalist heritage, remained a conservative Whig, an admirer of DANIEL WEBSTER, and a severe critic of the local radical abolitionists. In June 1848, however, friends talked him into chairing a Free Soil Society meeting in Boston, which led to his becoming a delegate to the national Free Soil party convention in Buffalo, at which he played a prominent role in the vice-presidential nomination of Charles Francis Adams, a family friend. Accepted thereafter as a leader among Massachusetts Free Soilers, and later influential among the Republicans of his state, Dana continued sporadically to allow politics to draw him away from his law practice, which had the effect of diminishing his eminence within his profession without satisfying his incessant craving for appointment and sometimes for election to high public office. Too fastidious, proud, and rigid to adapt to the rapidly increasing democratization of American politics, he was useful as an advisor and speaker for others who sought elective office, but he made a poor candidate himself. And, despite his need to support a growing young family and a sizable contingent of impecunious relatives, he continued his involvement in the liberal Free Soil movement, which so alienated many wealthy

New Englanders that it limited his ability to earn more than an average income for his time and location. According to a sympathetic biographer, he was for many years known as "the counsel of the sailor and the slave—persistent, courageous, hard-fighting, skillful, but still the advocate of the poor and the unpopular" (Adams 1890, 1:129).

Perhaps the best example of Dana's determination always to put principle before expediency was his connection with the famous Boston fugitive slave cases of the period 1851–1854. After Congress passed the controversial Fugitive Slave Act of 1850, it was inevitable that Southern slaveholders would attempt to compel enforcement of that law in Boston, the center of the abolitionist movement. In 1851 a black man called Shadrach was arrested on the charge of being a fugitive slave. Dana represented him pro bono before the local U.S. commissioner, but a trial never took place because Shadrach was set free by a mob and escaped to Canada. Dana then devoted considerable time to five separate trials defending local citizens accused of participating in the affair (Adams 1890, 1:179–183, 195–198; Gale 1969, 155).

In 1854, Dana eloquently defended Anthony Burns, charged with being a fugitive slave from Virginia. Burns was nevertheless returned to slavery and Dana, for his trouble, was assaulted on a Boston street by thugs and seriously injured, an occurrence that for the first time made him locally popular among a majority of Bostonians. Indeed, by dramatizing the issues involved in the seizure and return to Southern slavery of alleged fugitives, he had greatly assisted the antislavery cause in New England (Gale 1969, 155–156; Adams 1890, 1:262–288, 300–330, 344–346; Shapiro 1961, x).

Elected a delegate to the 1853 Massachusetts constitutional convention, Dana emerged that summer as the dominant force at the convention among many distinguished lawyers and political leaders, including RUFUS CHOATE, Charles Sumner, Henry Wilson, Anson Burlingame, Joel Parker, and Benjamin F. Butler. Again his law practice suffered from his public-spiritedness and all for naught; the revisions recommended by the convention were defeated in the November election (Adams 1890, 1:229–230, 233–251, 290–295).

Restoring his debilitated law practice to good health, Dana damaged his own health. Although he won a famous victory in the landmark case of the *Osprey* (1854), establishing the maritime rule governing the passage of steamships and sailing vessels (Dana 1968, 2:662–663), most of his practice was not lucrative, impelling him to devote most of his waking hours to legal labors, which led to his falling ill in July 1859, essentially from overwork. On the advice of his physician, he embarked at once on a round-the-world tour by way of Panama, California, Hawaii, China, Japan, Egypt, Greece, Italy, and England, which absented him from the United States for 433 days, until his arrival in New York City on September 27, 1860, at which time, refreshed, he resumed his law practice (Adams 1890, 2:176–247).

Soon after ABRAHAM LINCOLN became the first Republican president early in 1861, Dana was appointed to the position of U.S. attorney for Massachusetts, in which capacity he prepared and tried the celebrated Boston *Prize Cases* of the Civil War era, including the case of the *Amy Warwick*, which resulted in a decision of inestimable importance (Veeder 1903, 2:907–928).

From the time that seven Southern states seceded from the Union during the winter of 1860–1861, and an attack on Fort Sumter in South Carolina precipitated civil war, President Lincoln and his advisors persistently maintained that the subsequent struggle was no more than a widespread insurrection, or rebellion, and thus an internal matter, undeserving of recognition or any other action by foreign governments. At the same time, the Lincoln administration claimed belligerent rights under international law, not only against the Southern "rebels," but also against foreigners who attempted to assist them, including the right to close Southern ports by a naval blockade and the right to seize and condemn as prizes of war all foreign vessels and their cargoes violating the blockade, even though the exercise of such belligerent rights was bound to imply the existence of a state of war between two nations.

Called to Washington in 1863 to defend the government's maritime policy, Dana was faced with a daunting task. He had to convince skeptical Supreme Court justices that the U.S. government might, under international law, exercise belligerent rights of search, seizure, and confiscation of blockade runners without violating its claim that the Southerners were merely citizens in arms against its authority, whose so-called Confederate States government was a nullity under international law and who therefore had no belligerent rights or any legitimate claim to foreign recognition.

At the outset of the trial, in which several lawsuits by owners of foreign vessels seized by blockaders were combined, it was widely assumed that the government's two positions—that no actual war as defined by international law existed, and that while endeavoring to quell the Southern rebellion it was nevertheless entitled to exercise all of the belligerent rights recognized by international law as belonging to a nation at war—were irreconcilable. Either the Supreme Court would have to rule that the Civil War was *justum bellum* (real war)—the announcement of which would encourage foreign governments eager to grant full diplomatic recognition to the Confederate regime to do so at once, with increased military aid to follow, resulting almost inevitably in a permanent division of the American Union—or the Court would accept the administration's claim that the Civil War was not "real war" under international law, in which case it would be obliged to invalidate the Northern naval blockade of the South and all searches and seizures of prizes of war resulting from it. This would require the reopening of the Southern ports, resulting in the exchange of hoarded cotton for vastly increased military supplies from foreign sources and the appearance in the South of foreign mercenaries, which would likely insure the success of the rebellion. Either way there was great danger that an adverse Supreme Court decision would contribute to democratic government, as Lincoln put it at Gettysburg, "perish[ing] from the earth" (Adams 1890, 2:266–270, 273–274, 332, 413–415, 418).

Richard Henry Dana's greatest service to his country was his carefully prepared argument and eloquent presentation of it before the U.S. Supreme Court that convinced a majority of the justices that the U.S. government could constitutionally, without violating international law, treat the Confederates at the same time both as rebels and as belligerents without providing the owners of ships caught in the naval blockade, or their governments, any just cause of complaint. Indeed, the majority opinion of the Court closely followed not only Dana's reasoning, but also the very language of his brief. It was a triumph with the most momentous consequences (Shapiro 1961, 119–122, 225–226).

During his tenure as U.S. attorney for Massachusetts, Dana took on the task of editing a new edition of Henry Wheaton's classic text on international law, a project on which he labored diligently for more than two years when permitted to do so by his official duties. Although the compensation he ultimately received from the publisher scarcely matched his research expenses, he performed his editorial duties with his usual thoroughness, digesting the unwieldy mass of material added to the deceased Wheaton's original work by William Beach Lawrence in editions published in 1853 and 1863. While greatly reducing the size of the treatise, Dana provided new material and contributed exhaustive essays (the most influential of which dealt with the Monroe Doctrine) comparable in learning and in concise presentation to Wheaton's own writings. Unfortunately, Dana neglected to give credit to Lawrence's massive compilations of authorities that had so weighted down the two previous editions so that both Wheaton's family and his publisher had sought a different editor. The wealthy Lawrence filed a lawsuit alleging plagiarism and literary piracy and launched a relentless public attack on Dana that lasted from 1866 until Lawrence died in 1881. Although Dana was ultimately exonerated on all but a few technical counts, Lawrence's interminable lawsuit, and his long-lasting deluge of vitriolic letters to newspapers and public figures, blighted the final fifteen years of Dana's life (Shapiro 1961, 155–159; Adams 1890, 2:282–327, 389–461).

Feeling the added burden of brief service in the Massachusetts legislature, and strongly disagreeing with President Andrew Johnson's post–Civil War reconstruction policies, Dana resigned as U.S. attorney on September 29, 1866, and sought once more to rebuild his private law practice. He took only a short recess in 1867 when he accepted an appointment to act with his old friend WILLIAM M. EVARTS in representing the U.S. government in the treason trial of former Confederate president Jefferson Davis, a trial several times postponed on the recommendation of Dana and others, until the charge was finally dropped (Adams 1890, 2:338–341).

In 1868, as a reform candidate to oust the notorious Benjamin F. Butler from Congress, Dana was the recipient of a typical Butler onslaught of mendacious mudslinging, in which his nemesis, Lawrence, eagerly joined. Further handicapped by his lifelong notion that to solicit public office was dishonorable, he lost the election by a large margin (Adams 1890, 2:342–348).

From this time on, his hopes for further public service fading, Dana devoted himself with decreasing enthusiasm to his law practice. In the age of the Robber Barons, a Boston Brahmin, as Dana's friend Henry Adams lamented, was no more than an archaic irritant. Remonstrances by Lawrence with a former law partner, Secretary of State Hamilton Fish, prevented Dana's appointment as counsel to the U.S. delegation at the *Alabama Claims* arbitration at Geneva, Switzerland, in 1871 and 1872, and Dana's nomination in 1876 by President Ulysses S. Grant to be U.S. minister to Great Britain, which momentarily reinvigorated his ambition for high office, was rejected by the Senate as a result of strenuous opposition by Lawrence, Butler, and Simon Cameron, chairman of the Foreign Relations Committee, who sneered at Dana as "one of those damn literary fellers" (Adams 1890, 2:362–377).

Briefly consoled by an appointment to act as counsel to the U.S. delegation meeting at Halifax, Nova Scota, during the summer of 1877 to settle a dispute over the Atlantic fisheries, Dana vainly opposed an excessive award to Canada, made possible by the ineffectiveness of the U.S. delegate and the unethical collusion of the Canadian and British delegates. Thereafter he seemed to lack vigor or a sense of purpose. In 1878, he abandoned his law practice and moved with his wife and two daughters to Paris, and then to Rome, expressing an intention in the evening of his life to author a treatise on international law. While lackadaisically engaged in this work, he died of pneumonia on January 6, 1882 (Shapiro 1961, 183–186).

As a lawyer, Dana was notable for meticulous preparation even for trials involving the most mundane issues, totally immersing himself in judicial precedents and the opinions of publicists, and then arguing at great length the cases of his clients with such eloquence and learning that his exhortations were almost irresistible to judges and juries alike. A perfectionist, he prepared and presented all of his cases without assistance from clerks or junior colleagues, personally locating and copying every legal reference, preparing every witness, taking every deposition, and laboriously composing and reworking all of his arguments before he offered them in court. He was the most persistent and tenacious of advocates; one observer remarked admiringly that it "seemed at times as if the only way to get rid of a lawsuit in which he was concerned was to have it decided in favor of his client" (Dana 1968, 2:134–147; Shapiro 1961, 46).

Year after year, and always with cool courtesy, he relished going to court against leading members of the Boston bar, sometimes opposing two or more of them together, frequently emerging from such trials as the winner; yet his code of honor and his pride in his profession would not allow him to profit exorbitantly from his practice or to confine it to matters of great moment. Hence he remained throughout his life without great wealth, supplementing his professional practice by delivering paid lectures, struggling with debt, and shrinking from opportunities to win further fame and fortune out of fear of financial failure (Shapiro 1961, 16, 21, 53–54, 107). As a result of these limitations, Dana's work as a lawyer had but little impact on the future of U.S. jurisprudence, and his brief periods of official activity produced no great reputation as a statesman. Nevertheless, compared with contemporaries, he deserves to be considered a lawyer of the first rank, whose greatest contributions were his advocacy of human rights in the Boston fugitive slave cases and his successful defense before the Supreme Court of the government's military and foreign policies during the American Civil War.

—*Norman B. Ferris*

Sources and Suggestions for Further Reading

Adams, Charles Francis, Jr. *Richard Henry Dana: A Biography.* 2 vols. Boston: Houghton Mifflin, 1890.

Dana, Richard Henry, Jr. *The Journal.* Edited by Robert F. Lucid. 3 vols. Cambridge: Belknap Press of Harvard University Press, 1968.

Gale, Robert L. *Richard Henry Dana, Jr.* New York: Twayne, 1969.

Shapiro, Samuel. *Richard Henry Dana, Jr: 1815–1882.* East Lansing: Michigan State University Press, 1961.

Veeder, Van Vechten, ed. *Legal Masterpieces: Specimens of Argumentation and Exposition by Eminent Lawyers.* 2 vols. St. Paul: Keefe-Davidson, 1903, 2:903–928.

DARROW, CLARENCE

(1857–1938)

CLARENCE DARROW

Clarence Darrow (standing), principal witness before the Judiciary Committee of the House during hearings on the McLeod Bill, which would abolish the death penalty in Washington, D.C., 1 February 1926. (Library of Congress)

PERHAPS THE FIRST TRIAL LAWYER OF NATIONAL RENOWN, CLARENCE Darrow built his reputation as a friend of labor and a fiery orator. He later became a household name for his role in both the Leopold and Loeb "thrill-killing" case, and the defense of John T. Scopes, a Dayton, Tennessee, schoolteacher who had attempted to teach the theory of evolution to his students.

Darrow was born in Kinsman, Ohio, on April 18, 1857. His father, Amirus Darrow, made a career of furniture making and was also an ardent abolitionist. Emily Darrow, his mother, worked as a homemaker and as a proponent of women's rights. Each instilled in Clarence the value of education, and at age sixteen he enrolled in Allegheny College in Meadville, Ohio. After only one year of schooling, he took a job as a district schoolteacher and did not return to college. During the next three years, as he carried out his teaching duties, he began to study the law on his own. His family convinced him to enroll at the law college at Ann Arbor, Michigan, but he again left after only one year and took a clerical job in a Youngstown, Ohio, law firm. A year later, in 1878, he was admitted to the bar and began ten years of legal practice in Ashtabula, Ohio.

In 1888, Darrow moved to Chicago (where he lived for the rest of his life) and worked for two years as junior partner to John Peter Altgeld, the future governor of Illinois. Darrow held a series of municipal appointments, including corporation counsel for the City of Chicago (where he worked to lower transit fares).

Darrow switched sides in 1894, however, when he resigned his position as counsel for the Chicago and North-Western Railway Company to represent Eugene V. Debs, leader of the American Railway Union, then on strike against the Pullman Palace Car Company. In the *Debs* case, Darrow dismissed the notion that the court was the forum to make peace between labor and management, and instead developed a confrontational approach to labor cases. He seethed with contempt for the prosecution and its charge of conspiracy to obstruct interstate commerce and the mails. As the prosecution presented its case, Darrow, in what became characteristic fashion, slouched in his chair with a derisive expression on his face. In a case in which U.S. Attorney General Richard Olney and the special government attorney, Edwin Walker, both had extensive ties to railroad interests (Walker had only a week before represented the General Managers Association, a group of twenty-two railroad companies in Chicago), Darrow challenged the use of the conspiracy charge against labor and implied that it would be better used against the railroad companies: "Conspiracy, from the day of tyranny in England down to the day the General Managers Association used it as a club, has been the favorite weapon of every tyrant. It is an effort to punish a crime of thought. If the government does not, we shall try to get the general managers here to tell what they know about conspiracy" (Tierney 1979, 105–106). When the judge adjourned the case because of an ill juror and chose not to reopen it, Debs went to prison for six months anyway. Darrow responded by directing his ire at judges, characterizing them, too, as friends of corporate chieftains and other opponents of labor. "It's no exaggeration to say that nine-tenths of the laws are made nowadays by the judges," he said, "and that they are made in the interests of the rich and powerful and to destroy the poor" (Ginger 1958, 214).

Although Darrow did not win the *Debs* case, it established him as an uncompromising advocate for labor, one who would combat the government and industry leaders at every turn. He soon found himself in demand for many labor cases, but the one that attracted the most attention was his 1907 defense of William D. "Big Bill" Haywood and two other leaders of the Western Federation of Miners (WFM) against charges of conspiring to assassinate Frank Steunenberg, the former governor of Idaho.

As he had foreshadowed in the *Debs* case, Darrow's primary tactic in the *Haywood* case was not to defend the defendants as much as to prosecute the prosecution in the court of public opinion. Such an approach proved especially effective in this case, because the state of Idaho had taken extralegal measures to apprehend the defendants, with Pinkerton detectives kidnapping the three men in Denver and shuttling them by overnight train to Boise. In his summation, Darrow again established a precedent for future trials by setting the case in a larger context of labor versus capital, justice versus injustice. He spoke for eleven hours, not once referring to notes, and remembered every key detail from the weeks of testimony. He told the jury that he had larger concerns than Haywood's fate. Like so many who had "worked for the poor and weak" and been sacrificed, Darrow said, Haywood "might face death, too. But, you shortsighted men of the prosecution," he charged, "you men of the Mine Owners' Association . . . you who are seeking to kill him not because it is Haywood but because he represents a class, don't be so blind; don't be so foolish as to believe you can strangle the Western Federation of Miners when you tie a rope around his neck. If at the behest of this mob you should kill Bill Haywood, he is mortal; he will die. But I want to say that a million men will grab up the banner of labor at the open grave where Haywood lays it down . . . [and] will carry it on to victory in the end" (Stone 1941, 236–237). Such statements seemed designed not to persuade the jury of weaknesses in the prosecution's case, but rather that the trial was merely another attempt by those in power, politically and economically, to defeat labor in an ongoing class war.

Some of Darrow's associates thought he went too far with such rhetoric. Harlan Garland once wrote that "as an advocate, Darrow weakens his cause by extreme expression . . . he is to me a lonely figure. In all that he writes, in all that he says, he insists relentlessly on the folly and injustice of human society" (Stone 1941, 253). Darrow's own co-counsel in the case, Edmund Richardson, remarked immediately after the trial that "preaching socialism and trying a law case are entirely different matters. If you don't believe it, look at Darrow's closing speech before the jury. It was rank. It was enough to hang any man regardless of the fact of his innocence or guilt" (Tierney 1979, 224). Yet, despite their lawyer's churlish approach, or because of it, the jury acquitted Haywood and the other WFM leaders.

The *Haywood* case proved so exhausting that Darrow promised his wife he would take no more labor cases. But in 1911, when American Federation of Labor president Samuel Gompers came to ask him to defend James and John McNamara against charges that they dynamited the *Los Angeles Times* building (killing twenty men inside), Darrow relented. He did so primarily because Gompers convinced him that he would go down in history as a traitor to the cause of labor if he refused the call. In the end, however, Darrow's handling of the case led the labor movement to regard him as a traitor anyway. Darrow's troubles began when he realized, despite his early unequivocal pronouncements of the McNamaras' innocence, that his clients were unquestionably guilty and that the prosecution would have little difficulty proving it. After months of investigating, Darrow worked through muckraking journalist Lincoln Steffens to arrange for the brothers to plead guilty in exchange for escaping the death penalty; James McNamara (who had personally perpetrated the crime) received a life sentence, and John, a sentence of fifteen years. Darrow, a lifetime opponent of capital punishment, saved his clients' lives, but he alienated the working people of America, who were convinced of the men's innocence. To add insult to injury, the state indicted Darrow himself on charges of jury tampering; he was subsequently acquitted, but not before the McNamara case had seemingly destroyed his career.

Darrow adopted a much lower profile during the next ten years, taking on a range of criminal cases that by the middle of the 1920s would eventually lead him back into the national spotlight. Among the quieter cases, Darrow achieved some distinction in joining forces with the newly formed American Civil Liberties Union (ACLU) to defend Benjamin Gitlow, a New York communist charged under a state antianarchy law. Although the lower court convicted Gitlow, his appeal led the Supreme Court to adopt the principle that the Bill of Rights could be applied to states through the due process clause of the Fourteenth Amendment. In 1922, he also published a book, *Crime: Its Cause and Treatment*, which brought into focus many of his criticisms of the U.S. legal system but offered few concrete proposals to alleviate criminal behavior.

The two cases for which Clarence Darrow is best known, however, came a year apart, in 1924 and 1925, and could not have been more different. In the first, Darrow agreed to defend Nathan Leopold and Richard Loeb, two very rich young Chicago men (ages 18 and 19) who had confessed to the kidnapping and murder of fourteen-year-old Bobby Franks. The crime shocked the public for its senselessness, particularly when it was learned that the two men committed it purely for the thrill, in an effort to carry out the "perfect crime." Public outrage soared even higher when Darrow took the case; most Chicagoans believed that the families of the boys were trying to buy their sons' freedom and that Darrow would receive upwards of one million dollars for his services (he was paid thirty thousand dollars). Darrow, who had built his career as a defender of the poor, again heard charges of being a traitor.

In fact, however, Darrow took the case because he believed that the two men were mentally ill and therefore did not deserve to die; here again he found an opportunity to fight capital punishment. In an unprecedented move, rather than enter pleas of not guilty by reason of insanity, Darrow, seeking to avoid a jury trial, had his clients plead guilty but asked to present evidence of their mental condition "in mitigation of their punishment." At a time when psychiatry had only recently become respectable (although much of the general public remained unpersuaded), Darrow led a long line of psychiatrists through testimony before a courtroom filled with the Midwest's leading lawyers and judges (many of whom had traveled great distances to see this unusual case unfold).

After hearing detailed descriptions of the defendants' mental illnesses, including "diseased motivations" and "pathological discord" between their intellectual and emotional life, and a lesson on the functioning of the endocrine glands and the effect of their secretions on the central nervous system, Darrow worked toward a conclusion that such levels of mental disease, while not sufficient to constitute insanity, still rendered his clients guiltless for their actions. Darrow's summation lasted three days, and it hinged on the inhumanity of killing two mentally ill men who could not "feel the moral shocks which come to men that are educated and who have not been deprived of an emotional system or emotional feelings" (Tierney 1979, 310). While scientists and criminologists investigated the causes of crime, he said, the law goes "on and on and on, punishing and hanging and thinking that by general terror we can stamp out crime" (Stone 1941, 416). In an appeal that Darrow himself later said he could never again match, he challenged Judge John Caverly to consider his place between the past and the future. "You may hang these boys," he said. "But in doing it, you will turn your face toward the past. In doing it you are making it harder for every other boy who in ignorance and darkness must grope his way through the mazes which only childhood knows" (Stone 1941, 417). Leopold and Loeb each received a life sentence for murder and a ninety-nine-year sentence for the kidnaping. Darrow had prevailed again.

The case for which Darrow is best known is the *Tennessee v. Scopes* trial of 1925. At sixty-eight years old, "the Great Defender" (as he was so often called) brought his outspoken agnosticism to Dayton, Tennessee, to face William Jennings Bryan, the former Populist, Democratic candidate for president, and secretary of war, in a great contest of science versus religion. Darrow led a team of ACLU lawyers in defense of John T. Scopes, a local schoolteacher who had volunteered to test the Tennessee law that outlawed the teaching of evolution.

Darrow did not deny that Scopes had taught evolution; rather, much of the proceedings centered on arguments for and against introducing expert scientific and theological testimony to determine if Scopes fit the law's spe-

Clarence Darrow is the only attorney who participated in the *Scopes* "monkey" trial whose biography is contained in this volume, but almost equally famous was his primary opponent, William Jennings Bryan, "the Great Commoner," who is better known for his politics than for his law degree. The golden-throated orator from Nebraska stirred populist and Democratic passions with his "Cross of Gold" speech at the Democratic National Convention in 1896, which helped him gain his party's nomination. Bryan ran unsuccessfully for president on three occasions before involving himself in the Scopes controversy. Although a religious conservative, Bryan was also convinced that the Scopes prosecution vindicated the rights of the people to decide what would be taught in public schools. Bryan died shortly after the *Scopes* trial, and a religiously affiliated college named after him, and which still exists today, was founded in Dayton, Tennessee, to honor his memory.

Also involved in the trial as prosecutors were brothers Herbert and Sue Hicks, the latter of whom was named after his mother, who had died when he was born. Sue Hicks later served as inspiration for a hit by singer Johnny Cash entitled "A Boy Named Sue."

Among those who assisted Darrow in Scopes's defense was Arthur Garfield Hays, the chief counsel for the American Civil Liberties Union. Born to a solidly Republican family in 1881, Hays used much of the money he earned defending corporate clients in New York to represent radicals, including individuals charged in Germany with the burning of the Reichstag. The *New York Times* described Hays as "the lawyer who grew rich representing corporations and who became famous defending civil liberties without pay" (Walker 1990, 53).

REFERENCES

Hays, Arthur Garfield. *City Lawyer: The Autobiography of a Law Practice*. New York: Simon & Schuster, 1942.

Larson, Edward J. *Summer for the Gods: The Scopes Trial and America's Continuing Debate over Science and Religion*. New York: Basic Books, 1997.

Walker, Samuel. *In Defense of American Liberties: A History of the ACLU*. 2d ed. Carbondale: Southern Illinois University Press, 1990.

cific definition of someone who denied the Bible's story of creation. When the judge ruled out expert testimony, it appeared that the defense had lost the case. Darrow then surprised the court by calling Bryan, one of the prosecutors in the case, as a witness. Darrow quizzed Bryan, a self-proclaimed Bible expert, on whether he believed various Old Testament stories. Bryan consistently responded that he accepted the Bible literally. But Darrow soon caught Bryan in an inconsistency when he asked about the origins of the universe as described in Genesis:

"Do you think the sun was made on the fourth day?"

"Yes."

"And they had evening and morning without the sun ?"

"I am simply saying it is a period."

"They had evening and morning for four periods without the sun, do you think?"

"I believe in creation as there told, and if I am not able to explain it I will accept it." (Larson 1997, 189)

But Bryan had already acknowledged that even he at times made his own interpretation of biblical passages. This constituted a major break for the defense, for if the Bible was subject to interpretation by Bryan, couldn't a teacher introduce students to evolution without denying the biblical story of creation, *as he interpreted it?* Ultimately, the jury convicted Scopes, but not before Darrow had seemingly defeated fundamentalism with his cross-examination of Bryan.

Two years after the *Scopes* case, Darrow retired, but thanks to his notoriety, he found himself in demand for frequent lectures and debates; he published his autobiography in 1932. He did not appear in the national limelight again until 1934, when he served as chairman of a New Deal review board aimed at evaluating the fairness of the National Industrial Recovery Act. Four years later, on March 13, 1938, Darrow died at home in Chicago.

Clarence Darrow's career has been the subject of several dramatic interpretations, most notably by Spencer Tracy in the fictionalized—and flawed—depiction of the *Scopes* trial in the film version of *Inherit the Wind* (1960). Although it is kind to Darrow, the film oversimplified the issues of the case and made the Bryan character particularly unsympathetic. That said, if Darrow lingers in popular memory today, it is largely due to the film's success and not his own.

—*Michael S. Foley*

SOURCES AND SUGGESTIONS FOR FURTHER READING

Darrow, Clarence. *The Story of My Life*. New York: Scribner, 1932.

Ginger, Ray. *Altgeld's America, 1890–1905*. New York: Funk & Wagnalls, 1958.

Gurko, Miriam. *Clarence Darrow*. New York: Thomas Y. Crowell, 1965.

Larson, Edward J. *Summer for the Gods: The Scopes Trial and America's Continuing Debate over Science and Religion*. Cambridge: Harvard University Press, 1997.

Lukas, J. Anthony. *Big Trouble: A Murder in a Small Western Town Sets Off a Struggle for the Soul of America*. New York: Simon & Schuster, 1997.

Stone, Irving. *Clarence Darrow for the Defense*. New York: Doubleday, 1941.

Tierney, John. *Darrow: A Biography*. New York: Thomas Y. Crowell, 1979.

Weinberg, Arthur, and Lila Weinberg. *Clarence Darrow: Sentimental Rebel*. New York: Putnam, 1980.

DAVIS, JOHN W.

(1873–1955)

JOHN W. DAVIS
Library of Congress

JOHN W. DAVIS WAS PERHAPS the most celebrated and successful attorney of the twentieth century. He made 140 oral arguments before the U.S. Supreme Court, many of them while he was solicitor general of the United States. The consensus among the bench and bar of his time held him to be the most clear and effective advocate in practice. Although several political ventures drew him away temporarily from the active practice of law, Davis always eagerly returned to the bar, which remained his greatest passion.

Davis was born April 13, 1873, to John J. Davis and Anna Kennedy Davis of Clarksburg, West Virginia. He was raised in the Presbyterian faith, believed in God, but rejected organized religion from an early age and seldom attended church after reaching adulthood. Davis received his early education at a private Clarksburg seminary, and in 1887 he enrolled at a preparatory school. In the fall of 1889, Davis entered Washington and Lee University, from which he graduated in 1892. Davis married Julia McDonald on June 20, 1899. The couple lived with Davis's parents, and Julia gave birth to a daughter in July 1900. Julia died shortly afterward. Davis's mother and sisters raised the child, whom Davis named Julia after her mother. He was remarried in 1912 to Ellen G. Bassel, the marriage lasting until she died in 1943.

In June 1893, Davis began to study law in his father's Clarksburg office. After fourteen months, he returned to Washington and Lee and enrolled in the school of law, as his father had done forty years earlier when the school was still called the Lexington Law School. Graduating after one year, Davis was admitted to the West Virginia bar in 1895 and joined his father in a Clarksburg law practice. A year later he was offered an assistant professorship at Washington and Lee, which he accepted for a one-year term. This was the first in a line of difficult decisions Davis would make to leave, even if only temporarily, the active practice of law. When one of the school's two senior professors died, Davis was offered an advancement in salary and position, but he declined in order to resume practice with his father.

Davis early entered the world of litigation. He at first handled many criminal cases but quickly grew to dislike this type of case and ceased to accept them. One of Davis's first cases was dramatic. A mining strike had occurred in West Virginia, and a court had entered an injunction against strikers who were marching along a public road that ran through a mine that was still operating. Their presence, although they marched silently, was meant as a message to nonstrikers. Thus the mine operators sought an injunction. Although he was inexperienced, Davis represented the strikers after they were arrested for violating the injunctive order and held his own against two experienced attorneys. His clients received only three days in jail, a considerable victory in light of the antiunion attitudes of the particular bench.

By 1900, the business and personal relationships between Davis and his father changed. Davis assumed the management of the office. Furthermore, John W. was gaining a reputation as a fine attorney and as the better advocate. Davis's surpassing his father in the professional arena strained their relationship, despite the regard with which the son continued to treat his father.

A lifelong Democrat, Davis held various political offices during his life, beginning with membership in the 1899 session of the West Virginia House of Delegates. In 1910, he was nominated for the U.S. House of Representatives, and it was with reluctance that he agreed to run. During the campaign he protested the drainage of government resources brought about by various social services. Davis labeled such public spending as "the wild reign of extravagance in the disbursement of the people's money" (Harbaugh 1973, 65). Elected in 1910 and assigned to the Judiciary Committee, Davis was reelected in 1912.

While a member of Congress, Davis was able to correct what he saw as an abuse of the injunction, which dated back to its use to hamper strikes in his home state. He drafted a bill that precluded federal judges from granting injunctions in labor disputes unless they were necessary to prevent irreparable injury to property. The bill also protected the right to protest as well as the right to persuade others to do so. The bill became part of the Clayton Antitrust Act of 1914.

Although political involvement was a integral part of Davis's life, the only office he actively sought was a federal judgeship on the U.S. Court of Appeals for the Fourth Circuit. Despite wide public support, Davis did not receive the nomination. Still, President Woodrow Wilson recognized Davis's talents, and a few months later, in 1913, he nominated Davis as solicitor general of the United States. Davis was pleased to receive this position because it accommodated his affection for the practice of law, and he served in this office until 1918.

Throughout his life, Davis was unwavering in his political convictions, but he was also able to put them wholly aside when making an argument with which he did not agree. This ability becomes evident on examining Davis's arguments to the Supreme Court while solicitor general. For example, Davis did not support African-American voting rights, but in *Guinn v. United States* (1915) he argued that an Oklahoma grandfather clause that effectively excluded illiterate African-Americans from the polls while allowing illiterate white persons to vote violated the Fifteenth Amendment. His personal disinterest in the result did not diminish his efforts in the courtroom. The Supreme Court unanimously agreed with Davis's argument, and for the first time it held a state statute unconstitutional under the Fifteenth Amendment.

While he was solicitor general, Davis's skill as an advocate developed greatly. An example of his improving ability is exemplified in the case of *Wilson v. New* (1917). Davis defended the Adamson eight-hour law for railroad employees. This was a controversial measure, enacted in response to a threatened strike if the eight-hour work day on railroads did not become law. Davis was opposed by Santa Fe Railroad's general counsel, Walker D. Hines, and John G. Johnson from Philadelphia, the most renowned business attorney of the time. Davis based his argument to sustain the law on Congress's commerce power, and the Court, although divided, held the law constitutional. Later, Davis himself admitted that the connection between wage regulation and the facilitation of interstate commerce was tenuous.

By 1917, Davis had grown restless in his position as solicitor general and was considering a return to private practice. However, he felt a duty to continue with his work due to the imminence of U.S. entry into World War I. Nine months after the United States entered World War I, Davis defended the Selective Draft Act of 1917. The case aroused public feelings of patriotism, and in an opinion by Chief Justice Edward D. White, the Court unanimously upheld the act. While Davis was in office, every Supreme Court justice expressed his desire that President Wilson appoint him to the Court, but Wilson did not heed these suggestions. Davis resigned from the office of solicitor general in 1918. In that capacity he had orally argued sixty-seven cases before the Supreme Court and had won forty-eight of them.

Despite his resignation, Davis's desire to return to private practice was further postponed by his appointment in 1918 as ambassador to the Court of St. James in England. After he was appointed but before he began his work as ambassador, Davis traveled to Switzerland to serve as commissioner to the Conference with Germany on the Treatment and Exchange of Prisoners. While still ambassador, Davis became a public favorite for the presidential race, but he did not receive the Democratic nomination in 1920. When Davis resigned from his position as ambassador in March 1921, he had been in public service for over ten years.

Toward the end of his time as ambassador, Davis was offered positions with private New York and Washington firms, as well as with private corporations. With firms actively competing for his services, Davis selected Stetson, Jennings & Russell in New York. The promise of assuming the leadership of the Stetson firm was a critical inducement, and Davis became a Wall Street lawyer. The firm's clients included major businesses such as J. P. Morgan, the Guaranty Trust Company of New York, the Associated Press, and Erie Railroad.

Soon after joining Stetson, Jennings & Russell, Davis was again considered for a seat on the Supreme Court. Chief Justice William Howard Taft asked Davis to consider an appointment, but Davis declined. He had not been back in private practice long, was enjoying the practice of law in the New York courts, and was committed to becoming financially secure after his ten years in office. Thus, although Davis regarded membership on the Supreme Court as the highest honor an attorney could achieve, he never became a justice.

In late 1923, Davis was again in the path of the presidential election. He did not actively seek support; it arose spontaneously, just as it had in 1920. Backers urged him to give up his practice and actively campaign, as his connection to J. P. Morgan would be detrimental to his chances for the Democratic party nomination. On March 4, 1924, Davis wrote a public letter stating that it would be dishonorable to tailor his career to further his political aspirations. The public saw Davis as principled and honest, and appreciation for these qualities diminished the negative effect that Davis's J. P. Morgan connection would have imposed. Davis refused to take any action that would be seen as campaigning for the nomination, but after prolonged balloting, he received the Democratic nomination for president in July. However, Republican Calvin Coolidge won the election handily.

After the election, Davis returned to work on Wall Street; his partners renamed the firm Davis, Polk, Wardwell, Gardiner & Reed. Davis led the firm for the remainder of his career. During the 1930s, Davis joined efforts to resist Franklin D. Roosevelt's New Deal program. He was an organizer of the anti–New Deal Liberty League, argued several cases challenging important New Deal laws, and informally advised opponents to Roosevelt's court-packing plan. In 1933, the Senate Banking Committee began investigating J. P. Morgan concerning the company's securities transactions. Davis, who represented Morgan during the three-month ordeal, was convinced that the investigation was unwarranted. He questioned the scope of the committee's investigation. In the end, the committee concluded that Morgan had not engaged in abusive lending practices and was prudent in making its investments.

Two of the most noted Supreme Court cases Davis argued were the last two cases of his career. The first, *Youngstown Sheet & Tube Co. v. Sawyer,* better known as the *Steel Seizure* case, arose in 1951, while the United States was in the midst of the Korean War. Negotiations between United Steelworkers and steel producers broke down, and the threat of a strike loomed. President Harry S Truman seized the mills to keep them operating, concerned that a halt of steel production would jeopardize U.S. troops abroad. Davis argued the case before the Supreme Court on May 12, 1952, at age seventy-nine. Solicitor General Philip Perlman argued for the government. Davis maintained from the beginning of the crisis that the president had neither statutory authority nor general inherent power to effect the seizure. In an oral argument that lasted eighty-seven minutes, he noted that no seizure of property in a labor dispute had ever occurred when a statute provided for an alternative. His reference was to the Taft-Hartley Act, which gave the president power to obtain an eighty-day injunction in such circumstances. Justice Hugo Black wrote the opinion for a 6–3 majority that the seizure was unconstitutional, thereby vindicating Davis's position.

The final case that Davis argued before the Supreme Court was the landmark school segregation case of *Brown v. Board of Education* (1954). In the companion case to *Brown, Briggs v. Elliott,* Davis defended South Carolina in its 1952 appeal to the Supreme Court in a desegregation suit brought by the National Association for the Advancement of Colored People (NAACP). Several partners and even his daughter suggested that he not take the case, believing South Carolina to be in the wrong, but Davis would not back down. He believed precedent and the Constitution supported South Carolina's position. Even as they headed for battle, NAACP attorney THURGOOD MARSHALL considered Davis an idol. He regarded Davis as the best solicitor general the country would ever see and had often lamented that he would never be as great an advocate as Davis.

Davis tried to persuade the Court that social wisdom, in addition to the law, called for segregation. Initially split 6 to 3 in favor of desegregation, the Court called for reargument of five questions on December 7, 1953. After the second hearing, the new chief justice, Earl Warren, told the justices that the Court could not evade the question of the constitutionality of segregation per se. On May 17, 1954, Warren ruled for a unanimous Court that segregation based solely on race violated the equal protection clause of the Fourteenth Amendment. Davis was greatly disappointed by the loss of his final Supreme Court argument and was equally upset because of his personal view that segregation was beneficial.

Throughout his life, Davis considered himself a conservative, and he was a delegate to every Democratic National Convention from 1904 to 1932. He was a Jeffersonian Democrat and believed that limited governmental power was needed only to suppress monopolies, preserve national security, and protect individual liberty and property. To Davis, respect for property rights was closely linked with the preservation of individual liberty. Davis espoused the political ideas of laissez-faire economics, limited taxation, and states' rights. He favored a textual adherence to the language of the Constitution, a conviction that never wavered throughout his career. Davis adhered to the concept of stare decisis and despised legal realist notions that the Constitution and common law must be organic to accommodate a changing society. Similarly, he disliked the formation of administrative law by regulatory agencies.

In "The Argument of an Appeal," a paper Davis delivered in the fall of 1940, he emphasized the need for brevity, clarity, and simplicity in legal arguments, and he set forth ten cardinal rules of oral advocacy. Quoting DANIEL WEBSTER, Davis stated that the one sentence that "should be written on the walls of every law school, courtroom and law office" was that "the power of clear statement is the great power of the bar" (Wellman 1941, 232).

In addition to the many governmental offices, Davis also held leadership positions in the bar. In 1906, he was elected president of the West Virginia Bar Association, after serving as its secretary for several prior years. He served as president of the American Bar Association in 1922, and he was elected president of the Association of the Bar of the City of New York in 1931.

John W. Davis died on March 24, 1955, after several years of deteriorating health.

—*James W. Ely Jr.*

Harbaugh, William H. *Lawyer's Lawyer: The Life of John W. Davis*. New York: Oxford University Press, 1973.

Kluger, Richard. *Simple Justice: The History of Brown v. Board of Education and Black America's Struggle for Equality*. New York: Alfred A. Knopf, 1976.

Marcus, Maeva. *Truman and the Steel Seizure Case: The Limits of Presidential Power*. New York: Columbia University Press, 1977.

Wellman, Francis L. *Success in Court*. New York: Macmillan, 1941.

DEES, MORRIS, JR.

(1936–)

SINCE THE EARLY 1970S, attorney Morris Dees Jr. has fought
in the courts for racial justice. By
developing innovative approaches
to attacking the activities of various Ku Klux Klan–affiliated organizations while representing
numerous victims, Dees has expanded the legal profession's arsenal for combating organized violence. As such, Dees has helped to
make the United States a safer
place for all its citizens.

Born to Morris and Annie Ruth
Dees in Shorter, Alabama, on December 16, 1936, Morris Dees Jr.
spent his early years working in
his father's cotton fields (Dees and
Fiffer 1991, 65). As the son of a
tenant farmer, he shared the experiences of his family's hired hands
and developed many relationships
that influenced his perceptions of
justice and equity (Dees and Fiffer
1991, 336). The prodding of his
father, coupled with the first-hand
experience of injustice, pushed
Dees first to obtain his undergraduate degree and then a degree in
law in 1960 from the University
of Alabama. Nevertheless, it was
his earlier experiences—seeing his
father drink from the same gourd

MORRIS DEES JR.
*Morris Dees photographed at a conference on bigotry in
Montgomery, Alabama, 8 October 1990. (AP Photo/Dave
Martin, File)*

as an African-American field hand, being whipped for using the word *nig-ger,* and feeling used after successfully litigating a contractual dispute for a friend—that developed in Dees a "passion for justice" (Dees and Fiffer 1991, 63; Dees 1995, 548), which can be considered the true force behind all his efforts.

Certainly, it was this passion for justice that led Dees and law partner Joseph J. Levin Jr. to begin the practice that would become the Southern Poverty Law Center (SPLC) in Montgomery, Alabama, in 1971. At that time, Dees's business dealings had placed him in a secure financial position. Having been reared as a poor tenant farmer, Dees developed a distinct need to establish self-sufficiency. Starting with a plan to send birthday cakes to students on campus, Dees and partner Millard Fuller (the future founder of Habitat for Humanity) as undergraduates founded a mail-order business that had sales of nearly half a million dollars a year (Emert 1996, 139). Through their business acumen and tenacity, Dees and Fuller were able to build a small publishing company, which they eventually sold to the Times Mirror Company for $6 million. As a result of his success in business, Dees had no monetary reasons for pursuing the various discrimination cases in which the SPLC specialized (Dees and Fiffer 1991, 130). Furthermore, the SPLC's original mission, to provide pro bono representation on behalf of death-row inmates and low-income individuals, reflects Dees's belief that the effects of money hopelessly taint the justice system (Dees and Fiffer 1991, 149–150). By providing the kind of services the SPLC offers, Dees and other lawyers have advanced the cause of racial justice along a number of fronts, including the desegregation of the Alabama State Troopers, the Montgomery YMCA, and the jury system in Alabama. These accomplishments alone can be considered major contributions to the cause of justice.

Nevertheless, Dees's greatest contribution lies not with these accomplishments but with his "agency theory" tactic used in the civil case between Beulah Mae Donald and Bobby Shelton's United Klans of America (UKA) (Dees and Fiffer 1991, 222). Although Dees has employed these same strategies in several cases, this case offers the best illustration of Dees's method of connecting national extremist organizations with the illegal actions of its members (Marshall 1999; Dees and Fiffer 1991, 222; Dees 1995, 551).

In *State v. Henry Hays,* James "Tiger" Knowles testified that he, Henry Hays, and Frank Cox randomly selected Michael Donald, an African-American youth walking alone at night, "to show the strength of the Klan" and to be an example to the city of Mobile of their disgust for the outcome of the Josephus Anderson trial, a closely watched murder/self-defense case involving a white police officer, an African-American defendant, and a majority African-American jury that was unable to reach a verdict (Dees and

Fiffer 1991, 212). The verdict in the *State v. Hays* trial sent Hays to death row; however, as Dees notes, the district attorney's failure to indict any of the other conspirators effectively resulted in the vast majority of individuals involved in this crime going free (Dees and Fiffer 1991, 213, 225, 237). Given Dees's passion for justice and his personal mission of "bankrupting bigots," one should not find it surprising that the SPLC would become involved in this case (Eichel 1998).

Dees's explanation of his "agency theory" is deceptively simple. As he notes, a lending business would become liable for the illegal collection tactics of its agents only if it "had a practice of encouraging strong-arm collection tactics"; in the same way, an organization such as the Klan would be liable for the actions of its members if those members acted with (or believed they were acting with) the approval of the parent organization (Dees and Fiffer 1991, 222). In practice this strategy takes two sometimes overlapping forms, the aiding and abetting claim and the civil conspiracy claim (Dees and Bowden 1995).

In the *Hays* case, Dees established the first link in the chain of legal culpability from Hays and his compatriots to the United Klans with the deposition of Johnny Jones. According to Jones's testimony, the membership of the local Klan unit had discussed the possibility of retaliating for the outcome of the Anderson trial, and the unit's senior officer, Bennie Hays, had directed Henry Hays, the unit's secretary, to "get this down." Therefore, Dees argued, the entire unit could be held liable (Dees and Fiffer 1991, 232). Since aiding and abetting theory does not require direct physical assistance, Bennie Hays's direction of the retaliation discussion constituted "encouragement." However, aiding and abetting theory in cases involving an agent also requires demonstration of the fact that the defendant authorized the agent to engage in criminal acts (Dees and Bowden 1995). In this case, Jones testified that he consulted Frank Cox, the unit's president, about lending his gun to Hays and Knowles (Dees and Fiffer 1991, 233). Cox's encouragement while acting as a superior officer fulfills this authorization requirement.

A more recent example of this tactic can be found in the civil case against Tom Metzger, White Aryan Resistance, and East Side White Pride arising from the 1988 murder of Mulugeta Serau (Dees 1995, 551). This case also closely resembles a classic aiding and abetting claim; testimony in the case revealed that David Mazzella, one of the perpetrators of the crime, was also the vice-president of Metzger's White Aryan Resistance movement and had been dispatched to Portland with the express purpose of "encourag[ing] racial violence" (Dees and Bowden 1995; Dees 1995, 552).

However, the aiding and abetting strategy is of limited value in many hate group–related cases because it specifically incorporates the idea of *sub-*

Few individuals have better epitomized the lawyer as hero than Atticus Finch, the attorney in Harper Lee's only published novel, *To Kill a Mockingbird*. Published by J. B. Lippincott in 1960 after more than two and a half years of rewriting, this book was awarded a Pulitzer Prize in 1961 and was made into a movie starring Gregory Peck in 1962.

Lee, an Alabama native, studied law at the University of Alabama from 1945 to 1949 but moved to New York to pursue a writing career rather than joining her father's law firm. Lee patterned Atticus (Lee's mother's maiden name) Finch after her father, Amasa Lee, a one-time newspaper editor, state senator, and Alabama lawyer.

In Lee's book (which is narrated by Finch's daughter, Scout), Finch, a fearless white attorney, unsuccessfully defends an African-American man falsely accused of raping a white woman, who was romantically interested in him and had apparently been beaten by her father for crossing the color line. Dill, a friend of Scout, is patterned in part on Truman Capote, one of Lee's childhood friends, for whom she later served as a research assistant when he wrote *In Cold Blood*.

To Kill a Mockingbird is one of the legal classics reviewed in the 1999 issue of the *Michigan Law Review*.

REFERENCES

"Harper Lee." <http://www.kirjasto.sci.fi/harperle.htm>.

"Harper Lee Biography." <http://www.chebucto.ns.ca/Culture/HarperLee/bio.html>.

---

stantial aid or encouragement between the actors, thus limiting the range of prosecution. As Dees has suggested, truly to cripple the operations of hate groups, one must interfere with the fiscal viability of the national organizations (Marshall 1999). Demonstrating substantial aid between a national organization and an independent actor would be difficult at best.

To overcome this difficulty, agency claims usually incorporate civil conspiracy theory to link the national organizations to local criminal acts (Dees and Bowden 1995). The key to this strategy lies in establishing both close links between the various agents and an agreement between those agents to commit the act. In the *Hays* case, several pieces of evidence, including the unit's charter from the UKA (signed by Shelton) and a copy of the *Kloran Klan in Action Constitution*, and testimony established that the structure of the local unit was directly responsible to the national leadership of UKA (Dees and Fiffer 1991, 237). In the case of the Klan constitution, the sections detailing organizational charts especially strengthened the link between Shelton as the "Imperial Wizard" and Bennie Hays (the father of Henry Hays) as the local "Titan" (Dees and Fiffer 1991, 249).

However, a civil conspiracy claim requires evidence of an *agreement* between the conspiring parties to commit the specific act or to follow a particular course of action that would include the criminal act. This being the case, testimony from FBI informants regarding the UKA's repeated use and encouragement of violence to further its agenda of maintaining the "God-given superiority of the white race" (Dees and Fiffer 1991, 250) was crucial to the assertion that, even if the Donald murder was not specifically authorized by the national organization, the long-standing pattern of violence employed by the UKA produced an atmosphere in which violence was perpetually encouraged and condoned.

The *Metzger* case provides another example of this tactic. As Dees and Bowden note, the fact that Metzger provided Mazzella (one of the defendants) with both training in fomenting racial violence and a letter of introduction to the East Side White Pride establishes the close relationship between the various actors necessary to defend a conspiracy claim (Dees and Bowden 1995). Furthermore, Mazzella's testimony that he was sent to Portland with the express purpose of encouraging racial violence establishes an agreement between Metzger and his agent to follow a course of action that would include illegal acts.

In developing and honing these strategies, Dees has greatly expanded the arsenal of tools prosecutors and attorneys can use to curtail the activities of national hate groups. Even a cursory examination of the various groups that have suffered setbacks as a result of Dees's personal courtroom involvement reveals the magnitude of this contribution. Louis Beam's Texas Emergency Reserve, Bobby Shelton's United Klans of America, Glenn Miller's Carolina Knights and his White Patriot party, Metzger's White Aryan Resistance, and the Invisible Empire, Inc., have all folded or severely curtailed their operations because of civil suits brought by Dees and the SPLC.

Nevertheless, cases are not usually won through clever courtroom antics but through vigorous pretrial investigations and legwork (Dees and Fiffer 1991, 220). Therefore, one may consider Dees's establishment of the Klanwatch project as his second great contribution to the field of jurisprudence. Although one may argue that Klanwatch does not directly relate to the field of legal practice, its mission to gather information about Klan activities and related hate groups has accumulated over twelve thousand computerized photographs and over sixty-five thousand records on individuals and events (Dees and Corcoran 1996, 6). Although this activity appears seriously to infringe on individual privacy, by cataloging the associations of extremists, Klanwatch has furthered investigations into hate crimes. As such, it is a contribution to the practice of law because it provides attorneys with easy access to the facts they require to build the kind of complaints described above.

Morris Dees Jr.'s forty-year history as a civil rights lawyer is a study of landmark victories for integration, equitable sentencing, and the protection of minorities. However important these contributions may be individually, they sum to a much larger picture; through his innovations Dees has helped to change the field of jurisprudence by bringing cases that might never have been litigated without the help of the SPLC. Furthermore, the application of "agency theory" to other areas, such as linking radical antiabortion groups to antiabortion violence, has increased the scope of prosecutions in other fields (Dees 1995, 547). In short, Dees's legal innovations have affected areas of jurisprudence beyond the domain of civil rights; he stands as an example of the difference attorneys can make by litigating cases.

—*Matthew Vile*

Sources and Suggestions for Further Reading

Dees, Morris, Jr. *A Passion for Justice*. Krinock Lecture Series, vol. 12. Lansing: Thomas M. Cooley Law Review, 1995, 547–558.

Dees, Morris, Jr., and Ellen Bowden. "Taking Hate Groups to Court." *Trial*, February 1995. Available at <http://www.splcenter.org/legalaction/la-3.html>.

Dees, Morris, Jr., and James Corcoran. *Gathering Storm: America's Militia Threat*. New York: HarperCollins, 1996.

Dees, Morris, Jr., and Steve Fiffer. *A Season for Justice: The Life and Times of Civil Rights Lawyer Morris Dees*. New York: Scribner, 1991.

Eichel, Henry. "In Church Suit against Klan, Dees Goes after Top Officials." *Boston Globe*, 19 July 1998, sec. A.

Emert, Phyllis Raybin. *Top Lawyers & Their Famous Cases*. Minneapolis: Oliver Press, 1996.

Marshall, Mike. "Civil Rights Activist Sees the Changing Face of Hate: Morris Dees' Goal is to 'Bankrupt Bigots.'" *New Orleans Times-Picayune*, 12 September 1999, sec. A.

Weisbrot, Robert. *Freedom Bound: A History of America's Civil Rights Movement*. New York: W. W. Norton, 1990.

DERSHOWITZ, ALAN MORTON

(1938–)

Alan Dershowitz is a world-renowned appellate criminal lawyer and public intellectual. He has represented defendants in the highest-profile legal actions in recent history. His books have been widely read around the world, and his various writings and public appearances cover nearly every aspect of public life. Much can be said about Alan Dershowitz, but much also remains enigmatic. He is an absolutist about free speech, believing there can be no good reason for censorship. He staunchly defends the right of the accused to the best defense available and the right of criminals to fair treatment by the government. He is a media figure, and this status certainly helps his career as an attorney. A liberal and a Democrat, he nonetheless supported the right of all citizens to litigate against the president, a position opposed by many in his party.

Newsweek magazine has described Alan Dershowitz as "the nation's most peripatetic civil liberties lawyer and one of its most distinguished defenders of individual rights." The Italian news-

Alan Dershowitz
Wally McNamee/Corbis

paper *Oggi* reported that he is "the best-known criminal lawyer in the world." *Time* magazine, in addition to including him in a cover story entitled "50 Faces for the Future," called him a "legal star" and "the top lawyer of last resort in the country—a sort of judicial St. Jude." *Business Week* characterized him as "a feisty civil libertarian and one of the nation's most prominent legal educators." ABC Commentator Jeffrey Toobin characterized him as "a national treasure," and Floyd Abrams, the eminent First Amendment lawyer, called him "an international treasure." He has been profiled by every major magazine, ranging from *Life* ("iconoclast and self-appointed scourge of the criminal justice system"), to *Esquire* ("the country's most articulate and uncompromising protector of criminal defendants"), to *Fortune* (an "impassioned civil libertarian" who has "put up the best defense for a Dickensian lineup of suspects"), to *People* ("defense attorney extraordinaire"), to *New York Magazine* ("one of the country's foremost appellate lawyers"), to *TV Guide* (one of "America's top attorneys"). He has been featured on the covers of many magazines, including the *American Bar Association Journal*, *New York* magazine, the *Jerusalem Post*, Italy's *Oggi*, and *Newsday*. He has been interviewed by a diverse range of U.S. magazines and newspapers, including the *New York Times*, *U.S. News and World Report*, *Playboy*, and *Boston* magazine, as well as by the foreign media throughout the world.

Alan Dershowitz was born in Brooklyn, New York, on September 1, 1938, to Harry and Clair (Ringel) Dershowitz. He attended Yeshiva University High School and Brooklyn College, where he was president of the debate society and graduated magna cum laude in 1959. After college, he attended Yale Law School, graduating magna cum laude in 1962, having served as editor-in-chief of the *Yale Law Journal*. He is married to Carolyn Cohen and has three children, Elon, Jamin, and Ella.

After graduating from Yale, Dershowitz was offered a teaching position at Harvard Law School. He declined this position in order to clerk for Chief Judge David L. Bazelon of the U.S. Court of Appeals in Washington, D.C. Dershowitz was a clerk for Bazelon in 1962 and 1963 and was a clerk for Justice Arthur Goldberg of the U.S. Supreme Court in 1963 and 1964. In 1964, Dershowitz joined the faculty of Harvard Law School. Dershowitz recalled fondly that Bazelon and Goldberg were "two of the finest and most humane judges in American history"; he viewed these judges as having such integrity that when he entered his academic career he did so with no small amount of naiveté (Dershowitz 1982, xiii–xiv). In 1967, *Psychoanalysis, Psychiatry and the Law*, which Dershowitz co-wrote with Jay Katz and Joseph Goldstein, was published, at which time Dershowitz became, at twenty-eight, the youngest full professor in the history of Harvard Law School. In 1993, he was named Felix Frankfurter Professor of Law.

Alan Dershowitz's specialty is the crafting of appeals to higher-level courts of criminal cases decided in lower courts. As an appellate lawyer, he becomes involved in most cases only after the defendant has lost at the trial court level and has already exhausted almost every possible legal avenue. He thinks of himself as a "lawyer of last resort." He writes, "O. J. Simpson referred to me as his 'God forbid' lawyer—'God forbid there should be a conviction, you've got to get it reversed on appeal'" (Dershowitz 1996, 13). In the *Tison v. Arizona*, 481 U.S. 137 (1987), and *Snepp v. United States*, 444 U.S. 507 (1980), cases, Dershowitz became involved when the cases went to the Supreme Court.

Dershowitz takes cases that he sees as having underlying constitutional issues and that he regards as "the most challenging, the most difficult and precedent-setting cases" (Dershowitz 1982, xv). Dershowitz's focus on constitutional questions, especially on issues of improper government conduct, allows him to frequently gain dismissal of determinations of his clients' guilt in lower courts. Dershowitz seems motivated by a belief in widespread misconduct, especially by the investigative wing of the criminal justice system. He writes, "it is often necessary to put the government on trial for *its* misconduct" (Dershowitz 1982, xiv). He has employed this tactic in several cases. For example, in the trial of Sheldon Siegel for the bombing murder of a woman, Dershowitz used tapes to prove that the government had lied about offering Siegel a deal. Siegel was acquitted; Dershowitz recounts that he cried for the victim that night.

In one of the highest-profile criminal trials in the twentieth century, Dershowitz successfully argued in the trial of Claus von Bülow for the murder of his wife that there had been an illegal search and seizure. A new trial was granted, and von Bülow was acquitted. Dershowitz wrote the book *Reversal of Fortune* (1986) about the von Bülow trial, which was later made into a film that garnered an Academy Award. However, some of his cases, like that of the Tison brothers, do not present an easily identifiable government violation of rights. In *Tison*, two brothers who had helped their father escape from prison faced the death penalty for a murder in which their father subsequently took part. Arguing before the Supreme Court, Dershowitz had their death sentences vacated on the grounds that they had not actually taken part in the murder. In a high-profile case in New York City, Dershowitz unsuccessfully argued that Bernard Bergman, who was convicted of fraud in his New York City nursing homes, was denied his rights because the prosecutor had violated a plea bargain.

Dershowitz, a staunch and absolute supporter of free speech, has been involved in many cases involving First Amendment free-speech rights. Several of these cases were precipitated by the Vietnam War. Dershowitz was on the successful defense team of Vietnam protester Dr. Benjamin Spock, and he successfully appealed William Kunstler's conviction for contempt of court for his actions as counsel for the defense in the trial of the "Chicago Eight" protesters at the 1968 Democratic convention. Later, he unsuccessfully represented former CIA analyst Frank Snepp in his bid in the Supreme Court to prevent the CIA from seizing the profits from Snepp's book about his experiences working for the agency. However, Dershowitz was successful in representing Mike Gravel, the U.S. senator from Alaska who released the Pentagon Papers.

Dershowitz has also worked as counsel for those accused of producing obscene and pornographic materials. In his first appearance before the Supreme Court, he successfully argued against the Boston ban on the Swedish film *I am Curious, Yellow,* which was considered at the time to be sexually explicit. He obtained an acquittal in 1976 for Harry Reems, star of the pornographic film *Deep Throat,* on charges of interstate trafficking in obscene materials. More recently, he represented Miramax Studios in winning an appeal to change the rating of the comedy *Clerks.* He has also represented *Penthouse* magazine.

Dershowitz is bothered by governmental attempts to use national security arguments to deprive accused persons of a full and proper defense. One of his clients, Jonathan Pollard, has been imprisoned for spying for Israel. However, he could not testify at an open public trial because of the sensitive nature of the issues. Dershowitz considers this an "abuse of the classification system to serve political rather than national security interests" (Dershowitz 1994, 219).

Dershowitz is best known for representing celebrities. He was a member of the defense "Dream Team" that won an acquittal in the murder trial of O. J. Simpson. Dershowitz's experiences and thoughts on the Simpson trial are collected in his book *Reasonable Doubts* (1996). Professor Dershowitz achieved a reduction of televangelist Jim Bakker's sentence from forty years to five years. He represented Senator Alan Cranston, one of the "Keating Five" senators, in a case involving improper influence peddling and fundraising activities; Dershowitz was able to win a reduction in sanctions. However, he was unable to overturn the conviction of Patricia Hearst, the young newspaper heiress turned terrorist, who went to jail and was later pardoned. He successfully represented Mia Farrow against Woody Allen when the two ended their long relationship. This particular case was satirized in a sketch on the television program *Saturday Night Live,* in which Dershowitz and Farrow encounter Allen on the way to a movie. Dershowitz has also represented boxer Mike Tyson, musicians David Crosby, John Lennon, Axl Rose, and Kenny Rogers, and former Louisiana governor Edwin W. Edwards.

Alan Dershowitz the litigator is quite different from Alan Dershowitz the public figure. When seeking an appeal in court, he is very respectful of the judge and the power of a court to provide justice to rich and poor alike. As a litigator, he draws on other legal experts, forensic scientists, law school students, and social scientists to make the best case he can regarding why a lower court failed to follow the law, legal process, or the evidence that was placed before it. For appeals courts, Dershowitz prepares well, leaving no stone unturned, trying to keep the court on point as to his reasons why justice was not served in lower courts. When advising at the trial court level, Dershowitz usually plays the role of supporting trial lawyers on possible bases for appeals. This role usually makes the trial judge aware of possible avenues of appeal, which tends to ensure the best possible hearing at the trial level.

On radio, television, and in the print media, Dershowitz has a quite different persona; he is showy and argumentative and at times appears outrageous and willing to do anything to exonerate a client. This occurs because he takes cases for famous clients, many of whom are quite out of favor with the public because of the crimes of which they have been accused, their riches, their personalities, or their lack of contrition. Dershowitz is always educating the public that the United States has an adversarial legal process, that the state must prove its criminal cases beyond a reasonable doubt, and that rich and poor both have the right to the best defense, whether or not they are guilty.

Dershowitz is widely credited as being a key innovator in the use of media as a legal tool, as in the O. J. Simpson case. In addition to public appearances on issues of general interest, such as his appearance on the *Larry King Live* television program during the execution of Gary Graham, he often appears on television and writes in newspapers as part of the defense of his clients. On one occasion he purchased a full-page ad in the *New York Times* on behalf of his client, Michael Milken, who was on trial for securities fraud.

Dershowitz has been awarded numerous honors by many prestigious institutions. He was a fellow at the Center for Advanced Study in the Behavioral Sciences at Stanford University in 1971–1972, and he was awarded a Guggenheim fellowship to pursue his work in human rights in 1979. Dershowitz holds honorary degrees from Yeshiva University, Syracuse University, Hebrew Union College, the University of Haifa, Monmouth College, Fitchburg College, and Brooklyn College.

Dershowitz's academic and social prominence have made him a highly coveted speaker in the United States and abroad. He has lectured at Rutgers Law School, the University of Pennsylvania Law School, the University of Texas Law School, the University of Cincinnati, and Brooklyn College. Dershowitz has taught at a diverse range of institutions, including Stanford Law School, McLean Hospital in Washington, D.C., the Vera Institute of Justice in New York, and Hebrew University Law School.

Dershowitz served as counselor to the director of the National Institute of Mental Health from 1967 to 1969; he was a member of the President's Commissions on Civil Disorder in 1967, the President's Commission on the Causes and Prevention of Violence in 1968, and the President's Commission on Marijuana and Drug Abuse in 1972; he participated in the Ford Foundation Studies on Law and Justice from 1973 to 1976; and he was rapporteur to the Twentieth Century Fund Study of Sentencing from 1975 to 1976.

Dershowitz has also gained international stature as an expert on criminal law. He has served as a consultant on criminal law to the Chinese government in 1981, as the John F. Kennedy Fulbright lecturer on the Bill of Rights in New Zealand in 1987, and as visiting professor of law at Hebrew University, Jerusalem, in 1988, where he lectured on civil liberties during times of crisis. In 1990, he lectured in Moscow on human rights.

Dershowitz, who has been characterized as a "public intellectual par excellence," has been a pioneer in making the legal profession accessible to the general public. He was the first law professor to write regularly for the *New York Times* in its Week in Review, op-ed, and Book Review sections. He was also the first to appear regularly on such stalwart television news and information shows as *Nightline, The McNeil-Lehrer News Hour, Firing Line, Larry King Live, Today,* and *Geraldo Rivera.* As a weekly columnist for United Features Syndicate, his articles have appeared in fifty U.S. daily newspapers, including the *Los Angeles Times,* the *San Francisco Chronicle,* the *Boston Herald,* and the *Chicago Sun-Times.* He has written more than one thousand editorial articles. His essay "Shouting Fire" was selected for inclusion in *The Best American Essays of 1990* and has been reprinted more than one hundred times. For two years, Dershowitz hosted a radio talk show about the law, for which he received the 1996 Freedom of Speech Award from the National Association of Radio Talk Show Hosts. William Buckley, a nationally respected conservative public intellectual, has described Dershowitz as a "deeply thoughtful man," "a master of the law," and "a masterful advocate." Dershowitz has even appeared as a guest star on the television show *Picket Fences,* in which, appearing as himself, he advised a small-town lawyer on how to argue before the Supreme Court.

Dershowitz is actively involved in important and controversial public issues, usually involving conflicts between politics and legal rights. During the impeachment proceedings of President Richard Nixon, he urged the American Civil Liberties Union to support President Nixon against violations of his civil liberties. He was heavily involved with the sequence of events up to and including the impeachment trial of President Bill Clinton. Unlike many liberals, he supported the appointment of an independent counsel for the Whitewater investigation and the apparently related of-

John Grisham: The Lawyer as Novelist

Few lawyers have had the popular literary success of John Grisham (b. 1955), who has published twelve novels since 1988, most of which have been bestsellers and a number of which have been made into popular films. Grisham's novels, which include *A Time to Kill, The Pelican Brief, The Client, The Chamber,* and *The Testament,* all deal in one or another way with the legal profession and are known for their fast-paced action.

After earning a law degree at the University of Mississippi in 1981, Grisham practiced for about a decade and served in the Mississippi state legislature from 1984 to 1990. Although he is an attorney, in his writing Grisham often plays on stereotypes that portray lawyers and politicians as greedy and crooked. As much of the action in Grisham's novels takes place within law firms and on the street as in the courtroom.

In 1996, Grisham received extensive publicity when he returned to Brookhaven, Mississippi (Grisham now splits his time between homes in Mississippi and Virginia), to litigate a case that he had accepted before his writing career took off involving the family of a railroad brakeman who was killed on the job. Admitting to being jittery after not having tried a case for seven years, Grisham won an award of $683,500 for his client, the largest of his career. Despite his success in this case, Grisham will be remembered more for what he has written about the bar than for his own cases.

REFERENCES

"About John Grisham." <http://www.random-house.com/features/grisham/about.html>.

Goodman, Walter. "Court of Public Opinion: Legal Thrillers Obey the Laws of Commerce." *New York Times,* 29 February 2000, B1–B2.

fenses. He also believed that it was proper to allow Paula Jones's lawsuit against the president to continue—and that the president should have settled early in the case to preserve the dignity of the office and keep the settlement low, an option he faults Washington lawyer Robert Bennett for not bringing to the president's attention. Dershowitz's criticism brought Bennett's wrath down on him; Dershowitz accused Bennett of not handling the case competently, a claim that Bennett has refuted on numerous occasions. Dershowitz also publicly debated Jerry Falwell, a conservative Republican and a leading supporter of Clinton's impeachment. During the impeachment trial, Dershowitz testified before Congress, vigorously defending the president and denouncing the impeachment as politically motivated. These comments were welcomed by Democrats and angered Republicans, among them Senator Henry Hyde, who made light of Dershowitz in a press conference a few days later. Dershowitz wrote about the Clinton impeachment in

Sexual McCarthyism (1998). He has spoken out on the trial of New York City police officers for the murder of Amadou Diallo, defending the change of venue of the trial from the Bronx to Albany. Dershowitz argued, against most liberals, that the status of the young Cuban boy Elián Gonzalez should have been determined by the courts. In a recent controversy, Dershowitz has claimed that he is owed $34 million for his part in the Florida tobacco settlement, saying that he would donate most of the money to charity. His views on police misconduct have earned him the ire of many in both the United States and Israel. At a press conference, Minnesota governor Jesse Ventura noticed him and said, "Look, there's Dershowitz. Now I've really gotta watch what I say." Later that day, Dershowitz was part of a roundtable discussion about the flamboyant politician. In the spring of 2000, Dershowitz argued that, notwithstanding an individual's First Amendment rights to free speech, professional baseball was within its legal rights to penalize John Rocker, an Atlanta Braves pitcher, who made offensive racial comments.

Dershowitz is active in Jewish affairs, which brought him his first case, in which he argued in support of Sheldon Siegel of the Jewish Defense League. Over the years, he has worked on behalf of religious freedom, Soviet Jewry, and a respectful place for Jews in U.S. society. The title of one of his books, *Chutzpah* (1991), suggests he is not bashful. He once said, "Anybody who votes for Pat Buchanan knowing that he is anti-Semitic, knowing of his bigotry, is committing a political sin. You cannot live with yourself and vote for a man as evil and bigoted and as anti-Semitic . . . as Pat Buchanan." Buchanan responded, "What does he do for a living? He defends guys who murder their wives—[Claus] von Bülow and O. J. Simpson. And he runs around to get all this publicity. My view of the guy is that there is nothing that can pull him away from a television camera but the distant wail of an ambulance siren."

In 1983, the Anti-Defamation League of B'nai B'rith presented him with the William O. Douglas First Amendment Award for his "compassionate eloquent leadership and persistent advocacy in the struggle for civil and human rights." In presenting the award, Nobel laureate Elie Wiesel said, "If there had been a few people like Alan Dershowitz during the 1930s and 1940s, the history of European Jewry might have been different." Rabbi Irving Greenberg included Dershowitz, along with Wiesel, as prime examples of "modern-day rabbis" who teach Torah in a secular context.

Professor Dershowitz has held many positions in legal institutions and professional organizations. He is a member of the District of Columbia, Massachusetts, and U.S. Supreme Court bars. He has served on the boards of directors of the Society of American Law Teachers and the American Civil Liberties Union, the advisory boards of the Civil Liberties Union of

Massachusetts and the International Parliamentary Group for Human Rights in the Soviet Union, and as a member of the executive committee of the Assembly of Behavioral and Social Sciences of the National Academy of Sciences.

The New York Criminal Bar Association honored Dershowitz for his "outstanding contribution as a scholar and dedicated defender of human rights." The Lawyers' Club of San Francisco has honored him as a "Legend of the Law," and the Atlanta Bar Association included him in the category of legal "superstar." NBC selected Dershowitz as a participant on the U.S. team to debate a trio of Soviet representatives on a nationally televised confrontation, and, after the debate, William F. Buckley proposed the U.S. team for Medals of Freedom.

Dershowitz is a prolific author, and his literary achievements include not only works on law but critiques of Jewish life in the United States and fiction. His books on law demonstrate great variety, ranging from his early work on psychiatry and law to his most recent title, *The Genesis of Justice: 10 Stories of Biblical Injustice That Led to the 10 Commandments and Modern Law* (2000), and include *Sexual McCarthyism* (1998), *Reasonable Doubts* (1996), *The Abuse Excuse* (1994), *Contrary to Popular Opinion* (1992), and *The Best Defense* (1982). In *The Vanishing American Jew* (1997) and *Chutzpah* (1991), Dershowitz writes about the consequences of assimilation for American Jews and their place in U.S. society.

He has also published hundreds of articles in a wide range of magazines and journals. These include the most prestigious of scholarly journals, such as the *Harvard Law Review*, *Yale Law Journal*, *Stanford Law Review*, the *Journal of Legal Education*, *American Bar Review Journal*, and *Israel Law Review*. His articles appear regularly in the top periodicals that emphasize commentary on public issues, such as *The Nation*, *New York Review*, *Saturday Review*, *Commentary*, *The New Republic*, and *Harper's*. Dershowitz has even been published in such diverse publications as *New Woman*, *TV Guide*, *Sports Illustrated*, *American Film*, *Good Housekeeping*, and *Penthouse*.

His novels, *Just Revenge* (1999) and *The Advocate's Devil* (1994), tell stories about complex issues in legal ethics. Dershowitz's writing on legal ethics strike many of his detractors as odd. He admits, "Almost all of my own clients have been guilty," (Dershowitz 1982, xiv). He receives hate mail, both of an anti-Semitic nature and related to his clients. He received an especially large amount of hate mail after O. J. Simpson's acquittal in the murder of his wife. Pundits on the right and the left, including radical lawyer and former friend WILLIAM KUNSTLER, see Dershowitz as greedy and attention seeking. During the O. J. Simpson trial, Dershowitz's comments incensed the Los Angeles Police Department, whose chief, Willie Williams, called him a liar and demanded an apology. Dershowitz is rumored to charge some four hundred dollars an hour for his services, but about half his casework is done pro bono. He claims, "I have never in my life done anything for the money."

— *Ronald Kahn*

Sources and Suggestions for Further Reading

Dershowitz, Alan M. *The Abuse Excuse*. New York: Little, Brown, 1994.

_____. *The Best Defense*. New York: Random House, 1982.

_____. *Reasonable Doubts*. New York: Simon & Schuster, 1996.

_____. *Reversal of Fortune*. New York: Random House, 1986.

"Dershowitz, Alan Morton." In *West's Dictionary of American Law*. Vol. 4. St. Paul: West Group, 1984, 71–73.

"*Snepp v. United States*." In *Great American Courts*. Vol. 1, *Individual Liberties*. Detroit: Gale Group, 1998.

DEWEY, THOMAS E.

(1902–1971)

BETTER KNOWN TODAY AS A two-time unsuccessful Republican candidate for president, Thomas E. Dewey first came into the public eye as a hard-driving New York prosecutor. He served three terms as governor of New York and was a counselor to Presidents Dwight D. Eisenhower and Richard Nixon, although by the time they came to office he had resumed the full-time practice of law and generally avoided the public spotlight.

Dewey was born in 1902 in Owosso, Michigan, to George and Annie Dewey; Dewey's father was a Republican newspaper editor who eventually became a postmaster. Dewey, who had a well-trained baritone voice, initially attended the University of Michigan (and the Chicago Musical College where he met Francis Eileen Hutt from Oklahoma, whom he would later wed) with a serious interest in music, but he gradually directed his attention toward law, attending Columbia Law School after graduating from Michigan.

After visiting Europe, where he first grew his signature mustache

THOMAS E. DEWEY
Library of Congress

(with his boyish but handsome face and somewhat distant demeanor, Dewey would later be likened to the plastic groom on the wedding cake), Dewey returned to New York, working first with the firm of Larkin, Rathbone & Perry and then with MacNamara & Seymour. Dewey also became active in local Republican politics. Then offered a job by U.S. attorney George Z. Medalie as chief assistant with responsibility over fifty to sixty other lawyers, Dewey quickly proved himself under Medalie's able tutelage, helping to win a conviction for James J. Quinliven, a vice squad officer accused of taking bribes from speakeasies and brothels, and winning a stock manipulation case against the Manhattan Electrical Supply Company. A federal agent working with Dewey during this period described him as "the perfectionist to end all perfectionists" and noted that "his thoroughness is beyond description" (Smith 1982, 115). In addition to his reputation for meticulous combing through financial records, Dewey also developed a reputation for arrogance.

Continuously groomed by Medalie, Dewey was chosen by nine federal judges to serve out the five weeks remaining in Medalie's term when Medalie returned to private practice. Dewey was the youngest person in New York ever to serve in this capacity. In this role, Dewey was able to win an income tax evasion case (sometimes compared with the prosecution of Al Capone) against bootlegger Waxey Gordon. A Dewey biographer notes that Dewey and his agents sifted through more than two hundred thousand deposit slips "piecing together earlier transactions, tracing wealth and its sources deeply camouflaged behind Gordon's subordinates" (Smith 1982, 134). At trial's end, Dewey won the accolades of the judge, Frank J. Coleman, who said, "It is my firm conviction that never in this court or in any other has such fine work been done for the government" (Walker 1944, 43).

Democrats replaced Dewey at the end of his term, and he returned briefly to private practice, but his reputation as a prosecutor had not been forgotten, and he was named as counsel for the New York Bar in the prosecution of Judge Harold L. Kunstler for being on the take, and he was appointed as a special assistant to the attorney general to handle the appeal of Waxey Gordon. From 1935 to 1937, Dewey was appointed by New York governor Herbert Lehman as a special prosecutor charged with investigating organized crime, and it was in this capacity, as well as in his subsequent role as district attorney for New York City, that Dewey garnered his greatest encomiums and criticisms.

Appointed special prosecutor in part by pressure brought about by outspoken New York clergyman G. Drew Egbert and in part by a semi-runaway grand jury that brought pressure to bear on elected officials, Dewey had the finances and staff resources that were typically unavailable to ordinary district attorneys. Dewey set up shop on the fourteenth floor of Woolworth's sixty-story Cathedral of Commerce, where he could seal off the operation from unwanted intruders and where he and his fellow prosecutors had 10,500 square feet of space in which to pursue their work at the frenetic pace that Dewey demanded and in which to temporarily house individuals arrested in mass roundups. Beginning with a half-hour radio address in which Dewey assured New Yorkers that he was out to prosecute racketeers and not to get labor (a particular concern among New York Democrats), Dewey developed friendly relations with the press, worked through blue-ribbon juries and judges who were free of Tammany Hall influence, utilized the element of surprise in rounding up the accused, and used the "joinder indictment," or "Dewey Law," through which he was able to combine several prosecutions into one.

As a special prosecutor, Dewey busted rackets involving the trucking industry, restaurants, the poultry industry, electrical contractors, brickmakers, and the garment trading industry. Altogether, Dewey won seventy-two of seventy-three prosecutions (Beyer 1979, 21). His most famous prosecution was that of "Lucky" Luciano, who was charged with masterminding the New York prostitution racket—and who appears to have been responsible for ordering the killing of Dutch Schultz, when, during Dewey's earlier investigations, Schultz had attempted to put out a contract on him (Smith 1982, 170–173). Initially skeptical of Luciano's influence, after being persuaded of Luciano's role by an assistant, Eunice Carter, Dewey eventually fingered him as the prostitution kingpin of New York, thereby taking some of the luster off Luciano's more glamorous connections with bootlegging. Dewey succeeded in extracting Luciano from Hot Springs, Arkansas, and returning him to New York—after Luciano's conviction, entertainer George Jessel answered the question, "What's the fastest way of getting to Hot Springs?" by answering, "Join a mob and have your name brought to Dewey's attention" (Smith 1982, 207).

During the prosecution, Dewey noted that "we can't get bishops to testify in a case involving prostitution" and "we have to use the testimony of bad men to convict other bad men" (Walker 1944, 54). Dewey succeeded in convincing New York editors and reporters that Luciano was the prostitution kingpin, although there are still those who remain skeptical about Dewey's mass arrests and continuing incarceration of prostitutes before trial, the inducements that Dewey offered to witnesses who testified against Luciano, and about the breadth of Luciano's own power. Nonetheless, Dewey's exploits captured the popular imagination and were celebrated in the movies and on the radio series *Gangbusters*.

Dewey had committed to become a senior trial attorney with John Foster Dulles in the well-heeled New York firm of Sullivan & Cromwell (Beyer

1979, 26), but he ran successfully instead for the office of district attorney of New York under the fusion ticket with the colorful Fiorello La Guardia. As district attorney, Dewey continued to focus on prosecuting governmental corruption and organized crime, and did so fearlessly. Once threatened by a caller who promised to kill him on the way home from work, Dewey carefully followed his usual route home, insisting only that the lights in the car be turned on (Smith 1982, 30). Largely due to press reports of his exploits, Dewey, who was second only to Walt Disney in being named Man of the Year in 1936 (Beyer 1979, 21) and was often referred to as "Jack the Giant Killer," launched an unsuccessful campaign against Lehman for governor of New York in 1938 and went into 1940 with some hope for the Republican nomination for president. The nomination went instead to Wendell Willkie, who was considered more experienced in foreign affairs.

Still in the limelight, Dewey successfully ran for governor of New York in 1942 and served three successive four-year terms in this office (the first Republican to be reelected in over thirty years), establishing a record as a progressive but fiscally conservative politician. His accomplishments included the establishment of New York's state university system, construction of the New York State Thruway, reform of the state's mental hospitals, reform of the state police, and the adoption of strong civil rights legislation (Rae 1999, 522).

In 1944 and 1948, Dewey ran as the Republican nominee for president. Although ultimately unsuccessful, his 1944 campaign was the Republican party's strongest showing in almost two decades. Dewey recaptured the Republican nomination in 1948, partly as a result of a successful radio debate in Oregon in which Dewey affirmed his civil libertarian principles by arguing against rival Harold Stassen's proposal to outlaw the U.S. Communist party by contending that "you can't shoot an idea." The 1948 campaign, in which he ran as head of the ticket with former New York governor and future chief justice Earl Warren of California, is the better known of his two presidential races. Dewey's apparent complacency in the face of Harry Truman's successful attacks on the Republican "do-nothing" Congress apparently contributed to Truman's successful upset and Dewey's continuation in the New York state house. Alice Roosevelt Longworth reacted acidly, "We should have known he couldn't win. A soufflé never rises twice" (Stolberg 1995, 260).

Strongly committed to a bipartisan foreign policy and to internationalism, Dewey helped Dwight D. Eisenhower beat back the threat he himself had earlier faced from the isolationist senator Robert Taft of Ohio and capture the Republican nomination in 1952. Dewey, who identified with Richard Nixon's working-class background, was also influential in the selection of Nixon as vice-president. In 1955, Dewey, who had early in his career stated his ambition to head a major law firm, retired from elective office and founded Dewey, Ballantine, Bushby, Palmer & Wood, a successor of sorts to the Root-Clark firm originally founded by Elihu Root in 1909. Announcing, "I'm going to be a full-time lawyer," and that "when people come to see Thomas E. Dewey, he's going to be here," Dewey became an active partner and administrator and was rumored to have brought in an additional ten million dollars in business, including business from the Chase Manhattan Bank and several foreign clients (Smith 1982, 620–621).

Although Dewey focused on his legal practice, presidents often consulted him. However, Dewey eschewed the spotlight and turned down an offer by president-elect Nixon to appoint him as chief justice of the United States. (It is not clear whether Eisenhower had made a similar offer when Chief Justice Frederick Vinson retired.) (Smith 1982, 605) Dewey relished his return to the practice of law and enjoyed foreign travel.

Dewey's wife (with whom he had two sons) died of cancer in 1970; Dewey subsequently pursued a romantic relationship with Kitty Carlisle Hart, but she had turned down a marriage proposal shortly before his death of a heart attack in Bal Harbor, Florida, on March 16, 1971.

At a time when special prosecutors and the laws that created them are being reexamined, it seems clear that Dewey parlayed his successes as a prosecutor into political capital. Critics who believe that Dewey's ambitions were more prominent than his desire for justice argue that Dewey saw his prosecutorial work "as a stepping-stone to the governorship and the White House" (Stolberg 1995, 65). Similarly, such critics have argued that the Dewey trials "stand as testament to the elasticity and fragility of constitutional rights during perceived crime waves" (Stolberg 1995, 5). Dewey could alternate between extreme cockiness and self-righteousness both in the courtroom and on the stump; he also was known for his fastidiousness, often waiting for someone else to open doors and wiping his hands with a handkerchief when he had to touch the handle.

When on a roll, Dewey could be an extremely effective cross-examiner, but in a trial involving Tammany boss Jimmy Hines, Dewey arguably made a mistake in introducing improper evidence (remedied in a retrial after Dewey calmly announced, "We're going to start all over") that suggested "a weak understanding of evidential rules" (Stolberg 1995, 242). It might be argued that he was at best "a prosecutor, an administrator, the head of an office," rather than a "trial lawyer" (Stolberg 1995, 242). Dewey's inventiveness as a prosecutor and his ability to muster public opinion against crime were formidable, however, and there were times when Dewey's courtroom tactics would rival those of the best trial lawyer. Thus, during the retrial of Jimmy Hines, Dewey psychologically dissuaded him from testifying by bringing in a large file cabinet and preparing to call Hines's mistress to contradict him had he decided to take the stand (Stolberg 1995, 241).

— *John R. Vile*

Sources and Suggestions for Further Reading

Beyer, Barry K. *Thomas E. Dewey, 1937–1947: A Study in Political Leadership*. New York: Garland, 1979.

Rae, Nicol C. "Dewey, Thomas Edmund." In *American National Biography*, edited by John A. Garraty and Mark C. Carnes. Vol. 6. New York: Oxford University Press, 1999.

Smith, Richard Norton. *Thomas E. Dewey and His Times*. New York: Simon & Schuster, 1982.

Stolberg, Mary. *Fighting Organized Crime: Politics, Justice, and the Legacy of Thomas E. Dewey*. Boston: Northeastern University Press, 1995.

Walker, Stanley. *Dewey: An American of This Century*. New York: McGraw-Hill, 1944.

DILLON, JOHN FORREST

(1831–1914)

JOHN FORREST DILLON'S LEGAL practice and scholarship complemented the development of the railroad industry and the Republican party, two entities that were often intertwined during his lifetime. The Irish-descended Dillon was born to Thomas Forrest Dillon and Rosannah Forrest Dillon in Montgomery County, New York. The family moved to Davenport, Iowa, when John was seven. Although he lacked a formal education, Dillon was a voracious reader, and after three years of study, he earned a Doctor of Medicine degree from a branch of the University of Iowa in Davenport in 1850. Within six months, a hernia, which rendered unsafe the horseback riding necessary for the practice of medicine in mid-nineteenth century Iowa, motivated him to emulate a friend by the name of Howe, whom he had met in Farmington, Iowa, and study law. Appropriately enough in light of his background, Dillon would go on to spend most of the winters of the 1870s lecturing on medical jurisprudence at the University of Iowa (Cushman 1928, 311).

JOHN FORREST DILLON
North Wind Picture Archives

214

Struggling for a legal education in a mode similar to that of another future prominent Republican officeholder and supporter of railroads, ABRAHAM LINCOLN, by diligently studying books that Mr. Howe had recommended, Dillon gained admission to the Scott County bar in 1852. His election to the position of county prosecuting attorney came within months and was rapidly followed by both election and appointment to higher judicial positions. He won election in 1858 as judge of the Seventh Judicial District of Iowa, and in 1862—the same year he was awarded an honorary LL.D. degree by Iowa College and Cornell College of Iowa—he was elected to the Iowa Supreme Court as a Republican (Chase et al. 1976, 72). He served in the capacity of chief justice during his last two years of service on the court. During that time—first in *Clinton v. Cedar Rapids and Missouri Railroad Co.* (1868) and subsequently in *Merriam v. Moody's Executors*, 25 Iowa 163, 170 (1868)—he initially enunciated what has become known, to virtually all students of state and local government, as Dillon's Rule. This rule has been accurately summarized as "a rule that limits the powers of local governments to those expressly granted by the state or those closely linked to expressed powers" (Bowman and Kearney 1999, 37).

The already-published Dillon went on to be most noted as a prolific legal scholar and has been most frequently cited for his volume *Commentaries on the Law of Municipal Corporations*, which ran into five editions. He dedicated the fifth edition to the American Bar Association, which elected him as its president in 1891. Dillon had been elected to membership in l'Institut de Droit International in 1884. Although he was neither an original nor a philosophical thinker, he wrote well and produced renowned compilations of nineteenth-century legal thought (Twiss 1962, 184). Besides his magnum opus, *Municipal Corporations*, other works he produced include *U.S. Circuit Court Reports* (5 vols., 1871–1880), *Removal of Causes from State to Federal Courts* (1875), and *Municipal Bonds* (1876) (Johnson 1904).

In 1869, President Ulysses S. Grant appointed Dillon to a position on the newly created Eighth Judicial Circuit, where he served for a decade. From this vantage point, he became acquainted with lawyers throughout what was then the western section of the nation; this served to propel him into active participation in the newly formed American Bar Association. The circuit included Arkansas, Kansas, Missouri, Nebraska, and Minnesota during the entirety of his tenure, and Colorado, after it was admitted to the Union in 1876. All of these state bars honored Dillon when he resigned in 1879 ("Ex-Judge Dillon" 1914).

Dillon resigned to accept a law professorship at Columbia College, where he served for three years. Early in the presidency of Rutherford B. Hayes in March 1877, he was considered for a vacancy on the U.S. Supreme Court (Warren 1926, 565), but, in a practice that was common until the last decades of the twentieth century, Hayes appointed John Marshall Harlan of Kentucky, a man who had never served in high judicial office (Warren 1926, 566). In *Atkins v. Kansas* (1903), Harlan concurred with the majority of the Supreme Court when they held, in a view thoroughly compatible with the outlook of Dillon, that municipal corporations are but agents of states. Indeed, Harlan quoted an opinion that Dillon had delivered as chief justice of Iowa to bolster his argument (191 U.S. 207, 221).

While he taught real property and equity at Columbia, Dillon opened a law office in New York City. Following his resignation from Columbia in 1882, he actively practiced law in New York until shortly before his death. In addition to teaching at Columbia, Dillon accepted the position of Storrs Professor at Yale University for the 1891–1892 academic year, in which capacity he delivered thirteen lectures. The premier theme of his lectures, as well as of his 1892 presidential address to the American Bar Association, was that it is "the peculiar function of the lawyer and jurist to uphold the 'great primordial rights' of contracts and private property, and thus to protect the people against their own temporary caprice" (Twiss 1962, 185). Law in the United States, he argued, was based on English aristocratic notions, not on French conceptions of democracy, so they did not preclude the concentration of wealth (Twiss 1962, 188–189). In addition to being influenced by English ideas, Dillon also cited and was strongly influenced by the Social Darwinist thought of Yale University sociology professor Herbert Spencer.

As one who frequently appeared before the Supreme Court, one of its decisions that appalled Dillon was its opinion affirming a New York Court of Appeals decision upholding legislation prohibiting the manufacture of oleomargarine. Dillon believed that individuals engaged in the manufacture of a legal, in this case even beneficial, product should not be impeded. Yet Dillon also reasoned that a municipal corporation could exercise no power that state legislatures did not expressly grant. It could neither fund lavish banquets without state legislative authorization (since that would lead to increased taxation that would impose on the productive members of society), nor could it purchase uniforms for individuals to participate in Fourth of July parades. Municipal corporations should always leave to private enterprise those tasks that such enterprise can perform more ably. Legislatures should exercise care as to where they grant municipalities discretion, as Dillon notes in the following passage:

> Some of the evil effects of municipal rule have arisen from legislation unwisely conferring upon municipalities, at the suggestion often of interested individuals or corporations, powers foreign to the nature of these institutions, and not necessary to enable them to discharge the appropriate functions and

duties of local administration. Among the most conspicuous instances of such legislation may be mentioned the power to aid in the building of railways, to incur debts, often without any limit or any which is effectual, and to issue negotiable securities. (Dillon 1890, 29)

Dillon's lectures were published as a volume entitled *The Laws and Jurisprudence of England and America,* which he dedicated to his wife, Anna Price Dillon, the daughter of Hiram Price of Iowa. They had married in 1853 and had two sons and a daughter. Anna and their daughter, Mrs. Oliver, were lost at sea in the catastrophic sinking of the *Bourgogne* in 1898. Dillon was not with them because he was incapacitated with a broken leg at his estate, Knollcrest, in rural Far Hills, New Jersey. There he would live a full and socially engaged life at his beloved home in Far Hills until shortly before his death at age eighty-three on May 5, 1914. At the time of his death, he had been ailing for six months but had given up his legal practice only a month before his death. He spent his last month in the home of his daughter-in-law, Mrs. John M. Dillon. His surviving son, attorney Hiram Price of Topeka, Kansas, never left his bedside during the two weeks preceding his death.

Among other achievements that Dillon attained at Knollcrest was his editing of and writing a fifty-eight-page introduction to his masterful volume, *John Marshall: Life, Character and Judicial Services,* which he completed in December 1902. Dillon also worked on numerous addresses there, including "The Inns of Court and Westminster Hall," "Iowa's Contribution to the Jurisprudence of the United States," "Chancellor Kent, his Career and Labors," "Law Reports and Law Reporting," and "Bentham and His School of Jursiprudence." His legal outlook and practice certainly garnered favor from the wealthy and major corporate interests in the United States.

Among the clients of Dillon's firm of Dillon, Thomson & Clay at 115 Broadway in New York City was the railroad magnate Jay Gould. Dillon served as general counsel for the Union Pacific Railroad, of which his uncle, Sidney Dillon, was president, and he handled an important case for the Manhattan Elevated Railway Company, of which the same uncle was a director (Twiss 1962, 183). He was also general counsel of the Western Union Telegraph Company (Chase et al. 1976, 73), and he wrote extensively about both railroad and telegraph companies in his treatise on municipal corporations. He dealt with such topics as the location of telegraph poles and issues arising from the rights of way granted to horse-drawn trolleys and elevated railroads. Benjamin R. Twiss has written that "He successfully defended the Western Union against the imposition of a state tax on messages on the ground that it was an unconstitutional burden upon interstate commerce"(Twiss 1962, 183). Similarly, Dillon made notable arguments in

United States v. Trans-Missouri Freight Association, 166 U.S. 290 (1897). Benjamin R. Twiss has summarized Dillon's interpretation of the Sherman Anti-Trust Act:

> But the contribution for which Dillon was given the greatest credit in later years was his assertion that the Sherman Act did not prohibit *reasonable* restraints of trade not detrimental to public interests. He based this on a declaration that the statute merely enacted the common law on restraint of trade, which had of late come to uphold contracts similar to the railroad agreement as not contrary to public policy although in general restraint of trade. Surrounding circumstances are to be considered in determining *whether the contract is or is not unreasonable,* was the correct doctrine. (Twiss, 1962, p. 191)

Still, Dillon's outlook was about more than corporate advocacy. He agitated strongly against slavery before the Civil War. On the bench he ruled that a Memphis ordinance prohibiting African-Americans from being on the streets after dark was an unconstitutional denial of the Fourteenth Amendment's guarantee of equal protection.

In a prophesy that proved sadly incorrect, Dillon predicted in the thirteenth of his lectures delivered at Yale University that arbitration would make war a rare occurrence in the twentieth century.

Dillon was ecstatic about the development of telegraph communication and railroad transportation in the United States, particularly as they affected the practice of law. Known for his own lengthy orations, he firmly believed that printed briefs were woefully inadequate substitutes for oral presentations and arguments. Consequently, he reveled in the fact that it was now possible, due to the greater ease of transportation made possible by railroads, for lawyers to present their own cases to the U.S. Supreme Court without having to rely on members of the Washington or Baltimore bars to do so. Most laudably, he posited that the advent of the national railroad and telegraph systems were making lawyers less provincial and leading to a greater uniformity among laws throughout the nation. Dillon himself argued hundreds of cases and addressed bar associations throughout the nation. In the obituary published the day after his death, the *New York Times* observed that during his courtroom presentations, Dillon would sometimes note that "'I decided that point when I was on the bench,' whereupon he would send for a volume of his circuit court reports and quickly turn to the particular case, establishing a precedent." Dillon's interest in railroads complemented his work on municipal corporations. Municipal corporations were heavily involved in subsidizing and promoting railroad development in the nineteenth century. Indeed, municipalities as varied as Chicago, Atlanta, and Crowley, Louisiana, would prosper as the railroads developed. Others incurred debilitating financial liabilities.

If a state legislature granted a railroad the right of way through a city, the municipality had to defer to its judgment. This was at a time when a number of state legislatures and state governments in general were considered to be under the undue influence of railroads. This was particularly true with respect to California, where Republican railroad magnate Leland Stanford served as governor of the state and was chosen by the state legislature to serve in the U.S. Senate. Concern about such influence was one reason California was a pioneer in the development of the initiative and referendum as a mechanism to circumvent state legislatures.

In *Commentaries on the Law of Municipal Corporations*, Dillon lucidly distinguished between the degrees of authority that municipal corporations may exercise. With regard to ordinary steam railroads that connect towns, he points out that explicit "legislative authority is necessary to warrant them to be placed in the streets or highways" (Dillon 1890, 878). Still, he observes, "The legislature may delegate to municipal or local bodies the right to grant or refuse such authority" (Dillon 1890, 878). With respect to the construction of horse railways that are to be used for transportation within the municipality, an express grant of power is not required for their construction, although implied power is not sufficient for a municipal corporation to "confer franchises or authorize the taking of tolls. This must come from the legislature" (Dillon 1890, 879).

The New York legislature appointed Dillon to serve on the commission that wrote the charter for the City of New York, which took effect on January 1, 1898. By uniting four boroughs, this document propelled New York ahead of Chicago to make it the largest city in the United States, a status that it still retains.

Whereas Plato and Aristotle founded the discipline of political science largely if not entirely because of their concern that an informed citizenry should be able to function properly in the polis, or city-state, Dillon took the stand that the Greek view of the polity was not pertinent to modern times, since the Greeks did not have our conception of the nation-state. Hence, the municipal corporation could in nearly all circumstances only perform functions that were clearly delegated to it by its state constitutions and legislatures.

One obvious flaw in his view that municipalities derive all their powers from states is that so many of them predate their respective states. Natchitoches, the oldest settlement in what would become the Louisiana Purchase, long predates the modern state of Louisiana and the United States itself. The same is true vis-à-vis St. Augustine and the state of Florida.

Nonetheless, the reasoning of John Forrest Dillon has become a canon of jurisprudence in the United States with no serious competitive theories about the nature of state government and local government relations. Most other state courts have upheld this precedent, which was upheld by the U.S. Supreme Court in *Atkin v. Kansas*, 191 U.S. 207 (1903) (Grant and Omdahl 1997, 305–306, 315). Undercutting the thrust of the decision with respect to municipal corporations was the increasing tendency of legislatures in the twentieth century to grant "home rule" charters, which permitted local communities to structure their local governments as they deemed most appropriate. Still, Dillon's reasoning prevails even today among members of the bench with respect to the quasi-corporations that are counties (Grant and Omdahl 1997, 320).

—Henry B. Sirgo

Sources and Suggestions for Further Reading

Atkin v. Kansas, 191 U.S. 207 (1903).

Bowman, Ann O'M., and Richard C. Kearney. *State and Local Government*. 4th ed. Boston: Houghton Mifflin, 1999.

Chase, Harold, Samuel Krislov, Keith O. Boyum, and Jerry N. Clark. *Biographical Dictionary of the Federal Judiciary*. Detroit: Gale Research, 1976.

City of Clinton v. Cedar Rapids & Missouri R.R. Co., 24 Iowa 455 (1868).

Cushman, Robert E. "Dillon, John Forrest." In *Dictionary of American Biography*, edited by John H. Finley. Vol. 5. New York: Scribner, 1928.

Dillon, John F. *Commentaries on the Law of Municipal Corporations*. Boston: Little, Brown, 1890.

———. *John Marshall: Life, Character and Judicial Services as Portrayed in the Centenary and Memorial Addresses and Proceedings throughout the United States on Marshall Day, 1901, and in the Classic Orations of Binney, Story, Phelps, Waite and Rawle*. Chicago: Callaghan, 1903.

———. *The Laws and Jurisprudence of England and America: Being a Series of Lectures Delivered before Yale University*. Boston: Little, Brown, 1895.

"Ex-Judge Dillon, Noted Lawyer Dies." *New York Times*, 6 May 1914, 11.

Grant, Daniel R., and Lloyd B. Omdahl. *State and Local Government in America*. Madison: WCB Brown & Benchmark, 1997.

Johnson, Rossiter, ed. *Twentieth Century Biographical Dictionary of Notable Americans*. 10 Vols. Boston: Biographical Society, 1904. Available at <http://www.ancestry.com/search/rectype/inddbs/2022.htm> (registration required for access).

Twiss, Benjamin R. *Lawyers and the Constitution: How Laissez Faire Came to the Supreme Court*. New York: Russell & Russell, 1962.

Warren, Charles. *The Supreme Court in United States History*. Vol. 2. Boston: Little, Brown, 1926.

DOAR, JOHN MICHAEL

(1921–)

JOHN DOAR

Sam Garrison (assistant minority council), Albert Jenner (middle), and John Doar (right) deliver the minority report during the Judiciary Committee meeting for Nixon's impeachment, July 1974. (Wally McNamee/Corbis)

PERHAPS ONE OF THE MOST influential lawyers playing a role in the civil rights movement, John Michael Doar was an effective trial lawyer whose ability to achieve results landed him a place in U.S. history. He has become famous for his accomplishments both inside and outside of the courtroom and is credited by many for helping turn the tide in the civil rights movement. Doar selected his battles carefully and won the battles that he chose to fight. His commitment to the movement led to his position as lead counsel in a jury trial that changed the course of U.S. history. That case, *U.S. v. Cecil Price* (1967), culminated in the trial that became infamously known as the *Mississippi Burning* trial. Very few jury trials in the United States had a more substantial impact on our nation, and very few trial lawyers have had as much commitment to their causes as did John Doar. Throughout his legal career, Doar perfected the art of persuading judges and jurors in hostile environments, and in the process, he persuaded our nation as well.

John Doar was no stranger to the law or to legal success. He was born into a family of lawyers on December 3, 1921, in Minneapolis, Minnesota. His father founded a law firm in New Richmond, Wisconsin, that became one of the most prominent firms in Wisconsin. It was in Wisconsin that John Doar grew up and was encouraged to pursue the law as a profession by his father.

Doar left Wisconsin in 1940 to pursue his undergraduate studies at Princeton University. He received his A.B. degree in 1944 and then attended Boalt Hall School of Law at the University of California, where he earned his LL.B. in 1949. After successfully completing his legal education, he was admitted to the California and Wisconsin bars in 1950, and he returned to Wisconsin and practiced privately for ten years. It did not take long, however, for Doar to become bored with the everyday rigors of private practice. His political mindset compelled him to leave the world of private practice behind and pursue greater legal endeavors with governmental affairs.

Doar came to the civil rights movement in an unusual manner. In 1960, he became an attorney with the U.S. Department of Justice. Contrary to popular belief, he did not join the Justice Department because he had any visions of coming to the aid of the oppressed African-American men and women. Rather, his political affiliation as an active member of the Republican party greatly influenced and prompted this move. Doar joined the Justice Department because he wanted to enforce federal voting rights laws more vigorously, and he desperately wanted to break the political monopoly that Democrats then had in the South. He experienced an epiphany when he went to Tennessee and prosecuted his first voting rights case. While there, he saw firsthand the violence and fear that southerners used to prevent African-Americans from voting. Doar left Tennessee a changed man. He knew that his calling was to help the oppressed. As one civil rights historian put it, "the experience would make it impossible for him ever to go home to Wisconsin" ("Wisconsin's Legal History" n.d.).

After his awakening in Tennessee, Doar threw himself headlong into the civil rights movement. He became a proven success as an advocate, both inside the courtroom and out. In 1962, a federal court ordered the University of Mississippi to accept James Meredith as the university's first African-American student. The governor of Mississippi, Ross Barnett, stood at the steps of the university and twice turned Meredith away, refusing to let him register. John Doar appeared with Meredith, and Doar used his advocacy skills in an attempt to convince Governor Barnett that Meredith should be permitted to register for classes. He stood with Meredith on the university's steps arguing and demanding that Governor Barnett's attempts to block the registration cease. Doar addressed Governor Barnett in an aggressive tone shouting, "I call on you [Governor] to permit us to go in and see Mr. Ellis and get this young man registered" ("Wisconsin's Legal History" n.d.). His demands were met with shouts and jeers from the hundreds of angry protesters. Doar's aggression and persistence eventually prevailed, however, and James Meredith was escorted into the university by armed troops and allowed to register for classes on that day.

Moman Pruiett

Few lawyers have lived more colorful lives than did attorney Moman Pruiett (1872–1944), who practiced law in the Indian territory in the American Southwest. If his autobiography is accurate, Pruiett defended 342 men accused of murder and won 304 acquittals and had only one client, later pardoned by President William McKinley, who received the death penalty (Pruiett 1945, 32).

Few individuals would have appeared to be unlikelier candidates for the bar. Born aboard a riverboat to parents (his father was a butcher) who always seemed to be in financial distress, Pruiett, who had only the most rudimentary education, was sent to jail in Arkansas at age sixteen for forgery and still later in Texas for robbery, after evidence of his previous offense was introduced at his trial. It was here that Pruiett, who professed his innocence, made a most unlikely threat. After attributing his conviction to the introduction of his prior record and "the trail of the serpent following me," Pruiett proclaimed,

> You think you can break me with it, but by God, you can't. As sure as I live I'll make you sorry. I'll empty your damned jails, an' I'll turn the murderers an' thieves a'loose in your midst. But I'll do it in a legal way. (Pruiett 1945, 52)

After serving his time and changing his first name from Moorman to Moman, Pruiett began hanging around courthouses and caught the attention, at age twenty-three, of U.S. district judge David E. Bryant, who fulfilled Pruiett's mother's dream by swearing him in as a lawyer.

Pruiett has been likened to P. T. Barnum (Uelmen 1982, 36), who learned from the streets rather than from books of law. In one notable case, Pruiett conducted a thorough voir dire of the jury pool that demonstrated that at least one of the jurors whom the judge had seated had come believing the defendant to be guilty and thus set the stage for a successful appeal (Uelmen 1982, 36). On yet another occasion when the evidence clearly pointed to the guilt of his client in killing his lover's husband, Pruiett was able to hang the jury on the question as to whether the husband was in fact dead or whether he was participating in insurance fraud (Uelmen 1982, 37).

In 1935, the Oklahoma Supreme Court, recognizing Pruiett's failing health and his service to the profession of law for more than forty years, gave Pruiett a one-year suspended sentence for his involvement in an extortion scheme (Uelmen 1982, 37).

Pruiett was criticized more for his role in exonerating so many defendants than for his own personal failing. Pruiett answered his critics in his autobiography:

> I made a lot of money, but I never turned down a criminal defense 'cause the accused didn't have the money to pay me. Maybe I have been indiscreet in my time. Maybe I have been a hypocrite, in some of the acts I've put on before juries, but let me tell you this. All the crookedness I ever poured into all the lawsuits I ever tried wouldn't amount to a tenth of what any of these big railroads or oil companies has crammed into a single case, just to cheat honest landholders out of their just rights. I can look 'em in the eye an' tell 'em to go to hell. I done mine for mercy. They done theirs for greedy gold. (Pruiett 1945, 574–575)

References

Pruiett, Moman. *Moman Pruiett: Criminal Lawyer.* Oklahoma City, Okla.: Harlow, 1945.

Uelmen, Gerald F. "Legends and Landmarks: Moman Pruiett, Criminal Lawyer." *Criminal Defense* (May/June 1982).

In June 1963, Doar found himself in downtown Jackson, Mississippi, in the aftermath of the assassination of civil rights leader Medgar Evers. As tensions mounted and rioting crowds swelled, Doar became an advocate for peace and placed himself between angry African-American youths and lines of heavily armed police ready to move in with clubs and guns. "My name is John Doar," he shouted. "I'm from the Justice Department, and anybody around here knows I stand for what is right" ("Wisconsin's Legal History" n.d.). Once again John Doar prevailed by helping to prevent a full-scale riot from taking place on that day.

By 1965, Doar was the assistant attorney general heading the civil rights division of the U.S. Department of Justice and had become a key player in the civil rights movement. Doar then began making waves and achieving success inside the courtroom as well. He became known as the most forceful advocate within the Justice Department, and he aggressively prosecuted his voting rights cases. Doar declared that the Voting Rights Act of 1965 was "one of the greatest pieces of legislation ever enacted," and he worked tirelessly to combat the inequities of the law's enforcement ("Wisconsin's Legal History" n.d.). He traveled extensively throughout the South, ensuring that African-American applicants were not unfairly subjected to literacy tests, that voting registration centers remained open for required periods of time, and that local municipalities did not gerrymander African-American residents outside of voting districts. Doar experienced so much success with voting rights endeavors that he befriended then–Attorney General Robert Kennedy and began to serve as Kennedy's chief aide in the prosecution of voting rights violators throughout the South ("Wisconsin's Legal History" n.d.).

Doar's first major courtroom victory outside of the voting rights discipline occurred not in front of a jury, but in front of a federal judge by the name of Frank Johnson. In 1961, busloads of people waged a cross-country campaign to try to end racial discrimination at bus terminals. This group became known as the Freedom Riders, and their nonviolent protest was brutally received at many stops along the way. As a participant in many seminal civil rights movement events in the South, Doar witnessed firsthand the violent assaults in Alabama against the Freedom Riders, and he took it upon himself to seek an injunction based on the 1946 U.S. Supreme Court case of *Morgan v. Virginia*, which held that segregation on interstate buses was unconstitutional. This injunction was granted by Judge Johnson, and it helped prevent any future violent attacks on the Freedom Riders. This achievement, while seemingly small, was a precursor to Doar's role in the biggest civil rights trial of the era.

The stage was set for a major civil rights courtroom drama when three civil rights workers were killed in Neshoba County, Mississippi. Doar, who was head of the Justice Department's Civil Rights Division, got the call to lead the prosecution in the case. In fact, Doar was the first federal official notified of the disappearance of the three workers near Philadelphia, Mississippi. At 1:30 A.M. on June 22, 1964, Doar received a telephone call from a Student Non-Violent Coordinating Committee worker from Atlanta who told him that the three workers were hours overdue from their trip to Neshoba County. Doar advised the worker to contact the Mississippi Highway Safety Patrol, and soon thereafter he authorized the FBI to enter the case.

After more than three years of investigation into Mississippi's deeply rooted and powerful Ku Klux Klan, Doar indicted and brought to trial eighteen men who were accused of participating in a Klan conspiracy to murder the three youths. The *Mississippi Burning* trial (*U.S. v. Cecil Price*) began on October 7, 1967, and throughout it Doar insisted that he was not accustomed to the role he had been called on to play in the case. After all, he had prosecuted several voting rights cases for the Justice Department, but those were civil matters. Remarkably, the *Mississippi Burning* trial was only his second criminal trial.

> May it please the Court, ladies and gentlemen of the jury, I'm not accustomed to the duty which I have attempted to perform here in Meridian for the last few days. Only once before have I acted as prosecutor for the government in a criminal case. I hope very much that you will understand the reasons I have come here, it's not because of any skilled experience that I am here, but only because I hold the office as head of the division with the Department of Justice, and it is my responsibility to try and enforce the law in which these defendants have been charged. (Doar "Closing Argument" n.d.)

Doar's obvious overplay of his "fish out of water" role as prosecutor in this racially and politically charged climate was somewhat disingenuous, however. It was certainly no accident that John Doar led this prosecution team. In fact, he was the obvious choice as lead prosecutor for this trial. Just two years earlier, he had successfully prosecuted a white supremacist named Collie Leroy Wilkings for the murder of Viola Liuzza in Alabama. This conviction was the first ever in Alabama for the death of a civil rights worker. As if that feat were not remarkable enough, he obtained that conviction in Alabama in front of an all-white jury. Here stood John Doar once again in front of an all-white jury attempting to convict several white supremacists in a southern town in a southern state.

This time, however, Doar had one more card stacked against him. He was not only attempting to convince an all-white jury to convict members of their own race, but he was trying this conspiracy case before one of the most determined segregationist judges in the country, William Harold Cox. Judge Cox had been a constant source of problems for Justice Department lawyers who sought to enforce civil rights laws in Mississippi. For example, in one incident, Judge Cox referred to a group of African-Americans who were about to testify in a voting rights case as "a bunch of chimpanzees." Other examples of Judge Cox's obvious bias in favor of the white supremacist defendants were evident throughout the entire criminal process. He initially dismissed seventeen of the indictments on the ground that the men were not acting "under color of state law." The U.S. Supreme Court later overruled this decision, and eventually Doar successfully persuaded Cox to indict eighteen Klansmen.

John Doar's trial strategy was simple. Present the hard facts and evidence as in any other trial, while ensuring that members of the jury did not feel that the federal government had invaded or attempted to take over and govern this southern corner of the nation. He did a remarkable job of delivering this message and easing jurors' fears of the outside world taking over their state. He cleverly emphasized that this was a local matter, being handled by local folks, and that this was Mississippi's matter and would be handled as such.

> The federal government is not invading Philadelphia or Neshoba County . . . [but rather] these defendants are tried for a crime under federal law in a Mississippi City, before a Mississippi federal judge, in a Mississippi courtroom, before twelve men and women from the state of Mississippi. The sole responsibility of the determination of guilt or innocence of these men remains in the hands where it should remain, the hands of twelve citizens from the state of Mississippi. (Doar "Closing Argument" n.d.)

While downplaying the government's role, Doar skillfully focused the jurors on the national significance of their decision.

> This is an important case. It is important to the government, it is important to the defendants, but most of all . . . it's important to the state of Mississippi. What I say, what the other lawyers say here today, will soon be forgotten, but what you twelve people do here today will long be remembered. . . . If you find that these men are not guilty you will declare the law of Neshoba County to be the law of the state of Mississippi. (Doar "Closing Argument" n.d.)

John Doar battled not only the judge, opposing counsel, the jurors, and the rules of evidence in that Mississippi courtroom, but he also did battle with the entire southern mindset. Convincing twelve persons in a jury box was one thing. Converting thinking that had become a way of life was an altogether different task. But Doar knew how to fight these uphill battles and to emerge victorious. After all, he had been winning one-sided fights since he joined the Justice Department in 1960. On October 21, 1967, after more than two days of deliberation, "Allen charges" (supplementary judge's instructions to a jury finding it difficult to reach a decision), motions for mistrials, and five unanswered notes to Judge Cox from the jury, John Doar got his convictions. This federal court jury convicted seven men for participating in a Ku Klux Klan conspiracy to murder three young civil rights workers.

The significance of Doar's victory cannot be overemphasized. Not only had he achieved a remarkable trial lawyer's feat by winning his case against all odds, but he had toppled one of the most powerful holdout hate groups in the South. His victory effectively brought an end to the Klan's rule and oppression of the Mississippi African-Americans and signaled the dawning of a new era in a nation of equality.

After winning what was undoubtedly the biggest case of his career, Doar left the Department of Justice in 1967 and moved to New York. There he became active in other areas of the civil rights movement, such as the local school desegregation controversy. His advocacy then again took a political turn in 1973 when he was chosen as chief counsel for the House Judiciary Committee's investigation of the Watergate scandal. Doar's ability to deliver the facts effectively in a hostile environment made him an excellent choice for this position. When he presented his proposed impeachment articles to the committee in 1974, he said that President Richard Nixon's actions constituted an obstruction of justice and involved "a continued, contrived, and continuing deception of the American people" (Aukofer 1998, 1). Doar won bipartisan praise for his efficient and effective presentation of the evidence that helped persuade many of his own Republican party that, notwithstanding party loyalty, they had to vote to impeach President Nixon. After Nixon resigned in 1974, Doar returned to private practice, and he continues to practice law in Washington with the firm of Doar, DeVorking & Reick, concentrating on general litigation in all federal and state courts. John Doar's civil rights activism and advocacy made him a living legend, which is honored each time the Justice Department presents the John Doar Award to people who have also distinguished themselves in the fight for civil rights. Fellow civil rights attorney William Taylor has said that Doar had "a clear vision of what was unjust and intolerable, and he kept focused on that." Doar is, Taylor said, "a great man, a hero" ("Wisconsin's Legal History" n.d.).

—*Robert D. Howell*

Aukofer, Frank A. "The President in Crisis." *Milwaukee Journal Sentinel*, 11 December 1998. Available at <http://www.jsonline.com/news/president/1211counsel.asp>.

Doar, John. "Closing Argument in the Mississippi Burning Trial." *Famous American Trials*. <http://www.law.umkc.edu/faculty/projects/ftrials/price&bowers/doarclose.htm>.

Doar, John. "The Work of the Civil Rights Division in Enforcing Voting Rights under the Civil Rights Acts of 1957 and 1960." *Florida State University Law Review* 25 (1997): 1.

Linder, Douglas O. "The Mississippi Burning Trial: A Bibliography." *Famous American Trials*. <http://www.law.umkc.edu/faculty/projects/ftrials/price&bowers/bibliography.html>.

_____. "Mississippi Burning Trial: The Jury's Decision." *Famous American Trials*. <http://www.law.umkc.edu/faculty/projects/ftrials/price&bowers/jury.html>.

_____. "The Mississippi Burning Trial (*United States vs. Price et al.*): A Trial Account." *Famous American Trials*. <http://www.law.umkc.edu/faculty/projects/ftrials/price&bowers/Account.html>.

"The Need for Change." *We Shall Overcome—Historic Places of the Civil Rights Movement*. National Park Service, 2000. <http://www.cr.nps.gov/nr/travel/civilrights/change.htm>.

"Wisconsin's Legal History: John Doar." *Wisconsin Lawyer*. <http://www.wisbar.org/wislawmag/archive/history/doar.html>.

DOUGLAS, STEPHEN A.

(1813–1861)

STEPHEN ARNOLD DOUGLAS
Library of Congress

ALTHOUGH HE IS BEST KNOWN as one of the most influential political leaders of the 1850s, Stephen Arnold Douglas spent his early adult years as a respected lawyer and judge in Illinois, where he polished his political skills and extended his contacts, riding circuit with companions like his famous rival, ABRAHAM LINCOLN. Born of Scottish ancestry on April 23, 1813, in the village of Brandon, Vermont, Douglas was only several weeks old when his physician father, Stephen A. Douglass, died of a stroke. The infant's mother, the former Sarah Fisk, then went to live with a bachelor brother, Edward Fisk, on a nearby farm, where Stephen from an early age worked in fields and barns, apprenticed as a cabinetmaker, and attended a district school three months a year.

In 1830, after his mother married Gehazi Granger of Clifton Springs, New York, and his sister married Granger's son, Douglas followed them to Ontario County in the burned-over district, so named for its frequent religious revivals, where his stepfather en-

229

rolled him in the Canandaigua Academy. There he was active in political debate, arguing in favor of the reelection of Andrew Jackson as president in 1832. In January 1833, he began the study of law with a local attorney, but he soon discovered that to meet New York's requirements for a law license he would have to continue such studies for four more years. This impelled him to depart for the West in June 1833, seeking less rigorous requirements.

At that time, Douglas, having by then dropped the second s from his family name, was barely five feet tall and weighed no more than one hundred pounds, with an oversized head surmounting a frail body. He was ambitious and extremely assertive. A bout with malaria in Cleveland and a failure to secure clerical positions in law offices in Cincinnati, Louisville, and St. Louis kept him determinedly on the move until, sickly and impoverished, he finally managed to find employment teaching school in the village of Winchester in central Illinois. The following spring, still a month short of age twenty-one, he moved to Jacksonville, where he persuaded a justice of the Illinois Supreme Court to grant him a license to practice law, rented office space in the Morgan County courthouse, and advertised his services in the local newspaper (Capers 1959, 5–8).

In 1834, Jacksonville, described by contemporaries as "an island of New England influence" in a region of Illinois that had been settled mostly by border-state Southerners, had more lawyers than was warranted by the available legal business, and Douglas at first had few clients. His fortunes changed drastically, however, when he attended an overflow public meeting called to win support for a petition to request Congress to recharter the second National Bank, on which President Jackson had declared political war. After several of the community's leading lawyers, all Whigs, had attacked Jackson and his Democratic supporters, young Douglas spoke for an hour in the president's defense. So convincing were his arguments that the gathering proceeded to pass resolutions, presented by Douglas, backing Jackson and condemning the bank. Carried away on the shoulders of his new admirers, the "Little Giant," as they had begun to call him, soon saw his law practice flourish (Johannsen 1997, 24–26).

As a result of statewide publicity that Douglas himself did much to procure for the foregoing event, he rapidly became known as one of the leaders of the Jacksonian Democrats in central Illinois. This reputation followed him to the state capital, Vandalia, during the legislative session beginning in December 1834, at which time he worked as a lobbyist to pass laws taking the power of appointing men to certain state offices away from the Whig governor and vesting it in the legislature. After his bills passed, he was rewarded by being elected (by a margin of four votes) in a joint legislative session on February 10, 1835, to the office of state's attorney for the

First Judicial District of Illinois. Still very short and slight, and only twenty-one years old, he had little legal experience, owned no law books, and was interested mainly in politics, not in the practice of law. Nevertheless, he traveled with the court through the eight counties of his sprawling district, cementing valuable political alliances while prosecuting all criminal cases and some civil cases in which the state of Illinois was involved. Although his knowledge of the law remained meager, he was effective with juries, and his quick wit compensated for his lack of legal learning and made him more than a match for older and more experienced opponents (Pratt 1949, 12–14; Johannsen 1997, 26–33).

An early encounter with John T. Stuart made Douglas a local legal legend. Stuart—a veteran Whig attorney, law partner of Abraham Lincoln, member of the legislature, and future member of Congress—was determined to humble the obnoxious stripling who had masterminded the ouster of Stuart's Whig friend, John J. Hardin, from the state's attorney job. In a pompous and contemptuous manner, Stuart moved that all of the indictments that Douglas had hurriedly drawn up for McLean County be quashed because the state's attorney had allegedly misspelled the name of the county in each one of them. When Judge Stephen T. Logan, also a Whig and Lincoln's second law partner, and a future congressman as well, asked for Douglas's response, he was able, because of what was later proved to be an error in the locally printed version of the law establishing McLean County, to show that his spelling was identical with that enactment, and the attempt to chastise and humiliate him therefore failed. Nevertheless, his indictments and briefs continued to be carelessly composed during the short period remaining of his service as state's attorney, as he gravitated more and more toward politics and away from the law. Not required to ride circuit from late October until early March, during which time the legislature was in session, he spent most of the winter months at the capital, neglecting both his duties as state's attorney and his private law practice, working to strengthen the Illinois Democratic party and undermine the Whigs (Johannsen 1997, 32–35).

One of Douglas's achievements during this period was the successful introduction of the nominating convention system, based on the practices of New York's Albany "Regency," into Illinois Democratic party politics. As an active member of such conventions, he soon won election to the state house of representatives, joining the tenth general assembly at Vandalia in November 1836. His energetic backing of the candidacy of Martin Van Buren for president that year procured for him a presidential appointment in March 1837 to become the register of the Illinois Land Office at Springfield, the new state capital. Even though he promptly resigned both his legislative seat and his state's attorney position, the salary of this office, and the relative leisure it provided, enabled him vastly to increase the number of his many real estate speculations and to travel freely on the far-flung Eighth Judicial Circuit promoting the Democratic party and, naturally, himself. In November 1837, although he was still a year short of the constitutional age of twenty-five for members of Congress, he was nevertheless nominated for U.S. representative by his party at a district convention at Peoria. His Whig opponent in the 1838 election was his former antagonist, John T. Stuart, who with the aid of his law partner, Abraham Lincoln, won the election by only thirty-six votes (Capers 1959, 10–12; Pratt 1950, 37).

After briefly contesting the election results, Douglas resigned his land office position in March 1839 to become virtually a full-time organizer, lobbyist, and campaigner for the Illinois Democratic party, while continuing to travel the judicial circuit. It was during the years 1839 and 1840 that he first engaged in a series of political debates with Abraham Lincoln (at the time a state legislator from Springfield), precursors of their more famous debates in 1858. Douglas's incessant campaigning resulted in his selection by a Democratic governor and his confirmation by the state senate on November 30, 1840, as Illinois secretary of state (Johannsen 1997, 73–87).

As he moved rapidly from one public office to another, Douglas had relied on his law practice to provide economic stability. Preferring to work alone, he did not form partnerships with other lawyers, except temporarily for specific purposes. One of these alliances resulted in a famous courtroom confrontation with Lincoln. One of Douglas's backers for Congress in 1838 had been Jacob M. Early, a physician and Methodist preacher. Henry L. Truett, the son-in-law of Congressman William L. May (who had been deprived of renomination on the Democratic party ticket by Douglas), accused Early of slandering May and then shot him. Three days later, Early died and Truett was tried for murder. Douglas volunteered to assist his successor as state's attorney, Daniel Woodson, in prosecuting the case. Representing the defendant were John T. Stuart, who at the time was campaigning for Congress against Douglas, and Lincoln. Much to Douglas's disappointment, Lincoln won an acquittal for his client by convincing the jury that there was reasonable doubt whether Truett had not fired in defense against a chair that Early had picked up to try to shield himself against a gunshot (Johannsen 1997, 90–91).

Between 1835 and 1841, Douglas argued twenty cases before the Illinois Supreme Court. Of these, he won fifteen and lost five. Although he was admitted to practice before the U.S. Supreme Court in 1849, there is no record of his ever appearing before that body. Indeed, once Douglas became Illinois secretary of state, his law practice languished, as he devoted himself almost entirely to politics. Although he never completely abandoned his profession, moving his office to Chicago in 1847, his appearances as an attorney in court were rare after 1840 (Pratt 1950, 38; Johannsen 1997, 91–92).

During the winter of 1840–1841, Douglas lobbied behind the scenes in the Illinois legislature for a bill to increase the membership of the state supreme court from four justices (of those sitting at that time, three were Whigs) to nine, and requiring them to perform circuit court duties. The Democratic legislature enacted the measure early in 1841 and selected Douglas (then age twenty-seven) as one of the five additional justices. From that time forward he was widely known as "Judge Douglas." Assigned to the Fifth Judicial Circuit in west central Illinois, he moved his residence to Quincy, a Mississippi River town in his district. Later he referred to his acceptance of the judgeship as one of his "youthful indiscretions," a phrase later used by an eminent Congressman from the same area to explain an admitted adultery (Johannsen 1997, 93–98).

During Douglas's two years on the state supreme court bench, he held thirty-eight sessions in his circuit court district and attended four sessions of the high court, during which he wrote twenty-two of its opinions, in one of which he reversed his own earlier ruling in a circuit court case. Perhaps his most momentous decision, later upheld by the U.S. Supreme Court, was rendered against Richard Eells, an abolitionist accused of assisting a fugitive slave in violation of a state statute. Eells's lawyers argued that the U.S. Supreme Court decision in the case of *Prigg v. Pennsylvania* (1842), declaring that the power to deal with fugitive slaves was vested exclusively in the federal government, had invalidated Illinois's fugitive slave law. Douglas, however, ruled in circuit court that the purpose of that law was not to return fugitive slaves but rather to preserve the peace. As the exercise of the inherent police power of a state, which extended to all its civil and criminal policies, the Illinois fugitive slave act was constitutional. Moreover, Congress could not, by mere legislation, deprive a state of its right of police power. Here was the essence of Douglas's later defense of his notorious doctrine of "popular sovereignty" as the solution to all controversies regarding the place of slavery in the national territories, when it came under attack by Abraham Lincoln and others during the decade preceding the Civil War (Johannsen 1997, 99–103).

Described by an observer from the East as a "steam engine in breeches" on the bench, and "the most democratic [and informal judge] I ever knew," Douglas, despite his youth, impressed contemporaries with his judicial acumen. Justin Butterfield, a prominent Whig attorney, wrote, " . . . damn that squatty Democrat. He is the best and most acute judge in all this Democratic State. He listens patiently, comprehends the law and grasps the facts by intuition; then decides calmly, clearly and quietly and then makes the lawyers sit down. Douglas is the ablest man on the bench today in Illinois" (Capers 1959, 17).

In December 1842, as a candidate for the U.S. Senate at age twenty-nine, Douglas lost his party's nomination in the Democratic caucus by a five-vote margin when opponents argued that he would not have reached the constitutional age requirement for serving in the Senate by the time his term would have begun. He then announced his candidacy for one of the four new seats in Congress awarded to Illinois following the 1840 census. Belatedly receiving the Democratic party's nomination in June 1843 for the fifth congressional district, corresponding roughly to his judicial district, he resigned his judgeship, campaigned hard against the Whig nominee, Orville H. Browning, and on August 7 was elected by a margin of 461 votes (Capers 1959, 116–123).

Easily reelected to a second congressional term in August 1844, Douglas concentrated thereafter on the presidential contest of that year, delivering speeches in favor of James K. Polk in both Missouri and Tennessee, as well as in Illinois, which Polk easily carried on his way to victory over the Whig candidate, HENRY CLAY. As the new chairman of the House Committee on Territories, Douglas supported Polk's war against Mexico, advocated war against England if the British did not yield all of the disputed Oregon region to the United States, supported the "gag rule" to prohibit any discussion of the alleviation of Southern slavery, and opposed the Wilmot Proviso to ban slavery from the western territories. In 1846, he was elected against token Whig opposition to a third term in Congress. However, he soon resigned his seat when the Illinois legislature promoted him to the Senate in January 1847, at which time he transferred his residence to the quickly growing town of Chicago and began rapidly buying up real estate there. In 1848, he married Martha Merton, the daughter of a wealthy North Carolina planter. Douglas began almost at once to manage a Mississippi cotton plantation of more than twenty-five thousand acres worked by more than one hundred slaves. Ownership of the plantation had been transferred to his new wife by her father, and Douglas received 20 percent of its annual income (Johannsen 1997, 148–217).

When he took his seat in the U.S. Senate in December 1847, Douglas was immediately made chairman of its Committee on Territories. Utilizing the leverage provided by this position, he assumed direction of the forces that enacted the Compromise of 1850, which wrote into law his doctrine of "popular sovereignty" to let each new state formed out of the western territories decide for itself whether or not to allow slavery within its boundaries. In the early 1850s he became the leader of Young America, an extreme "manifest destiny" expansionist movement. A leading candidate for the

Democratic party's presidential nomination during the decade, he lost in 1852 to Franklin Pierce and in 1856 to James Buchanan, two presidents whose deficiencies helped to bring on the Civil War (Johnson 1964, 398–401).

In 1854, Douglas sponsored the Kansas-Nebraska Act, the passage of which greatly exasperated those who opposed the introduction of slavery into the western territories. During the furor that followed, the Whig and American parties virtually disappeared, a new antislavery Republican party was born, and the notion of secession from the Union began to take hold throughout the South. Vainly Douglas tried to impede the impending "irrepressible conflict" by preaching compromise based on popular sovereignty, but the Supreme Court's decision early in 1857 declaring all U.S. territories open to slavery, the ineptness of the Buchanan administration, and the intense insistence of Southern leaders on their continued political dominance of the national government as the price of their region remaining in the Union made it unlikely that a rupture could be postponed much longer.

Campaigning for reelection to the Senate in 1858, Douglas engaged in a series of seven debates with the Whig candidate, Abraham Lincoln, during which Lincoln pushed him into expounding the idea that, despite the *Dred Scott* decision of 1857, territorial governments could still exclude slavery by denying it "police" protection, a position that was unacceptable to many Southern Democrats. After a close vote in the Illinois legislature, Douglas was able to retain his Senate seat, but Southern opposition, as well as the hostility of some Northern Democrats stemming from Douglas's refusal to support President Buchanan's efforts to turn the territorial government of Kansas over to a slaveholding minority, prevented him from receiving the 1860 presidential nomination of a united Democratic party (Johnson 1964, 400–402).

Divided between Northern and Southern factions, the one having nominated Douglas and the other Vice-President John Breckinridge for president, the Democratic party went down to defeat in November 1860 when Abraham Lincoln, the candidate of the united Republican party, won a majority of electoral votes, entirely in the Northern and Western states. Lincoln's election provided Southern secessionists with a pretext for withdrawing their states from the Union, and his inauguration was soon followed by civil war. Having labored for conciliation and compromise until the fighting began, Douglas then energetically supported the military actions of the U.S. government, but chronic alcoholism and rheumatism weakened him to the point that he was unable to fight off an attack of typhoid fever, from which he died on June 3, 1861, at age forty-eight (Johnson 1964, 402–403).

—*Norman B. Ferris*

Capers, Gerald M. *Stephen A Douglas: Defender of the Union*. Boston: Little, Brown, 1959.

Johannsen, Robert W. *Stephen A. Douglas*. Urbana: University of Illinois Press, 1997.

Johnson, Allen. "Douglas, Stephen Arnold." In *Dictionary of American Biography*, edited by Allen Johnson and Dumas Malone. Vol. 3, pt. 1. New York: Scribner, 1964, 397–403.

Pratt, Henry E. "Stephen A. Douglas, Lawyer, Legislator, Register and Judge, 1833–1843." *Lincoln Herald* 51 (December 1949): 11–16; 52 (February 1950): 37–43.

EDELMAN, MARIAN WRIGHT

(1939–)

MARIAN WRIGHT EDELMAN
AP Photo/Bob Burgess

MARIAN WRIGHT EDELMAN is founder and president of the Children's Defense Fund (CDF), former director of the Center for Law and Education at Harvard University, and staff attorney for the National Association for the Advancement of Colored People (NAACP) Legal Defense and Educational Fund. She was the first African-American woman admitted to the Mississippi bar in 1965. The daughter of a Baptist minister and a church worker, Edelman grew up in an environment that emphasized the importance of family values, the sanctity of life, community responsibility, and advocacy for the poor. She turned these life lessons into a well-chronicled life of advocacy for children and government's responsibility in protecting the lives of children. In 1992, John D. Feerick, president of the Association of the Bar of the City of New York and dean of Fordham University School of Law, called Edelman the "preeminent children's advocate" for her tireless work in raising awareness about the plight of children in the United States. Edelman's early experiences with community-based activism as a member of the executive committee of the civil rights group the Student Non-Violent Coordinating Committee (1961–1963) structured her interactions with southern culture and northeastern intelligentsia and influenced her perspectives on children's rights, education, and poverty.

Marian Wright was born in Bennettsville, South Carolina, the youngest of five children born to Arthur J. and Maggie (Bowen) Wright. She studied as a Merrill scholar at the Universities of Paris and Geneva in 1958 and 1959, and then attended the all-female Spelman College in Atlanta, Georgia, graduating in 1960. She obtained a J. H. Whitney fellowship (1960–1961) and later earned her LL.B. and an honorary LL.D. degree from Yale University in 1963.

Shortly after graduating from Yale, Wright was admitted to practice in 1963 and gained employment as a staff attorney for the New York City office of the NAACP (1963–1964). In 1963, she found herself on assignment in Greenwood, Mississippi, which was known for its anti–civil rights campaigns. Greenwood, like other southern cities and towns, was a target of NAACP pro–civil rights activity, including community empowerment and legal defense of civil rights activists. It was an intense assignment, even for an experienced civil rights activist, and Wright was soon center stage in Mississippi's turbulent struggle with civil rights. Some even attempted to use violence and intimidation to discourage Wright and the NAACP, and in one incident someone shoved the young community advocate to the bottom of the courthouse steps. In an interview of prominent female attorneys for the *American Bar Association Journal,* Wright later recalled how its "outrageousness" solidified her commitment to practice law in Greenwood, saying, "It was awful, it was a challenge, and there was a need." Noting her courage and commitment, NAACP officials made Wright responsible for opening and directing the Mississippi office of the NAACP Legal Defense and Educational Fund. She held the director's position from 1964 to 1968, stationed in Jackson, Mississippi. Wright became the first African-American woman admitted to the Mississippi bar in 1965, received the *Mademoiselle* magazine award in that year, and was later named one of the outstanding young women of America in 1966.

Wright's success in jurisprudence, community empowerment, and advocacy for the poor in Mississippi caught the attention of members of Congress, in particular then–New York senator Robert F. Kennedy. She convinced Senator Kennedy to travel to Mississippi, to see firsthand the effects of government inaction in the lives of rural poor children. Kennedy and staffers accompanied Wright to the homes of several poor Mississippians. Her efforts proved fruitful in two ways: it garnered national attention to the plight of America's hungry, and it refocused attention on the dilemmas of the national food stamp program. Wright's efforts also helped to gather attention to the state's efforts in implementing programs targeted at children, specifically the state's first Head Start program. During Kennedy's visit to Mississippi, Wright befriended a Kennedy staff member named Peter Edelman. Their friendship blossomed into love, and they were married on July 14, 1968. The couple have three sons, Joshua, Jonah, and Ezra. During the same summer, Marian Wright Edelman moved to Washington, D.C., to assist civil rights activist Martin Luther King Jr. as the congressional and federal liaison for the Poor People's March on Washington, coordinated by the Southern Christian Leadership Conference. In the midst of planning for his 1968 Poor People's March to Washington, King took a trip to Memphis, Tennessee, in support of striking sanitation workers. On April 4, 1968, King was shot and fatally wounded on the balcony of the Memphis hotel where he was staying. The march eventually took place, led by King's successor, Ralph Abernathy, in May 1968.

From 1968 to 1973, Edelman served as partner in the Washington Research Project of the Southern Center for Public Policy, a public interest law firm. Edelman served simultaneously as an associate of the Center for Law and Education at Harvard University, becoming director from 1971 to 1973. From 1971 to 1977, Edelman also served on the Carnegie Council on Children and as a member of the Yale University Corporation. Given her commitment to advocacy and government action, coupled with her network of contacts inside and outside the Washington beltway, Edelman decided to develop the Washington Research Project into a larger children's advocacy organization, the Children's Defense Fund (CDF), to serve as a lobbying force for all children, families, and the poor. Edelman, the president and founder of the CDF, once referred to the organization as an advocate for a "constituency with no voice." Edelman and the organization have been commended numerous times for exemplary work and for the CDF's commitment to advancing children's interest by raising awareness about the connection between mental, physical, spiritual, and nutritional well-being and educational success. The CDF's programmatic focus includes numerous efforts designed to target all facets of child and family development, including Head Start and Healthy Start. It has an average annual budget over $2.5 million, funded by corporate and foundation grants with little if any financial assistance from government money. The prominence of the CDF has earned Edelman a reputation as an effective leader and has earned her numerous awards and prizes, including the MacArthur Fellow Prize in 1985, an Essence Award, and the Albert Schweitzer Humanitarian prize from Johns Hopkins University in 1987.

Edelman's jurisprudence was displayed in the courtroom and in her selection of particular court cases in which the CDF offered amici curiae briefs on behalf of children's rights. Edelman displayed her keen understanding of the law in a landmark case concerning desegregation in South Boston High School. In *Morgan v. Kerrigan,* 409 F. Supp. 1141; 401 F. Supp. 216 (1975), Edelman and other Massachusetts attorneys argued passionately that the actions of school administrators and white students supported a racially hostile environment that rebuffed the implementation of student desegregation plans, particularly one ordered by the U.S. District Court on May 10, 1975. The court ordered South Boston High School into receivership under the guidance of the superintendent, citing numerous examples of implicit and explicit overtones of racial segregation found through evidentiary hearings and two unannounced visits. The vehement opposition to desegregation and busing in Boston has been the subject of numerous books and documentaries.

In *Washington v. Davis,* 426 U.S. 229 (1976), Edelman joined five other attorneys in presenting a racial discrimination case to the Supreme Court, arguing that the recruiting procedures of the police department of the District of Columbia, which included a written personnel test, violated the due process clause of the Fifth Amendment. The case originated in 1970 when two African-American police officers and unsuccessful applicants filed a suit against members of the District of Columbia's police department and the Office of the Commissioner, who made appointments to the police department subject to the provisions of Title 5 of the U.S. Code relating to the classified civil service. The case focused on the validity of a qualifying test administered to applicants for positions as police officers and on the proper standard required to differentiate between laws written with the intention of enabling racial discrimination and laws having a racially disproportionate impact. The Supreme Court reversed a court of appeals decision that invalidated Test 21 (designed to test applicant vocabulary, verbal ability, and reading comprehension and developed by the Civil Service Commission), concluding that its disproportionate impact on African-American applicants did not warrant a conclusion that the test was indeed a discriminatory device. It further ruled that the court of appeals erred by misapplying the statutory standards enunciated in *Griggs v. Duke Power Co.* (1971), which held that Title VII of the Civil Rights Act of 1964 prohibited the use of exclusionary tests unless the employer demonstrated its substantial relation to job performance. Edelman's determination to use federal government power to protect the civil rights of "voiceless" constituents was evidenced three years later in a case before the U.S. Court of Appeals for the Fifth Circuit.

In another case, Edelman supported the role of the federal government, specifically the judicial branch, in overseeing the actions of states, particularly when such actions jeopardized the adequate protection of children's lives. In *Gary W. v. Louisiana*, 601 F.2d 240 (1979), Edelman argued for proper enforcement of Rule 53 of the Federal Rules of Civil Procedure calling for the judicial appointment of a special master to advise Louisiana and monitor implementation of a 1976 court order forcing the state to provide mentally retarded or emotionally disturbed children medical care and treatment. In the 1976 case, the state of Louisiana's policy of placing or financially supporting the placement of such children in Texas institutions was found to violate the constitutional and statutory rights of the children. In a victory for children's rights advocates, in 1979 the circuit court ruled that the district court did not err in denying Louisiana an evidentiary hearing about the appointment of a special master, nor did it abuse its discretion in the granting of authority given to the special master. Citing precedents and statutory language, the circuit court ruled that the special master would have power to make reports and recommendations, that either party could object to the recommendations, and finally, that the district court retained the authority to reject or modify recommendations. In deciding in the appellees' favor, the circuit court affirmed the right of the plaintiffs to ask for judicial relief given their dissatisfaction with the progress toward implementation of the district court orders.

Edelman also effectively used interest group access to judicial proceedings in hopes of influencing judicial decisions. In *Goss v. Lopez*, 419 U.S. 565 (1975), the CDF filed a brief of amicus curiae urging the Supreme Court to support the ruling of a three-judge district court in Ohio affirming the constitutional right of Ohio public high school students, who had been suspended for up to 10 days, to have an administrative hearing either before suspension or within a reasonable time thereafter. The Supreme Court joined the district court in ruling the Ohio statute unconstitutional. It concluded that the statute granted high school administrators arbitrary and unilateral discretion in administering suspensions and directly violated the Fourteenth Amendment's prohibition against arbitrary deprivation of liberty (i.e., access to academic environments and due process).

In a landmark case that became the first major constitutional test of affirmative action policy, *University of California Regents v. Bakke*, 438 U.S. 265 (1978), Edelman's organization joined several other organizations in asking the Supreme Court to reverse a California Supreme Court ruling that ordered Allan Bakke be admitted to the University of California Medical School at Davis. The Supreme Court ruled that the special admissions program, by using racial classification to award admittance, violated the equal protection clause of the Fourteenth Amendment. The Court concluded that the program was not the least intrusive means of racially diversifying the medical profession and increasing the number of doctors willing to serve minority communities.

Linda Fairstein

Women have played an increasingly important role in modern law, and Linda Fairstein (1947–) helps exemplify such influence. Born to a doctor and nurse in Mount Vernon, New York, Fairstein majored in English at Vassar College and earned her law degree from the University of Virginia.

Despite being told by the Manhattan district attorney that he thought his office was "no place for a woman like you" (Calabro 1996, 141), she was nonetheless hired in 1972. She was subsequently asked by the next district attorney to head up the Sex Crimes Prosecution Unit that has subsequently been copied in many other cities. The establishment of the unit came at a time when rape laws began to change to give more credibility to the testimony of women, and Fairstein attempts to see that investigators thoroughly prepare such women for courtroom testimony so that there are no surprises.

Due to the nature of her unit, Fairstein and her department often prosecute highly controversial cases from date rape to gang rapes by strangers. Fairstein prosecuted assailants who participated in the "wilding" and gang rape of a Central Park jogger. She tried Robert Chambers, the "preppy" murderer accused of committing his crime during rough sex in Central Park (when jury deliberations stalled, Fairstein accepted a plea of manslaughter). She has tried the "Playboy Bunny Rapist," the "Greenwich Village Rapist," and the "Midtown Rapist" (Couric 1988, 42).

One of Fairstein's most difficult cases involved the prosecution of dentist Marvin Teicher, a Manhattan doctor accused of molesting patients while they were under sedation. Fairstein used evidence from a video camera hidden in the doctor's office, from an undercover agent, and from numerous expert witnesses in a case successfully prosecuted in front of a judge rather than a jury.

Fairstein has earned a reputation for professionalism and for thorough preparation. She is married to attorney Justin Feldman.

References

Calabro, Marian. *Great Courtroom Lawyers: Fighting the Cases That Made History.* New York: Facts on File, 1996.

Couric, Emily. *The Trial Lawyers: The Nation's Top Litigators Tell How They Win.* New York: St. Martin's Press, 1988.

Ever the vigilant warrior for children, in *Miller v. Youakim*, 440 U.S. 125 (1979), the CDF filed an amicus curiae brief urging the Supreme Court to affirm a court of appeals ruling that an Illinois statute distinguishing between related and unrelated foster parents, for purposes of disproportionately administering its Aid to Families with Dependent Children foster care program, was unconstitutional. The CDF argued that the law violated the intent and history of the Social Security Act and was invalid under the supremacy clause giving the Department of Health, Education, and Welfare's formal interpretations of the act primacy over state action. Later, in *Parham v. J.R.*, 442 U.S. 584 (1979), Edelman joined with members of the American Orthopsychiatric Association and William B. Spann Jr., John H. Lashly, and Daniel L. Skoler from the American Bar Association in offering briefs of amici curiae urging the Supreme Court to affirm a ruling by the U.S. District Court establishing the unconstitutionality of Georgia's procedures for voluntary commitment of children under age eighteen. The federal district court ruled that Georgia's procedures committing children to state hospitals violated constitutional rights of due process and, more important, failed adequately to protect due process rights by neglecting to include a minimal right to an adversary-type hearing before an impartial tribunal. The Supreme Court reversed the ruling and remanded the decision, ruling against the class action suit brought against Georgia mental health officials. The Court concluded that the district court erred in holding unconstitutional Georgia's procedures for admitting children for treatment and that the state's medical processes were consistent with constitutional guarantees.

In *Pickett v. Brown*, 462 U.S. 1 (1983), the CDF filed an amicus curiae brief urging reversal of a Tennessee Supreme Court ruling that upheld the constitutionality of a two-year time limitation on establishing the paternity of illegitimate children for the enforcement of obligatory support. The Supreme Court ruled that the two-year limitation denied certain illegitimate children the equal protection of the law guaranteed by the Fourteenth Amendment, particularly given idiosyncratic circumstances (i.e., socioeconomic condition, emotional strain and confusion, familial relations, affection for the father) that may prevent a mother from filing a paternity suit within two years after the birth of an illegitimate child. In *Paulussen v. Herion*, 475 U.S. 557 (1986), the CDF offered a brief urging reversal of a Pennsylvania superior court ruling that rejected an appellant's contention that the state's statute of limitations shielding the appellee from being forced to make contributions to his daughter's support after paternity was established violated the equal protection clause of the Fourteenth Amendment. In supporting children's rights, Edelman supported the appellant's decision to file a paternity and child support petition in a Pennsylvania court on behalf of her seven-year-old daughter born out of wedlock five years after the appellee's last contribution, although the state statute required that such paternity actions be commenced within six years of the child's birth or within two years of the last voluntary contribution or written acknowledgment of paternity. The Supreme Court vacated the Pennsylvania superior court judgment and remanded it for further consideration given a new law enacted in Pennsylvania providing individuals with an eighteen-year window of opportunity after a child's birth for the commencement of paternity actions.

Rounding out Edelman's accomplishments as an attorney are numerous awards, recognitions, honorary degrees, and memberships on the boards of prestigious organizations. Along with serving as president of the CDF, Edelman currently serves as a member of the advisory council to the Martin Luther King Jr. Memorial Library and the Martin Luther King Jr. Memorial Center. She is also on the board of directors for the NAACP Legal Defense Fund and the advisory board of Hampshire College. She served on the trustee board for Spelman College, her undergraduate alma mater, which she chaired from 1976 to 1987. In 1970, she was awarded the Louise Waterman Wise award and nine years later earned the Whitney M. Young Award. In 1977, Edelman was appointed to the Presidential Commission on Missing in Action and has traveled to Hanoi to assess whether the embattled region may hold the remains of U.S. military personnel. Two years later, Edelman was appointed to the Presidential Commission on the International Year of the Child, and one year later she joined the Presidential Commission on the Agenda for the 1980s. Her commitment to change earned her the John W. Gardner Leadership Award for independent-sector public service achievement awarded by Common Cause. Her leadership in furthering civil rights and the interests of the poor earned her the Hubert Humphrey Civil Rights Award and a Gandhi Peace Award in 1990. Other memberships on boards of directors include Aetna Life Casualty Foundation, the Citizens for Constitutional Concerns, U.S. Commission of UNICEF as the U.S. representative, the Leadership Conference of Civil Rights, City Lights, the National Alliance of Businesses, Skadden Fellowship Foundation, and Parents as Teachers National Center, Inc. Edelman is also an active member of the U.S. Olympic Commission.

Ever the supporter of women's issues as well, in 1980 Edelman was awarded both the Leadership Award by the National Women's Political Caucus and the Black Women's Forum Award. Three years later, Edelman was reported to have taken a privately sponsored two-week mission to South Africa to explore women's issues in the country and on the continent. This mission took place long before the celebrated conference on women attended by Edelman's long-time personal and professional associate Hillary Rodham Clinton and other foreign dignitaries interested in the role of women's issue in the process of South African democratization.

Edelman holds many honorary degrees from prestigious colleges and universities, including an LL.D. from Smith College and a D.H.L from Trinity College, Washington. Her awarders include Smith College, Trinity College in Washington, Brown University, Notre Dame University, Williams College, the University of Massachusetts, Howard University, the New School of Social Research, Lesley College, Harvard University, Duke University, and Princeton. Edelman is a member of the bar associations of the District of Columbia, Mississippi, and Massachusetts. She also holds honorary membership in Phi Beta Kappa and is an honorary fellow of the University of Pennsylvania Law School.

Edelman is reported to have had some influence over the Clinton administration's domestic programs related to children and was very critical of President Clinton when the Democratic president signed Republican-led welfare reform legislation into law. Edelman referred to the potential damaging effect of the legislation as a "policy of national child abandonment."

Edelman is also author of several books, including *Families in Peril: An Agenda for Social Change* (1987), *The Measure of Our Success: A Letter to My Children and Yours* (1992), *Guide My Feet: Meditations and Prayers on Loving and Working for Children* (1996), *Stand for Children* (1998), and *Lanterns: A Memoir of Mentors* (1999).

—*Tyson King-Meadows*

Sources and Suggestions for Further Reading

Edelman, Marian Wright. "Dynamics of Change." In *Rebels in Law: Voices in History of Black Women Lawyers*, edited by J. Clay Smith. Ann Arbor: University of Michigan Press, 1998.

———. "Say No to This Welfare Reform." *Washington Post*, 3 November 1995, A23.

Fager, Charles E. *Uncertain Resurrection: The Poor People's Washington Campaign.* Grand Rapids, Mich.: Eerdmans, 1969.

Gardner, Dana, Jessica Levin, Dan Pink, and Lisa Weil. "The YLPR Interview: Marian Wright Edelman." *Yale Law and Policy Review* 9 (Spring 1991): 92–107.

International Who's Who of Women. 2d ed. London: Europa Publications, 1997.

Lowery, Charles D., and John F. Marszalek, eds. *Encyclopedia of African-American Civil Rights: From Emancipation to the Present.* New York: Greenwood Press, 1992.

Mandulo, Rhea. "Edelman Urges Advocacy for Children." *New York Law Journal* 208 (December 1992).

Middlebrooks, James G. "Book Review: The Measure of Our Success." *North Carolina State Bar Quarterly* 40 (Spring 1993): 31.

Quade, Vicki. "Women in the Law: Twelve Success Stories." *American Bar Association Journal* 69 (October 1983): 1400–1412.

Who's Who of American Women: 1999–2000. 21st ed. Chicago: Marquis Who's Who, 1999.

EMMET, THOMAS ADDIS

(1764–1827)

LIKE JUDAH P. BENJAMIN, Thomas Addis Emmet distinguished himself as a leader of the bar in two countries. Whereas Benjamin fled the defeated Southern Confederacy for a legal career in England, Emmet, after a brief European stopover, left Ireland for a career in America, where he founded a law firm in New York City that now displays information about its founder on the Internet.

Born in Cork County, Ireland, Thomas was one of four of Robert and Elizabeth Emmet's seventeen children who survived into adulthood. Thomas's father was a prominent physician in Dublin, who, despite his position as a state physician, remained an ardent Irish patriot. Thomas attended Trinity College and then earned a medical degree at the University of Edinburgh in Scotland in 1784. Thomas subse-

THOMAS ADDIS EMMET
Library of Congress

quently spent two years in residency at Guy's Hospital in London and began a tour of Europe. A brother, Christopher Temple Emmet, who had, like Thomas, been an outstanding academic success at Trinity College, died soon thereafter, and Thomas, apparently in part at the urgings of his father, who doubted the capacity of medicine to support a family, decided to study law at the Inner Temple in London. Emmet was admitted to the Irish bar in 1790, and the following year he married Jan Patten, with whom he would have eight children (two of whom also became lawyers) who survived to adulthood.

At that time, Ireland's ties to Britain were not much different than those in which the American colonies had earlier found themselves. Emmet joined the Dublin Society of United Irishmen in 1792 and, in addition to advocating independence, he supported a host of Lockean liberal reforms, including religious freedom for Irish Catholics (Emmet was Protestant) and universal manhood suffrage. His association with Irish patriots both furthered his successful legal practice and put him into jeopardy. In one dramatic case, Emmet successfully defended a client for taking an alleged test oath by swearing the same oath before the court trying the case. After an unsuccessful revolution, Emmet—who could well have become the first president of an independent Ireland—and other leaders of the United Irishmen were arrested in 1798 and incarcerated for more than three years. During that time, Rufus King, a Federalist who was then a U.S. minister to England in the same year that the Alien and Sedition Acts were adopted in the United States, opposed Emmet's immigration to America.

After being incarcerated in Newgate Prison, Dublin, and Fort George, Scotland, Emmet and his family were allowed to go to Europe in 1802. Emmet spent most of his time in France, where, as an official emissary of the United Irishmen, he was frustrated in his hope to secure military aid from Napoleon Bonaparte (similar to the aid that France had provided during the American Revolutionary War) for a revolution in Ireland. His gifted brother Robert, who was also a lawyer, returned to Ireland and was hanged by the British after another unsuccessful attempt at revolution there.

Seeing the cause of Irish liberty lost for the near future, Thomas and his family left for New York in October 1804, having decided not to live in the South, where slavery still prevailed. Emmet was forty when he arrived in New York. Overcoming some opposition by New York Federalists, including James Kent, who distrusted Irish immigrants with their generally Republican sympathies, Emmet was admitted to the New York bar in 1805 even though he had not yet obtained his American citizenship. However, by the following year, when the New York Supreme Court admitted him to practice, he had become a citizen. Emmet made forty-five appearances before this court within the next six years (Robinson 1955, 232).

Emmet's first case dealt with fugitive slaves. He soon had a thriving legal practice that brought in from ten thousand to fifteen thousand dollars a year. His practice was undoubtedly aided by the fact that although there were many anti-Federalist citizens, there were few anti-Federalist lawyers, whereas Federalist lawyers abounded (Hagan 1923, 101). In an early case, Emmet unsuccessfully defended the editor of the *American Citizen* against a libel charge brought about when the editor, an opponent of Governor

George Clinton, published resolutions accusing the governor of a variety of offenses.

Emmet spent the rest of his life in the legal profession, remaining loyal to Governor Clinton and his nephew, Mayor DeWitt Clinton, and other New York Republican supporters while also winning over a number of the Federalists who initially opposed him. He served briefly in 1812 as attorney general for the state of New York, and he wrote a pamphlet entitled *Hints to Immigrants* (1816). Emmet also served as counselor to the New York Medical Society (he was later given an honorary doctor of laws degree by the Columbia College Corporation) and the New York Manumission Society and as first president of the New York Irish Emigrant Society and of the Shamrock Friendly Society. Emmet participated in a number of political campaigns, including one in which he opposed the candidacy of his old nemesis, Rufus King, for New York governor in 1807. Emmet also joined the movement for court reform in New York. However, Emmet primarily distinguished himself as an advocate in the field of law. In this field he established a reputation as a somber, prematurely aged advocate who bent slightly forward because of nearsightedness. Emmet was known for thorough preparation, for long work hours, for his impressive oratorical skills, and for the ardor with which he defended his clients, whether he initially believed in their cases or not.

Among the significant cases in which Emmet involved himself was a dispute between John Yates and New York Chancellor John Lansing. Lansing had reincarcerated Yates for contempt after Yates had obtained release through a writ of habeas corpus from another judge. Emmet succeeded in having Yates released from custody after establishing that Lansing had exceeded his judicial authority. Emmet lost a civil case, however, in which Yates sought monetary damages, thereby indirectly helping to establish a doctrine of judicial immunity for official actions that remains relatively unchanged to this day.

Emmet first argued before the U.S. Supreme Court in 1815 in four maritime cases (the *Mary,* the *Frances,* the *Adeline,* and the *Nereide*) in which he was pitted against Maryland's esteemed WILLIAM PINKNEY. In one of these cases, in which Pinkney had charged that Emmet was mistaken in every statement of law and fact that he had made, Emmet offered a manly response that elicited an apology from Pinkney. An observer writing in the *National Intelligencer* compared the two legal giants:

In amplification both Mr. Pinkney and Mr. Emmet excel: the former is more impressive, and the latter more convincing. Mr. P. improves the understanding—Mr. E. convinces it. The former is more of a logician and philosopher. The former addresses the passions, imagination—and judgment—the latter the judgment only. In listening to Mr. P. we seem to stroll through lanes of bliss and "to repose by the water-falls of Elysian gardens"—in hearing Mr. E. we loiter through academic bowers, or Wander along the ancient Lyceum—the mind is enchained and the senses Lose their operation. In correct and elegant pronunciation and in all the Graces and embellishments of oratory, Mr. P. had decidedly the Superiority. In short Mr. P. has more genius—Mr. E. more judgment—Mr. P. more learning, taste, and elegance—Mr. E. is a more constant and Persevering reasoner, a more skillful artificer of the weapons of logic. (Robinson 1955, 360)

If this quotation seems to indicate that Emmet appealed primarily to logic, he was nonetheless quite capable of defending his clients and himself with emotion. In one notable exchange, probably with Francis Hopkinson of Philadelphia, Emmet turned an attack on his Irish ancestry on his opposing attorney in such a way as to highlight Emmet's own love for freedom and his native country:

I am not ashamed of my country or my political conduct. In the storms of those tumultuous scenes through which I passed, I sought to make her free, and to deliver her from that tyranny which prevented her from the enjoyment of freedom . . . and I essayed it by honorable means. . . . I discovered the value of civil liberty . . . the people were the source of all legislative power, and that for their happiness and true interest all government ought to be administered. (Robinson 1955, 360)

While serving as New York attorney general, Emmet likewise defended his honor against charges of partisanship made by a rival attorney by saying that, "The office which I have the honor to hold is the reward of useful days and sleepless nights devoted to the acquisition and exercise of my profession, and of a life of unspotted integrity,—claims and qualifications which that gentleman can never put forth for any office, humble or exalted" (Hagan 1923, 118). Legal historian G. Edward White has identified Emmet's "distinctive combination of contentiousness and grace" (White 1991, 210).

U.S. Supreme Court justice JOSEPH STORY, who observed Emmet on a number of occasions, and who identified Emmet as being "by universal consent in the first rank of American advocates" (Hagan 1923, 116), further adds to this picture:

That [Emmet] had great qualities as an orator cannot be doubted by anyone who had heard him. His mind possessed a great deal of the fervor which characterizes his countrymen. He was quick, vigorous, searching and buoyant. He kindled as he spoke. There was a spontaneous combustion, as it were, not sparkling, but clear and glowing. His rhetoric was never florid; and his diction, though select and pure, seemed the common dress of his thoughts as they arose, rather than any studied effort at ornament. Without being deficient in imagination, he seldom drew upon it for resources to aid the effect of his arguments or to illustrate his thoughts. His object seemed to be, not to excite wonder or surprise, to captivate by bright pictures and varied images and graceful groups and startling apparitions but by earnest and close reasoning to invoke the judgment or to overwhelm the heart by awakening its most profound emotion.

Story continued:

His own feelings were warm and easily touched. His sensibility was keen, and refined itself almost into a melting tenderness. His knowledge of the human heart was various and exact. He was fairly captivated by the belief that his own cause was just. Hence his eloquence was most striking for its persuasiveness. He said what he felt, and felt what he said. His command over the passions of others was instantaneous and sympathetic. The tones of his voice, when he touched topics calling for deep feeling, were themselves instinct with meaning. They were utterances of the soul as well as of the lips. (Robinson 1955, 347–348)

The most famous case that Emmet argued before the U.S. Supreme Court was *Gibbons v. Ogden* (1824), in which Emmet represented the New York steamboat monopoly interest of long-time friend Robert Fulton and Robert Livingston. Emmet had also argued before the state legislature against claims that this monopoly interfered with federal power over interstate commerce. Although, consistent with his views in other areas, he had privately advised his clients that their case was weak in light of national constitutional powers, Emmet gave no hint of such reservations in court and argued their case to the best of his ability. He prevailed at the lower New York court presided over by Chancellor James Kent before losing to DANIEL WEBSTER and WILLIAM WIRT before JOHN MARSHALL's Supreme Court. Emmet made his arguments over the course of three days, and although they did not succeed in convincing Marshall that New York's monopoly was valid, they may have helped keep open the doctrine of concurrent state and federal powers over certain areas of commerce, a position eventually articulated in *Cooley v. Board of Wardens* (1851).

In 1827, Emmet took on another major case when he defended the claims of John Jacob Astor to a large tract of land in New York that the state had confiscated from Tories Roger and Mary Morris. The state had sold this land to buyers on the assumption that the Morrises had absolute title to the property rather than a mere life estate. Recognizing that the latter was the case, Astor had cheaply purchased rights of remainderman (Robinson 1955, 404) and subsequently claimed the property. Emmet and Webster argued rival sides of the case before a federal court for five days; the U.S. Supreme Court later upheld the jury's judgment for Astor.

In 1827, Emmet suffered a stroke and fell to the courtroom floor while arguing another case before a U.S. circuit court defending a will that had established the Trustees of the Sailors' Snug Harbor. He died that same evening. His funeral was attended by the governor, both New York senators (one of whom was future president Martin Van Buren), and by leading members of the bench and bar who paid tribute to an immigrant who had reached the top of his profession in two countries. In an address to the New York Bar Association, Daniel Lord would later describe Emmet as one "whose enlarged and extensive learning was equaled by his simplicity of heart" (Hagan 1923, 137).

Thomas Addis Emmet (1828–1919), a noted surgeon and gynecologist, was born to Emmet's son, John Patten Emmet, a professor at the University of Virginia who had been invited to teach there by the university's founder, Thomas Jefferson.

—*John R. Vile*

Sources and Suggestions for Further Reading

Hagan, Horace H. "Thomas Addis Emmet." In *Eight Great American Lawyers*. Oklahoma City: Harlow, 1923, 85–141.

Robinson, Thomas P. "The Life of Thomas Addis Emmet." Ph.D. dissertation, New York University, 1955.

"Thomas Addis Emmet, 1764–1827." <http://www.emmetmarvin.com/thomas.htm>.

White, G. Edward. *The Marshall Court and Cultural Change, 1815–1835*. New York: Oxford University Press, 1991.

EVARTS, WILLIAM M.

(1818–1901)

WILLIAM M. EVARTS WAS CON-sidered one of the great lawyers, orators, and public servants of the nineteenth century. A New York lawyer who distinguished himself as an advocate in high-profile cases, he was most well known for his spirited defense of President Andrew Johnson during the im-peachment trial of 1868. Many ob-servers credited Evarts—through his sharp intellect, adherence to constitutional principle, and ap-peal to reason—with gaining the president's narrow acquittal in the Senate.

William Maxwell Evarts was born in Boston on February 6, 1818. His father, Jeremiah Evarts, was a Puritan who became editor of the *Panoplist*, one of leading re-ligious papers of the time. Al-though he was trained as a lawyer, Jeremiah Evarts spent his life as a publisher and a missionary, dying when William was only thir-teen. William's mother, Mehetabel Sherman Evarts, also came from a distinguished Puritan line. She was the daughter of Roger Sher-man, signer of the Declaration of Independence, the Articles of Confederation, and the Constitu-

WILLIAM EVARTS
Library of Congress

252

tion. Thus, William M. Evarts was reared in an environment that emphasized culture, scholarship, and the importance of public service. (His great-grandson, Archibald Cox, would emerge from this same mold a century later. See entry for Archibald Cox, above.)

Evarts attended Bowdoin Grammar School in Boston, where he won a prize, instituted by Benjamin Franklin, for the leading pupil in each grammar school. After completing studies at the Boston Latin School, Evarts traveled 240 miles by stage coach to attend Yale for his college training, wishing to expand his horizons beyond Boston. (His father had received a degree from Yale, and his grandfather, Roger Sherman, had been treasurer at the college.) At Yale, Evarts became one of the founders of the *Yale Literary Magazine* and stood out as a formidable debater.

For a year after college, Evarts taught in a local school in the bucolic New England town of Windsor, Vermont, where his sister lived, giving lessons in Latin and reading law with Horace Everett. Thus prepared, in 1838 Evarts entered Harvard Law School (then Dane Law School), where he immediately impressed his professor, Judge JOSEPH STORY. When Evarts decided to seek a job in New York after receiving his law degree, he carried with him a letter from Judge Story, which described him as a young man with "very uncommon talents and professional attainments for his years," who was "destined to take a very elevated rank in the profession" (Hagan 1923, 257).

Evarts began his preceptorship in law in New York City in 1840, under the tutelage of Daniel Lord, one of the preeminent New York lawyers of the time. In late 1841, Evarts was admitted to practice law in New York, opened his own office at 60 Wall Street, and was quickly retained as junior counsel in a case defending Monroe Edwards, a notorious forger. Although Edwards was convicted, Evarts delivered a two-hour opening speech to the jury that drew repeated cheers from the crowded courtroom, earning him immediate attention among the New York bar. He soon formed a partnership with Charles E. Butler, Charles F. Southmayd, JOSEPH H. CHOATE, and Charles C. Beaman Jr. This law firm (with minor changes in personnel) would remain his home until his death almost sixty years later.

Evarts formed another lasting partnership at this time. In Windsor, he had met Helen Minerva Wardner, the daughter of a local banker. Now that Evarts was able to support a wife and a family, he married Helen Wardner in 1843 and remained married to her for fifty-four years. They established their home in New York City and produced twelve children.

Evarts also acquired a farm in Windsor, along the banks of the Connecticut River situated beneath picturesque Mt. Ascutney, to escape the heat of the summers and provide a country retreat for his family. This beautiful estate he later named Runnemede, after the place where King John had signed the Magna Carta in 1215. It would later become a place where

Evarts entertained presidents and diplomats; it would also become a focal point for the Evarts family for generations.

In 1849, Evarts accepted an appointment as deputy U.S. district attorney in New York, a position that he held (while continuing his private practice of law) until 1853. In conjunction with his blossoming law practice, Evarts became active in political affairs in New York. He was a conservative Whig and a great supporter of DANIEL WEBSTER, pushing for Webster's candidacy for president in 1852. After Webster's defeat and his premature death in 1852 (Evarts attended the funeral as a representative of the New York bar), Evarts became a founder of the Republican party in New York. As chairman of that state's delegation, he supported the candidacy of William H. Seward for president in 1860, but after Seward's defeat, Evarts moved to make the nomination of ABRAHAM LINCOLN unanimous.

Evarts himself was nominated for the U.S. Senate seat made vacant, in 1861, when Seward resigned to become President Lincoln's secretary of state. But Evarts eventually withdrew and threw his votes to another candidate—Judge Ira Harris—when it appeared that the obstreperous editor of the *New York Tribune*, Horace Greeley, might secure the nomination and drive a wedge into the Republican party.

It was in the period shortly before the Civil War that Evarts established a national reputation as a lawyer, arguing the landmark *Lemmon Slave Case* on behalf of New York. An ardent abolitionist, Evarts was well suited to represent his state in this dramatic clash between North and South that foreshadowed a broader conflict within the nation. In 1852, Jonathan Lemmon and his wife had departed from Virginia, en route to Texas, taking with them a number of slaves. They stopped in the port of New York to switch boats. Here, their slaves were seized pursuant to state law, and the question was joined as to whether transient slaves could be emancipated. In the federal court of appeals, Evarts argued the case in January of 1860 against Charles O'Conor, the recognized leader of the New York bar and one of the nation's leading attorneys.

This clash between New York and Virginia, during a particularly incendiary period, captured the attention of political observers around the country. The arguments of O'Conor and Evarts were described as equally masterful. Evarts stated poignantly that "the status of slavery is not a natural relation, but is contrary to nature, and at every moment it subsists it is an ever new and active violation of the law of nature" (Evarts 1919, 1:66; Hutton 1966, 11). The court of appeals affirmed the right of New York to emancipate slaves passing through its ports, giving Evarts a resounding victory. The case would have undoubtedly made history in the Supreme Court, were it not for the arrival of the Civil War in the interim.

One noted commentator of the time, A. Oakley Hall, described Evarts's uncommon talent as an advocate and appellate oralist with poetic flair: "Evarts cut into a legal problem, as one would cut into a pineapple—laying aside deftly the skin and rind and getting at once at the pulp and juice of the controversy, and then sugaring it with a clear style" (Barrows 1941, 48).

After the arrival of the Civil War, Evarts was hired by Attorney General EDWARD BATES to assist in representing the United States in the controversial *Prize Cases*. In these four cases, decided together by the Supreme Court in 1863, Evarts successfully argued that President Lincoln's blockade of Southern ports and his seizure of Confederate vessels at the outbreak of the Civil War were constitutional.

When Chief Justice Roger Taney died unexpectedly in 1864, the Court of Appeals of New York unanimously signed a petition to President Lincoln urging that he appoint Evarts to fill the vacancy on the high court. However, Evarts was passed up for Salmon P. Chase, with the understanding that if Chase turned down the appointment, Evarts would be next in line. Chase accepted the appointment. (Ironically, Chase would later preside over the impeachment trial of Andrew Johnson, at which Evarts found himself a reluctant counsel.)

The assassination of President Lincoln stunned the nation; Evarts was selected as a member of a small New York delegation dispatched to attend the funeral in Washington. Upon returning to deliver a short address to the New York Historical Society, Evarts stated, "No more wonderful career than that of Abraham Lincoln is told in sacred history or furnished in romance. He has been a direct example of what any one may come to under our constitution" (Barrows 1941, 127).

In the wake of Lincoln's death, Evarts would play his most dramatic role as a lawyer, sealing his place in American history. Congress (driven by Evarts's own Republican party) sought to impeach Lincoln's successor, President Andrew Johnson—ostensibly because of his violation of the Tenure of Office Act (which made it a "high misdemeanor" for the president to remove his own cabinet officers without the Senate's consent). In reality, the Radical Republicans disagreed with Johnson's lax policy toward Reconstruction in the South—some even spread the dark rumor that Johnson was involved in the assassination of Abraham Lincoln—and seized on the Tenure of Office Act controversy to remove him from office.

Evarts agreed to represent President Johnson (a Democrat), even though they were members of opposing political parties. The Radical newspaper *Independent* called Evarts a "hireling counsel" who had "pawned his honor for a lawyer's fee." Yet Evarts believed with every ounce of his reasoning that the charges against the president were "pure political poppycock"; it was important to defend the words and soul of the Constitution to which he had pledged adherence (Gormley 1997, xvi–xvii).

When Attorney General Henry Stanberry (who had resigned his cabinet post to act as lead counsel for the president) collapsed from exhaustion and withdrew from the case, Evarts stepped into the leading role. His oration in the Senate chambers is considered a masterpiece in political and legal rhetoric. He spoke, without prepared script, for four days and fourteen hours. After challenging the senators to adhere to their oaths of office, "for the Lord will not hold them guiltless who taketh his name in vain" (Hagan 1923, 274), Evarts proceeded to pull the articles of impeachment to shreds with his methodical logic.

Henry Cabot Lodge would later say that Evarts possessed a "phosphorescent" wit that flashed constantly (Gormley 1997, xix). He pounced on the House managers leading the impeachment and reduced them to intellectual laughingstocks. When manager George S. Boutwell of Massachusetts suggested that there was a "hole in the sky" where President Johnson should be thrown into exile, Evarts proceeded to describe this imaginary hole in the sky from which Boutwell would attempt to launch the president— shouting "*Sic itur ad astra!*"—at which point (he said) the manager would be hurled into orbit himself, making it difficult to determine "which is the sun and which is the moon."

Not only did Evarts bring shouts and laughter to the spectator seats, but he was able to speak with such power and emotion that he gradually spellbound the Senate jurors. One historian wrote that Evarts "lifted the whole proceedings, from the murky atmosphere in which it had its origin, to a region of lofty and patriotic wisdom" (Hutton 1966, 24). Evarts told the senators,

> And oh, if you could only carry yourselves back to the spirit and the purpose and the wisdom and the courage of the framers of the Government, how safe it would be in your hands! How safe it is now in your hands, for you who have entered into their labors will see to it that the structure of your work comports in durability and excellency with theirs. (Evarts 1919, 1:525)

By the end of the proceedings, the momentum of the Radical Republicans had been halted. A. Oakley Hall later wrote, "The logical strength of the Evarts argument . . . unquestionably decided wavering senators, and gave his client a majority of one for acquittal" (Hutton 1966, 24–25, n. 53).

After Evarts's historic role in saving Andrew Johnson's presidency in 1868, he remained in the public eye until his death. He served a brief eight-month stint as attorney general under President Johnson, during which time he appeared in the Supreme Court on behalf of the U.S. government and participated (among other things) in the prosecution of Confederate president Jefferson Davis for treason. After resigning as attorney general to return to private law practice, Evarts cofounded the Bar Association of the City of New York in 1869, helping to dismantle the corrupt "Tweed Ring" that was tainting the legal profession. He saved the Republican party from defeat in the contested Hayes-Tilden election of 1876, acting as lead counsel for the Republicans and successfully battling to obtain electoral college votes in four states that ultimately gave the election to Rutherford B. Hayes. Once Hayes moved into the White House, Evarts was named secretary of state, serving from 1877 to 1881.

Evarts was again prominently mentioned for a seat on the Supreme Court when Salmon Chase died of a stroke in 1888, but he was passed over for Morrison Waite, never to have the pendulum of history swing back in his direction. In old age, Evarts was elected to the U.S. Senate by the New York legislature, serving from 1885 until 1891—a final role in public service that ended with his vanishing eyesight. Evarts died in New York in 1901 at age eighty-three; he was buried in Windsor, Vermont.

When the cornerstone was placed on the tomb of President Ulysses S. Grant in New York in 1891, Evarts had delivered a moving speech, observing that "it is difficult to understand, until the work is completed, how the fabric of great men's lives is woven, for much of the playing of the loom is unnoticed until the conciliated colors are united and presented as the complete fabric of their lives" (Barrows 1941, 485).

When it came to the life of William M. Evarts, he would be remembered as a rare public servant "who did not seek office, but let it seek him" (Barrows 1941, 493). He was a lawyer of unbounded talent who defended the integrity of the Constitution, even when it was not politically expedient. Evarts left an indelible mark on the U.S. constitutional system through a unique combination of intellectual agility, brilliance in the courtroom, enthusiasm for public service, and deep-seated moral conviction.

—*Ken Gormley*

Sources and Suggestions for Further Reading

Barrows, Chester L. *William M. Evarts: Lawyer, Diplomat, Statesman.* Chapel Hill: University of North Carolina Press, 1941.

Dyer, Brainerd. *The Public Career of William M. Evarts.* Berkeley: University of California Press, 1933.

Evarts, Sherman, ed. *Arguments and Speeches of William Maxwell Evarts.* 3 vols. New York: Macmillan, 1919.

Gormley, Ken. *Archibald Cox: Conscience of a Nation*. Boston: Addison-Wesley, 1997.

Hagan, Horace H. *Eight Great American Lawyers*. Oklahoma City: Harlow, 1923.

Hutton, Sister M. George Bernard. "William M. Evarts: Secretary of State, 1877–1881." Ph.D. dissertation, Catholic University of America, 1966.

Ross, Edmund G. *History of the Impeachment of Andrew Johnson, President of the United States by the House of Representatives, and His Trial by the Senate, for High Crimes and Misdemeanors in Office, 1868*. New York: Burt Franklin, 1965.

Trefousse, Hans L. *Impeachment of a President: Andrew Johnson, the Blacks, and Reconstruction*. Knoxville: University of Tennessee Press, 1975.

FALLON, WILLIAM J.

(1886–1927)

WILLAM J. FALLON
The Corcoran Gallery of Art

WILLIAM JOSEPH FALLON, known through much of his life as "The Great Mouthpiece," has been classified along with Clarence Darrow and Earl Rogers (with whom his life shares many parallels) as one of the three greatest criminal attorneys in the first half of the twentieth century (Hynd 1960, 8). Talented, vain, and flamboyant, Fallon has been called "a beloved rogue" (Hynd 1960, 130).

Born in 1886 in New York City to Ellen and Joseph Fallon, immigrants from Ireland who owned a market, William was the third of four children whose family later moved to Westchester County, New York. The physically striking William, who had red hair and blue eyes, grew to five feet eleven inches. Maintaining an almost obsessive love of his mother, Fallon obtained both his undergraduate degree and his law degree at New York's Catholic Fordham University. In college, Fallon developed a reputation for his pranks and petty thievery, his appetite, his generosity, his beautiful singing voice, and his ability to speak. He graduated in 1906 as

259

the valedictorian of his class and received an award for obtaining the highest grade in philosophy (Fowler 1931, 76). After three additional years of achievements at the law school, the dean proclaimed, "Here is a new star in the constellation of law" (Fowler 1931, 79).

Fallon began his practice of law in White Plains, New York, and in 1912 he married Agnes Rafter, who would bear his two daughters. Fallon had a fairly inauspicious beginning as a lawyer in partnership with David Hunt. Fallon developed a reputation for devoting a great deal of attention to cases, especially in criminal law, that interested him and little to those that did not. Fallon subsequently became an assistant prosecuting attorney in Westchester County but apparently sometimes shared his earnings with the families of individuals he prosecuted (Fowler 1931, 96). His most dramatic case, which he lost, involved prosecution of penologist Tom Osborne for immorality with prison inmates. Fallon claimed that his defeat was instructive, helping him to understand the difference between "prosecution" and "persecution" (Fowler 1931, 126), a distinction that Fallon would later use to save himself. In making this same defense, Fallon would tell how he abandoned prosecutorial work after he discovered, as the result of a confession from another criminal, that he had sent the wrong person (for whom he later helped secure a pardon) to jail for robbery and that the mother of the accused had died of a stroke while he was imprisoned (Hynd 1960, 139).

Fallon soon moved to the Bronx, where he had a brief partnership with Edward J. Glennon before establishing a more permanent and successful partnership with Eugene F. McGee (who had taught some classes at Fordham) on Broadway. Their firm was often referred to as "the Broadway and Forty-second Street Bar Association" (Hynd 1960, 130). In the early years of their partnership, McGee treated Fallon with an exaggerated deference that impressed both jurors and members of the press with Fallon's importance. With a nearly photographic memory, Fallon was particularly impressive at appealing to juries and at bringing out inconsistencies in witnesses' testimony. However, he apparently could also cast doubt on the testimony of truthful witnesses simply by reading sinister implications into ordinary behavior. Noting Fallon's "sure, confident manner" and his ability to play "on the failure of human memory for details," a biographer cites an example of Fallon's questioning and described his demeanor as follows:

> His habit, after asking such a question, was to look terribly pained; to turn away swiftly after putting the question. To act as though he dreaded to hear the "lying" answer. To gaze knowingly at the jury. . . . (Fowler 1931, 136)

A consummate dramatist, it was no surprise that Fallon especially enjoyed the company of people from the theatre.

As Broadway's wealth expanded, so did the underworld that surrounded it. Fallon became the first lawyer to gain the confidence and lucrative fees of this group; his typical clients have been described as "gunmen, gangsters, prohibition racketeers, income-tax evaders [and] underworld big shots" (Hynd 1960, 125). Although Fallon insisted on shining his own shoes, cutting his own hair, and taking women on the subway rather than paying for taxi fares, he otherwise had a reputation as a spendthrift who could always dispose of money faster than he earned it, and who on occasion had his office furniture dispossessed. Moreover, Fallon and his partner cared little for precise bookkeeping, and, as a ladies' man, Fallon often accepted the cases of beautiful women without charge.

Once referred to as "Eleven-to-One Fallon" (Hynd 1960, 176), Fallon was perhaps better known for getting hung juries, often by a single vote, than for outright acquittals, but prosecutors often gave up after such experiences, and Fallon became known as "the Jail Robber." Although he was apparently not beyond using illegal means to buy a juror, Fallon also had an uncanny ability to divert jurors' attention to himself rather than to the defendant or to find a single member of a jury with whom he could make an emotional connection. Fallon did not always respect those whom he influenced. On one occasion he told a client's wife, "All I have to do is to pick out the dumbest of the dozen, concentrate everything on him, and my client is sure of a hung jury" (Hynd 1960, 126). On another occasion, in defending a beautiful woman accused of having tried to blackmail an Armenian rug merchant, Fallon chose his jurors largely by how distracted they were by her legs (Hynd 1960, 150).

Although many of his clients were engaged in less bloody activities, Fallon defended 126 homicide cases, including 22 capital cases, and never lost one (Fowler 1931, 212). Occasionally blamed by clients (especially those who saw evidence of Fallon's alcoholism in the courtroom) expecting near miracles, Fallon once responded to a convicted bootlegger's complaints by saying, "Well, sometimes the rabbit doesn't come out of the magician's hat" (Fowler 1931, 316).

There were certainly times when Fallon's solution seemed almost magical, if not altogether ethical. In a story credibly attributed to him, when a bank teller came to him after embezzling $10,000 that the bank had not yet discovered missing, Fallon is said to have advised the teller to secure $50,000 more. Taking $10,000 of this as his fee, Fallon then called the bank and reputedly convinced its managers that he could recover $40,000 from his client if the bank agreed not to prosecute him and if its officials would write a letter of positive recommendation on the teller's behalf so that he could secure another job (Hynd 1960, 123–125).

In addition to questions that arose over whether Fallon was using illegal means to influence nullifying jurors, opponents sometimes found that their files disappeared during the course of a trial. As he increasingly associated with gamblers, Fallon sometimes participated in fraudulent schemes involving cards or other games of chance to catch the unwary. A teetotaler until he was twenty-nine, Fallon eventually ruined his life with alcohol, becoming increasingly susceptible to intoxication and alcohol-related diseases as he aged. Once questioned by a judge about whether he had alcohol on his breath in court, Fallon won the judge's favor by responding, "If your Honor's sense of justice is as keen as Your Honor's sense of smell, I shall have no fear that my client's bail will be reduced" (Hynd 1960, 133). The once faithful family man also felt the allure of Broadway's actresses and developed a reputation as a playboy who rarely sought to hide his extramarital indiscretions, although he did from time to time return home for forgiveness before striking out again for the thrills of high living.

Fallon's ability to read and digest books, often on highly technical subjects, was legendary, as was his proclivity for waiting for the last week, or even the day, before the start of a trial to begin preparation. During a high-profile defense of a chauffeur whose lover had bled and died during an extramarital affair in the back of his taxicab, Fallon so impressed a doctor with his knowledge of gynecology that the doctor said, "I did not know you were an M.D. When did you get your degree?" Fallon responded in characteristic cocky fashion, "I received my degree last night. I began practice this morning" (Fowler 1931, 213–214). In this case, Fallon persuaded the jury that the woman's death had been accidental and actually turned the prosecution experts as well as the woman's former husband into defense witnesses. Always the dramatist, Fallon brought the taxicab into court, helped establish his client's own honesty by having him admit that he, and not the woman, had first suggested that the couple move to the back seat of the taxi, and disposed of his confessions by introducing evidence that the police had extracted them through use of force (Hynd 1960, 165–166).

In another trial, in which Fallon was defending an individual accused of arson, a fireman testified that he had smelled kerosene on rags discovered at the site but subsequently discarded. Questioning both the fireman's predisposition in the case and his ability to distinguish kerosene from water through his sense of smell, Fallon presented the fireman with five bottles of liquid and asked him to identify each. Fallon had filled the first four with kerosene and the last with water. Fallon realized that, by the time the fireman got to the last vial, his nose would be so filled with kerosene fumes that he would identify it as kerosene also. After this misidentification, Fallon confidently took a swig and offered the same privilege to the jurors, who, not surprisingly, acquitted his client (Hynd 1960, 174–175).

Eugene A. Rerat

Born in Minneapolis in 1898, Eugene (Gene) Rerat was embarked on a career with Goodyear Tire and Rubber Company before reading a newspaper account of a murder trial that convinced him to become an attorney. He subsequently took night classes at the Minnesota College of Law, where his teachers included Floyd B. Olson, a fiery criminal lawyer and soon-to-be governor. When Rerat graduated, he discovered that he could not take the bar examination until he took a course to get a high school diploma.

Rerat spent his first fifteen years of practice in criminal law, and he is said to have achieved acquittals for 99 percent of his clients (Sevareid 1963, 32). Rerat was as famed for his persistence as for his masterful control of the courtroom. Rerat successfully defended Robert V. Newbern in one bank robbery trial only to lose a second in another state. Still not giving up, Rerat eventually helped secure a second trial that eventually secured Newbern's release. Rerat also successfully worked to get the state parole board to release Leonard Hankins, who, Rerat also believed, had been falsely identified and accused in the case.

After practicing law for about fifteen years, Rerat became a personal injury attorney, often battling the railroads and frequently obtaining record-breaking judgments for his clients. In one case, Rerat had to try a case three times, each time proving to the jury's satisfaction that his client's blindness had been precipitated by an accident at the railroad.

Rerat's work eventually resulted in charges that he had violated the American Bar Association's Canons of Professional and Judicial Ethics by soliciting business (then considered to be illegal). Rerat was exonerated in a hearing that seemed to point to railroad complicity in attempting to derail one of their most formidable legal adversaries. Far from ending Rerat's career, the hearing only brought him more publicity and more clients.

Reference

Sevareid, Paul A. *The People's Lawyer: The Life of Eugene A. Rerat.* Minneapolis: Ross & Haines, 1963.

Fallon defended Jules Arnstein, who was suspected of participating in a $5 million stock robbery, successfully appearing before the U.S. Supreme Court in the case to invoke his client's Fifth Amendment right against self-incrimination in an involuntary bankruptcy proceeding that had resulted in a citation for contempt. It was during this appearance that Fallon met a young dancer named Gertrude Vanderbilt, with whom he would maintain a longstanding romantic relationship, although not to the exclusion of others.

Long interested in sports, and particularly in the New York Giants baseball team, Fallon successfully represented former flyweight boxing champion Abe Attell, who was accused in the 1919 baseball scandal. Fallon often enraged both opposing counsel and judges, using behavior—including numerous trial delays—that often came close to bringing him into contempt of court, to evoke inappropriate emotional reactions by opposing counsel or to lay the grounds for mistrials. Fallon would often feign illness to delay trials or engender sympathy with the jurors (a technique that he sometimes had his clients employ as well), and, on at least one occasion, he pretended to have lost his hearing in order that he might practically shout questions to an adverse witness.

One biographer identified Fallon's defense of Phil Kastel and others involved in stock fraud as having "laid a foundation for ethical dry rot and professional ruin," which the biographer describes as "the spectacle of a man failing through success" (Fowler 1931, 317). Although Fallon's cases often provided good copy in New York City, these cases led to eventual conflict with the editors of the Hearst papers, who in characteristic journalistic fashion labeled Fallon as the "King Kleagle of the Kriminal Clan" (Fowler 1931, 331). After hiding out for some time, Fallon was arrested, but, in arguments that drew on the distinction between *prosecution* and *persecution*, Fallon equaled his defense of others whom he had represented and successfully questioned and defended himself against charges that he had bribed a juror. In his characteristically brash style, after his acquittal, Fallon told a reporter, "I'll never bribe another juror" (Fowler 1931, 384).

Fallon also escaped subsequent attempts to disbar him from the practice of law, but his reputation had clearly been tarnished, and his later successes never equaled his earlier ones. Caught by one woman when he was in a compromising situation with another in 1926, Fallon had acid thrown on his face but almost miraculously ended up being neither seriously scarred nor blinded by the attack (Fowler 1931, 392–393).

As one who lived constantly on the edge and burned the candle on both ends, Fallon died at age forty-one in April 1927 after suffering a gastric hemorrhage and heart attack. More than a thousand persons, including many dignitaries and acquaintances and professors from Fordham, attended his funeral at New York's Church of the Ascension. Fallon stands as an example of a brilliant practitioner, whose many successes and innovations in and out of the courtroom were marred not only by the alcoholism that destroyed him but also by unethical and illegal conduct.

— *John R. Vile*

SOURCES AND SUGGESTIONS FOR FURTHER READING

Arndstein v. McCarthy, 254 U.S. 71 (1920).
Fowler, Gene. *The Great Mouthpiece: A Life Story of William J. Fallon.* New York: P. F. Collier, 1931.
Hynd, Alan. *Defenders of the Damned.* New York: A. S. Barnes, 1960, 123–182.

FIELD, DAVID DUDLEY

(1805–1894)

DAVID DUDLEY FIELD
Library of Congress

DAVID DUDLEY FIELD WAS A leading business attorney, legal reformer, and constitutional lawyer from the 1840s to the 1880s. He was born in Haddam, Connecticut, on February 13, 1805.

Field's father, also named David Dudley Field (1781–1867), graduated from Yale before serving as a Congregational minister in Connecticut and western Massachusetts and receiving a doctorate from Williams College. The elder Field was the son of Captain Timothy Field of Guilford, Connecticut, who served in the American Revolution. Field's mother, Submit Dickinson Field (1782–1861), was the daughter of Noah Dickinson, who served in both the French and Indian War and the Revolution.

The younger David Dudley Field was the eldest of nine Field children, whose achievements were, as a group, remarkable. Matthew Dickinson Field (1811–1870) was a successful engineer who built the world's then-longest suspension bridge and collaborated with younger brother Cyrus in planning the transatlantic cable. Jonathan Edwards Field (1813–1868) became president of the Massachusetts Senate and helped revise the laws of that state. Stephen Johnson Field (1816–1899) left a successful legal practice with his elder brother David during the Gold Rush of 1849 and moved to California, where he quickly entered public life, ascended to membership on the California Supreme Court—of which he became chief justice—and was appointed by President ABRAHAM LINCOLN to the U.S. Supreme Court, where he served more than thirty-four years and articulated a constitutional order that lasted fifty years. Cyrus West Field (1819–1892) had already retired in his mid-thirties from manufacturing paper before successfully laying the transatlantic telegraph cable. Henry Martyn Field (1822–1907) became a nationally prominent Congregational minister, editor, and author who debated with "The Great Agnostic," Robert Ingersoll. A sister, Emilia Ann Field (1807–1861), served as a missionary and was the mother of David Josiah Brewer (1837–1910), who was appointed a justice of the Supreme Court, where he served more than twenty-one years—the first seven with his uncle.

In 1821, David Dudley Field entered Williams College. After three years he was asked to leave because of his leadership of a student protest against a faculty member's treatment of another student. Although he was offered the opportunity to return to Williams, in the spring of 1825 Field took a clerk's position in an Albany law office. A few months later, Field moved to a similar position in New York City with family friends who had a growing practice. In 1828, Field was admitted to the bar as an attorney and became a partner in the firm. Field expanded the firm's predominantly admiralty practice into commercial law and real estate. Field's friends included James Kent, Samuel F. B. Morse, and William Cullen Bryant. Field once hosted a picnic attended by, among others, Oliver Wendell Holmes Jr., Nathaniel Hawthorne, and Herman Melville. By the 1850s, Field's practice involved mostly municipal law. He also defended the *New York Herald*'s publisher in several high-profile libel suits. In the late 1860s and early 1870s, Field advised Jim Fisk and Jay Gould during "the Erie Wars"—a controversial series of corporate and legal clashes with "Commodore" Cornelius Vanderbilt over the Erie Railroad and the control of rail traffic between New York and the Great Lakes. In the mid-1870s, not having been chosen to prosecute the infamous "Boss Tweed" on charges of criminal corruption, Field and his partners defended Tweed instead. In 1882, at age seventy-seven, Field presented the oral argument for New York State before the Supreme Court in *New York v. Louisiana* (1882).

Parallel to Field's highly paid legal practice was his personal campaign to demystify the law by "codification." Previously, the body of American legal procedure and substance could be known only from volumes of opinions explaining decisions in specific cases. Field was a leader in the movement to simplify and organize the law by identifying its main principles and compiling it as a written code. Codification was opposed by those in the legal profession, who had acquired their expertise by years of study and felt that changes that reduced the law to a single well-organized and clearly written book were both threatening and demeaning to their profession. In the 1840s, the New York state legislature created a commission, to which Field was appointed, to reform that state's laws. The so-called "Field Code"—nominally the product of the commission but mostly the work of Field himself—became the basis for state legal procedure in twenty-four (principally western) states and in much of the British Empire. Field's later proposed code to govern substance was less widely accepted and had less influence. In 1872, Field offered his own draft of an outline of a code of international law providing for disputes between nations to be arbitrated. Four years later, he published a revised version complete with laws of war. Field paid out of his own pocket for many of his expenses to advance codification.

In politics, Field was a states-rights Democrat who broke with his party in the late 1840s over the issue of slavery and the annexation of Texas, allying himself first with the Free Soil party and then with the Republican party. Field attended the Republican party convention in 1860—though not as a delegate—and William H. Seward's supporters blamed Field and Horace Greeley for persuading the delegates to nominate Lincoln instead. After the Civil War, Field returned to the Democratic party because of his disagreements with the Radical Republicans. When the election of 1876 resulted in a dispute over whether Republican Rutherford Hayes or Democrat Samuel Tilden had been elected president, Congress created an electoral commission to decide how disputed electoral votes should be counted. Although he had voted for the Republican Hayes, Field was elected as a Democrat to complete the remaining two months of a vacant seat in the House of Representatives, where he presented the Democrats' argument that the commission should reject several states' officially certified results and decide for itself whom to certify. However, the final vote broke along straight party lines.

As a courtroom litigator, Field left his most lasting marks by presenting to the Supreme Court persuasive arguments that national governmental powers—executive and congressional—were limited to those explicitly enumerated or clearly implied by the Constitution. In *Ex parte Milligan* (1866), Field argued on behalf of Lambdin P. Milligan, whom a military court (called a "commission") convicted and sentenced to hang for conspiring and inciting to insurrection in Indiana during 1863 and 1864. Milligan's attorney, a former attorney general of Indiana, appealed Milligan's conviction to the U.S. Supreme Court, where the defense team added JEREMIAH BLACK (previously a chief justice of the Pennsylvania Supreme Court, U.S. attorney general, and secretary of state under President Buchanan), James Garfield (previously a Union general, then congressman from Ohio, and future president), and Field. Black and Field served pro bono. Field delivered the oral argument for Milligan, beginning with a factual recitation establishing that (1) Milligan was a civilian convicted of crimes for which he could have been tried and punished in the ordinary civil courts; (2) the military court was established pursuant to executive order rather than congressional legislation; and (3) Indiana was untouched by military conflict at the time of the alleged crimes. Thus, said Field, the question was this: "Has the President, in time of war, by his own mere will and judgment of the exigency, the power to bring before his military officers any man or woman in the land, to be there subject to trial and punishment, even to death?" Field urged that no military court could have jurisdiction to try civilians in a state untouched by war when the civil courts were open, and the Court accepted Field's argument.

Cummings v. Missouri (1866) arose soon after the enactment in 1865 of a new Missouri Constitution requiring state officeholders, lawyers, voters, and even clergymen to take an oath not only that they would be loyal to the Missouri and federal governments prospectively but that they had never been disloyal to either of those governments in any way—not even by sympathetic feeling—in the past. Cummings, a young Catholic priest, preached after failing to take the oath within the prescribed time and was promptly indicted, tried, convicted, and sentenced. Unsuccessful appeals in the state courts were followed by an appeal to the U.S. Supreme Court, where Cummings was represented by Field and REVERDY JOHNSON, a U.S. senator from Maryland and former U.S. attorney general. In his oral argument, Field attacked the Missouri test oath as (1) requiring an affirmation of past *disloyalty* to the federal government, since it affirmed past loyalty to the government of the State of Missouri, which had itself been disloyal at the outbreak of the Civil War; and (2) violating the Constitution's prohibitions of bills of attainder and ex post facto laws, since it effectively imposed punishment without trial for past deeds which were not unlawful at the time they were committed. In a 5–4 opinion written by Field's brother, Stephen, the Court agreed on the basis of Field's second argument.

In *Ex parte McCardle* (1869), Field raised a constitutional challenge to the entire post–Civil War military occupation and Reconstruction of the South. McCardle, a Mississippi editor, was tried and convicted by a military court for publishing intemperate white supremacist criticisms of military officers and state officials and for advising voters either to refrain from voting or to vote a particular way. Before the Supreme Court, Jeremiah Black presented the first part of McCardle's argument and was followed by Field, who attacked McCardle's conviction because (1) the Constitution prohibited military government, since the power of Congress to substitute military government for civilian government in states was neither enumerated nor implied in the Constitution; and (2) the factual premise of the Military Reconstruction Acts—that no legal state governments or adequate protection for life or property existed in the South—were false. However, before the Court rendered a decision, there were plausible reports that the Court would overturn McCardle's conviction, and Congress passed legislation ending the Court's jurisdiction over such cases. Although President Andrew Johnson vetoed the law, Congress overrode the veto, and the Court decided it had no jurisdiction to review McCardle's appeal whatsoever. Although the case is remembered today chiefly for the Court's opinion as to the extent of congressional authority over the Court's appellate jurisdiction, at that time it was a step in dismantling the Reconstruction program of the Radical Republicans, because Congress also repealed the act under which McCardle had been prosecuted.

U.S. v. Cruikshank (1875) arose after a riot in Colfax, Louisiana, on Easter Sunday, April 13, 1873, when political opponents massacred between 60 and 150 African-Americans and three white men. Cruikshank and more than one hundred other whites were indicted under the federal Enforcement Act of 1870 of conspiring to deprive African-Americans of the free exercise and enjoyment of rights and privileges granted and guaranteed to them by the Constitution and laws of the United States. At oral argument before the Supreme Court, Field asserted the equality of the freedpeople could have been provided after the Civil War by either (1) federalizing all those rights previously enjoyed as the result of citizenship in the states; or (2) barring states from discriminating against freedpeople with regard to those already existing rights they possessed as citizens of states. He argued that the Thirteenth, Fourteenth, and Fifteenth Amendments represented the second of these possible choices. That is, the amendments (1) prohibited only action by the states and did not give Congress the constitutional power to prohibit the actions of individuals; and (2) applied only to the rights freedpeople possessed because of citizenship in states and not to rights they possessed because of citizenship in the nation. In this case, Field argued, the rights with which Cruikshank allegedly interfered were based exclusively on state citizenship, so laws exercising constitutional powers of the federal government did not apply to him. Reasoning along the lines laid out by Field, the Court ruled in favor of Cruikshank.

Field charged for his services—following normal practice—according to their value to his clients. Although Fisk and Gould disputed his fees continually, they continued to retain Field. On one occasion, a client requested an opinion that took Field only a few days to prepare but for which he charged the considerable sum of five thousand dollars. When his client protested, Field replied,

> Why did you come to me? You knew that I am not a cheap lawyer. You knew that you could get an opinion to the same effect for a fifth of the money from any one of half a dozen lawyers which would have commanded respect, but for some reason you came to me. Now I think you came to me because you believed that my opinion would be more influential in effecting the result which you desired, and I believe that end has been accomplished, and that my opinion contributed largely toward it. Am I not right? Very well, then, gentlemen, you have benefited to a vast amount through my opinion, and you must pay me my charge, which, all things considered, is a very small one. (Bergan 1986, 50–51)

Field took satisfaction in the fact that he probably earned more money by the practice of law than any contemporary.

For more than fifty years, Field was, in the words of a contemporary member of the New York bar, "the most commanding figure at the American bar" (Hoy 1908, 132). The adjective *commanding* is important, for Field's courtroom success was not due to oratory or personality but to great learning, prodigious energy, thorough preparation, decisiveness, and persistence. Convinced his opinions were right and his conduct above reproach, the straitlaced and humorless Field saw himself as a "fighter" braving personal ridicule and hostility to fulfill obligations both personal and professional. Thus, to those outside his circle of personal friends, Field maintained a cool professional distance and gentlemanly reserve. He could be sarcastic, overbearing, and uncivil toward opponents. Many judges thought he was insufficiently respectful of the bench. But at trial, Field was master of all the minutiae of procedure, law and fact, while he reduced a dispute to its essential issues and constructed an elegant argument favoring his client. When his case was fatally weak, Field did not have the charm and sophistical skill to get away with evasion and pettifoggery. But when there was something to his case, Field went straight to the crux and overpowered by force of logic, fact, and precise statement.

Field was a founder (1873) and honorary president of the Association for the Reform and Codification of the Law of Nations, the founding U.S. member of the International Law Institute (1873), and a president of the American Bar Association (1888–1889). Blessed with excellent health, Field outlived three wives and was both mentally and physically vigorous until, only two days after returning from his annual voyage to Europe, he died at home at age eighty-nine in New York City on April 13, 1894.

Field's surviving papers are in the William Perkins Library at Duke University.

—*James A. Keim*

Sources and Suggestions for Further Reading

Bergan, Philip J. "David Dudley Field: A Lawyer's Life." In *The Fields and the Law*, by Philip J. Bergan, Owen M. Fiss, and Charles W. McCurdy. New York: Federal Bar Council, 1986.

Field, Henry M. *The Life of David Dudley Field*. New York: Scribner, 1898.

Hoy, Helen K. "David Dudley Field." In *Great American Lawyers*, edited by William Draper Lewis. Philadelphia: John C. Winston, 1908, 5:125–174.

Reppy, Alison. *David Dudley Field: Centenary Essays Celebrating One Hundred Years of Legal Reform*. New York: New York University School of Law, 1949.

Sprague, A. P., and T. M. Coan, eds. *Speeches, Arguments and Miscellaneous Papers, David Dudley Field*. 3 vols. New York: Appleton, 1884–1890.

Van Ee, Daun. *David Dudley Field and the Reconstruction of the Law*. New York: Garland, 1986.

FOREMAN, PERCY

(1902–1988)

LIKE THE STATE OF TEXAS, WHERE he was born and died, criminal defense and divorce attorney Percy Foreman established a reputation to match his large size: he stood six feet four inches tall and weighed 250 pounds or more. Born in a small house in Bold Springs, Texas, in the piney woods area of Polk County, Foreman was a third cousin to comedian Will Rogers, with whom he shared Cherokee ancestry. Foreman's father, R. P. Foreman, was a sheriff and jailer; at age eight, Percy—who would later do so much to defend individuals accused of murder and who would later advocate resuming public executions—witnessed the public execution of an African-American man accused of killing several whites.

Believing that he "knew everything they would teach me" (Dorman 1969, 43), Foreman dropped out of school at age fifteen, but he subsequently worked shining shoes, collecting bills, delivering goods, and loading cotton and won a scholarship to the Staunton Military Academy in Virginia. Afterwards he enrolled in the University of Texas at Austin, where he continued to increase his personal fortune by giving

PERCY FOREMAN

American defense lawyer Percy Foreman points from the assassin's hiding place to the verandah where Dr. Martin Luther King Jr. fell. (Express Newspapers/Archive Photos)

lectures on the Chautauqua circle, preparing the ground for future greatness by learning to give two-and-a-half-hour orations on such topics as "The High Mission of Women in the Twentieth Century." Not surprisingly, Foreman distinguished himself in law school by winning an oratorical contest with "A Tribute to Stephen F. Austin as the Father of Texas."

After he graduated, Houston attorney J. W. Lockett offered to take Foreman into his partnership, but Foreman later joined the Houston district attorney's office, where he worked on and off until 1935, when he established his own practice. In an early case defending Jewish peddlers who were accused of selling their wares without a license, Foreman let hundreds of indictments pile up, then brought in sixty or more bearded clients and challenged the arresting officers to identify them. The only conviction was of one Muscowitz, who apparently stood up during the proceedings to identify himself (Dorman 1969, 51).

Foreman's greatest claim to fame during his career was the fact that he handled from one thousand to fifteen hundred death penalty cases. Few of his clients served jail time, and Furman lost only one—Steve Mitchell, who was convicted of shooting his wife through a door while she was sitting on a bathroom commode—to the executioner. Foreman clearly considered criminal law to be his specialty. Defending this preference, Foreman noted that

> the civil lawyer defends money. He represents money. The criminal lawyer is primarily concerned with life and liberty. When I talk to young law students I tell them that, if they love money more than life and liberty, they should stay in their sequestered cells. But, if they value life and liberty, they should join us. (Dorman 1969, 30)

Foreman referred to many of his own cases as "misdemeanor murders" (Dorman 1969, 85). He further argued that in jail such individuals were often "the best characters—the most trusted, reliable, dependable people, the people most likely to be readjusted to society" (Dorman 1969, 318).

Early in life, his fellow Baptists—who had ordained him as a deacon—criticized Foreman for defending too many criminals. Subsequently remaining "ordained but unchurched," Foreman indicated his belief that all were entitled to a defense by asking his fellow parishioners, "Does a barber cut an infidel's hair?" (Dorman 1969, 51).

Foreman ran for district attorney in 1940 and lost, and he stuck ever thereafter to defense work, serving as one-time president of the National Association of Defense Lawyers in Criminal Cases and winning the American Academy of Achievement's Golden Plaque award for excellence (Dorman 1969, xii). His most notorious cases have involved murders and divorces.

One of the stories told at the 1986 Festival of American Folklife was that of an attorney defending a client accused of murdering his wife in a case based solely on circumstantial evidence. A body had been found, but there was controversy as to whether the body that was found was that of the alleged victim.

Attempting to highlight this lack of identity, the attorney pointed to the door and promised that the wife would walk through it. When the jurors looked in that direction, the attorney noted, "the fact that you looked at the door clearly demonstrates that you didn't believe that it was the defendant's wife they found."

Nearly certain of victory, the defense attorney was shocked when the jury convicted his client after only five minutes of deliberation. Asking a juror how they could possibly have found his client guilty when all the jurors had looked at the door, the juror noted that, while they had looked, "your client didn't!"

Reference

Schrager, Sam. *The Trial Lawyer's Art*. Philadelphia: Temple University Press, 1999, 186–187.

Many of his cases were quite dramatic. In 1962, Foreman defended Dr. Harold Eidinoff for the murder of Theodore Andress, the president of the El Paso School Board and member of the board of directors of the National School Board Association. Andress had come into possession of nude photographs of Eidinoff and his first wife (taken on their honeymoon), and Eidinoff had stalked Andress in disguise and killed him at an airport. Foreman used a novel "Ivory Soap" defense, claiming that Eidinoff was "ninety-nine and forty-four one-hundredths percent sane" but was obsessive over the nude pictures and his feud with Andress (Dorman 1969, 95). Although Eidinoff was declared not guilty by reason of insanity, he was subsequently confined to a mental institution.

Not all Foreman's cases have involved murder. In 1962, he defended conservative former major general Edwin Walker against charges that he had incited the uprising that led to rioting and death at the University of Mississippi when African-American James Meredith was admitted. Ironically, Foreman would later serve as a de facto attorney for Lee Harvey Oswald (who had tried to assassinate Walker before killing President John F. Kennedy) and briefly for Jack Ruby (Oswald's assassin), whose family later hired MELVIN BELLI instead.

Foreman was known for a variety of distinctive traits. Almost always in a hurry, Foreman balanced numerous cases at once and often lined up defendants almost in an assembly-line fashion. Rarely humble, Foreman reputedly said, "It's not that I'm vain, proud or egotistical. I just don't have anything to be modest about" (Dorman 1969, 29). Foreman often listed his address simply as "PERCY 77002," indicating that all the post office needed to know was his first name and zip code. Similarly, he handed out calling cards indicating that he belonged to the law firm of "Moses, Justinian, Blackstone, Webster and Foreman" (Dorman 1969, 117).

Foreman's legendary memory was aided by prodigious preparation, which was fueled by a high energy level—he showed up for work every day, including Sundays, and worked most days from early in the morning until late at night. Foreman once told a colleague, "For me, practicing law is the be-all and end-all. I don't practice law to take vacations and play golf" (Draper 1994).

Foreman consulted with his clients as early as possible, trying to prevent them from confessing to anything, and he was an apparent master of jury selection techniques. Like EARL ROGERS, Foreman reveled in courtroom demonstrations, once cracking a whip with which the murdered husband of a defendant had allegedly beaten her, in the courtroom (Barron 1988, 15). In another trial, Foreman's client, a safecracker who usually walked on a wooden leg, came into court, presumably at Foreman's direction, without the leg and was on at least one occasion carried to the stand by Foreman himself (Dorman 1969, 142).

Foreman's large height and size have helped him dominate the courtroom. One reporter referred to his "attention-getting black-and-white plaid sports jackets and bow ties" as well as to the "wisps of his iron-gray hair" that tumbled over his forehead (Barron 1988). Foreman, whose biographer described him as "vain, stubborn, and arrogant," also called him "an original" (Dorman 1969, 326).

Foreman was known as a relentless cross-examiner whose knowledge of the facts often confounded witnesses. Foreman was often able to undermine confessions by suggesting that they had been coerced by police officers. Similarly, he often suggested that police had gone easy on prosecution witnesses who were willing to tell them what they wanted to hear.

One of Foreman's chief strategies was to divert attention away from the defendant onto himself, the police, the opposing witnesses, or society itself. Foreman was quoted as saying, "You should never allow the defendant to be tried. Try someone else—the husband, the lover, the police, or, if the case has social implications, society generally. But never the defendant" (Dorman 1969, 1). During his trials, Foreman often directed attention to red herrings, which seemed at the time to be significant but often had little to do with the case.

In 1964, Foreman successfully employed this strategy in his defense of John Whitfield Bonds, a forty-two-year-old man who had shot a fifteen-year-old named William John Walden III in front of a grocery store; at the time, the trial was the longest in the state's history. Foreman portrayed Walden as a juvenile delinquent and used psychiatric analysis of an essay

Walden had written in the seventh grade to show that Walden was deeply troubled. Foreman advanced Bonds's seemingly contradictory defenses that the killing had been an accident but had been committed in self-defense. During a two-hour closing argument in which he seemingly put society as a whole on trial, Foreman sobbed convulsively at times but ended by quoting from Sir Walter Scott's *Lady of the Lake* (Dorman 1969, 26).

Similarly, in defending Mrs. Virginia Deane Thomson in the killing of her husband, Foreman accused Mr. Thomson of having tried to put out a contract on her, of sexual deviance, and of abuse of his wife and of pets. In his summation to the jury, Foreman said, "The Almighty intended Arthur Francis Thomas to die. Perhaps he died that others might live in peace. He lived by force, and he died by force and violence" (Dorman 1969, 271).

Although he lost a case to District Attorney A. C. Winborn, who was also known for his fine closing arguments, Foreman had a stenographer copy down Winborn's closing, and Foreman memorized it. In the next case, he caught Winborn off guard by telling jurors word for word in advance what Winborn planned to say and leaving him to improvise unsuccessfully (Dorman 1969, 141).

Although he frequently quoted the Bible and a host of other great works of literature, Foreman never lost the common touch. Thus, in defending individuals accused of distributing obscene literature, Foreman told jurors that prosecutors cut the defendants out of the herd "to be branded and barbequed" but that, although the prosecutors were asking for a barbecue, "they haven't given you enough firewood" (Dorman 1969, 284).

Foreman earned a reputation for aggressiveness, and, on several occasions, Foreman was challenged to fisticuffs in the courtroom by prosecuting attorneys. On one occasion, after likening two lawmen, Kern and Klevenhagen, and an associate (Kain) to the Ku Klux Klan for torturing a defendant into confessing, Foreman was physically beaten by the lawmen in the courtroom after the jury announced a not guilty verdict. On another occasion, he talked a woman defendant out of shooting him by saying, "You don't want to shoot me, honey. I'm the only one who can get you off" (Dorman 1969, 212–213).

Ironically, Foreman's defendants are often the most aggrieved with him. A Foreman biographer explained that he enraged some by his high fees, some by his contemptuous treatment, and some by the fact that he had them plead insane as a way of avoiding the death penalty (Dorman 1969, 213). Foreman, who had shown a proclivity for making money before he ever entered the legal profession, died a multimillionaire with a great deal of property. He was known for accepting insurance policies, ranches, and jewelry from his clients—on one occasion, he even accepted circus elephants. At one time, Foreman owned more than forty cars, all of which he had received in payment from clients (Draper 1994). Foreman said, "I don't represent wealthy clients. If they weren't poor when they came to me, they are when they leave." Further indicating that his fees exacted a rough form of justice (albeit somewhat contradicting the view that defendants are innocent until proven guilty), Foreman once said that, "My fee is my client's punishment" (Dorman 1969, 60).

Despite his love of money, Foreman claimed to turn down divorce cases when he thought the couple could be reconciled. On occasion, his own insults apparently drove the couple to defend one another and reconcile. When a woman answered his query about why she wanted a divorce by saying, "I'm just not happy," Foreman saved her marriage by responding, "You don't need a lawyer! You need a pharmacist! You'll never find someone who treats you as well as this man does! Now get out of my office!" (Draper 1994).

Foreman's most controversial case may have been his defense of James Earl Ray for the assassination of Dr. Martin Luther King Jr. in Memphis, Tennessee. After consulting with Ray for more than fifty hours, Foreman was convinced that he was guilty and that a jury was likely to give Ray the death penalty. Although he convinced Ray to take a ninety-nine-year sentence in a plea bargain, Ray subsequently claimed—a claim that Foreman later disputed and for which he could find no evidence—that he was simply a pawn in a much larger conspiracy.

Through most of his career, Foreman was a sole practitioner who relied on but one solitary secretary for permanent support. He did, however, often share cases with other counselors, especially if his interest waned in a case or he found that his client was unwilling to let him run the show. In about 1976, Foreman took on some partners, including Dick and Mike DeGuerin, who have gone on to make solid reputations as criminal lawyers in their own right, but relationships were often rocky, and a number of his partners set out on their own.

Foreman was married twice. He and his first wife divorced. He married his second wife, Marguerite Obert, a native German, in 1957, a year after he met her on an overseas trip. Foreman had an adopted son by his first marriage, William Pinckney Foreman, and a daughter by his second marriage. Foreman died of cardiac arrest at Methodist Hospital in Houston in 1988.

—*John R. Vile*

SOURCES AND SUGGESTIONS FOR FURTHER READING

Barron, James. "Percy Foreman, Texas Lawyer, 86: Defended the Assassin of Dr. King." *New York Times*, 16 August 1988.

Dorman, Michael. *King of the Courtroom: Percy Foreman for the Defense*. New York: Delacorte Press, 1969.

Draper, Robert. "The Great Defenders." *Texas Monthly*, January 1994, 96.

FORTAS, ABE

(1910–1982)

ABE FORTAS HAD THE TALENT to be among the twentieth century's most influential lawyers and backroom policymakers, but instead his belief that he was beyond the rules led him to be remembered as the only Supreme Court justice ever to be forced to resign from the bench.

Fortas grew up as a marginalized Jewish boy in Memphis, Tennessee, where he was born on June 19, 1910. During this childhood and his education both at Southeastern (now Rhodes) College and Yale Law School, Fortas displayed remarkable intuitive genius, which was tempered by his realization that in anti-Semitic times he had to downplay his status as a Jew in order to get ahead. In addition, Fortas internalized the belief that holding onto one political or ideological philosophy would be a detriment, as it would limit his personal ambitions. All of this created a man lacking in strong ideological beliefs, but rather with a view of being able to mold himself to those around him to realize his personal ambitions.

ABE FORTAS
Ehrenhaft/Collection of the Supreme Court of the United States

Fortas's legal mentors at Yale Law School, who helped mold his legal philosophy, included such legendary professors as Walton Hamilton, Wes Sturges, THURMAN ARNOLD, and William O. Douglas. These professors, especially Douglas, believed that law was not an end unto itself; instead, it was a mechanism through which positive social change could occur. One of

Douglas's pet projects while at Yale was the integration of the study of law and business, as he began a curriculum taught in conjunction with Harvard Business School. While Fortas was at Yale, the Great Depression gripped the world, and Douglas's integrative law-business curriculum became increasingly important, as many viewed it as the avenue through which the economic downturn could be understood and solved. When Douglas went to Washington to begin work on President Franklin Roosevelt's New Deal, he sought a capable student to take over his law/business program, and that student was Fortas. Fortas began to learn about Douglas's socioeconomic policy by doing casework in Chicago while still a student at Yale, as he studied the impact of the overextension of consumer credit by employers.

During the summer after his graduation from law school in 1933, Fortas received an offer from his former professor, Wes Sturges, to work for the newly created Agricultural Adjustment Agency (AAA) in the legal department. Fortas began his legal work in the canned peach business, and though lacking in specific knowledge of the field, he excelled in the process of setting prices and output for the government to such an extent that he became the symbol of the young revolutionary New Dealers who were making policy. It was in this service that Fortas distinguished himself from other New Dealers by using pragmatic views rather than ideological theory to solve the problems of the Great Depression in this field. In this initial venture into commercial reform, Fortas also displayed the full confidence that any societal problem could be solved using hard work and logical thinking. All of this, combined with his deft ability to mediate a compromise position between opposing sides, displayed the kinds of skills that would guide the rest of Fortas's career.

After capably serving the AAA through the summer of 1934, Fortas joined his old mentor William O. Douglas at the newly created Securities and Exchange Commission (SEC), where the two men investigated the abuses of the protective committees that were formed to resolve bankruptcy cases. Since Fortas's responsibilities at the SEC were less demanding than those at the AAA, he was also able to commute back and forth between Washington and New Haven, Connecticut, where he started his teaching career at Yale Law School. Although he was skeptical of the activities of big business in this study, Fortas was pragmatic enough to understand that for the U.S. economy to function effectively, Wall Street should not be hamstrung by strict government regulation.

In 1938, after resigning from teaching at Yale, Fortas returned to work full time as the assistant director of the SEC's public utilities division, where he regulated the large utilities conglomerates that had been broken up by the Public Utility Holding Company Act of 1935. While at this job, Fortas's role was essentially to make the extremely powerful utilities companies justify their existence or face Section 11 of the SEC code, known as the "death sentence," which empowered the SEC to dissolve companies whose existence was superfluous. Here Fortas followed the general New Deal retreat from planning economics toward the restoration of the natural competition necessary for capitalism to flourish.

When his mentor, William O. Douglas, was appointed to the Supreme Court in 1939, Fortas accepted a position in the Department of the Interior under Harold Ickes as the general counsel to the Public Works Administration in 1939. After some bureaucratic shuffling, Fortas was named counsel to the Bituminous Coal Division, where he worked to reduce competition in the industry by regulating the price of different types of coal. In the spring of 1941, Fortas was named chairman of the newly formed Division of Power, which represented the Department of the Interior on matters of public power. Here, Fortas battled once more against both the powerful utilities conglomerates and members of the National Power Policy Committee (NPPC), who were less enthusiastic toward government control over public power. Because of his excellent work in all of these positions, when Jack Dempsey resigned as undersecretary of the interior in January 1942, Fortas was appointed to the position, becoming the number two person in the department at the young age of thirty-two. Despite the conservative direction taken by much of Roosevelt's government during wartime, Fortas continued to pursue a liberal course, pressing for land reform and the support of civil liberties, as shown by his opposition to martial law in Hawaii and internment of Japanese-Americans in the western United States. During his time at the Department of the Interior, Fortas also became interested in socioeconomic reform for Puerto Rico, an island whose people he would champion for the rest of his life. Fortas's main role at the department, though, was to coordinate the war production effort, including mediating a well-reported conflict with powerful United Mine Workers union leader John L Lewis. After the death of President Roosevelt in April 1945, Fortas decided to quit government service and explore the benefits of private practice. Fortas's record as a New Deal bureaucrat from 1933 to 1945 had been exemplary, embodying the values of hard work, progressive thinking, and social conscience. For him, such bureaucratic work was a good fit as, lacking a solid ideological base from which to operate, Fortas did his best work in a legal arena. Once he left governmental service for public work, this lack of an ideological center, combined with his pragmatic and mediating skills, would serve him well in private legal practice. However, they were in direct opposition to the progressive ideology that he had pursued while working in the New Deal.

After leaving the Interior Department, Fortas, along with two other government lawyers, Thurman Arnold and Paul Porter, launched the law firm of Arnold, Fortas & Porter. Specializing in corporate law, this firm assisted businesses in navigating their way through the web of government bureaucracy. Only five years after the founding of the firm, Arnold, Fortas & Porter had a client list that would be the envy of any corporate law firm, with notable clients such as Lever Brothers, Philip Morris, American Broadcasting Company, and Pan American Airways.

Fortas reveled in his new role as a Washington lawyer for corporate interests, aggressively representing the interests of his clients. Rather than just representing his clients, Fortas became an overt advocate of their firm's interests, never challenging their assumptions or goals. Frequently, their actions were just the opposite of the New Deal philosophy he had once espoused. Seeking to justify this change of direction, Fortas rationalized his position by compartmentalizing his life, claiming that his legal career was a separate entity from his political beliefs.

Perhaps out of a feeling of guilt because of his abandonment of progressive ideals, during the late 1940s and early 1950s, Fortas's firm was one of the few law firms to take on the courageous pro bono defense of Americans accused by the government loyalty boards of being Communists. The firm took the case of Dorothy Bailey, a personnel expert in the U.S. Employment Service who was accused of being a Communist, all the way to the Supreme Court, only to lose because of the conservative direction of that body. When Senator Joseph McCarthy accused Johns Hopkins University government professor Owen Lattimore of being a Communist, it was Abe Fortas who defended him. After waging a vigorous public relations campaign for him and preparing Lattimore for his grilling by the Senate investigating committee, the firm was able to clear the professor of perjury charges. Although Fortas's defense of these people was courageous, it also gave him even more publicity, thus allowing him to make an even better living.

Fortas's firm also did progressive work on behalf of such causes as protection of animal rights; changing legal codes for the mentally ill, thus making it easier for defendants to prove their innocence by reason of insanity; and improving conditions in Fortas's beloved Puerto Rico. Also, Fortas was counsel in the landmark Supreme Court case *Gideon v. Wainwright* (1963), which established by a unanimous decision that all those accused of a felony offense are entitled to an attorney, resulting in the creation of the position of public defender nationwide. These cases, like Fortas's pro bono defense of those before loyalty boards, showed that Fortas still had a progressive streak and social conscience from his days working on the New Deal. However, he drew criticism for his work on behalf of corporations such as tobacco giant Philip Morris.

While in private practice, Abe Fortas also increasingly spent his time as an advisor to those in power in Washington. Fortas's most powerful ally was Lyndon Johnson, whom Fortas had helped win a legal challenge to his nomination for the Senate and who later served as Senate majority leader, vice-president, then president after John F. Kennedy's assassination in 1963. This relationship, though based on a foundation of friendship and mutual respect, also served Fortas's business concerns, as Fortas used his influence with Johnson as a selling point to potential clients. As a result of this friendship, over Fortas's objections, Johnson appointed him to the Supreme Court in July 1965.

Fortas's performance as a Supreme Court justice was very representative of his overall legal ideology. Fortas was a realist on the Court, basing his decisions on his calculations of their social consequences rather than his personal ideology. A majority of Fortas's decisions while on the Court were liberal, as he protected the rights of criminals, freedom of speech, and the right to privacy. Typical of these decisions was *In re Gault* (1967), which created a set of Bill of Rights protections for juveniles in criminal cases. Conversely, Fortas's decisions in the business law area were strongly pro-business, following his work as a corporate lawyer rather than in the New Deal. Unlike many of his contemporaries on the bench, Fortas did not view his decisions as a finite body of legal thought, rather seeing them as tools by which U.S. society could be improved. Overall, Fortas's performance as a justice was considered above average, although liberals felt he was too conservative on business issues and conservatives despised his consistent representation on the liberal Earl Warren bloc on social issues.

In June of 1968, Fortas was nominated to become chief justice, replacing the retiring chief justice, Earl Warren. Republicans and conservative Southern Democrats decided to hold up the Senate's confirmation of the nomination in the hopes that the Republican Richard Nixon would win the presidency in November 1968 and appoint a more conservative chief justice. Days of investigations by the Senate Judiciary Committee uncovered that Fortas had continued to serve as a private political advisor for President Johnson on such issues as the Vietnam War, civil rights, and various speeches as well as bills for congressional consideration. The nomination died when the Senate uncovered that Fortas had accepted money from former legal clients to teach a seminar at American University law school in juvenile justice. Because of the inability to break a Senate filibuster on the nomination, Fortas withdrew his name, Warren returned to his seat for a year, and eventually Richard Nixon replaced him with Warren Earl Burger, thus changing the entire ideological direction of the Court.

Fortas's legal ethics came under attack in the late spring of 1969 when it was uncovered that he had accepted money from a foundation dealing with civil rights for juveniles in Florida that had been established by industrialist

Louis Wolfson, who had been indicted by the SEC for stock irregularities. When the Nixon administration worked with members of the press to leak accounts of this relationship to the public, Fortas resigned from the Court in disgrace, moving the Court further in the conservative direction.

After his resignation from the Supreme Court, Fortas returned to his roots as a private lawyer. Although members of his old law firm would not take him back, he set up a small law firm in Georgetown, far from the arena of power and influence that he had once dominated. In his final years, Fortas advised some of his former clients on antitrust and securities matters and remained involved in matters of constitutional law, contributing law review articles on subjects such as antitrust law, civil liberties, the patent system, and criminal justice. Fortas even returned once to the Supreme Court, arguing a case before the Court in 1982 regarding a dispute between two of Puerto Rico's political parties involving succession of power in the legislature. Unfortunately, he did not live to learn that he had won this case, as he died of a burst aortic valve on April 5, 1982.

Abe Fortas's career was one of missed opportunity and unsuited position for a man of his legal skills. Among his contemporaries, Fortas was a lawyer of unmatched brilliance, and when he put his intelligence to good use, most vividly during the New Deal, the results were spectacular. When Fortas's legal work was motivated by monetary interests, such as in his corporate work at Arnold, Fortas & Porter, the results were better for his pocketbook than for the nation as a whole. And when he was trapped into a position on the Supreme Court for which he was not suited due to his lack of an ethical center and ideological backbone, the results were tragic.

—*Bruce Murphy and Scott Featherman*

Sources and Suggestions for Further Reading

Kalman, Laura. *Abe Fortas: A Biography*. New Haven: Yale University Press, 1990.
Murphy, Bruce Allen. *Fortas: The Rise and Ruin of a Supreme Court Justice*. New York: William Morrow, 1988.

GINSBURG, RUTH BADER

(1933–)

RUTH BADER GINSBURG IS best known as the lawyer and litigator primarily responsible for raising the issue of equal rights for women to the level of constitutional principle. She was "a critical participant in the Court's dialogue about the role of women in society and their status in the law, and she awakened the Court's conscience about the meaning of equality" (*Report* 1993, 5). Her imprint can be found on virtually every gender equity case decided by the Supreme Court during the 1970s. When, on June 14, 1993, President William Jefferson Clinton nominated Ginsburg to be an associate justice of the Supreme Court, he spoke of her "pioneering work on behalf of the women of this country." Having been a successful advocate and the victorious counsel of record before the Supreme Court in the first handful of gender discrimination suits, Ginsburg was, Clinton remarked, "to the women's movement what Thurgood Marshall was to the movement for the rights of African-Americans."

RUTH BADER GINSBURG
Collection of the Supreme Court of the United States

Ruth Bader Ginsburg was born Joan Ruth Bader into a Jewish family in Brooklyn, New York, on March 15, 1933. She was the second daughter of Nathan Bader, a garment manufacturer and salesman, and Cecelia Amster Bader, a homemaker. Ginsburg was raised in Brooklyn, in a nation mired in the Great Depression, in a world that discriminated against Jews and women. She received her diploma from James Madison High School in 1950. Four years later Ginsburg obtained the B.A. degree, graduating Phi Beta Kappa and "with high honors in government and distinction in all subjects," from Cornell University in Ithaca, New York. That same year, she married Martin D. Ginsburg, who had just completed his first year at Harvard Law School. (Her husband later become a well-respected lawyer and law professor at Georgetown University Law Center.) When the military required the services of her husband, the family relocated to Oklahoma. There, as a clerk-typist in a Social Security office, Ginsburg experienced firsthand discrimination in the workplace: Because of her "pregnant condition," she was denied the opportunity for promotion. The memory of that injustice later sparked her accomplishments in the field of women's rights.

After two years in Oklahoma—and the birth of her first child—Ginsburg matriculated at Harvard Law School in 1956. There, she experienced discrimination in education firsthand. Women were denied access to the old periodicals room in the library, for example. In the classroom, women were called upon more often than were men. "It wasn't harassment as much as it was fun and games: Let's call on the woman for comic relief," Ginsburg explained (Friedman 1994, 12). The dean of the law school, ERWIN GRIS-WOLD, even went so far as to ask the women students how they could justify taking up a classroom seat that could be occupied by a man (Gilbert and Moore 1981, 156). Ginsburg responded by being named to the law review. Following two years at Harvard, Ginsburg, for financial and family reasons, transferred to Columbia Law School, where she served on law review—the first person to be named to both Harvard and Columbia law reviews—and was named a Kent Scholar. She earned the LL.B. (J.D.) in 1959, finishing first in her class. That same year she was admitted to the New York bar.

Despite all of her academic successes, Ginsburg continued to face discrimination. Supreme Court justice Felix Frankfurter turned her down for a clerkship "simply because he wasn't ready to hire a woman" (Kaplan and Cohn 1993, A1). The legendary federal judge Learned Hand refused to offer her a clerkship because he feared that his "salty" language might be offensive to a woman (Margolick 1993, 29). Nevertheless, Ginsburg was able to secure employment from Edmund L. Palmieri of the U.S. District Court for the Southern District of New York, for whom she clerked from 1959 to 1961. In 1961, Ginsburg was admitted to the bars of the U.S. District Courts for the Southern and Eastern Districts of New York. The following year she was permitted to practice before the U.S. Court of Appeals for the Second Circuit.

In 1961, Ginsburg became a research associate and, one year later, associate director of Columbia Law School's Project on International Procedure, where her assignment was to study and write about Sweden's procedural system and the practices of Scandinavian countries with respect to international judicial assistance. In 1963, Ginsburg joined the faculty of Rutgers University Law School as an assistant professor. As a professor she quickly established herself as a leading expert on gender discrimination law. Ginsburg rose to associate professor three years later; she attained the rank of full professor in 1969. It was during this professorship—in 1967—that she was admitted to the bar of the U.S. Supreme Court. In 1972, Ginsburg became the first female professor at Columbia Law School, where she taught until 1980.

While on the faculty at Columbia, Ginsburg became the first director of the Women's Rights Project of the American Civil Liberties Union (ACLU). This project was soon recognized as the leading women's rights advocacy group in the courts. Between 1973 and 1980, Ginsburg served as general legal counsel to the ACLU, which participated in more than sixty gender-bias cases before the Supreme Court. In 1975, she was admitted to practice before the District of Columbia Court, the U.S. District Court for the District of Columbia, and the U.S. Courts of Appeals for the Fifth and District of Columbia Circuits.

Ginsburg's only courtroom experiences were between 1971 and 1979. Although her tenure was brief, her contributions were large. During those years, Ginsburg practiced exclusively at the federal level and almost entirely in appellate courts. Although she was the author of numerous amicus curiae briefs filed in state courts and was regularly consulted by ACLU attorneys in matters pending in state courts, Ginsburg never appeared as an attorney in a state court. Moreover, although she initiated several federal district court actions, most of these "first-instance" cases were resolved at the pretrial stage. The two cases she personally argued in the district court were before special three-judge panels. Thus, not once during her legal career did Ginsburg argue to a jury. She did, however, have significant appellate experience: In fifteen cases she was the attorney of record for a party, and she was the sole or principal author of many amicus curiae briefs filed in appellate tribunals.

The bulk of Ginsburg's legal work addressed the equal protection clause of the Fourteenth Amendment and gender discrimination. She developed a brilliant legal strategy that included using men as plaintiffs in gender discrimination suits. This tactic was designed to persuade the all-male justices that gender-biased laws—discriminating against either men or women—

Leslie Abramson

Although some lawyers try to avoid murder cases, Leslie Abramson clearly thrives on them. As she writes, "In homicides you are learning about human nature at its most explosive" (Abramson and Flaste 1997, 60). Born and raised in New York, Abramson attended Queens College and went to law school at the University of California at Los Angeles. She then worked for seven years in a variety of capacities in California as a public defender before going into private practice in 1976.

In a book that she wrote, Abramson details work on behalf of parents accused of killing their children, of individuals charged with committing murder in the course of other felonies, and of women accused of killing their husbands. In a highly emotional case in which the district attorney had effectively sought to convict her client in public, Abramson was able to show that Dr. Khalid Parwez, accused of killing his eleven-year-old son, carving up his body, and leaving it in a dumpster, was on duty at a hospital as an obstetrician when the murder occurred and that the more likely murderer was Parwez's brother Sattar, who had fled to his native Pakistan.

Abramson believes that a defense attorney has an obligation to defend clients, regardless of whether they believe them to be guilty or innocent; she argues that a lawyer defending a client has no more cause to question the client's guilt than does a doctor who is about to operate (Abramson and Flaste 1997, 150). Abramson believes that solid preparation and knowledge of scientific evidence is often critical in winning verdicts. In an early case that she took while in private practice and whose outcome was likened to a Perry Mason story, Abramson was able to use neutron activation analysis to trace the bullets used in a murder pinned on her client (Shirelle Crane) to her client's accuser, Frank Ruopoli. Abramson is more skeptical of eyewitness testimony, noting that, contrary to its often positive reputation, it "is inherently unreliable, the human mind being what it is" (Abramson and Flaste 1997, 149).

Abramson acknowledges being aggressive in the courtroom, believing that jurors will respect an attorney who goes all out in a client's defense. Abramson also considers closing arguments to be important and believes that she does them well (Abramson and Flaste 1997, 14). The only major case in which Abramson's client was sentenced to death involved the conviction of Ricky Sanders for participation in the shooting of eleven people, four of whom died, in a walk-in freezer in a Bob's Big Boy restaurant in Los Angeles.

Abramson served as a commentator for ABC News during the O. J. Simpson murder trial. She had been through a similar media circus (which has persuaded her that cameras do not belong in the courtroom) in defending Eric Menendez, who along with his brother Lyle, killed his parents with a shotgun. Although evidence of longtime parental sexual abuse did not prevent the brothers from being convicted of first-degree murder, they were sentenced to life in prison rather than being given the death penalty.

The Los Angeles Criminal Courts Bar Association has twice named Abramson its Trial Lawyer of the Year, and Abramson was the first woman to serve as president of the California Attorneys for Criminal Justice.

REFERENCE

Abramson, Leslie, with Richard Flaste. *The Defense Is Ready: Life in the Trenches of Criminal Law*. New York: Simon & Schuster, 1997.

were incompatible with the great principle of equal protection under the law.

Beginning in 1971, Ginsburg participated either by direct argument or by assisting in the preparation of the legal brief in nine cases brought before the Supreme Court. In six cases she participated by authoring the legal brief and presenting argument; she was victorious in five. In three other cases Ginsburg prepared the legal brief; her position was affirmed in two, and an adverse lower court decision vacated in the other. These cases constitute much of the significant gender equity litigation of the twentieth century and had great constitutional and societal significance. And it was Ginsburg who "virtually steered" the Court to its current jurisprudence on the subject.

Until the 1970s, the equal protection clause of the Fourteenth Amendment offered little protection for women. Gender classifications were routinely upheld so long as they were rationally related to a legitimate government objective. Under this standard—known as the "rational basis" test—little scrutiny was involved. Thus, the justices had held, for example, that women could be barred from the legal profession (1873), had no constitutional right to vote (1875), and could be disqualified from serving on a jury (1961). By the 1970s, changing social and economic conditions demanded a reassessment of laws that discriminated against women based on stereotypical notions of women's roles and capabilities. *Reed v. Reed* (1971) provided that opportunity.

The Idaho statute challenged in *Reed* declared that between persons "equally entitled" to administer a decedent's estate, "males must be preferred to females." Ginsburg was the principal author of the legal brief for Sally Reed. Her primary argument was that the Court should analyze gender-based classifications in the same manner that it analyzed race-based classifications. Race-based classifications were upheld only if the state had a compelling state interest in the classification, and the classification was necessary to accomplish that interest. Under this higher standard—known as the "strict scrutiny" test—much examination was involved. "Legislative discrimination grounded on sex, for purposes unrelated to any biological differences between the sexes, ranks with legislative discrimination based on race, another congenital, unalterable trait of birth, and merits no greater judicial deference," her brief noted. Although the Court was unwilling to accept Ginsburg's primary argument, it did accept her alternate position— the statute failed the "rational basis" test because it lacked "the constitutionally required fair and reasonable relation to a legitimate state interest." Thus *Reed* was the first occasion on which the Court held a gender-based classification inconsistent with the equal protection clause.

Buoyed yet undeterred, Ginsburg continued to encourage the Court to elevate gender to a "suspect classification." In *Frontiero v. Richardson*

(1973), in which she was responsible for both the writing of the brief and the oral argument, she came quite close: Four justices agreed with her, one short of the requisite five needed to establish a precedent. Nevertheless, the Court held that married women in the military were entitled to the same benefits as married men. Her opposing counsel in this case was Erwin N. Griswold, then solicitor general of the United States and former dean of the Harvard Law School—the same man who, some years earlier, had questioned Ginsburg on the role of women in the legal profession. *Reed* and *Frontiero*, read together, intimated that gender was a quasi-suspect category, deserving some form of heightened scrutiny.

Ginsburg's only defeat before the high court was *Kahn v. Shevin* (1975), in which the justices sustained a real property tax exemption for widows but not widowers. In this case, in which she was the principal author of the brief and presented oral argument, the Court reasoned that women faced greater financial difficulty when their spouses died than men did when their spouses died. Ginsburg later remarked that this holding was indicative of the widely held proposition that women needed a "boost . . . because they [could not] make it on their own" (Ginsburg 1988, 25).

The following year, Ginsburg altered her methodology. Instead of requesting that gender be elevated to a "suspect classification," she argued, per her brief and in oral argument in *Wienberger v. Wiesenfield* (1975), that gender should be placed in a yet-to-be-recognized intermediate level of scrutiny. While the Court did not *officially* adopt her argument, it did strike down a section of federal law that granted survivor's benefits to widows and minor children but not to widowers. The fact that men were more likely to be employed was not a "compelling reason" to distinguish between men and women, the justices reasoned. Thus, without so acknowledging, the Court was embracing Ginsburg's argument. And, in fact, the Court would formally adopt an intermediate standard of review for gender discrimination the following year, in *Craig v. Boren* (1976). Although Ginsburg was not directly involved in this case, she did file an amicus curiae brief and advised the attorney of record of the pointlessness of requesting "strict scrutiny." Her advice was well heeded.

During the late 1970s, Ginsburg also participated in a number of other important cases: *Edwards v. Healy* (1975) and its companion case *Taylor v. Louisiana* (1975), in which the Court struck down a Louisiana law exempting from jury duty all women except those who volunteered; *Turner v. Department of Employment Security* (1975), in which the justices declared unconstitutional a Utah provision that denied to pregnant women certain unemployment benefits on the presumption that pregnant women were unable to work; *Goldfarb v. Califano* (1977), in which the Court concluded that a federal law that provided Social Security benefits for widows based on the earnings of deceased husbands, but no benefits for widowers unless they had received half of their financial support from their deceased spouses, constituted invidious discrimination against female wage earners; and *Duren v. Missouri* (1979), in which the Court struck down a Missouri statute that permitted women to opt out of jury service and which had, in practice, produced jury venues averaging less than 15 percent female. *Duren* was Ginsburg's last participation as a lawyer before the Court.

The following year, President Jimmy Carter nominated Ginsburg for a seat on the U.S. Court of Appeals for the District of Columbia circuit. The Senate confirmed her on June 30, 1980, by a vote of 99 to 1. On June 14, 1993, President Clinton nominated Ginsburg to succeed Justice Byron White on the Supreme Court. Her nomination sailed through the Senate Judiciary Committee by an 18–0 vote. The full Senate confirmed her appointment on August 3, 1993, by a vote of 96 to 3. Ginsburg thus became the second woman to sit on the Court and the first Jewish justice since Arthur J. Goldberg's retirement in 1965. After joining the high court, Ginsburg continued to interpret the Constitution as a prohibition against artificial barriers to equal opportunity for all persons. To witness, she authored the majority opinion in *United States v. Virginia* (1996), in which the justices declared Virginia's exclusion of capable women from certain educational opportunities violative of the equal protection clause. "State actors," she wrote, "may not exclude qualified individuals based on 'fixed notions concerning the roles and abilities of males and females.'"

During her years as an advocate, judge, and justice, Ginsburg visited several faculties, including New York University School of Law, Harvard Law School, University of Amsterdam, University of Strasbourg, the Salzburg Seminar in American Studies, Aspen Institute, and Dickinson College of Law.

Ginsburg has received numerous awards and honors, including recognition as one of the most outstanding law professors in the United States from *Time* magazine in 1977; the Outstanding Teacher of Law Award from the Society of American Law Teachers in 1979; the Woman of Achievement Award from Barnard College in 1980; and the Margaret Brent Women Lawyers of Achievement Award from the American Bar Association Commission on Women in the Profession in 1993. In addition, Ginsburg became the first woman recognized in the "Gallery of Greats" at Columbia University School of Law, when her alma mater placed her portrait next to those of former justices Charles Evans Hughes and Harlan Fiske Stone. She also received honorary degrees from more than a dozen universities or law schools.

During her career, Ginsburg has had numerous publications. She co-authored or edited four books, including *Civil Procedure in Sweden* (1965),

Swedish Code of Judicial Procedure (1968), Business Regulation in the Common Market Nations (1969), and Text, Cases, and Materials on Sex-Based Discrimination (1974). She authored or coauthored three monographs, including "The Legal Status of Women under Federal Law: A Report to the U.S. Commission on Civil Rights" and "Constitutional Aspects of Sex-Based Discrimination," both published in 1974. In addition, Ginsburg has had over seventy articles published in respected national and international journals. A fair number of Ginsburg's lectures have also been published.

—*Richard A. Glenn*

Sources and Suggestions for Further Reading

Ayer, Eleanor H. *Ruth Bader Ginsburg: Fire and Steel on the Supreme Court.* New York: Macmillan, 1994.

Friedman, Jeanette. "Ruth Bader Ginsburg: A Rare Interview." *Lifestyles*, March 1994.

Gilbert, Lynn, and Gaylen Moore. *Particular Passions: Talks with Women Who Have Shaped Our Times.* New York: Crown Books, 1981.

Ginsburg, Ruth B. "Biographical Data." Washington: Public Affairs Office, U.S. Supreme Court, 1993.

———. "Remarks on Women Becoming Part of the Constitution." *Journal of Law and Inequality* 6 (1988): 17.

Kaplan, David A., and Bob Cohn. "A Frankfurter, Not a Hot Dog." *Newsweek*, 28 June 1993.

Margolick, David. "Trial by Adversity Shapes Jurist's Outlook." *New York Times*, 25 June 1993.

Report on the Nomination of Judge Ruth Bader Ginsburg to the United States Supreme Court. Washington: Alliance for Justice, 1993.

U.S. Senate Committee on the Judiciary. *Hearings on the Nomination of Judge Ruth Bader Ginsburg, to be Associate Justice of the Supreme Court.* 103d Congress, 1st sess., July 20–23, 1993.

GREENBERG, JACK

(1925–)

JACK GREENBERG IS AN AT-torney who early in life deter-mined that African-American citizens' civil rights and liberties must receive full constitutional protection. His principles have remained constant. Over the years he has initiated changes in judicial constitutional interpreta-tion and has submitted new remedies for eliminating inequi-ties. Greenberg was born in New York City in 1925. His parents, Bertha Rosenberg Greenberg and certified public accountant Max Greenberg, were immigrants, re-spectively, from Romania and Poland. Greenberg said, among other people, his parents were part of a "mosaic" of factors that influenced his attitude through-out his life. He grew up in a closely knit family in Brook-lyn and Bronx neighborhoods.

JACK GREENBERG

James Meredith (center) and his attorneys, Mrs. Constance Motley (left) and Jack Greenberg (right), pause briefly to talk with reporters in front of the Federal Courts Building, 28 September 1962. (Bettmann/Corbis)

Greenberg remembers no occasion during his boyhood when he saw dis-crimination against African-Americans (Greenberg 1994b, 46–53). He re-mained oblivious to flagrant violations of civil rights and liberties while at-tending Columbia University. During his service in the navy after graduating from Columbia with an A.B. degree in 1945, Greenberg became concerned about the rigidity with which the lowest-level positions were as-signed to African-Americans and his inability to convince superiors to pro-mote an African-American steward mate. It was his first experience in directly trying to change a racially biased system (Kluger 1975, 274; Greenberg 1994b, 42, 46–47).

Greenberg was named Harlan Fiske Stone scholar while a student at Columbia University Law School. Professor Walter Gelhorn, who taught civil rights courses, later recommended Greenberg for an assistant counsel position in the Legal Defense Fund (LDF) of the National Association for the Advancement of Colored People (NAACP). The professor was instrumental in shaping Greenberg's intense dedication to providing constitutional protections for African-Americans. After the young attorney's brief employment in the New York State Law Revision Commission, he entered his new position in the LDF office and served thirty-five years as a member of the legal staff (1949–1961) and later as director (1961–1984). His advocacy for civil rights in the United States and other countries never wavered (Kluger 1975, 274, 436, 437; Greenberg 1994b, 45, 588; see also Greenberg 1979a, 1983a, 1997b; and Greenberg and Shalit 1993).

After Greenberg was awarded his LL.B. in 1948, his legal skills were immediately put to the test in both trial and appellate cases. Three of the following trial cases illustrate his techniques and his determination to make constitutional law viable for African-Americans. For example, when African-American students were denied admission to a white university under Delaware's de jure segregation system, Greenberg was assigned his first important case, *Parker v. University of Delaware* (1950). He and local attorney Louis Redding gathered evidence to show discriminatory administrative policies and practices by submitting expert research findings and data on Delaware State College for Negroes that included a very limited curriculum, loss of accreditation, and a library with only one-tenth the number of books in the library of a white university of equivalent size. Greenberg exposed rampant discrimination against African-American college faculty members who were denied tenure-track opportunities afforded white counterparts and who were paid less than public school teachers. Greenberg and Redding visited the University of Delaware president, who appeared embarrassed about the segregated state university system. African-American witnesses feared reprisals for their cooperation in arguing against segregation. During the trial, white state attorneys denied that Delaware State College was a state institution, although all evidence proved the contrary. The state attorneys maintained that the African-American college provided educational opportunities equal to those available in white universities. Greenberg and Redding were amazed by these blatant lies. They asked the judge to visit African-American and white campuses and compare buildings and equipment; the judge found that the Delaware State College buildings were "shabby" and decrepit." The Greenberg-Redding plan worked. They celebrated a resounding victory when for the first time in our country a federal court ordered desegregation of university undergraduate students. The state did not appeal the case (Greenberg 1994b, 46, 88, 89; Kluger 1975, 289, 290).

Young attorney Greenberg was almost immediately counted among the inner circle of LDF director THURGOOD MARSHALL. At the same time, Greenberg declined an offer for a position in a major law firm because, unlike the law firm's cases and clientele, LDF clientele, civil rights issues, and their outcome were important to him. He also rejected an offer to teach at Rutgers University Law School because, as he later explained, he had engaged in "the action and thrill of actual combat in a cause I cared about" (Greenberg 1994b, 91, 92). His continued intense passion for civil rights is well documented (see Greenberg 1959a, 1959b, 1968, 1974b, 1975, 1979b, 1991, 1994a, 1997a).

The issues and Greenberg's pursuit of constitutional protections through the judicial system were so controversial that at times he was portrayed in the press as a "Boleshevik" and "the Jew Jack Greenberg" (Greenberg 1994b, 46). He was especially not welcomed by most whites when he worked on cases in the South, but he remained undeterred. Public school desegregation was among his top priorities. One of his first major cases, *Gebhart v. Belton* (1912), dealt with public school desegregation in Wilmington, Delaware. Greenberg and Redding were an effective team. Their clients included thirteen African-American and white students who traveled on five occasions to the Lafarque Clinic in New York, where experts performed research and presented evidence that illustrated the negative effects of segregation on children. The trial court decision was stunning because, for the first time in the United States, the court mandated desegregation of a white public school, which was required to enroll African-American students. Though it was not the perfect constitutional solution, it was a significant leap forward. During that period, Greenberg worked on several cases. LDF lawyers worked simultaneously on many school de jure segregation cases throughout the South. For instance, Greenberg and colleagues orchestrated the search for midwestern expert witnesses who would testify at the *Brown v. Topeka Board of Education* (1954) trial. The task was difficult. Prominent specialists turned down Greenberg's request. Dr. Karl Menninger of the renowned Menninger Clinic in Topeka, Kansas, ignored the request. Dr. Arnold Gunnar of the University of Minnesota eventually declined to participate as an expert witness. Within a few days of the trial, however, Greenberg finally found eight midwestern experts who agreed to testify (Kluger 1975, 274, 430, 442–449, 557; Greenberg 1994b, 134–138, 150).

Osmond Fraenkel

The American Civil Liberties Union (ACLU) has been one of the most influential advocacy groups in modern U.S. history. Founded in 1920 by social worker Roger Baldwin—who was an earlier co-founder of the American Union Against Militarism, which had a Civil Liberties Bureau—the ACLU continues as a non-profit organization whose fifty state affiliates and three hundred local chapters often take cases on behalf of individuals whose rights are threatened. The ACLU has been especially prominent in its defense of First Amendment freedoms (including the rights of American Nazis to engage in peaceful demonstrations) and of the right to privacy, often filing amicus curiae (friend of the court) briefs in cases in which it is not directly representing a client. Osmond Fraenkel served as general counsel of the ACLU from 1954 to 1977.

Beginning with *DeJonge v. Oregon* (1937), a case involving the successful defense of a Communist organizer against charges of "criminal syndicalism," Fraenkel presented twenty-six oral arguments before the U.S. Supreme Court and helped draft 103 briefs filed before that body (Walker 1990, 106). His cases included his defense of Japanese-Americans for violations of curfews during World War II; his defense on appeal of two of the African-American Scottsboro Boys accused of the rape of two white women; cases involving challenges to the Smith Act and its suppression of freedom of speech and associa-

tion; his defense of a birth control pamphlet and *Esquire* magazine against obscenity charges; and his defense of one's right to distribute pamphlets without a permit. Fraenkel said that he believed that "people should do whatever they wanted as long as they didn't hurt anyone else" (Margolick 1983). Fraenkel was a week away from his eighty-fifth birthday when he argued his last case before the U.S. Supreme Court (Walker 1990, photo insert, n.p.n.), and he continued his work as a lawyer until he was felled by a heart attack on his way to work at age ninety-four (Margolick 1983).

Born in New York City, Fraenkel (1888–1983) graduated from Harvard College and Columbia Law School. The author of an obituary noted that "the 'Osmond K. Fraenkel brief' became synonymous with clarity and conciseness" (Margolick 1983). Fraenkel authored more than one hundred articles and several books, including one about the historic *Sacco and Vanzetti* case, and he served from 1936 to 1951 as chair of the New York City Welfare Department Hearing Board.

References

Margolick, David. "Osmond K. Fraenkel Dies at 94; Former Counsel to the A.C.L.U." *New York Times*, 17 May 1983, B-6.

Walker, Samuel. *In Defense of American Liberties: A History of the ACLU*. 2d ed. Carbondale: Southern Illinois University Press, 1990.

Greenberg was an especially effective attorney in dealing with diverse issues on the trial and appellate levels. The LDF agenda eventually included cases dealing with discrimination against African-Americans in the workplace, businesses and government agencies that either denied services or provided inadequate services, and the judicial system itself. Greenberg recognized the necessity for a lawyer to engage in thorough research, to develop effective writing skills, to select witnesses carefully, and to find and submit, when appropriate, sociological data, surveys, and unique remedies. He phrased arguments so that judicial biases did not interfere with convincing and original approaches in legal reasoning. Nevertheless, although the trial court's decision in *Gebhart,* the Delaware public school desegregation case, was a major step forward, it fell short of ensuring full constitutional protection for African-American students. School desegregation cases required significant time and concentration for the preparation of briefs. The Supreme Court justices were independent minded. Greenberg worked with colleagues as they carefully crafted legal strategies that, among other considerations, addressed Justice Felix Frankfurter's constitutional frame of reference and the technical questions that he would be likely to pose. Greenberg's first experience of oral argument before the Supreme Court was exciting for the twenty-eight-year-old attorney (Kluger 1975, 557).

School desegregation cases were a priority for Greenberg, but his determination to fight legal battles for other constitutional rights was equally important from the beginning of his career. Almost immediately after joining the LDF, Marshall worked with Greenberg on a capital-punishment rape case in Florida, *Shepherd v. Florida.* The defendants and the African-American community itself were subjected to an atmosphere of terrorism. After the African-American defendants were convicted, the LDF entered the case, and Marshall assigned Greenberg the task of writing the petition for the writ of certiorari on appeal to the U.S. Supreme Court and later the brief. During the trial, Greenberg, who had diligently read dusty volumes containing old English cases to impress Justice Frankfurter, experienced sneezing fits (Greenberg 1994b, 94–99). For the second trial, Marshall and Greenberg found new witnesses, relied on a detective's evaluation of evidence entered in the first trial, conducted a public opinion poll that showed the impossibility of a fair trial in Lake County, and conducted investigations that proved illegal conduct of the sheriff and his deputies. In the evening during the preliminary motions process, Greenberg watched white hecklers drive around his hotel while blowing horns, waving Confederate flags, and carrying torches. One demonstrator wore a Ku Klux Klan robe. The next morning, the local press reported that the sheriff had killed one of the defendants and severely injured the other defendant, Walter Irvin. Terror prevailed. The Florida NAACP state secretary and his wife were killed by a bomb detonated at their home. The governor offered the severely injured Irvin a sentence of life in prison if he confessed to raping the white woman, but Irvin refused to plead guilty to something that he did not do. The trial itself was a sham, and the judge's rulings were bizarre. Testimony by African-American witnesses for the state was inaccurate. An African-American newspaper labeled one African-American witness as "a turncoat." Testimony by witnesses for Irvin was described as "not terribly powerful." Despite an unfair trial, Irvin received the death sentence. Much later, the Florida governor commuted Irvin's sentence (Greenberg 1994b, 134, 135, 140–145; Greenberg 1994c, 590–594). The tragedy of the trial left its mark on Greenberg. Afterward, his mission was directed toward convincing the legal community that the capital-punishment system in reality does not accomplish the goal of our constitutional framers (see Greenberg 1986, 1992, 1994c).

Greenberg, armed with supporting data, has strongly maintained that the U.S. judicial system in practice unevenly applies the death sentence against white and African-American criminals and is especially biased against African-Americans. Recognizing that proponents of death sentences are motivated by moral principles and/or the idea that the prospect of a death sentence deters crime, he urges supporters of those laws to examine "the hard facts of the actual American system of capital punishment." Yet after all of the years in explaining statistics and other facts, Greenberg remains an optimist. He believes that eventually the Supreme Court will consider evidence of long-term erratic and uneven applications of capital punishment laws and decide that the system itself fosters cruel and unusual punishment in violation of the Eighth Amendment (Greenberg 1986, 1677, 1679; see also Greenberg 1977, 1982).

Greenberg's style as a lawyer handling difficult cases has attracted admirers and detractors. Assessments of Greenberg as a practicing attorney range from "a frostiness to his exterior," "a first-rate analytical mind," to a "substratum of deep emotional commitment." Walter Gelhorn has said that his former student's record shows that Greenberg "can stand controversy and developing animosity" and has lauded his intellectual approach, which Gelhorn felt was the most appropriate technique for arguing civil rights cases in the South. Attorney Robert Carter noted that Greenberg "was obviously a very bright lawyer, though perhaps with more of an intellectual than emotional commitment to his tasks." Professor Louis Pollak explained that Greenberg's abstract manner reminded him of a surgeon. His demeanor was a form of "self-protection from the drain of emotional energy that his work could so easily cause . . ." Attorney and former colleague

Louis Redding, based on his close association with Greenberg, said that his friend is a private individual. Redding never doubted his "genuineness about the Negro cause" (Kluger 1975, 274, 436, 438, 439).

Flexibility is a major strength of Greenberg as an attorney. For example, he changed legal strategies over a period of time in school desegregation cases. In the early Wilmington school desegregation case, he argued convincingly that African-American students should attend neighborhood white schools rather than travel on a school bus sometimes up to thirty-mile round trips to their assigned African-American schools (Kluger 1975, 442, 443). Several years later, Director Greenberg approved a new desegregation remedy in the celebrated and controversial busing-for-desegregation case of *Swann v. Charlotte-Mecklenburg School Board* (1971). In a 1978 interview, Greenberg justified his radical change in strategies. When questioned about his arguments against racial classification of students for school assignments in earlier cases and later his arguments that supported racial classification for student assignments, Greenberg responded,

> It became apparent that centuries of racial discrimination had so imbedded segregation into society, human habit, into a variety of educational practices, and that resistance to integration was so deeply imbedded, so severe, and that devious methods were being used, as well as all sorts of other types of resistance, that the only way that you could undo the segregation . . . and have some objective standard against which performance could be measured was by making racial classifications for the purpose of abolishing discrimination. (Mauney 1978, 169)

In contrast to earlier arguments in *Monroe v. Board of Education of Jackson* (1968) and other cases, the legal strategy changed to remedies focused on percentages of African-Americans and whites enrolled in individual schools. Director Greenberg reminisced,

> Well, I really don't know when people first began thinking about that, and I might say that we don't disparage the virtue of the neighborhood schools. There is something to be said for it, but there is something to be said about a great many other values. [You must] look at the total picture, take into account all of the various factors, and decide whether whatever benefit neighborhood schools have outweighs disadvantages that they might present in some circumstances. (Mauney 1978, 169)

Greenberg promoted freedom of choice in his 1959 book *Race Relations and American Law* (Greenberg 1959a, 239) and earlier cases. During the 1978 interview, Greenberg said that he was asked the same question during oral argument in 1968. At that time he admitted to Justice William J. Brennan that if he had known when he proposed freedom of choice plans what he learned later, he would never have proposed freedom of choice (Greenberg 1994b, 383). He explained the change:

> I think people began to think of [freedom of choice] when they began to see that nothing was happening as a result of resistance, deviousness, settled habits, and things of that sort. So the only way that the pre-existing situation could change would be if some sort of benchmark was established. (Mauney 1978, 170)

Throughout his productive life as counsel and LDF director; as Columbia Law School professor and dean; in visiting professorships at Yale, Harvard, and Saint Louis University law schools; as consultant; as speaker; as recipient of honorary doctorates from Columbia University, Morgan State College, Central State College, and Lincoln University; and as author of articles and books, Greenberg has championed constitutional protections for African-American citizens (Greenberg 1991, 117n; Greenberg 1997, 129n; *Who's Who* 1998, 1671). Yet he balanced his unusually heavy schedule with responsibilities at home. As an attorney, his wife, Debby Greenberg, often was out of town, and husband and father Jack Greenberg "played a more than active role at home." Eventually, four of six children entered college, but they came home from time to time. Preparing dinners for his large family afforded an opportunity for chief cook Greenberg to develop expertise in the kitchen. Greenberg recalled that when "Debby called home from out of town, the kids, to her chagrin, usually seemed to be having a good time." She eventually returned to New York when she was appointed president of the Legal Action Center and later member of the Columbia Law School faculty (Greenberg 1994b, 428).

The U.S. Constitution is often described as a living and breathing document. Jack Greenberg has played key roles in challenging courts to adapt their constitutional interpretations to protect the rights of African-American citizens. At times he lamented how politicians in the legislative and executive branches sought to negate the accomplishments that guaranteed civil rights during his years as trial and appellate lawyer (see Greenberg 1983a, 1991, 1992, 1997a). He is a bold advocate for the elimination of grave injustices, both in the United States and in other countries. He was willing to find new legal approaches when old ones failed. His courage is well grounded in knowledge based on study, close observations, thoughtful analysis, and practice. Jack Greenberg remains a great American lawyer in every sense of the term.

—*Connie Mauney*

Brown v. Topeka Board of Education, 347 U.S. 489 (1954); 349 U.S. 294 (1955).

Gebhart v. Belton, 87 A. 2d 862 (Del.Ch. 1952); 91 A. 2d 137 (1953); 347 U.S. 483 (1954).

Greenberg, Jack. "Against the American System of Capital Punishment." *Harvard Law Review* 99 (1986): 1670–1680.

_____. "Burger Court and the Constitution: 15th Annual Columbia Law Symposium." *Columbia Journal of Law and Social Problems* 11 (1974a): 35–71.

_____. "Capital Punishment as a System." *Yale Law Journal* 91 (1992): 908–936.

_____. "Civil Rights Class Actions: Procedural Means of Obtaining Substance." *Arizona Law Review* 39 (1997a): 575–586.

_____. "Civil Rights Enforcement Activity of the Department of Justice." *Black Law Journal* 8 (1983a): 60–67.

_____. "A Crusader in the Court: Comments on the Civil Rights Movement." *University of Missouri-Kansas City Law Review* 63 (1994a): 207–227.

_____. *Crusaders in the Courts: How a Dedicated Band of Lawyers Fought for the Civil Rights Revolution.* New York: Basic Books, 1994b.

_____. "Death Penalty: Where Do We Go from Here?" *NLADA Briefcase* 34 (1977): 55–57.

_____. "Evolving Strategies in Civil Rights." *Suffolk University Law Review* 25 (1991): 117–128.

_____. "Foreword: Symposium Commemorating the 25th Anniversary of *Brown v. Board of Education*." *Howard Law Journal* 23 (1980): 1–133.

_____. "Litigation for Social Change: Methods, Limits, and Role in Democracy." *Record* 29 (1974b): 320–375.

_____. "The Philippines: A Country in Crisis—A Report by the Lawyers Committee for International Human Rights." *Columbia Human Rights Law Review* 15 (1983b): 69–129.

_____. *Race Relations and American Law.* New York: Columbia University Press, 1959a.

_____. "Race Relations and Group Interests in the Law." *Rutgers Law Review* 13 (1959b): 503–510.

_____. "Reflections on Leading Issues in Civil Rights Then and Now." *Notre Dame Law* 57 (1982): 625–641.

_____. "Someone Has to Translate Rights and Realities." *Civil Liberties Review* 2 (1975): 104–128.

_____. "South Africa and the American Experience." *New York Law Review* 54 (1979a): 3–18.

_____. "Supreme Court, Civil Rights, and Civil Dissonance." *Yale Law Journal* 77 (1968): 1520–1544.

_____. "A Tale of Two Countries, United States and South Africa." *Saint Louis University Law Journal* 41 (1997b):1291–1299.

_____. "War Stories: Reflections on Thirty-Five Years with the NAACP Legal Defense Fund." *Saint Louis University Law Journal* 38 (1994c): 587–603.

_____. "Widening Circles of Freedom?" *Human Rights* 8 (1979b): 1013.

Greenberg, Jack, Alexander Bickel, N. Lent, and C. Mitchell. "Education in a Democracy: The Legal and Practical Problems of School Busing: A Symposium." *Human Rights* 3 (1973):53–92.

Greenberg, Jack, and J. Himmelstein. "Varieties of Attack on the Death Penalty." *Crime and Delinquency* 15 (1969): 112.

Greenberg, Jack, and Anthony Shalit. "New Horizons for Human Rights: The European Convention, Court, and Commission of Human Rights." *Columbia Law Review* 63 (1963): 1384–1412.

Keyes v. Denver School District, 413 U.S. 189 (1973).

Kluger, Richard. *Simple Justice*. New York: Vintage Books, 1975.

Mauney, Connie. *Evolving Equality*. Knoxville: University of Tennessee Bureau of Public Administration, 1978.

Monroe v. Board of Education of Jackson, 391 U.S. 450 (1968).

Parker v. University of Delaware, 75 A. 2d 225 (Del. 1950).

Shepherd v. Florida, 339 U.S. 282 (1950); 341 U.S. 50 (1951).

Sobel, Richard. "A Colloquy with Jack Greenberg about *Brown v. Board of Education*: Experiences and Reflections." *Constitutional Commentary* 14 (1997): 347–364.

Swann v. Charlotte-Mecklenburg Board of Education, 402 U.S. 1 (1971).

Who's Who in America. 52d ed. Vol. 1. New Providence, N.J.: Marquis Who's Who, 1998.

GRISWOLD, ERWIN NATHANIEL

(1904–1994)

ERWIN NATHANIEL GRISWOLD had a distinguished career as a professor and dean of Harvard Law School and as a practicing attorney, including a stint as solicitor general of the United States. He is one of the few individuals who has argued more than one hundred cases before the Supreme Court. During his lengthy and varied career, he made important contributions as an educator, scholar, and litigator in the areas of civil liberties and civil rights.

Griswold was born on July 14, 1904, in East Cleveland, Ohio, to James Harlen Griswold and Hope Erwin Griswold. The elder Griswold spent his career as an attorney in Cleveland, most of it as senior partner in the firm Griswold, Palmer & Hadden, so in a sense, Erwin Griswold was born to a career in the law. In May 1921, Erwin graduated from Shaw Public High School in East Cleveland as valedictorian of his class. By his own account, he received an "excellent preparatory education" grounded in a classical curriculum (Griswold 1992, 19). He followed in the footsteps of both of his parents by attending nearby Oberlin College

ERWIN NATHANIEL GRISWOLD
Corbis/Bettmann-UPI

rather than following many of his friends to the Ivy League. He wrote in his autobiography that, although tempted by Yale, he suffered from shyness and found somewhat troubling the elitism associated with an East Coast education. "I never regarded myself as any sort of Brahmin, any sort of an elite. Most of the people who went from Cleveland to the big eastern universities had a superior attitude, which I did not feel" (Griswold 1992, 27).

Griswold graduated from Oberlin in May 1925. Although he toyed briefly with the idea of graduate studies in physics, he decided instead to follow his father into the law. Harlen Griswold had spent his entire career practicing law in Cleveland and was eager to provide Erwin with the Harvard Law School degree that his own parents had been unable to afford. Despite his earlier misgivings about elite eastern universities, Erwin entered Harvard Law School in September 1925.

In keeping with his previous academic record, Griswold excelled in law school. In 1927, his peers elected him president of the *Harvard Law Review*. He completed the LL.B. degree in 1928, fully expecting to return to Cleveland and join his father's firm. His mentor, Professor Austin Scott, instead persuaded Griswold to remain at Harvard for another year to pursue the higher law degree of S.J.D. Scott hired Griswold to assist him in his position as reporter on trusts for the American Law Institute. Griswold found his dissertation topic in that work, completing "Spendthrift Trusts" in time to graduate in the spring of 1929. His work for Scott and his dissertation research provided him with the foundation of a lifelong interest and expertise in tax law.

Griswold returned to Cleveland in September 1929 to work in his father's firm. That career was short lived, however. In October, at Scott's recommendation, U.S. Solicitor General Charles Evans Hughes Jr. offered Griswold a position on his staff. Griswold accepted, and on December 2 he became one of two junior attorneys on a staff of five in the solicitor general's Washington, D.C., office. The solicitor general's office was responsible for representing the government in Supreme Court cases. With virtually no practical experience, Griswold began assisting his seniors on important cases and soon began writing his own briefs. He also astutely carved a niche for himself. At the time, tax law was in its infancy as a specialty; Harvard Law School had not even offered a course on the subject. No one else in the solicitor general's office wanted to deal with tax law cases, so Griswold industriously took on the task. He soon gained a reputation as the resident expert on tax law in the Department of Justice and, before long, he began arguing tax cases before the Supreme Court.

Griswold continued on the solicitor general's staff until 1934. Besides laying the foundation for a lifelong interest and expertise in tax law, he made one other significant contribution to jurisprudence during that period. In

1934, the *Harvard Law Review* published an article by Griswold entitled "Government in Ignorance of the Law—A Plea for Better Publication of Executive Legislation." In one of the cases assigned to him by the solicitor general, he had discovered that it was virtually impossible to determine what federal regulations were operative in the case. This was during the early years of Franklin Roosevelt's New Deal. As the number of federal government agencies rapidly expanded, the regulations that those agencies issued multiplied exponentially. Such federal regulations, coming from the executive branch of government along with the president's own executive orders, carried the force of law. Unlike legislation emanating from Congress, however, no effective mechanism for publishing and cross-referencing federal regulations existed. Thus it was difficult to determine when one rule had superseded another, or even if a rule existed in the first place, since the basic mechanism for publishing federal regulations was through press releases. Griswold's article proposed congressional legislation to create a mechanism for systematically tracking and publishing orders and regulations issued by the executive branch of government. The end result of Griswold's effort was the law passed by Congress on July 26, 1935 (49 Stat. 501) creating the *Federal Register*. The first issue of the *Register* appeared on March 14, 1936. Although, as Griswold noted, it is probably the "dullest publication distributed widely in the United States," it allows any citizen to comment on proposed regulations and to read the exact wording of approved regulations and has doubtless "saved many mistakes by courts and enormous amounts of time for lawyers" (Griswold 1992, 118–119).

In 1934, Griswold left the solicitor general's office to join the faculty of Harvard Law School as an assistant professor, thus beginning a long and distinguished career in legal education. He began by teaching taxation, conflict of laws, and a seminar on legislation. His first major scholarly publication was a revision of his dissertation, *Spendthrift Trusts* (1936). In 1936, he was made full professor and also began developing a full-fledged curriculum on taxation. He produced a textbook, *Cases on Federal Taxation*, in 1940; it eventually appeared in six editions. He also collaborated with others on *Cases in Conflict of Laws* (1941).

In 1946, the Harvard Corporation, with the approval of the law school's board of overseers, named Griswold the Charles Stebbins Fairchild Professor of Law and simultaneously appointed him dean of the law school. In 1950, he was named Langdell Professor of Law, but he continued to hold the deanship until 1967. One of his first contributions to legal education as dean was his joint effort with the deans of the law schools at Yale and Columbia to persuade the Educational Testing Service to develop a standardized entrance examination for law schools (now the LSAT). He also immediately faced the challenge of rebuilding the law school faculty following

the lean war years, while simultaneously coping with enrollments burgeon-
ing from the return of students whose legal education had been interrupted
by wartime service and by new students coming under the auspices of the
G.I. Bill.

Dean Griswold presided over a dramatic expansion of facilities and financial resources during his time at the helm of Harvard Law School. He took
particular pride in having established the Harvard Law School Fund in
1950. The law school's first systematic annual giving program for alumni, it
raised $80 million in its first forty years of existence.

During his career at Harvard, Griswold remained professionally active.
He served as a consultant with private law firms in numerous tax cases and
argued seven cases before the Supreme Court. Because of his interest in the
complex issues surrounding the conflict between laws of different states, he
was long involved in the American Law Institute. The institute, established
in the 1920s, published *Restatements of the Law*, a reference tool that
sought, in Griswold's words, "to organize and systematize our chaotic system
of varying State laws" (Griswold 1964). Griswold served for thirty-seven
years on the governing council of the institute. He was also a founding
member of the section on taxation of the American Bar Association
(ABA) and served on the section's council. On being elected as president
of the Association of American Law Schools in December 1957, he auto-
matically became a member of the ABA's house of delegates and continued
to serve in that body for twenty-seven years. Griswold left Harvard in 1967
to assume the position of solicitor general of the United States during the
tumultuous years 1967–1973. During that period, he argued before the
Supreme Court the government's side in dozens of cases on a wide range of
issues.

Apart from his sizable contributions to legal education, Griswold's career
also had a significant impact in two broad areas of social and political life in
mid-twentieth-century America: civil liberties and civil rights. Griswold's
first foray into public commentary on the issue of civil liberties arose in the
intensely anticommunist climate of the early 1950s. In 1951, the president
of the Massachusetts Bar Association, Samuel P. Sears, demanded that Harvard Law School disband the Harvard Lawyers Guild, a student organization that Sears suspected of harboring Communist sympathizers. Griswold,
then dean of the law school, refused on the grounds that such a step "would
be an improper interference with the legitimate freedom of our students"
("Erwin Nathaniel Griswold" 1956, 239, citing *New York Times* article of
6 March 1951).

Griswold found further scope for his concerns about the suppression of
civil liberties in Congress's anticommunism crusade of this period. In 1953
and 1954, at the height of Senator Joseph R. McCarthy's "investigations"

Great Trials in American History

It is difficult to think about great lawyers without also thinking about great trials. Just as great cities often grow beside great rivers, so too, great lawyers often emerge from, and are drawn to, great trials. In recent years, there have been a number of volumes that have been devoted to such trials.

One of the most popular descriptions of trials is located on a web site created by Douglas O. Linder entitled *Famous Trials*. The trials covered to date include the *Leopold and Loeb* trial (1924), the *Scopes* "monkey" trial (1925), the *Rosenbergs* trial (1951), the *Amistad* trials (1839–1840), the *Bill Haywood* trial (1907), the Salem witchcraft trials (1692), the My Lai courts-martial (1970), the *Scottsboro Boys* trials (1931–1937), the *Dakota Conflict* trials (1862), the *Mississippi Burning* trial (1967), the *Chicago Seven* conspiracy trial (1969–1970), the Andrew Johnson impeachment trial (1868), and the *O. J. Simpson* trial (1995). Linder plans to add a description of the *Sacco and Vanzetti* trial (1921) and the *Chicago Black Sox* trial (1921) early in 2001.

Of all American trials, Linder thinks that the *Scopes* trial was the most dramatic. Long after William Jennings Bryan, Clarence Darrow, and the other participants have died, conflicts about school curricula and science and religion continue to stir public debate.

REFERENCE

Linder, Douglas O. "Famous Trials." <http://www.umkc.edu/famoustrials>.

into alleged Communist infiltration of the United States, the senator brought many people to testify before his committee regarding their supposed Communist ties. A refusal to testify by claiming the Fifth Amendment privilege against self-incrimination was interpreted as an admission of guilt. The "guilty" parties, branded Communist sympathizers, often found careers destroyed and reputations shattered as a result of McCarthy's tactics.

Griswold was appalled by the abuse that the Fifth Amendment privilege suffered at McCarthy's hands. He gave a series of speeches in 1954 that were subsequently published in 1955 under the title *The Fifth Amendment Today: Three Speeches by Erwin Griswold*. Using several hypothetical examples, he demonstrated the reasons why a claim of Fifth Amendment privilege could not legally be construed as an admission of guilt. Griswold argued that the Fifth Amendment right not to testify against oneself was a key element of due process and a "right of fundamental importance in our legal and social system" (Griswold 1955, 53). The Fifth Amendment, in fact, stood as a symbol of "the great tradition of individual liberty" (Griswold 1955, 53). He further maintained that the McCarthy hearings violated due process because they lacked appropriate legal procedure and violated the rights of those called to testify. Griswold expressed the view that "a legislative investigation is improper when its sole or basic purpose is to 'expose' people or to develop evidence for use in criminal prosecutions"(Griswold 1955, 48). Questioning the legality of a congressional subcommittee conducting such investigations in the first place, Griswold held the entire Congress responsible for McCarthy's actions, because members had delegated to McCarthy the power that he was abusing and they failed to intervene when matters got out of hand. Griswold's most scathing commentary was summed up when he wrote, "In protecting ourselves from the threat of Communism, we should not adopt methods of oppression here which the Communists themselves would use" (Griswold 1955, 50).

Griswold's next major foray into the area of civil liberties found him in a rather different position. While serving as solicitor general from 1967 through 1973, he found himself intimately involved in one of the most notorious Supreme Court cases of the twentieth century: *New York Times Co. v. United States*, 403 U.S. 713, 91 S. Ct. 2140, 29 L. Ed. 2d 822 (1971), popularly known as the *Pentagon Papers* case. At the height of public disillusionment over the Vietnam War, the *New York Times* and the *Washington Post* set out to publish excerpts from a top-secret history of U.S. involvement in Vietnam. Secretary of Defense Robert S. McNamara had ordered the preparation of the study in 1967. It covered the period from the end of World War II until 1968. One of the study's authors, Daniel Ellsberg, had by 1970 become radically opposed to the war and decided to leak a copy to *New York Times* reporter Neil Sheehan. Between June 12 and June 14, 1971, the *Times* published a series of articles based on the study; the *Washington Post* soon followed suit. The U.S. government sought injunctions for prior restraint of publication on the grounds that releasing information from the top-secret document could endanger the war effort and the lives of American prisoners of war. The papers fought in the courts on First Amendment grounds and on the grounds that all of the information contained in the report was more than three years old and therefore not likely to endanger national security. The complex legal maneuverings moved swiftly through the legal system, arriving before the Supreme Court on June 30, 1971. A divided Supreme Court ruled 6 to 3 in favor of the newspapers.

Erwin Griswold, as solicitor general of the United States, found himself arguing the government's side both before the Court of Appeals for the Second Circuit and before the Supreme Court. He later noted he was not even allowed to see the study before the Court of Appeals argument and had only a few hours to peruse the seven-thousand-page document before arguing the case before the Supreme Court. Although he thought the government's position was shaky at best, he proceeded with the government's argument on the grounds that a legitimate national security risk existed. He was arguing from a difficult position because he had so little time to assess the papers himself. He lost the case and later declared that the whole situation was a "tempest in a teapot." He acknowledged that no harm had come from the publication of the papers, but he maintained that, had a real national security threat existed, the government would have been justified in its argument for prior restraint of publication and that he could imagine situations in which national security trumped First Amendment freedom of the press. The case, however, is usually cited as a major triumph for the First Amendment guarantee of a free press, and Griswold did not contest that interpretation.

In the area of civil rights, Griswold had a distinguished record. For example, in 1949, as dean of the Harvard Law School, Griswold petitioned the Harvard Corporation to allow the admission of women. The first class of women entered in 1950. But Griswold left his most important mark in the area of racial equality.

In 1928–1929, the year that Griswold spent as a graduate student in the Harvard Law School, an African-American second-year law student named WILLIAM H. HASTIE was elected to the board of editors for the *Harvard Law Review*. Hastie's attendance at the *Review*'s annual formal dinner became a point of controversy that year. Hastie himself stated that he would not attend because of the controversy. Griswold later wrote that "a considerable number of the members of the Board, with whom I joined as an alumnus member, let it be known that we would not attend the dinner unless Hastie was welcomed and did attend, and the matter was worked out on this basis" (Griswold 1992, 182).

During the 1930s and 1940s, THURGOOD MARSHALL, then legal director of the National Association for the Advancement of Colored People, had developed a strategy of challenging segregation in public education by attacking the practice in graduate and professional schools. In 1950, Marshall approached Griswold and invited the dean to serve as an expert witness on cases involving legal education. Griswold first testified in North Carolina in a case challenging the legality of the refusal by the University of North Carolina at Chapel Hill to admit African-American students. A separate law school had been established in Durham at the North Carolina College for Negroes (now North Carolina Central University) but was clearly not "equal." Griswold recalled that he "testified, in short, that a segregated legal education *could not* be equal" (Griswold 1992, 184). He subsequently offered the same testimony in federal court in Oklahoma City in *McLaurin v. Oklahoma State Regents for Higher Education*, 339 U.S. 637 (1950). Griswold was also among the members of the Association of American Law Schools who filed an amicus brief in the landmark Supreme Court case *Sweatt v. Painter*, 339 U.S. 629 (1950). The *McLaurin* and *Sweatt* cases played an important role in establishing precedent for *Brown v. Board of Education* in 1954. Although Harvard Law School already admitted African-American students by the time Griswold became dean, he further promoted African-American legal education late in his career at Harvard by supporting a group of faculty members who received a grant to offer all-expense-paid summer prelaw institutes for African-American college students interested in the legal profession.

Griswold also served, under appointment by Presidents John F. Kennedy and Lyndon Baines Johnson, as a member of the U.S. Commission on Civil Rights from 1961 through 1966. In this capacity, he traveled throughout the United States presiding over hearings and gathering information that would then be used by the president and Congress to craft civil rights legislation.

Griswold's involvement in civil rights issues reached a climax during his term as solicitor general (1967–1973). In this role, he argued the government's side in Supreme Court cases involving school desegregation. Griswold viewed *United States v. Montgomery Board of Education*, 295 U.S. 225 (1969), as "one of the most important decisions in the desegregation struggle." In the Montgomery County, Alabama, schools, faculty and staff were segregated. A federal judge had declared that the school system thus violated the law and required that they achieve a consistent ratio of white and African-American faculty and staff in all of their schools. The school system appealed all the way to the Supreme Court, where Griswold argued the government's side, maintaining that the school board was violating both the spirit and the letter of the law. "If there is any one thing that makes a school a 'black school,'" he later wrote, "it is an all-black (or nearly all-black) faculty and vice versa" (Griswold 1992, 273).

One of the last major cases that Griswold argued before the Supreme Court was the landmark case *Swann v. Charlotte-Mecklenburg Board of Education*, 402 U.S. 1 (1971). A judge had ordered the desegregation of North Carolina's Charlotte Mecklenburg County elementary schools and included a provision that encouraged busing students to schools outside their neighborhoods to achieve desegregation. Griswold represented the government's side, arguing that the judge's order was directed at rectifying past discrimination and was therefore valid and should be upheld by the Supreme Court. The Court ruled unanimously in favor of the government.

Erwin Griswold retired to private legal practice in 1973. He continued serving clients until not long before his death at age ninety in 1994. In a memorial that appeared in the *Harvard Law Review* shortly after Griswold's death, retired Supreme Court justice Harry A. Blackmun wrote,

> As the years passed, I watched with pride and enthusiasm the progress of this man—his contributive years at the Harvard Law School, his professional in-

tegrity and responsibility in representing the United States as Solicitor General under both Democrat and Republican Administrations, and his careful appearances for clients when he returned to the embrace of the Washington office of his old Cleveland law firm. All this demonstrated the personal integrity, the professional ability, and the steadfastness that anyone could expect of a lawyer. He brought grace and a distinct sense of righteousness to the profession. . . . His arguments to the Court, when I was there, were always thoroughly prepared, attacked the issues directly, contained an answer for every question any Justice asked, and ended within the allotted thirty minutes. For me, it was a delight to have him listed as an advocate on the day's calendar. ("In Memoriam" 1995, 980)

—*Lisa Pruitt*

Sources and Suggestions for Further Reading

Abrams, Floyd. "The First Amendment: 1991." *Prologue* (Spring 1992): 48–54.

Bollinger, Lee. "Prior Restraint." In *Guide to American Law.* Vol. 8. New York: West, 1984, 273–275.

Dulles, Foster Rhea. *The Civil Rights Commission: 1957–1965.* Lansing: Michigan State University Press, 1968.

"Erwin Nathaniel Griswold." In *Current Biography Yearbook.* New York: H. W. Wilson, 1956, 231–233.

Griswold, Erwin N. *The Fifth Amendment Today: Three Speeches by Erwin Griswold.* Cambridge: Harvard University Press, 1955.

_____. "Government in Ignorance of the Law—A Plea for Better Publication of Executive Legislation." *Harvard Law Review* 48 (1934): 198–213.

_____. *Law and Lawyers in the United States: The Common Law under Stress.* Cambridge: Harvard University Press, 1964.

_____. *Ould Fields, New Corne: The Personal Memoirs of a Twentieth Century Lawyer.* St. Paul: West, 1992.

_____. "The Pentagon Papers Case: A Personal Footnote." *Supreme Court Historical Society Yearbook* (1984): 112–116.

"In Memoriam: Erwin Nathaniel Griswold." *Harvard Law Review* (March 1995).

Rudenstine, David. *The Day the Presses Stopped: A History of the Pentagon Papers Case.* Berkeley: University of California Press, 1996.

GUTHRIE, WILLIAM DAMERON

(1859–1935)

WILLIAM DAMERON GUTHRIE
Library of Congress

As a member of the Supreme Court bar, William Dameron Guthrie argued several critical constitutional cases before the justices. As an advocate of limited federal power and an opponent of economic regulation, Guthrie was instrumental in the striking down of the federal income tax and the development of the constitutional theory of dual federalism used by the Court. His arguments provided the legal and constitutional basis for Supreme Court decisions striking down the federal income tax and child labor and minimum-wage laws.

Born on February 3, 1859, in San Francisco, California, William Dameron Guthrie was the son of George and Emma Guthrie. As a child, William spent several years in France, where he developed a fondness for the country and its people. On his return to the United States, Guthrie began working as a messenger in the New York law offices of Blatchford, Seward, Griswold & DeCosta. After a few years he attended Columbia Law School and, although he did not earn a degree, he was admitted to the bar in 1880 at age twenty-one. In 1883, at age twenty-four, Guthrie became a partner in the firm that became known as Seward, DeCosta & Guthrie.

As a partner in the firm, Guthrie was involved with much of the railroad litigation that sprang up during the 1880s. Guthrie spent much of his early career arranging for financing for railroads and defending them against financial claims. He developed a reputation as a tough negotiator and a hard worker. His dedication, though, had negative consequences. He became surly and difficult to work with when handling a case. His hectic schedule created tension within the law firm. He bickered with his partners over their legal work and over such minor irritants as their smoking habits. With the arrival of new partners, Guthrie saw his contribution and importance to the firm begin to decline.

Guthrie's partnership in the firm continued until 1906, and during that time he became one of the most prominent attorneys in the country. His departure from the firm was controversial. A New York State investigation of the firm's business practices caused Guthrie publicly to criticize his partners. Although Guthrie was cleared of any wrongdoing, his acrimonious relationship with his partners required his leaving the firm. In 1907, he served as a lecturer at the Yale Law School, then in 1909 he became a partner in the firm of Guthrie, Bangs & Van Sendren. Guthrie continued the partnership until 1921, when he joined the firm of Guthrie, Jerome, Rand & Kresel. In 1924, he left this firm and developed his own private practice. Throughout the period he was a constitutional law professor at Columbia, serving until 1931. He also served as mayor of Letlingtown, New Jersey, in the 1930s. While his litigation rate declined, Guthrie continued arguing important cases and providing legal advice and commentary on political issues. He attacked everyone from William Howard Taft to the Roosevelt administration. He remained tied to his views on economic regulation and the rule of law.

During his early years as a lawyer, Guthrie became attached to the belief that government regulation was a threat to private property. As his career progressed, he earned a reputation as a zealous opponent of economic legislation and a man who had principles rather than positions. Among those principles was an overriding belief in judicial activism and the courts acting as a check on the passions of the legislature in holding back the wave of economic regulation. Guthrie's efforts on behalf of these ideas took a two-track approach. His legal arguments before the Supreme Court provided the justices with a constitutional framework for striking down legislation. He supplemented those legal arguments with a series of public addresses. In those speeches he provided a systematic view of state and federal relations and the limits of governmental regulatory power.

But Guthrie was more than a litigator. He served as president of the New York State Bar Association from 1921 to 1923, then as president of the New

Delphin Michael Delmas

Delphin Michael Delmas (1844–1928) was known as the "Napoleon of the Western bar," partly because of his small size and imperial demeanor and partly because of his successes in the courtroom. Delmas was known for having won nineteen acquittals in nineteen murder cases (Langford 1962, 50).

Delmas's most famous case was his 1907 defense of Harry Thaw for the murder of architect Stanford White in Madison Square Garden, which White had designed. Thaw, a wealthy playboy heir married to Elizabeth Nisbit, openly shot White as he observed a theatre performance apparently to vindicate his wife, whom White had allegedly raped when she was a showgirl. Describing White as having "crushed the poor little thing—the sweet little flower that was struggling toward the light and toward God," Delmas argued that Thaw suffered from "*dementia Americana*," a type of insanity that persuades an American to believe "that whoever violates the sanctity of his home or the purity of his wife or daughter has forfeited the protection of the laws of this state or any other state" (Langford 1962, 203–204).

The prosecutor, William Travers Jerome, answered with his own powerful argument, pointing out that "justifiable homicide does not mean dementia Americana. Justifiable means self-defense, and when a man sits with his head in his hands, quietly looking at a play, and is shot down by an enemy with a revolver, held so close that his very features are so disfigured that his brother-in-law does not recognize him, even the wildest stretch of imagination will hardly picture that to a jury east of the Mississippi River as a case of self-defense" (Uelmen 1982, 50). These arguments led to a hung jury in the first trial and to exoneration in a second trial not argued by Delmas.

During Thaw's trial, a reporter described Delmas's almost hypnotic effect upon a jury:

> Juries like Delmas for the same reasons that women do; and he is the manner of man who women instantly like. . . . There is [in his manner] the flattering unction that causes a washerwoman to forget that she is not a queen. He bends over an ordinary feminine hand as though it were a lily leaf that had floated downward from the gardens of paradise. And there is in his attitude toward the jury a subtle hint of good fellowship and yet a deference which intimates, "You are the twelfth and I am merely the thirteenth. If you will permit this lesser being for a short time your gracious attention, I shall be most honored." (Langford 1962, 91)

REFERENCES

Langford, Gerald. *The Murder of Stanford White*. Indianapolis: Bobbs-Merrill, 1962.

Turley, Jonathan. "The Trial Lawyers of the Century." *Recorder*, 15 December 1999, 4.

Uelmen, Gerald. "The Trial of the Century?" *Criminal Defense* (November-December 1982), 49–50.

York City Bar Association from 1925 to 1927. He was also the chairman of a state constitutional revision committee. As chairman he oversaw changes to the judicial section of the New York constitution.

His role as chairman also gave him a platform on which to speak about the direction of the law and the type of legal education being offered. Guthrie was a proponent of the Legal Aid Society, which provided the avenue for those without money to challenge the economic regulations passed by the states and the federal government. He noted in a commentary that society maintained a respect for law and government institutions among most citizens.

Guthrie also confronted those who criticized the values he argued in the courts. He charged that law schools and professors were undermining students' belief in the courts. He considered some law professors to pose a danger to the stability of the law and disagreed with the Legal Realism movement that was sweeping through the profession. As chairman of the Committee on Character and Fitness for the New York Bar from 1927 to 1930, he fought to restrict entrance to the bar, warning against allowing radical lawyers to practice and threaten legal institutions. He took umbrage at being considered a mouthpiece for corporate interests. Instead he believed in the interests he represented, seeing himself as more than a legal advocate.

In addition to his work with the bar, Guthrie was involved with the Catholic Church. He received awards and recognition for his legal and other activities on behalf of the church. Guthrie provided legal counsel, including the church litigation in *Pierce v. Society of Sisters* (1925), which challenged an Oregon law prohibiting students from attending private or parochial schools. He also wrote a legal brief arguing that the new Mexican constitution violated religious rights and undermined the Catholic Church within the country.

That same year, he was considered for the Supreme Court vacancy created by Justice Joseph McKenna's retirement. But by that time Guthrie was approaching seventy and was considered by President Calvin Coolidge to be too old. Passed over for the prestigious office he always wanted, Guthrie spent his last years fighting a rearguard action against those who challenged his views of government and society.

During the first decade of his career at the Seward law firm, Guthrie dealt with routine cases involving corporate financing and rights. Although he was known within the legal community for his hard-bargaining stances and tendency to lose his temper, Guthrie was not nationally known. His rise to prominence occurred during the battle over the federal income tax.

Guthrie's role as a driving force behind the litigation in *Pollock v. Farmers Loan and Trust Co.* (1895) provides an interesting picture of the dedication he felt toward his cause. The 1894 income tax focused on both corporate and individual incomes. Challenging the act, though, provided a special problem. It required that a litigant pay the tax, then challenge its constitutionality. Guthrie arranged for stockholders in the trust company to challenge the company's decision to pay the tax. That decision was prompted by Guthrie's suggestion that paying the tax provided the opportunity to challenge the law. Guthrie went even further. He worked with the federal government to expedite arguments for the case and took the additional step of suggesting a lawyer to oppose him. This collusion was not unusual during the era. The identical scenario prompted the challenge to the Louisiana segregation law in *Plessy v. Ferguson* (1896) and was not seen as a violation of ethics or the adversarial system.

The income tax cases attracted some of the best legal talent for oral arguments. Guthrie utilized the efforts of Senator George Edmunds of Vermont and RUFUS CHOATE, one of the best-known attorneys of the era. Opposing him was Attorney General Richard Olney and James Carter, former president of the American Bar Association.

In oral arguments before the Court, Guthrie limited himself to a technical argument as to whether the income tax represented a direct or indirect tax and how the constitutional prohibition against direct taxes would apply. His co-counsel, Rufus Choate, offered a sweeping constitutional argument on behalf of overturning precedent and the Court's understanding of congressional taxing power.

A narrow 5–4 majority of the Court agreed with the Guthrie definition of direct taxes and struck down the income tax. Hence, at age thirty-five, Guthrie initiated a lawsuit challenging the keystone of the Progressive political agenda and constructed an argument that convinced five justices to sweep aside precedent and overturn a major piece of federal legislation. With *Pollock* under his belt, Guthrie moved on to challenging other forms of federal regulation on property rights.

As the twentieth century began, Guthrie was at the forefront of corporate lawyers using the judiciary to attack economic legislation. He served as lead counsel in two prominent cases defining federal commerce and taxing power. In *Champion v. Ames* (1903) and *McCray v. United States* (1904), Guthrie argued that the federal government had exceeded its power to regulate interstate commerce.

In *Champion*, Guthrie used a two-tiered argument that lottery tickets, which were banned as interstate commerce, were not commerce. In addition, he noted in his oral argument that the power to regulate commerce did not include prohibiting the use of that article of commerce. In his arguments Guthrie presented his own vision of state and federal relations. He denied the existence of a federal police power protecting the safety and welfare of citizens. Instead, such power was delegated to the state governments under the Tenth Amendment. A closely divided Court rejected Guthrie's arguments in upholding the ban on interstate transport of lottery tickets.

In *McCray*, Guthrie represented margarine producers who were challenging a federal ten-cent-per-pound tax on their product. Guthrie's arguments on their behalf would be echoed in future challenges to federal taxing power. He also noted that the power to tax was to be used only for raising revenue, not restricting the use or manufacturing of a product. As with *Champion*, Guthrie's arguments convinced only a minority of the Court, as six justices voted to uphold the margarine tax.

During his many oral arguments in the Court, Guthrie served with several prominent attorneys and political figures. These included ELIHU ROOT, with whom he argued the *National Prohibition Cases*, and Charles Evans Hughes. His close relationship with Rufus Choate during the *Income Tax Cases* solidified his position as a leading attorney during the era. He also represented several major clients, including the Illinois Central and Santa Fe railroads and the Vanderbilt family.

Guthrie also participated in one of the few challenges to the constitutionality of a constitutional amendment. In the *National Prohibition Cases* (1920), a group of brewers challenged congressional and state power to amend the constitution so as to restrict individual behavior. A second challenge arose to congressional power to regulate alcohol without state consent.

As a defender of state power, Guthrie offered evidence in support of the second argument. He noted that while Congress could regulate the interstate transport or sale of alcohol, it could not regulate intrastate alcohol production without state approval. To do so would be an invasion of state prerogatives under the Tenth Amendment. Guthrie's arguments were ignored by the Court, as a seven-member majority upheld the Eighteenth Amendment and the Volstead Act as proper uses of federal power. The justices dismissed Guthrie's contention that states controlled intrastate trade in alcohol.

In one of his last great constitutional cases, Guthrie represented the Catholic Church in its challenge to an Oregon state law prohibiting children from attending private school. In *Pierce v. Society of Sisters* (1925), Guthrie utilized the same arguments used against economic regulation to challenge the law. He stated that the law exceeded the police power in attempting to destroy a nonharmful institution. Guthrie returned to the proposition that the state could regulate only harmful activities to protect its citizens. Private parochial schools represented no such danger. In *Pierce*, Guthrie's arguments convinced each member of the Court, as they unanimously struck down the Oregon law.

Guthrie's career as a constitutional lawyer extended beyond the courtroom. He used his prominent position as an attorney and the leader of the New York bar to expound on his constitutional theories. Taking on the task as constitutional proselytizer, he gave a series of speeches that served as seminars on government power. In those speeches, Guthrie offered a systematic theory of the separation of powers, judicial activism, government economic regulation, and federalism. Guthrie proposed limitations on federal power and a strict division of duties between the federal and state governments.

Guthrie was even more adamant in his defense of the judiciary as a legal bulwark against progressive economic policies. He saw judges as the last defenders of economic rights and sought to expand judicial power at the expense of the legislature. One of the avenues for that was a reinterpretation of the Eleventh Amendment and state sovereign immunity as a check on federal judicial power. In a 1908 speech before the New York State Bar Association, Guthrie proposed a constricted view of state sovereign immunity, one that would allow federal judges to prevent state officials from enforcing economic regulations the Court believed to be unconstitutional. He commented on the case of *Ex parte Young* (1908), in which the Court did just as Guthrie advised and allowed federal judges to rule against state officials.

Guthrie died of a heart attack on December 8, 1935. During that time the Court and the country were poised on the edge of a constitutional revolution that would sweep away the arguments and philosophy offered by Guthrie. Although his beliefs would barely outlast him, William Dameron Guthrie was one of the most powerful members of the bar during his life and had a dramatic effect on the development and application of the law.

—*Douglas Clouatre*

Sources and Suggestions for Further Reading

Auerbach, Jerold. *Unequal Justice*. London: Oxford University Press, 1976.

Bickel, Alexander, and Benno Schmidt Jr. *The Judiciary and Responsible Government*. New York: Macmillan, 1984.

Bloomfield, Maxwell. "Politics and Precedents: The Income Tax Case." In *Historic U.S. Court Cases 1690–1990, An Encyclopedia*, edited by John W. Johnson. New York: Garland, 1972.

Guthrie, William Dameron. *Lectures on the Fourteenth Amendment*. New York: Da Capo Press, 1998.

———. *Magna Carta and Other Addresses*. New York: Columbia University Press, 1916.

Swaine, Robert. *The Cravath Firm and Its Predecessors 1819–1947*. Vols. 1 and 2. New York: privately published, 1947.

Twiss, Benjamin R. *Lawyers and the Constitution: How Laissez Faire Came to the Supreme Court*. New York: Russell & Russell, 1962.

HAMILTON, ALEXANDER

(1757–1804)

ALEXANDER HAMILTON, USUALLY remembered for his role as a political figure and a framer of the U.S. Constitution, also maintained a far-ranging law practice and laid the foundation for several legal doctrines that are integral to modern judicial thought. His legal theories gave rise to the doctrine of judicial review, helped to enlarge freedom of the press, and encouraged a muscular interpretation of the contract clause. By any standard, Hamilton was one of the most able and creative lawyers of the early republic.

Hamilton was born out of wedlock on January 11, 1757, on the island of Nevis in the British West Indies. Hamilton's mother died when he was eleven and his father played little role in his life. Raised in St. Croix, Hamilton was sent to America at age fifteen by friends. He studied at King's College in New York City from 1773 to 1776. Hamilton served in the Revolutionary War as General George Washington's aide from 1777 to 1781, and he married Elizabeth Schuyler, a member of a leading New York family, in 1780. Before the war ended, Hamilton briefly studied law in Albany and was admitted to practice in various New York courts in the period 1782–1783. He soon gained success at the

ALEXANDER HAMILTON
Library of Congress

318

bar and was in demand by prominent clients throughout his career. He often acted as co-counsel, appearing several times with Aaron Burr.

Hamilton authored the earliest known treatise on the practice of law in New York. Written while Hamilton was a law student, the book, entitled *Practical Proceedings in the Supreme Court of the State of New York*, discusses the procedures of the Supreme Court of New York as well as aspects of the state's substantive law. The treatise, an important early work on private law in the Revolutionary era, indicates that Hamilton was well versed in many areas of English law, as well as the laws of other countries, such as Spain, Italy, and France.

Among the first cases Hamilton argued were those known as the *War Cases*. These consisted of about sixty-five cases involving three New York anti-Loyalist statutes passed in the wake of the Revolutionary War. In the most noted of his war cases, *Rutgers v. Waddington* (1784), Hamilton fashioned legal arguments that became a building block for the modern doctrine of judicial review. The case concerned the occupation by Loyalist Benjamin Waddington & Company of property belonging to Elizabeth Rutgers, who had fled due to British military occupation. Under New York's Trespass Act of 1783, a plaintiff could bring a suit for trespass against anyone who had occupied or destroyed his or her property. Rutgers sued Waddington for eight thousand pounds in rent; Hamilton served as defense counsel along with Brockholst Livingston and Morgan Lewis, and the case was argued before James Duane in the Mayor's court.

The law of nations sanctioned the use of abandoned property, when authorized by the commanding military officer during wartime. By precluding the defense that one's trespassory actions were pursuant to a military order, the Trespass Act directly conflicted with the law of nations. Hamilton argued first that the Trespass Act violated the law of nations and was thus void. Because the New York Constitution had adopted the common law, which included the law of nations, violation of the law of nations was thus a violation of the laws of New York. Second, he argued that Congress had exclusive power to enter into peace treaties, including the implied power to prescribe reasonable conditions necessary to carry out the treaties. Lastly, he maintained that if the act was invalid on either ground the court was obligated to declare the statute void.

The court did not directly address Hamilton's argument. Instead, it held that the use by the defendant under immediate authority of the British commander was defensible under the law of nations. Regarding the issue of whether the court was bound by the statute even if it was in conflict with the law of nations, the court noted that it did not profess to have the power to find the statute void, acknowledging the supremacy of the legislature. However, the court held that because the legislature had not expressed the intent to violate the law of nations, the court would read the statute so as to avoid this consequence. This necessitated the holding that the Trespass Act did not apply to the defendant's acts that were protected by the law of nations. Thereafter Hamilton represented Loyalists in a number of Trespass Act cases.

This early formulation of the concept of judicial review is one of Hamilton's most important contributions to the development of constitutional law. Hamilton further developed his thinking on judicial review in the famous essay No. 78 of the *Federalist Papers*. He endorsed the view that judges should strike down statutes that contradicted the Constitution, and he provided an intellectual foundation for judicial review.

In addition to his legal practice, Hamilton served in various political positions. He was a member of the New York legislature in 1787, served as a New York delegate to the Continental Congress from 1782 to 1783 and from 1787 to 1788, and was a New York delegate to the 1787 Philadelphia Constitutional Convention. Shortly after the Treasury Department was established in September 1789, Hamilton became the first secretary of the treasury, serving in this capacity from 1789 to 1795.

While secretary of the treasury, Hamilton proposed the creation of a national bank. In 1791, President Washington asked Hamilton for his views on the constitutionality of this measure. Hamilton responded with a classic formulation of the doctrine of implied congressional power derived from the "necessary and proper" clause of the Constitution. Hamilton's opinion was ultimately adopted by the U.S. Supreme Court in *McCulloch v. Maryland* (1819), a leading decision by Chief Justice JOHN MARSHALL.

Except for the years in which he served as secretary of the treasury, Hamilton argued cases before the New York Chancery Court every year from 1784 until he died in 1804. A primary focus of his chancery practice was commercial transactions, and this aspect of his work increased markedly when he returned to law in 1795. He handled numerous cases dealing with such matters as debt, creditors' rights, sales contracts, and promissory notes. Other cases involved disputes between shippers and merchants over which party should bear the burden of the loss of goods while en route.

Hamilton also developed an extensive marine insurance practice. He handled cases dealing with the interpretation of insurance contracts, refusal to pay on a loss due to suspected fraud, the extent of the application of a contract when an insured lied on the application, and the ability of a creditor to insure a vessel in the owner's name without his permission. Hamilton did not appear predominantly on either side of these types of disputes, having represented insurance companies as well as many policyholders. Related cases concerned admiralty and maritime jurisdiction, with many of these cases arising from violations of federal statutes. For example, the Slave Trade Acts prohibited American participation in the international slave trade. Hamilton participated in two cases in which his clients had allegedly violated these provisions. He was also retained in cases of civil salvage, in which the salvor of a distressed ship and/or its cargo received a fee for preventing a loss at sea.

Real property law was yet another of Hamilton's specialties. He represented both individuals and state governments in property boundary disputes, acting as counsel for New York in two boundary disputes with other states. The first, known as the *Massachusetts Dispute,* involved a portion of New York west of the Hudson River. Massachusetts claimed the land due to an overlapping colonial land grant. In 1785, New York retained Hamilton and Samuel Jones to represent the state in federal court. Massachusetts's argument was that discovery was the basis of title. Hamilton countered that occupancy and settlement were the appropriate elements by which to determine title, noting that the discovery doctrine would have entitled the Spanish to ownership of all of America due to prior discovery. This argument was never adjudicated, because the controversy was settled by the states in December 1786.

The second boundary dispute in which Hamilton represented New York was termed the Connecticut Gore controversy. This also encompassed British land grants that were vague about the exact location of boundaries. Connecticut claimed a small strip of land called "The Gore" along the New York–Pennsylvania border and had granted this land to two businessmen who owned the Gore Company. The men brought two ejectment actions in the U.S. Circuit Court for the District of Connecticut in 1796, against the grantees of the state of New York, for unlawful possession. Hamilton challenged the court's jurisdiction to try the case, suggesting that the U.S. Supreme Court should hear the case. Hamilton drafted a notice to the Gore Company, which had filed a petition to stay the ejectment action, while a bill in equity was filed in the Supreme Court. This notice appears to be the last action Hamilton took in the case. Both cases were eventually dismissed, and thus New York kept the land.

Similar to his role in the interstate boundary disputes, Hamilton represented individual property owners in boundary disputes arising from colonial land grants and also in disputes arising from land speculation deals. These cases were a substantial part of Hamilton's practice and predominantly consisted of ejectment and trespass actions. A major portion of the land in these disputes was that granted to three prominent families in the Hudson Valley, the Livingstons, the Schuylers, and the Van Rensselaers.

Criminal cases were not a large part of Hamilton's practice, but he represented a handful of criminal defendants, some of whom were court appointed. In *People v. Weeks* (1800), Hamilton, Aaron Burr, and Brockholst Livingston were defense counsel. Weeks was charged with murdering his fianceé and dumping her body in a well. The facts, as well as public opinion, were strongly against Weeks, but the defense put on a more organized case than the prosecution and convinced the jury that another man had committed the crime. Thus the jury found Weeks not guilty.

Hamilton also argued the significant case of *Hylton v. United States* (1796) before the U.S. Supreme Court. The immediate issue was the constitutionality of a carriage tax levied by Congress, but the larger question implicated the ability of the federal government to raise revenue. Arguing for the government at the request of the attorney general, Hamilton convinced the Court that the carriage tax was not a direct tax and was therefore a valid exercise of congressional power. Interestingly, the Court intimated that it would not enforce an act in violation of the Constitution, echoing Hamilton's views on judicial review.

One of Hamilton's noted contributions to the growth of constitutional law came in *People v. Croswell* (1804), the last important case of his career. On January 10, 1803, a grand jury indicted Harry Croswell, a Federalist newspaper editor, for seditious libel of President Thomas Jefferson. Croswell had published highly critical articles about Jefferson, accusing him of unconstitutional and partisan actions.

The defendant contended that his publication of this information was a public libel, in which truth should be a defense. This necessitated rejecting the English common law rule of libel, which did not allow truth as a defense.

The defendant also argued that the English law of libel was destructive of freedom of the press. Chief Justice Morgan Lewis, however, adhered to the common law doctrine, directing that a guilty verdict should be returned if the jury found that the defendant had in fact published the statements. He held that the issues of intent and falsity were matters of law for the court to decide.

Hamilton brilliantly argued Croswell's appeal to the Supreme Court of New York and helped to bring about a major change in the law. He insisted that freedom of the press required the defense of truth to charges of libel and that a jury, and not the court, should decide the question of guilt. Both of these, he said, were necessary to safeguard political discourse and to protect representative government. In his argument before the court, Hamilton declared, "I contend for the liberty of publishing truth, with good motives and for justifiable ends, even though it reflect on government, magistrates, or private persons" (Goebel 1964, 1:810). Although the court was equally divided and did not deliver an opinion, in 1805 the New York legislature enacted a statute that revamped the law of seditious libel and adopted much of Hamilton's position. Furthermore, at the Constitutional Convention of 1821, the section of the New York constitution on freedom of speech and of the press was amended to require that the jury in a libel case, rather than the court, determine the law and the facts, and that truth could be given as evidence. Hamilton's argument in *Croswell*, then, was a milestone in the development of freedom of the press.

Another of Hamilton's signal contributions to constitutional law came to fruition in *Fletcher v. Peck* (1810). Hamilton's legal advice, as well as the resulting Supreme Court decision, are known for their effect on the interpretation of the U.S. Constitution. Georgia had claimed a large tract of land called the Yazoo tract, in the Old Southwest. The Georgia legislature sold this land in 1795 to a group of land companies. Because the public was upset that the legislature had accepted bribes in exchange for enacting the bill, a repeal act was passed in February 1796, nullifying the sale of the Yazoo lands.

Rather than obtain a refund, for which the repeal act provided, some of the land companies chose to fight for their rights to the land. Apparently at the behest of the land companies, Hamilton prepared an influential legal opinion in 1796 that maintained that the Constitution's contract clause prevented state interference with public as well as private contracts. Therefore, he concluded that the repeal act was void and the original contract of sale was still enforceable.

In 1803, the companies instituted a collusive suit to obtain a Supreme Court decision on whether the repeal act was valid or was a violation of the contract clause of the Constitution. Fletcher sued Peck for allegedly selling him land that Peck did not rightfully own, which tract was part of the original 1795 Yazoo sale. In 1810, Chief Justice John Marshall delivered the Supreme Court's opinion, holding as Hamilton had predicted in his opinion to the land companies. The Court ruled that the original sale was valid and that the repeal act violated the contract clause of the U.S. Constitution. Hamilton's legal opinion pointed toward a vigorous application of the contract clause and shaped much of the jurisprudence of the Marshall Court.

In 1804, Hamilton's life was cut short by a political enemy, Aaron Burr. Hamilton had thwarted several of Burr's political endeavors, specifically his quest for the governorship of New York. Because Hamilton had spoken out against Burr, Burr challenged him to a duel. Hamilton accepted the challenge, and in July 1804, he died from a gunshot wound inflicted by Burr during the New Jersey duel.

—*James W. Ely Jr.*

Sources and Suggestions for Further Reading

Brookhiser, Richard. *Alexander Hamilton, American*. New York: Free Press, 1999.

Goebel, Julius, Jr., ed. *The Law Practice of Alexander Hamilton*. 5 vols. New York: Columbia University Press, 1964–1981.

Magrath, C. Peter. *Yazoo: Law and Politics in the New Republic: The Case of* Fletcher v. Peck. Providence: Brown University Press, 1966.

McDonald, Forrest. *Alexander Hamilton: A Biography*. New York: W. W. Norton, 1979.

Syrett, Harold C., ed. *The Papers of Alexander Hamilton*. New York: Columbia University Press, 1964–1981.

Who Was Who in America: Historical Volume, 1607–96. Rev. ed. Chicago: Marquis Who's Who, 1967.

HAMILTON, ANDREW

(1676–1741)

ANDREW HAMILTON
Archive Photos

THERE IS PROBABLY NO greater illustration of the principle that great cases identify great lawyers than the influence that the New York libel trial of John Peter Zenger has had on the reputation of Andrew Hamilton. Although Hamilton was a notable figure before this trial in his own right—indeed, one of the most notable colonial lawyers in America—his memory would have probably been largely lost along with other records of the cases of his period were it not for contemporary accounts of the *Zenger* case and its subsequent evocations by defenders of freedom of the press.

Little is known about Hamilton's background, although records indicate that he was born in 1676, probably in Scotland, that he may have graduated from St. Andrew's in Scotland (three men with this name graduated about the time he would have been there), and that about 1697 he moved to Virginia, where he may or may not for a time have assumed the name of Trent. The fact that he did not begin to practice law until three years after arriving in Virginia further suggests that he may have studied in the law offices of an attorney there. Captain and Mrs. Isaac Foxcroft, who had no children of their own and who later made him executor, and heir, of their estate, are known to have befriended Hamilton in Virginia (Nix 1964, 393). Hamilton began his practice in the Accomac County court in 1702 or 1703 and in other courts on Virginia's Eastern Shore, where his practice seems to have grown. In Virginia he married Ann Brown Preeson, the daughter of prominent Quaker Thomas Brown and Susanna Denwood Brown, and the childless widow of Susanna Brown's nephew, Joseph Preeson. Andrew and Ann would have a daughter and two sons, one of whom, James, would later serve as a lieutenant governor of Pennsylvania.

Amid evidence (including a negative comment by William Byrd) that he had stirred at least some opposition in Virginia, Hamilton moved to Kent County, on Maryland's Eastern Shore at about 1708 or 1709 and practiced there as well as in Delaware as he phased out his Virginia practice. Hamilton was chosen by agents of William Penn—whose wife noted that he was "an Ingenious man, and, for a Lawyer, I believe, a very honest one, & of very considerable Practice in these parts" (Loyd 1907, 7)—to bring a suit in 1712. In 1715, after Hamilton had sailed to England, where he was admitted to Gray's Inn—allowing him to practice law there—and returned (he would visit England again on business between 1724 and 1726), Kent County, Maryland, chose him as a deputy to the state legislature. He showed up late to the legislature because of a case he was arguing in Pennsylvania, where he soon moved.

Hamilton held a number of offices in Philadelphia, including that of attorney general (1717–1724), member of the provincial council (1720), judge of the court of vice admiralty (1737), master of the rolls, recorder of Philadelphia and prothonotary of the supreme court (1727), and an assemblyman from Bucks County (1735–1739) (Loyd 1907, 13). Hamilton was speaker of the Pennsylvania house (once being elected unanimously) for all but one year from 1729 to 1739, when he retired, largely because of his failing health. He appears to have been speaker of the Delaware legislature as well. Perhaps in part because of his associations with both states, Hamilton was influential in resolving a boundary dispute between Pennsylvania and Maryland. His tenure in Pennsylvania was marked by the passage of a law designed to aid insolvent debtors and by his personal superintendence and design of one of America's best-known public buildings, the Pennsylvania State House, now known as Independence Hall (Loyd 1907, 18).

The record of Hamilton's closing speech to the Pennsylvania assembly is a beautiful example of the kind of rhetoric that he might be supposed to have employed with good effect in the courts. Giving special note to the freedoms that the people of Pennsylvania exercised, Hamilton noted that it is not to the fertility of our soil, and the commodiousness of our rivers, that we ought chiefly to attribute the great progress this province has made, within so small a compass of years, in improvements, wealth, trade and navigation, and the extraordinary increase of people, who have been drawn hither from almost every country in Europe . . . it is principally and almost wholly owing to the excellency of our Constitution, under which we enjoy a greater share both of civil and religious liberty than any of our neighbors. (Loyd 1907, 20)

Hamilton further cautioned "against all personal animosity in public consultations," which he likened to a rock, which "the Constitution will at some time or other infallibly split upon" (Loyd 1907, 22).

Hamilton lived for two more years after retiring and died at his mansion in Bush Hill, Philadelphia (a house occupied after his death by his son, the lieutenant governor, and later by John Adams when he served as vice-president), in 1741. Initially buried on his family estate, his remains were later moved to the cemetery at Christ Church.

In writing his obituary, Benjamin Franklin, whom Hamilton had befriended on a passage back from England, noted that "he was no friend to power, as he had observed an ill-use had been frequently made of it in the Colonies; and therefore was seldom on good terms with the Governors." Franklin also noted, however, that "when he saw they meant well, he was for supporting them honourably, and was indefatigable in endeavoring to remove the prejudice of others." Franklin observed that "he spent much more time in hearing and reconciling differences in private (to the loss of his fees) than he did in pleading cases at the bar." Most interesting is Franklin's comment, that "his free manner of treating religious subjects gave offence to many, who, if a man may judge from their actions, were not themselves much in earnest. He feared God, loved mercy, and did justice. If he could not subscribe to the Creed of any particular Church, it was not for want of considering them all, for he had read much on religious subjects" (Loyd 1907, 24).

As a political figure, Hamilton was not above controversy, and there are a number of contemporary pamphlets that criticized him. A biographer explains that

his great success excited envy and stimulated calumny. The party leaders he opposed and frustrated, the rival lawyers whose ignorance and incompetence he exposed, the unfortunate litigants whom he disappointed, all were his enemies, or at least, ready to listen to his detractors. (Fisher 1892, 12)

Refuting most charges against him as baseless, a biographer further cites the *Zenger* case as one in which Hamilton, "with a professional reputation already established, [and] a fortune already acquired," "appeared before a Court which had already prejudged his case and a provincial jury very likely to be intimidated by the frowns of authority, to assert the great right of Freedom of the Press, without which most other rights would be valueless" (Fisher 1892, 13).

Hamilton conducted the defense of John Peter Zenger in a New York City courtroom in 1735. This case grew out of New York governor William Cosby's prosecution of Zenger for seditious libel in connection with articles and mock advertisements criticizing and ridiculing the governor that had been placed in the *New York Weekly Journal*. Zenger—a German immigrant who had once been an apprentice under the colony's royal printer, William Bradford, who edited the *New York Gazette*—edited the *Weekly Journal*, for which he received support from the powerful family of Lewis Morris, whom the Governor had dismissed from the supreme court. The *Journal* was also supported by James Alexander, an attorney who had defended Rip Van Dam, the prior interim governor who had refused to turn over half his salary to Cosby, a controversy that had been the basis of party division within the colony and the source of much initial opposition to Governor Cosby.

After a grand jury refused to do so, the governor and Attorney General Richard Bradley indicted Zenger "by information," which did not require grand jury approval. Zenger was arrested, and he spent eight months in prison awaiting trial and continuing to dictate the *Weekly Journal* to his wife, who maintained its publication. Chief Justice James Delancey, whom Cosby had appointed to replace Lewis Morris, further disbarred Zenger's would-be attorneys, James Alexander and William Smith, although he did subsequently appoint one John Chambers to represent Zenger. Although Chambers succeeded in ensuring that a jury was chosen that was not packed by the governor's forces, he was more than willing to turn the defense over to the fifty-nine-year-old Hamilton, who dramatically announced from the audience that he would take the case after Chambers's opening arguments (Katz 1963, 22), and who apparently argued the case without being paid—although he was given a five-ounce gold box for his efforts.

Few causes could have appeared bleaker than the one that Hamilton assumed. Precedents in both Great Britain and America suggested that negative critiques of governing authorities were serious offenses. Truth was not, at the time, regarded as a defense; indeed, the more truthful the publications, the greater the libel was considered to be! The limited role of the jury was simply that of deciding whether the accused was guilty of uttering such negative statements, and, in this case, Zenger did not deny editing the *Weekly Journal*.

Cotton Mather's First Address to Lawyers

Puritan clergyman Cotton Mather is credited with giving the first address to American lawyers in 1710. The speech indicates that in the early eighteenth century, as today, lawyers were viewed as individuals with a great capacity to do both good and harm. Although Mather's language is antiquated, his sentiments point lawyers toward the highest ideals:

GENTLEMEN: Your Opportunities to Do Good are such, and so Liberal and Gentlemanly is your Education . . . that Proposals of what you may do cannot but promise themselves as Obliging Reception with you. 'Tis not come to so sad a pass that an Honest Lawyer may, as of old the Honest Publican, require a Statue merely on the Score of Rarity. . . . A Lawyer should be a Scholar, but, Sirs, when you are called upon to be wise, the main Intention is that you may be wise to do Good. . . . A Lawyer that is a Knave deserves Death, more than a Band of Robbers; for he profanes the Sanctuary of the Distressed and Betrays the Liberties of the People. To ward off such a Censure, a Lawyer must shun all those Indirect Ways of making Hast to be Rich, in which a man cannot be Innocent; such ways as provoked the Father of Sir Matthew Hale to give over the Practice of the Law, because of the Extreme Difficulty to preserve a Good Conscience in it. Sirs, be prevailed withal to keep constantly a Court of Chancery in your Own Breast. . . . This Piety must Operate very particularly in the Pleading of Causes. You will abhor, Sir, to appear in a Dirty Cause. If you discern that your Client has an Unjust Cause, you will faithfully advise him of it. You will be sincerely desirous that Truth and Justice may take place. You will speak nothing which shall be to the Prejudice of Either. You will abominate the use of all unfair Arts to Confound Evidence, to Browbeat Testimonies, to Suppress what may give Light in the Case. . . . There has been an old Complaint, That a Good Lawyer seldom is a Good Neighbor. You know how to Confute it, Gentlemen, by making your skill in the Law, a Blessing to your Neighborhood. You may, Gentlemen, if you please, be a vast Accession to the Felicity of your Countreys. . . . Perhaps you may discover many things yet wanting in the Law; Mischiefs in the Execution and Application of the Laws, which ought to be better provided against; Mischiefs annoying of Mankind, against which no Laws are yet provided. The Reformation of the Law, and more Law for the Reformation of the World is what is mightily called for. (Warren 1966, ix–x)

REFERENCE

Warren, Charles. *A History of the American Bar.* New York: Howard Fertig, 1966.

As one who was reputed to be the best attorney in America (Katz 1963, 21), Hamilton undoubtedly knew what the law was. He also recognized that he might be able to make an appeal to the law as it might and should be against the law as it actually was. In brilliant arguments before the jury, Hamilton connected existing English precedents on libel law to the hated Star Chamber and suggested that, especially in the case of officials such as governors, who did not share actual sovereignty with the king, criticism was essential to the protection of liberty. Hamilton questioned the efficacy of English precedents in the New World setting. Denied by Justice Delancey the right to offer evidence to prove the truth of the accusations that had been printed, Hamilton in effect appealed to the jurors to recognize their truth anyway and to nullify existing law on behalf of a higher ideal. He succeeded in getting the jury to exonerate Zenger, to the huzzas of his audience, and he was subsequently feted before returning to Philadelphia. Heralded as this victory was in the colonies, it would be decades before the law to which Hamilton appealed would be recognized either in Great Britain or in America; curiously, it would be Alexander Hamilton who would later mention the Zenger precedent when defending a fellow Federalist, Henry Croswell, in 1804 against similar accusations raised by Democratic Republicans (Katz 1963, 32–33).

Andrew Hamilton clearly carried the day in the *Zenger* case by both the audaciousness of his arguments and the eloquence of his speaking. Hamilton's reasoning closely resembles that which would later find expression at the time of the American Revolution and the founding of the United States. At one point Hamilton argued that

> power may justly be compared to a great river; while kept within its due bounds, it is both beautiful and useful; but when it overflows it banks, it is then too impetuous to be stemmed; it bears down on all before it, and brings destruction and desolation whenever it comes. If then this is the nature of power, let us at least do our duty, and like wise men (who value freedom) use our utmost care to support liberty, the only bulwark against lawless power, which, in all ages, has sacrificed to its wild lust, and boundless ambition, the blood of the best men that ever lived. (Loyd 1907, 40)

Further pointing to his own advanced age, Hamilton said, "I should think it my duty, if required, to go to the utmost part of the land, where my service could be of any use, in assisting to quench the flame of prosecutions upon informations, set on foot by the government, to deprive a people of the right of remonstrating (and complaining too) of the arbitrary attempts of men in power" (Loyd 1907, 41). Much as WEBSTER would later evoke the small size of Dartmouth College in arguing its case before the U.S. Supreme Court, Hamilton said that Zenger's case was "not of small nor private concern." Rather than the mere cause of "a poor printer," he said that "It may, in its consequence, affect every freeman that lives under a British government on the main of America" (Loyd 1907, 41).

Just as JOHN ADAMS would later note that James Otis first fanned the flames of the American Revolution, Gouverneur Morris (a descendant of the displaced judge in the *Zenger* case) would later say that the *Zenger* case was "the germ of American freedom, the morning star of that liberty which subsequently revolutionized America" (McManus 1999, 914). Hamilton had the courage to see the law of freedom of speech not so much as it was as how it could be. Thus, a contemporary London correspondent of Benjamin Franklin's *Pennsylvania Gazette* noted that an English lawyer who heard about the case had said, "If it is not law, it is better than law, it ought to be law, and will always be law wherever justice prevails" (Konkle 1941, 109). Hamilton suggested that American liberty might be even wider than the liberty of Englishmen, and he arguably laid the foundation for freedom of the press that is as broad as that in any modern nation.

—**John R. Vile**

Sources and Suggestions for Further Reading

Fisher, Joshua Francis. "Andrew Hamilton, Esq., of Pennsylvania." *Pennsylvania Magazine of History and Biography* 16 (1892): 1–27.

Katz, Stanley Nider. Introduction to *A Brief Narrative of the Case and Trial of John Peter Zenger*, by James Alexander, edited by Stanley Nider Katz. Cambridge: Belknap Press of Harvard University Press, 1963.

Konkle, Burton Alva. *The Life of Andrew Hamilton, 1676–1741, "The Day-Star of the American Revolution."* Freeport, N.Y.: Books for Libraries Press, 1941.

Loyd, William Henry, Jr. "Andrew Hamilton." In *Great American Lawyers*, edited by William Draper Lewis. Philadelphia: John C. Winston, 1907, 1:1–48.

McManus, Edgar J. "Hamilton, Andrew." In *American National Biography*, edited by John A. Garraty and Mark C. Carnes. New York: Oxford University Press, 1999, 9:913–915.

Nix, Foster C. "Andrew Hamilton's Early Years in the American Colonies." *William and Mary Quarterly*, 3d ser., 21 (1964): 390–407.

HARLAN, JOHN MARSHALL, II

(1899–1971)

LONG BEFORE HIS YEARS ON the U.S. Supreme Court (1955–1971), John Marshall Harlan II was senior partner and chief litigator in one of Wall Street's most prestigious law firms. Grandson of the first Justice John Harlan (1833–1911), the complex Kentucky slaveholder and opponent of abolition who became a champion of civil rights on the Court, the younger Harlan was born in Chicago on May 20, 1899. His father, John Maynard Harlan, a colorful lawyer, was a Chicago alderman and unsuccessful mayoral candidate who railed against the city's traction (streetcar) interests and their grip on local officials, but ultimately made his peace with those same interests, becoming their counsel on a lucrative retainer. John Marshall's mother was the former Elizabeth Palmer Flagg of Yonkers, whom John Maynard met on one of his family's frequent summer holidays at Block Island, an exclusive resort off Long Island, and married in 1890.

His parents' at times turbulent and often unhappy union produced John Marshall and three

JOHN MARSHALL HARLAN II
Collection of the Supreme Court of the United States

daughters: Elizabeth, Janet, and Edith. The financial security John Maynard's traction clients provided, as well as the family's impeccable social connections, placed the Harlans at the center of Chicago society. But young John Marshall spent little of his life there. Packed off at an early age to a Canadian boarding school, where he excelled in academics and sports, he spent his summers with his family at their Quebec summer home. After a final year of preparatory education at the Lake Placid School in New York, he enrolled at Princeton in the class of 1920. After compiling an outstanding record at Princeton, where he was president of the student newspaper, he attended Oxford's Balliol College, the university's law school, finishing his three years of study there with a "First" in jurisprudence and placing seventh in a class of 120.

On his return from England, Roger A. Derby, the husband of Harlan's eldest sister Elizabeth, helped him to secure a position with Root, Clark, Buckner & Howland (now Dewey, Ballantine), one of New York's finest firms. Emory Buckner, Root, Clark's chief litigator, quickly became young Harlan's mentor and the greatest single influence on his professional development. Since Harlan's esoteric studies in jurisprudence at Oxford had hardly equipped him for an American law practice, Buckner insisted, over Harlan's initial objection, that his charge enroll at New York Law School, where he completed the two-year program in a year, winning admission to the bar in 1924. Under Buckner, Harlan also honed his litigator's skills, becoming a master of careful preparation and thorough attention to detail.

Soon, the young associate also got his first taste of public service. In 1925, Emory Buckner became U.S. attorney for the Southern District of New York. Harlan and other promising young lawyers—"Buckner's Boy Scouts," the press quickly dubbed them—joined his staff. With Harlan as his chief assistant in charge of the office's Prohibition division, Buckner launched a vigorous campaign to enforce the federal Prohibition law they—like most New Yorkers—personally detested. Given the office's limited budget, Buckner and Harlan decided to curtail the number of costly, time-consuming, and often fruitless criminal prosecutions, resorting instead to an approach that was proving successful in Chicago: the padlocking as public nuisances of nightclubs and other establishments found by the courts to be in violation of the Volstead Act. Not only were hundreds of clubs and restaurants closed, but thousands of criminal prosecutions were also processed. More than 70 defendants were acquitted after trial; the jury deadlocked in 10 cases; and nearly 700 cases were dismissed. But 3,880 guilty pleas were secured as well as 48 convictions after trial.

Among the criminal prosecutions, Harlan considered six major cases involving numerous defendants. In one, William V. ("Big Bill") Dwyer, one of the most notorious bootleggers of the period, received a two-year sentence and a ten-thousand-dollar fine. In another case, the mayor of Edgewater, New Jersey, and twenty-two confederates drew prison terms on numerous charges. But the most celebrated of the Buckner-Harlan Prohibition prosecutions involved Earl Carroll, the theater owner and producer. At midnight, February 22, 1926, following his *Vanities* showgirls' last performance of the evening at his Manhattan theater, Carroll hosted what the *New York Times* later characterized as an "all-night bacchanalian orgy" for five hundred guests, complete with two jazz bands, two large tables of food and drink, three large tubs of "iced liquid," and a chorus girl bathing nude in a bathtub of what appeared to be an illicit beverage.

Called by Buckner and Harlan before two grand juries, Carroll denied under oath that liquor had been served at his party or that a woman had bathed on his stage, as well as other details furnished by witnesses to the event. While the first grand jury adjourned without making any findings in the case, the second charged the producer with six counts of perjury. Carroll's trial before a packed courtroom, with Harlan presenting the prosecution, produced no firm evidence that liquor had been served at the defendant's bash. In fact, a representative of the Canada Dry Company testified that his firm had paid the defendant for the privilege of serving free ginger ale to *Vanities* audiences and that sixty to seventy thousand pints of the product had been consumed at Carroll's theater in the past year. The showman's conviction appeared to hinge, therefore, on his denials regarding the bathtub incident. Harlan's star witness on that point was to be the "Bathtub Venus," as the press called Joyce Hawley, the showgirl who testified that she had indeed bathed nude on Carroll's stage—and complained that he had reneged on his promise to pay her seven hundred to a thousand dollars for her appearance. Harlan's effort to portray Miss Hawley as a much-abused innocent was difficult at best. Although only seventeen, she had been posing nude as an artist's model since age fourteen; however traumatic she may have found the bathtub incident, moreover, she was now doing the same act nightly at a Greenwich Village theater. Ultimately, though, Hawley must have been a credible witness. At one point, the trial judge had brought smiles to Buckner's and Harlan's faces when he asked incredulously, "And were these men all standing around that bathtub just to get a drink of ginger ale?" (Yarbrough 1992, 28). Even so, the jury acquitted Carroll of lying about the consumption of liquor at the party. Jurors convicted the showman, however, of lying about the bathtub incident. Given New Yorkers' distaste for Prohibition, Harlan considered a conviction on any count a triumph.

Despite his success in dealing with Prohibition violators, Emory Buckner's tenure as U.S. attorney was hardly free of criticism. Critics charged that he was enforcing the law with undue enthusiasm—or not vigorously enough. Some thought he had his eye on the governor's mansion and that his Prohibition campaign was designed to bolster his popularity with voters, although the notion that Buckner's defense of the "dry" faith would endear him to most New Yorkers was questionable at best. Buckner was sensitive to such complaints, and charges of politics in his handling of the prosecution of two principals in the scandals of President Warren G. Harding's administration were the final straw; in 1926, Buckner resigned as U.S. attorney and returned with Harlan to Root, Clark. Two years later, however, Buckner and his protégé were back in public service. Buckner agreed to an appointment as a special assistant state attorney general in charge of an investigation and prosecution of Queens borough president Maurice E. Connolly on charges of municipal graft, with Harlan again serving as Buckner's chief assistant. Harlan's meticulously developed investigation, graphically depicted in a four-by-thirty-foot courtroom chart detailing the defendant's misdeeds, made Buckner's presentation at trial a relatively simple task. Connolly was convicted, and the appellate brief Harlan wrote effectively blocked the borough president's appeal efforts.

Harlan's successes as head of Buckner's Prohibition division in the U.S. attorney's office and his pivotal role in the Queens inquiry had enhanced his growing reputation in New York legal circles. On his return to Root, Clark after the Connolly case, he was clearly established as Emory Buckner's most valued assistant. That same year, Harlan also met and married Ethel Andrews, the strikingly attractive daughter of a Yale colonial history professor and sister of another Root, Clark associate. Ethel had been previously married to a New York architect twenty years her senior, from whom she had been divorced only a year. Divorce was rare in those days, and Harlan was nervous at the prospect of telling his mother that her only son was about to marry a divorcée. In appearance, personality, and disposition, however, the future justice had always been much closer to his refined, reserved mother than to his bombastic, temperamental father, who, continually pressed with financial problems in his later years, had become increasingly estranged from the family. When Elizabeth Harlan gave her blessing to the match, her son and Ethel were married on November 10, 1928, in Farmington, Connecticut. By all accounts, theirs was a generally happy marriage, producing a daughter and enduring until his death.

Soon, too, Harlan would become one of his firm's most important members. In 1931, he was made a junior partner. As Emory Buckner's health began to decline, Harlan also increasingly assumed leadership of Root, Clark's litigation team. His first major case in that capacity was also to be his most bizarre. In it, Harlan successfully defended heirs to the estate of the eccentric New York millionaire Ella Wendel from more than two thousand claimants. Miss Wendel's will left the bulk of the family's real estate fortune

Noah Walter Parden and Styles Hutchins

The first African-American lawyer ever to take the lead role in arguing a case before a justice of the U.S. Supreme Court was apparently Noah Walter Parden, who appeared before Justice John Marshall Harlan on March 17, 1906. Parden went before Justice Harlan on behalf of a twenty-three-year-old illiterate African-American named Ed Johnson, who had been accused and convicted of the assault and rape of a twenty-one-year-old white woman named Nevada Taylor in Chattanooga, Tennessee. The local sheriff, Joseph F. Shipp, and the judge, Sam McReynolds, were prepared to carry out Johnson's death sentence expeditiously after his court-appointed attorneys, Robert T. Cameron, W. G. M. Thomas, and Lewis Shepherd, agreed with the judge that an appeal of Johnson's conviction was likely to lead to mob violence like that which had first erupted when Johnson was arrested and incarcerated in the Chattanooga jail.

Unfortunately, Johnson's trial had been riddled with problems, and there is little evidence that he was guilty of the crime for which he was charged. African-Americans had been excluded from the jury, and Johnson's friends and family had not been able to attend. Judge McReynolds had met privately with attorneys and told them that he would not grant a change of venue. Although the victim believed Johnson to have been her attacker, she could not say for sure. The chief witness against Johnson, who had tried to link him to a leather strap that was found on the scene, had received a handsome monetary award. Numerous African-American witnesses who confirmed Johnson's alibi were apparently ignored, and one juror had threatened Johnson's life during the trial with no apparent response from the judge. Parden and his partner, Styles Hutchins, had entered the case after the three court-appointed attorneys decided that an appeal would be futile, and Johnson's father pleaded with them to take his son's case.

Although they were both African-Americans, Parden and Hutchins were quite different. Parden was a disciple of Booker T. Washington, who believed in trying to get along with white people. He was also deeply religious. Parden had studied law at Central Tennessee College in Nashville, Tennessee, and returned to Chattanooga, where he had attended high school. Unlike Parden, Hutchins was a follower of W. E. B. DuBois, who wanted more immediate equality for African-Americans. He had been one of the first African-American graduates of the University of South Carolina and had moved to Chattanooga after facing numerous obstacles to the practice of law in Georgia. Also very religious, Hutchins had convinced Parden to accept Johnson's appeal after noting that "much has been given to us by God and man. Now much is expected" (Curriden and Phillips 1999, 139).

When they appeared before the trial judge about the possibility of an appeal, the judge openly ridiculed them, asking,

> What can two Negro lawyers do that the defendant's previous three attorneys were unable to achieve? Do you know the law better than this court or the lawyers who represented the defendant? Are you aware of some legal principles that I have never heard of? What can a Negro lawyer know that a white lawyer does not? Do you think a Negro lawyer could possibly be smarter or know the law better than a white lawyer? (Curriden and Phillips 1999, 144)

Judge Reynolds further attempted to trick the lawyers by allowing them to be-

(continues)

(continued)

lieve that he would not count Sunday in the calculation of days within which an appeal had to be filed. Despite these obstacles, Parden and Hutchins filed an appeal to the Tennessee Supreme Court in *Ed Johnson v. State of Tennessee*. After losing in this venue, Parden and Hutchins filed an appeal in federal court under the Habeas Corpus Act of 1867. The U.S. district court judge, Charles Dickens Clark, stayed Johnson's execution until an appeal could be made to the U.S. Supreme Court, but he seemed unsure about his authority to issue orders to state officials.

It was in this capacity that Noah Parden appeared with an African-American attorney from Washington, D.C., named Emmanuel D. Molyneaux Hewlett in an ex parte proceeding before Justice John Marshall Harlan, who supervised the federal circuit that included Tennessee. Ironically, although he admired the work of Parden and Hutchins, W. E. B. Du Bois had urged them to turn the work over to more experienced attorneys. Much to the surprise and chagrin of many Chattanooga residents, Harlan—the only dissenter in the case of *Plessy v. Ferguson* (1896) upholding the system of Jim Crow segregation laws—issued an order postponing Johnson's execution and accepting his appeal to the U.S. Supreme Court.

It was at this point that mob rule raised its ugly head. After threats of a mob circulated, Sheriff Shipp left his Chattanooga jail practically unguarded, and, predictably, a mob stormed the jail. After Johnson was extricated by force from his cell, he continued to maintain his composure and to proclaim his innocence, saying (in words later inscribed on his tombstone), "God bless you all. I am an innocent man." He was nonetheless dragged by the mob to a bridge, hanged, and riddled with bullets; one observer subsequently cut off one of his fin-

gers for a souvenir. Sheriff Shipp, who had made no real attempt to quell the mob, subsequently issued a statement blaming the Supreme Court's decision for the turn to lawlessness.

In an extraordinary development, the Supreme Court charged Sheriff Shipp and leading ringleaders of the mob with contempt and ordered a trial to be held in Chattanooga before James D. Maher, a deputy clerk of the U.S. Supreme Court, acting as a commissioner. The U.S. Supreme Court subsequently upheld the conviction of Sheriff Shipp and five other defendants and sentenced them to jail.

By the time of Shipp's trial, Parden and Hutchins had both left Chattanooga. Although they had previously garnered numerous cases (often for little more than a free meal or two) from the African-American community, they had so antagonized Judge McReynolds and other local members of the bar that African-Americans no longer thought they could be effective in court. Lecturing for a time in the North, both apparently settled in the Oklahoma Territory, where Parden may have founded a small newspaper (Curriden and Phillips 1999, 349).

United States v. Shipp remains the only criminal trial that the U.S. Supreme Court has ever conducted. The case appears both to have helped reduce the number of lynchings and to have strengthened the resolve of sheriffs to intervene to stop such tragedies (Curriden and Phillips 1999, 339). Although they are not well known among American lawyers, Parden and Hutchins nonetheless demonstrated how lawyers with courage can make a difference.

REFERENCE

Curriden, Mark, and Leroy Phillips Jr. *Contempt of Court: The Turn-of-the-Century Lynching That Launched a Hundred Years of Federalism.* New York: Faber & Faber, 1999. [Contains photographs of both Parden and Hutchins.]

of about $75 million to a number of charitable institutions. But among phony heirs were several claimants who erected a tombstone bearing altered birth and death dates in a West Virginia cemetery, as well as Illinois claimants who produced letters from Wendel's father, dated 1836 and 1841, but written on paper purchased from Woolworth's and manufactured no earlier than 1930. The most audacious and, for those named in Wendel's will, potentially dangerous impostor was one Thomas Patrick Morris, a frail Scotsman who claimed to be the progeny of a secret marriage of Wendel's brother to an Edinburgh woman. With characteristic attention to detail, however, Harlan demolished the assertions of each fraudulent claimant. He established, for example, that the marriage certificate on which Morris largely based his claim to be the product of an 1876 marriage of Wendel's brother in Scotland was in fact torn from a book printed in 1913, thirty-seven years after the nuptials purportedly occurred!

Earlier, Harlan had assisted Emory Buckner in defending heavyweight boxer Gene Tunney in a suit for a piece of the champ's earnings from the 1926 Tunney-Dempsey match. And in 1940, he became involved briefly, but significantly, in a case that raised the sorts of fundamental civil liberties issues he would later confront on the Supreme Court. When the New York City Board of Higher Education offered noted British scholar Bertrand Russell a visiting professorship at City College, Russell's unorthodox life style and views on sex, morality, marriage, child-rearing, and education—especially his apparent support of sexual relations among college students and adultery as therapy for troubled marriages—provoked immediate controversy. In response to a taxpayer suit brought by a Brooklyn housewife challenging the board's action, a state judge who was a staunch Roman Catholic held the appointment invalid. Invoking a state law traditionally applied only to primary and secondary schoolteachers, the judge concluded that employment on City College's faculty was limited to U.S. citizens and those who had passed a qualifying examination. He also scorned Russell's "notorious immoral and salacious writings" and assumed authority to forbid creation of a "chair of indecency" at the college (Yarbrough 1992, 53). Volunteering his services without fee, Harlan filed a ninety-four-page appellate brief on the board's behalf. But two appeals courts upheld the trial judge. That defeat, a colleague later recalled, was the only time he ever saw Harlan truly angry.

As Harlan's battle over the Bertrand Russell appointment was reaching a frustrating conclusion, war erupted in Europe. By then in his early forties, Harlan was well past the usual age of military service, but he was anxious nonetheless to play a part in the great conflict. Enthusiastically accepting an opportunity to head the Army Air Corps' intelligence section in England, Harlan and his team of scientists and lawyers made numerous recommendations to military authorities, substantially improving the accuracy of air strikes. Toward the end of his tour of duty, he also served on a committee planning the postwar occupation of Germany.

After his separation from the service in December 1944, Harlan resumed his Wall Street law practice. As a senior partner in one of the city's leading firms, he was now at the top of his profession. He and Ethel had acquired a succession of increasingly commodious and comfortable Manhattan apartments and in 1937 had built a country home in Weston, Connecticut, on twenty acres of beautiful countryside. After the war as before, his principal clients were major corporate interests, including American Telephone and Telegraph and its subsidiary Western Electric, ITT, the American Optical Company, and the Gillette safety razor company. He also argued a number of important cases in the Supreme Court, including one in which he represented foreign diamond mining interests in an antitrust suit and another that produced a landmark decision in the fields of corporate law and civil procedure by erecting a substantial obstacle to suits by minor stockholders against companies in which they held stock.

Harlan's principal postwar clients, however, were members of the Du Pont family and a number of their corporate interests. In one antitrust suit, a district court rejected Harlan's arguments, holding that Du Pont and other companies were involved in an international conspiracy to eliminate competition in the trade of chemical products, arms, and ammunition. He successfully defended two of the Du Pont brothers, however, in another suit against their company, General Motors, and other businesses with large Du Pont holdings. For a Chicago phase of that litigation, a huge team of lawyers from several of the nation's leading corporate law firms descended on the city several months before the trial was to begin, taking over several floors of a local hotel and easily outgunning the government, which at one point was represented by a single lawyer. Perhaps discomfited by the stark contrast between the massive corporate and negligible government forces in the case, Harlan even offered the government's attorney—a "rabid New Dealer," the future justice's daughter later said—some of the space reserved for the defense team. After a nearly seven-month trial, the district judge accepted Harlan's central premise that the defendants' connections, however elaborate, established no conspiracy to violate the federal antitrust statutes. After Harlan's appointment to the Supreme Court, a majority, speaking through Justice William J. Brennan, overturned his trial victory in the Du Pont case. Given his earlier service as counsel in the case, Harlan had recused himself from participation in the Court's deliberations. As Brennan summarized the majority's opinion, however, Harlan penned a note to Justice Felix Frankfurter, one of two dissenters, decrying Brennan's "*superficial understanding of a really impressive record. . . . I hardly recognize the case as I listen to him speak*" (Yarbrough 1992, 135).

Even before the trial court's ruling in the Du Pont case, however, Harlan's career was taking a new and permanent direction. Although he was essentially uninterested in partisan politics, Harlan had participated over the years in a variety of Republican political campaigns as well as other political and civic activities. He enjoyed close relations with the moderate wing of the GOP and New York governor Thomas E. Dewey, the party's 1948 presidential candidate. When Dewey created a state crime commission to investigate ties between organized crime and government, the governor's selection of Harlan in March 1951 as the commission's chief counsel was thus hardly surprising. Harlan served without pay in the position until January of the following year, when the Du Pont suit began to require his exclusive attention. Augmenting his staff of lawyers were a number of full-time investigators, and local police were put at his disposal for temporary assignments. Investigating the influence of organized crime on the New York waterfront and in other areas, including the state judiciary, he and his staff conducted more than six thousand interviews and called more than two hundred witnesses before five public hearings. Their inquiry led to creation of the New York Waterfront Commission, among other reforms, made Harlan the target of death threats, and also generated charges, ultimately held to be unfounded, that he was using the commission and his staff for partisan political purposes.

By the time of Dwight D. Eisenhower's inauguration as president in January 1953, Harlan not only enjoyed a reputation as an outstanding corporate lawyer whose selection to the federal bench was likely to find favor with traditional Republican loyalists; he had also devoted a respectable share of his time and energy to party, bar, and public service causes. Of even greater significance to the future direction of his career were his ties to Governor Dewey, whose forces had supported Eisenhower at the 1952 GOP national convention; and Herbert Brownell, Eisenhower's attorney general and the key administration figure in the president's selection of federal judges, was a close Harlan friend of long standing. When a vacancy opened on the Court of Appeals for the Second Circuit, Brownell offered his friend the post, and Harlan accepted. His nomination went to the Senate for confirmation proceedings in mid-January 1954; on February 8, the Senate Judiciary Committee approved the nomination by a unanimous vote, and the next day the full Senate concurred.

On the Second Circuit, Harlan's caseload was confined largely to tax and other mundane issues. In *United States v. Flynn* (1954), the one notable exception to that pattern, Harlan spoke for a three-judge panel in upholding the convictions of twelve Communists under the Smith Act. The narrow construction Harlan assigned freedom of speech and related civil liberties claims in *Flynn* reminded one critical commentator of the archaic English law of constructed treason.

Harlan's circuit tenure was also to be quite brief. When Herbert Brownell had first approached his friend about the court of appeals vacancy, he frankly indicated that the appointment would give Harlan the prior judicial experience, however brief, that the White House, following Earl Warren's 1953 nomination as chief justice, was insisting Supreme Court nominees possess. When Justice ROBERT H. JACKSON, another New Yorker, died in October 1954, Harlan was Brownell's choice to fill the vacancy. Segregationist southern Democrats and conservative Republicans delayed Harlan's confirmation in the Senate for nearly five months, using the occasion for attacks on the Court's recent school desegregation ruling in the *Brown* case and on Harlan's nominal membership in the Atlantic Union Council, which critics considered a hotbed of "one-worlders" and a threat to U.S. sovereignty. Confirmation was never in doubt, but the Senate vote to approve the appointment was 71 to 11, with fourteen other senators abstaining.

On the supreme bench, Harlan quickly joined the restraintist voting bloc headed by Felix Frankfurter, whom the new justice had met years before through Harlan's mentor Emory Buckner, one of Frankfurter's closest friends. Like Frankfurter, Harlan developed his jurisprudence around a central premise that the political processes and principles of federalism and separation of powers ultimately were more effective safeguards of individual liberty than broad judicial interpretations of constitutional guarantees, as well as the corollary view that the policy preferences of elected public officials were entitled to substantial judicial deference in a free society. Consistent with such thinking, he generally supported governmental assertions of national security interests against First Amendment and related constitutional claims. In his last term, for example, he dissented when a 6–3 majority upheld free press claims in *New York Times v. United States* (1971), the *Pentagon Papers* case. He also opposed the Court's intervention in reapportionment cases, the *Miranda* restrictions on police interrogation of suspects, extension of the Fourth Amendment exclusionary rule to state cases, and the "incorporation" doctrine under which a majority applied most Bill of Rights safeguards to the states via the Fourteenth Amendment. After Justice Frankfurter's departure from the Court in 1962, at the beginning of the most "liberal-activist" period in the Warren Court's history, Harlan became the most significant critic of Warren Court constitutional trends.

His regard for the "passive virtues" did not mean, however, that Harlan invariably rejected civil liberties claims. His dissent in *Poe v. Ullman* (1961), for example, embraced a constitutional right of sexual privacy four years before the Court adopted that position in *Griswold v. Connecticut* (1965). And when his colleague, friend, and jurisprudential opponent Justice Hugo L. Black dissented in *Griswold*, emphasizing that judges should stick to the words of the Constitution and charging Harlan and others of the majority with writing their own notions of "natural law" into the document's meaning, Harlan decried in a concurring opinion what he considered the futility of Black's efforts to confine the Constitution to its literal meaning. For Harlan, trained at Oxford in a common-law jurisprudence, the judge's role was inherently creative, but was to be tempered with due regard for majoritarian institutions and federal principles.

Although he was virtually blind during the last several years of his tenure, Harlan served with distinction on the Court until the fall of 1971, when spinal cancer and related medical difficulties forced his departure from the bench. On September 23, a respectable ten days after Justice Black's retirement, Harlan sent his own retirement letter to President Nixon and the other justices. On December 29, 1971, he died. After his cremation, his ashes were interred at Emmanuel Episcopal Cemetery near his beloved Weston, Connecticut, estate. Harlan's judicial record confirmed his place as a "judge's judge" in Supreme Court history. Long before he served on the high bench, however, his illustrious career as one of the nation's finest corporate litigators had also justified his admirers' praise of Harlan as a "lawyer's lawyer."

—*Tinsley Yarbrough*

Sources and Suggestions for Further Reading

Dorsen, Norman. "The Second Mr. Justice Harlan: A Constitutional Conservative." *New York University Law Review* 44 (1969): 249–271.

Harlan, John M. *The Evolution of a Judicial Philosophy: Selected Opinions and Papers of Justice John M. Harlan*, edited by David L. Shapiro. Cambridge: Harvard University Press, 1969.

Laporte, Cloyd. "John M. Harlan Saves the Ella Wendel Estate." *American Bar Association Journal* 59 (1973): 868.

"Mr. Justice Harlan: A Symposium." *Harvard Law Review* 85 (1971): 369–391.

Yarbrough, Tinsley E. *John Marshall Harlan: Great Dissenter of the Warren Court.* New York: Oxford University Press, 1992.

HASTIE, WILLIAM HENRY

(1904–1976)

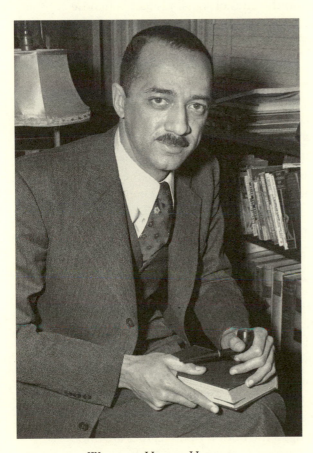

WILLIAM HENRY HASTIE
Bettmann/Corbis

WILLIAM HENRY HASTIE WAS A legal educator, civil rights litigator and activist, one of the foremost African-American lawyers of the mid-twentieth century, and the first African-American appointed to the federal judiciary. Hastie was born into a middle-class family in Knoxville, Tennessee. His father was William Henry Hastie, a graduate of Howard University's College of Pharmacy who worked as a clerk in the U.S. Patent Office; his mother was Roberta Childs, a schoolteacher educated at Fisk University and Talladega College. In 1921, Hastie graduated with honors from Paul Laurence Dunbar High School in the District of Columbia. Four years later, he graduated from Amherst College a member of Phi Beta Kappa and the class valedictorian.

As a result of his sterling academic performance at Amherst, Hastie had the opportunity to study abroad, either at Oxford University or the University of Paris. Instead, he decided to accept a faculty appointment at the Bordentown Manual Training School in New Jersey, an institution for African-American students that gave Hastie the opportunity to earn money to attend graduate school. The position also fulfilled Hastie's strong sense of obligation to teach as a way of returning knowledge into the African-American community. Hastie emerged as a gifted teacher and role model for his students, but after two years he decided to press forward with a career in the law. His decision to do so reflected Hastie's belief, shared with his cousin, the renowned African-American lawyer CHARLES HAMILTON HOUSTON, that law was a tool of social engineering that could be employed to advance the agenda of equality for African-Americans. Moreover, in the mind of Hastie, as was true of Houston, there was only one place to train for a life in the law: Harvard.

Hastie viewed Harvard as a means to the ends of social justice. When he entered law school in 1927 there were only about 1,230 African-American lawyers out of a total of about 160,000 attorneys in the nation. During this period, African-American lawyers were especially scarce in the South. Hastie believed that African-Americans had a particular duty to pursue social change through the law, since he concluded that white lawyers, no matter how well intentioned, could not be the most effective advocates in civil rights cases because, to some extent, they benefited from the exploitation that the civil rights movement sought to end. Hastie also learned a hard lesson about the assumptions behind even the most liberal members of the Harvard faculty. Hastie was one of only nine African-Americans on whom Harvard conferred LL.B. degrees between 1920 and 1930, the latter year that of Hastie's graduation. As previous law school dean and president of Harvard University Derek Bok has noted about the law school's provision of education to African-Americans, "If our tradition is long, it is also very thin" (Ware 1984, 30). Moreover, even as distinguished a figure as future Supreme Court Justice Felix Frankfurter embraced assumptions about African-Americans that upset Hastie. Obviously thinking that he was paying Hastie a compliment, Professor Frankfurter observed that the young African-American student was "not only the best colored man we have ever had but he is as good as all but three or four outstanding white men that have been here during the last twenty years" (Ware 1984, 30). Hastie observed in response that "this notion that Negroes have got to be better than other people is about as disgusting as the notion that Negroes are inferior. As a matter of fact, I very much fear that they are rationalizations of the same thing" (Ware 1984, 30).

Hastie had a brilliant career at Harvard. He was the second African-American man (Charles Hamilton Houston was the first) to become an editor of the *Harvard Law Review*, and he received his doctorate in juridical science in 1933. Hastie earned a reputation among his fellow students for brilliance, especially in response to the Socratic probing of Harvard's talented faculty.

When he graduated from Harvard, Hastie moved back to Washington, D.C. He joined the firm of Houston & Houston, where he worked with his mentor, Charles H. Houston, and taught at the Howard University Law School. He also served from 1932 to 1937 as an assistant solicitor in the Department of the Interior and became part of President Franklin D. Roosevelt's "black cabinet."

His most important contributions as a lawyer came through his connection with the National Association for the Advancement of Colored People (NAACP). Houston and, to a lesser extent, Nathan R. Margold, a fellow editor with Houston on the *Harvard Law Review*, framed the civil rights organization's legal strategy. They urged the directors of the NAACP's Legal Defense Fund to mount an incremental and indirect attack on the doctrine of "separate but equal," first enunciated in *Plessy v. Ferguson* (1896) and subsequently reaffirmed by the Supreme Court. In its simplest terms, "separate but equal" meant that as long as a state provided facilities of equal quality it could legally separate the races in public places. Houston, Margold, and Hastie also understood that the powerful emotional commitment of southerners to legal segregation presented a formidable barrier to change. They also believed that the legal system, if asked to do too much too quickly, might actually strengthen segregation's hold. Thus, they attacked segregation through a targeted campaign designed to erode the precedent gradually.

Hastie emerged as one of the NAACP's chief litigation weapons during the 1930s and 1940s. He played a central role in *Hocutt v. Wilson* (North Carolina, 1933), which dealt with discrimination in graduate education; *New Negro Alliance v. Sanitary Grocery Co.* (U.S., 1938), which turned on the issue of discrimination in employment; *Smith v. Allwright* (U.S., 1944), which involved voting rights for African-Americans; and *Morgan v. Virginia* (U.S., 1946), which treated segregation in public transportation. Hastie also exercised influence in other cases. For example, between 1939 and 1949 THURGOOD MARSHALL litigated nineteen cases before the U.S. Supreme Court, and of these Hastie served as a consultant or co-counsel in twelve. Through these efforts Hastie contributed to the NAACP's ultimate triumph in *Brown v. Board of Education* (1954), although by that time he was himself a member of the federal bench.

Hastie's first major civil rights case was *Hocutt*, and he lost. Margold and Houston believed that given the fears that white southerners had about mixing white and African-American children in elementary and high schools, the best strategy was to establish a beachhead in the area of higher education. Most southern states refused to admit African-Americans to graduate and professional education, but despite this practice they insisted that they were still complying with the dictates of "separate but equal." They did so by offering scholarships to African-Americans to attend universities in the North. In March 1933, Thomas R. Hocutt challenged this practice by attempting to enroll in the school of pharmacy at the University of North Carolina. The university refused on technical grounds to admit Hocutt, who failed to present a transcript of his college work.

At the time, Hastie was completing his studies at Harvard, but at Houston's urging he traveled to North Carolina to argue the case at trial. The North Carolina judge rejected Hastie's arguments and found for the state. Hastie, however, won broad respect on both sides of the issue for the clarity of his arguments and his poise before a hostile audience. Hastie also understood the importance of having argued the case, even in a losing cause. "It started something," Hastie recalled; "it was a first step toward eliminating the legal and moral contradiction of racism in the scheme of education for life in a democratic society" (Ware 1984, 53).

Hastie had greater success in two other major cases involving the rights of African-Americans, both of which became milestones in civil rights history. In *Smith v. Allwright*, the Supreme Court considered the constitutionality of the all-white primary. After Reconstruction, a Democratic primary victory assured success in the general election in Texas, where *Smith* arose, and throughout the rest of the one-party South. The Democratic party, however, which controlled southern politics, purposefully excluded African-Americans from participating in primary elections and thereby eliminated their voice in the general election. The Supreme Court accepted this practice in *Grovey v. Townsend* (1935) on the grounds that political parties were private organizations that could exclude anyone they wished, since "private discrimination" was beyond the reach of the Constitution.

Hastie decided that the best way to deal with the issue was to draw a distinction between state and federal elections. He understood that the high court itself had acknowledged such a distinction when it held in *United States v. Classic* (1941) that Congress could regulate primary elections that involved federal offices. In *Smith*, Marshall and Hastie expanded this opening by successfully arguing that the use of race to limit participation in primary elections violated the Fifteenth Amendment to the Constitution. The all-white primary was not a private practice, they insisted, because it was an integral part of the state's election procedures. The Democratic party of Texas, according to Hastie's view, was acting as a direct agent of the state and thereby unlawfully engaging in state-sanctioned, race-based discrimination. Justice Stanley Reed, who wrote for the majority in the case, agreed. He held that conducting primary elections was a state function that could not be shaped along racial lines by a private organization. Although the party was a private entity, it actually performed a public function, one subject to regulation as state action. The Court threw out the *Grovey* precedent and reduced the options available to keep African-Americans from voting to individual discrimination, such as the poll tax and literacy tests, rather than group discrimination.

Hastie's greatest success was *Morgan v. Virginia* (1946), another case that he argued with Marshall. In this instance, Irene Morgan, an African-American woman, boarded an interstate Greyhound bus in Gloucester County, Virginia, bound for Baltimore, Maryland. Virginia law required that African-Americans sit in the rear of the bus, but Morgan refused to obey the bus driver's order to do so. The Supreme Court of Virginia subsequently affirmed her conviction and fine, at which point the NAACP, Hastie, and Marshall stepped into the case, a somewhat unusual practice, since they had not handled it in the lower court.

Hastie emerged as the principal figure in *Morgan*. After Marshall presented the high court with the facts in the case, Hastie persuaded the justices of the need to change the law. He did so through a combination of legal skill and poise. Rather than focusing on the equal protection clause of the Fourteenth Amendment, Hastie rested his argument on the belief that a state could not impose a requirement to segregate passengers on a bus engaged in interstate travel because doing so violated the commerce clause of the Constitution. Hastie believed that if he rested his case on the equal protection concept, the justices would turn to *Plessy* for authority, with disastrous results. Justice Wiley E. Rutledge pressed Hastie on just this matter, but the lawyer refused to answer the question directly. "I pretended not to hear him," Hastie later explained. "I gave him fifteen minutes of irrelevancies" (Ware 1984, 189). Hastie, of course, believed that *Plessy* was wrong and that the Fourteenth Amendment should be applied to acts of discrimination in public transportation. He was also a pragmatic lawyer more interested in winning a small victory than losing a large battle, no matter its nobility. Still, in his brief, Hastie reminded the Court of the higher moral ground at issue, turning to the race-based discrimination practiced by Nazis. America, he warned, could not follow a similar path; interstate commerce should not be marked "by disruptive local practices bred of racial notions alien to our national ideals, and to the solemn undertakings of the community of civilized nations as well" (Ware 1984, 189).

The Supreme Court sided with Hastie by a vote of 7 to 1. As Hastie recognized, however, a legal victory did not immediately translate into practice. Throughout the South, buses continued to be segregated on an informal basis, even though it was clear that such practices on interstate vehicles would not survive legal challenge. Hastie also knew that he had nudged not only the Court but also the American people further along the path that led inexorably to *Brown* and the simple justice due all African-Americans.

Hastie's role in *Morgan* illustrated how indispensable he was to the NAACP's litigation strategy. Hastie was quick on his feet, gifted in debate, and a logician who exuded reasoned passion for the cause of African-American people. In short, he was the consummate appellate lawyer.

Hastie's career in the law extended beyond the courtroom. In 1937, President Franklin D. Roosevelt appointed him to the U.S. district court in the Virgin Islands, the first African-American elevated to the federal bench. He subsequently resigned that position in 1939 to become dean of the Howard University Law School, a post that he held for a year, when he took a leave of absence to become the civilian aide to Secretary of War Henry L. Stimson. The African-American community applauded Hastie's appointment, since he was given the responsibility of ensuring fair treatment for African-Americans in the military on the eve of World War II. In this and other positions, Hastie found himself confronted with a dilemma. As a leader in the African-American community, Hastie was one of the first African-Americans to enter white institutions, where he was typically given little power. He was often forced, as a result, to balance the need for African-Americans to maintain some foothold in the white institutions against the desire to avoid tokenism. In his role as adviser to Stimson, Hastie was given little actual power, but he nonetheless pressed for several reforms. He fought against the spread of segregation to integrated installations, advocated the protection of African-American soldiers from white civilian violence, and increased the number of African-Americans who received officer training.

In 1945, President Harry S Truman nominated Hastie to be governor of the Virgin Islands, the first African-American to hold that position. The nomination immediately ran into trouble from Senator James O. Eastland of Mississippi and several other southern senators. Hastie had during his career been involved with a number of left-wing political action groups. Eastland raised questions about these affiliations based on information supplied by the House Un-American Activities Committee. Eastland, for example, grilled Hastie about his possible Communist affiliations, notably his role in the National Lawyers Guild and the Washington Committee for Democratic Action. Hastie, however, maintained his poise while reminding the Senate Judiciary Committee that all Americans who had fought in the war deserved to be treated equally. The full Senate confirmed his nomination on May 1, 1946; Hastie served with distinction until 1949.

In 1945, President Truman had considered nominating Hastie to be judge of the U.S. Court of Appeals for the District of Columbia, but he decided not to do so in the face of strong opposition from the same southern Democratic senators who had opposed his appointment as governor. By 1949, however, Truman was grateful to Hastie for the support he had provided during the successful presidential campaign of a year earlier, one that Truman won surprisingly. The president decided to appoint Hastie judge of the Third U.S. Court of Appeals, which included Philadelphia. Opposition to the appointment came from several directions, some of them unexpected.

The African-American legal community in Philadelphia complained that Hastie had already been well rewarded; its members insisted that other African-American lawyers should benefit as well for their loyalty to the New Deal. White opponents charged that the governor of the Virgin Islands would be little more than a carpetbagger in the new position that most appropriately belonged to a Pennsylvanian. Hastie, as usual, remained above the fray, and the Senate ultimately confirmed his appointment. He became the first African-American to hold a federal appeals court judgeship.

Ironically, in his new office the great crusader for civil rights had few opportunities to advance the agenda he had pursued in the courtroom for more than two decades. Scarcely two dozen of his 486 opinions dealt with civil rights. Unlike Thurgood Marshall, who subsequently became a justice of the Supreme Court, Hastie was more restrained in his use of judicial power. For example, in *Lynch v. Torquato* (1965), he declined to expand the state-action concept that he had so actively advanced as a lawyer in *Smith v. Allwright*. He concluded that the equal protection and due process clauses of the Fourteenth Amendment did not embrace the management of the internal affairs of the Democratic party. Moreover, in his published writings he raised questions about the benefits of affirmative action programs that used race alone as a determinant of eligibility or qualification. Notably, a strong sense of Madisonian constitutionalism balanced his commitment to legal activism.

—*Kermit L. Hall*

Sources and Suggestions for Further Reading

Franklin, John Hope. *From Slavery to Freedom: A History of African Americans*. 8th ed. Boston: McGraw-Hill, 2000.

Hastie, William. "Charles Hamilton Houston." *Negro History Bulletin* 13 (1950): 207.

Kluger, Richard. *Simple Justice: The History of* Brown v. Board of Education *and Black America's Struggle for Equality*. New York: Alfred A. Knopf, 1975.

McGuire, Phillip. *He, Too, Spoke for Democracy: Judge Hastie, World War II, and the Black Soldier*. Westport, Conn: Greenwood Press, 1988.

McNeil, Gena Rae. *Groundwork: Charles Hamilton Houston and the Struggle for Civil Rights*. Philadelphia: University of Pennsylvania Press, 1983.

Rusch, Jonathan J. "William H. Hastie and the Vindication of Civil Rights." *Howard Law Journal* 21 (1978): 749–820.

Ware, Gilbert. *William Hastie: Grace under Pressure*. New York: Oxford University Press, 1984.

HAYNES, RICHARD "RACEHORSE"

(1927–   )

RICHARD "RACEHORSE" HAYNES is an archetypical representative of the lawyer as a champion fighter for his clients, and thus he is viewed either as a renowned folk hero or as an infamous villain, depending on the observer's perspective. Although this is a fairly normal situation for successful defense attorneys, "Racehorse" Haynes is particularly renowned for his dynamic courtroom style; he is a real crowd pleaser in the grand old tradition of the folksy, down-home lawyer. Perhaps the secrets of his success are his focused nature, his ability to pick a case thread and to weave it into a dramatic cloth, and the fact that his legal practice is conducted in the state of Texas, where such drama is appreciated. He is an artistic courtroom lawyer, and his artistic flair is manifested in both his professional life and his personal life. Past age seventy, he still enjoys flying his airplane, sailing his schooner, and motor racing around Texas.

Richard Haynes was born in Houston, Texas, on April 2, 1927. He was given the nickname "Racehorse" by a track coach dur-

RICHARD "RACEHORSE" HAYNES
Famed defense attorney Richard "Racehorse" Haynes, former lawyer for John Hill, talks about the "Blood and Money" trial during an interview at his Houston office, 10 March 1999. Haynes said "It had everything in it: the doctor, the socialite, high society." (AP Photo/David J. Phillip)

ing high school. His physical vigor was also demonstrated when he served both as a Marine and an army paratrooper and was decorated for heroism during the assault and capture of the Japanese island Iwo Jima during World War II. His high energy levels were also manifested during his subsequent service with the United Nations, first as a paratrooper officer with the Eleventh Airborne Division during the Korean War, and more recently his work with the Houston Human Rights Committee. Haynes has always been a person of unusual strength and ability.

After his military service, Haynes attended the University of Houston, graduating with his B.A. in 1951. He was admitted to the university's law school, which had been founded in 1912 with a commitment to egalitarian opportunity; and in 1956 he completed the J.D. degree and was admitted to the Texas bar in the same year.

Unlike many of the older Ivy League institutions, the organizational culture of the University of Houston law school is not particularly geared to theoretical principles but rather focuses on turning out competent practical lawyers. In the criminal defense field, practicality means looking for the element of reasonable doubt, showing it to the jury, and hammering away at the theme for the entire course of the trial. It takes a high-powered attorney to excel in this type of career, and Haynes has the prerequisite abilities.

Like many successful attorneys, Haynes had a role model. According to author David Phillips, Haynes grew up in the shadow of Percy Foreman, a Texas criminal defense lawyer of legendary ability (Phillips 1979, 71). Foreman not only had the same dynamic ability as Haynes, he also had several trial techniques that were particularly well suited to Texas trial practice: first, he routinely put the police on trial; second, if that did not seem sufficient, he would argue that "the S.O.B. should have been shot." Perhaps law school faculty members should not advocate this technique, but in the steamy law library at the University of Houston, the students grasped every survival technique they could. Haynes would add a few frills to Foreman's style; he learned to attack the prosecution as well as the police and to subject witnesses to grueling cross-examinations until tempers flared and mistrials could be won.

Haynes first came to national attention due to his spirited defense of Dr. John Hill, a renowned plastic surgeon who in the early 1970s was accused of causing his wife's death by failing to render medical treatment. A bestselling book by Thomas Thompson described the case, which ended in a mistrial when the doctor's second wife testified that he had tried to kill her as well (Thompson 1976). The prosecution scheduled a second trial, but Dr. Hill was mysteriously murdered before that case went to court. Years later, Thompson was attending a school reunion and took pleasure in recounting the tale (and the courtroom adroitness of Haynes) to an admiring crowd, members of an elite social stratum that delighted in messy scandals and divorces. Among his listeners was a man who was soon to have occasion to hire a defense attorney himself: T. Cullen Davis, the wealthy son of a Texas oil industry millionaire.

In 1979, Haynes was listed in *Who's Who in American Law*, undoubtedly because of his remarkable defense, in several proceedings, of T. Cullen Davis, perhaps the richest man ever accused of murder and subsequently of plotting the death of a trial judge. According to David Phillips, who wrote a spellbinding book about the affair, Haynes had successfully emulated his personal role model, Percy Foreman (Philips 1979, 71–72). As a result of this conscious career goal, Haynes may perhaps be portrayed as an anachronism: one of the last of the old-school populist lawyers, famous for his flamboyant trial tactics.

Haynes's style and success owe much to the fact that he bases his legal practice in Texas. The big, brash state represents the epitome of American entrepreneurial spirit and exalts the cowboy as the quintessence of rugged individualism. This cultural atmosphere sustains and rewards Haynes's trial technique of boiling down complex legal issues to the level of personal experience and gut reaction. This culture can be traced in part to the formation of the nation of Texas in 1836, when a group of Mexican citizens decided that they had had enough of dictatorial government and corrupt law enforcement. One of their number, Samuel Maverick, a graduate of Yale University, lent his name to what has become a focal point of Texas lore, the freewheeling radical lawyer who, in the name of common justice, challenges the high and mighty whenever necessary.

When his client Cullen Davis was tried for the attempted murder of his estranged wife and the murders of her daughter and boyfriend, Haynes's epic defense efforts made observers think of him as a combination hypnotist, psychologist, salesman, and legal sleuth. Steven Naifeh and Gregory Smith, in their popular work *Final Justice* (1994), compare Haynes to Rasputin, because of his gripping depiction of Davis's wife as a dissolute dweller in the slimy underbelly of Texas society. In *Law and American History* (1987), Steven B. Presser and Jamil Zainaldin describe how, in addition to following the precepts of defense practice generally and building on the lessons of Foreman, Haynes has refined his trial tactics by emphasizing changes of venue, voir dire, and publicity. After the original mistrial in Fort Worth, Haynes sought a more conservative venue and got the case removed to Amarillo, engaged in an elaborate (and expensive) process of juror research, and made sure that the community was deluged with news stories depicting Mrs. Davis's shortcomings and Mr. Davis's exceedingly generous contributions to local charities and worthy activities.

Another example of Haynes's technique, as noted by Phillips (1979, 80–81) during the Davis trial in Amarillo, is Haynes's use of a racy photograph of Mrs. Davis, enlarged on transparent film and held before a bright light during one of the Davis trials so that the jury could get a good view of the lady's indiscretion even if the exhibit might not be admitted into evidence. Instead of the cut-and-dried determination of whether an assault on the victim was committed, Haynes makes the jury experience an emotional reaction to the victim's own outrageous behavior, perhaps to justify the defendant's violent actions as righteous, or at least excusable behavior. According to Phillips (1979, 76), Haynes is perhaps the most famous living defense attorney in Texas.

In a subsequent trial, wherein Davis was accused of plotting the death of the judge hearing his wife's divorce case, venue was moved to Houston. Houston is a bigger and more sophisticated city than Amarillo, but it has a kindred culture. It is the same pioneering spirit that pushed the Apollo moon project to a successful conclusion and that drives the economic life of the state, and it is impatient with government rules and regulations. Among the compelling evidence submitted to the jury were FBI audiotapes of Davis apparently scheming; but after Haynes finished grilling the various FBI witnesses and informants and displayed the competing interests and factions within the FBI and other organizations, the Houston jury had no problem finding reasonable doubt whether Davis was a malefactor or the victim of overzealous police and prosecutors. Texas loves the underdog, and Haynes is an expert at uncovering the human motives of official investigators and witnesses in the courtroom—a surefire way to cast doubt over the objectivity of the criminal justice system.

Haynes has learned how to mine a rich field of public doubt over the fairness of the criminal justice system in Texas. That doubt is supported by pervasive official misconduct, such as was evident when the entire state prison system was placed under the supervision of the federal courts because of systematic constitutional violations. Of course, Texas was not the only state to be scrutinized in that regard. And some high-profile cases, particularly those involving Dallas prosecutor Henry Wade, have further undermined general confidence in criminal proceedings. Wade prosecuted Jack Ruby for the murder of Lee Harvey Oswald, fought to enforce abortion laws in *Roe v. Wade*, and prosecuted Lenell Geter, an African-American engineer, for armed robbery, despite the fact that he had clocked in at work and his coworkers swore he had an alibi. But after the police distributed so many photographs of him, labeled as a robbery suspect, that it became a mathematical probability that well-meaning citizens would come forth to testify against him, Henry Wade had little choice but to follow the police lead. After Errol Morris's television documentary hit *The Thin Blue Line* aroused national indignation and Geter was set free, Wade was quoted by Brian W. Wice of the *Houston Post* as saying that it did not bother him that appellate courts found fault with his prosecutions. "We convict 'em on the front page—and they reverse 'em on the back page." Haynes knows that a certain percentage of the jury pool will be sympathetic to insinuations about official misconduct and is an expert in seating juries and winning their confidence.

Haynes has won national recognition for his legal defense skills. In 1997, the National Association of Criminal Defense Lawyers held its annual meeting and seminar series in New York City. Among the illustrious attorneys participating were JOHNNIE COCHRAN, speaking on closing argument, and Arthur Miller, speaking on assessing the strengths, flaws, and ethics of former colleagues. Haynes was also a key participant, offering a seminar entitled "Integrating the Theme into Voir Dire, Opening, Cross & Closing." Haynes is particularly good at hammering away at a given theme until it is accepted.

Because Haynes is recognized as one of the greatest living defense attorneys, among his clients have been other distinguished attorneys, judges, and powerful politicians. It is a telling tribute when one famous attorney turns to another for help. In 1998, a nationally known attorney, John O'Quinn, did so. O'Quinn, identified by the *Wall Street Journal* as "the King of Torts" for his record-setting victories against big tobacco companies and breast-implant manufacturers, can be expected to know a good attorney when he sees one. O'Quinn, who has incurred the wrath of large corporations, was threatened with disbarment for allegedly violating state bar rules on solicitation of clients involving an airline crash. The Texas State Bar Association has a monthly report listing attorneys who are disbarred for violating its rules against solicitation of clients, and O'Quinn wanted to be sure that Haynes's innovative and energetic style and mastery of the art of defense lawyering would shield him from such a fate. O'Quinn hired not only the dramatic Haynes but also the more laid-back Arthur Miller of Court TV fame (Templer 1998). Miller combines a polished persona with a scholarly, analytic style of argument. It may be a challenge even for these talented lawyers to prevent O'Quinn from losing his law license, particularly since he has already been disciplined for a similar incident in the past.

Two other recent cases reported in the media show that Haynes's powers of persuasion are still in demand. One of them involved a state judge. The *Abilene Reporter-News* describes the case of a former Texas state judge, William Bell, who was indicted on perjury charges stemming out of the Kennedy Heights (Houston) toxic chemical contamination case ("Former Judge Indicted" 1998). An attorney came forward with an audiotape recording of her conversation with the judge purporting to show his interest in a sweetheart arrangement with Chevron Corporation officials. Judge

Bell engaged Haynes, who confidently advised that the tape would actually exonerate his client. After all, isn't a judge supposed to be friendly?

Houston Chronicle reporter Thom Marshall (1999) reported another case in which Haynes was called in to save former city councilman John Peavy Jr., who was being retried on charges of bribery and conspiracy resulting from an FBI sting operation in 1995 and 1996. The FBI was pretty confident of victory, based on its rather damning evidence that tapes of the undercover agent's discussions recorded. However, Haynes pointed out that much of the transcript of the tape was marked "UI" for unintelligible, presenting the possibility that the agent had modulated his voice deliberately to elicit out-of-context remarks from Peavy. And Haynes noted that at one point on the tape the agent asked another if the recorder was turned off, and then said, "turn it off before —." The unknown operator should turn it off before what?—before they record some valuable truth for a jury to hear? This gaping black hole of government control of the truth is guaranteed to raise a reasonable doubt in every juror winnowed through Haynes's exhaustive jury research team.

Haynes was joining this defense late, and only in the capacity of co-counsel, because the sitting judge in the trial, federal judge David Hittner, refused to allow Peavy's former attorney to vacate the top spot on the defense team. Judge Hittner also instructed that he would put up with no theater in his courtroom; but, noted by reporter Marshall, many people wondered whether it is possible to keep theater out of a courtroom or to prevent Haynes from winning a case. Haynes's argument, put before a public audience, was reminiscent of his facility with debunking the supposed infallibility of official government surveillance tapes.

Haynes's biographical information on the Houston Human Rights Committee web site ("Richard 'Racehorse' Haynes" 2000) shows that the International Academy of Trial Lawyers, the International Society of Barristers, the American Bar Association, the Texas Bar Association, and the American Judicature Society are among the prestigious organizations of which he is a member. He is also the recipient of numerous awards and recognitions, including the Outstanding Alumni and Law Alumni awards from the University of Houston and the Golden Plate Award from the American Academy of Achievement. He is a member of the permanent teaching faculty of the National College for Criminal Defense and has served as an adjunct professor of law at the University of Houston. He also serves on the boards of directors of several community organizations and is an active member of the United Nations Houston Human Rights Committee, which is not the most popular organization in Texas.

Richard "Racehorse" Haynes is a throwback to the good old days of spellbinding defense lawyers energetically defending their clients according to their oaths of office. Haynes does not hesitate to challenge the authority of law enforcement officers, prosecutors, and conservative judges. He looks for the shadow of a doubt in the case against his client, picks a defense theme, and vigorously hammers away at that theme in venue hearings, voir dire, and case argument. And Richard Haynes is a master of publicity and community culture. He and other attorneys like him are so good at getting criminal defendants released or acquitted that to many it may seem that the objectivity and functional effectiveness of the criminal justice system itself may be placed in jeopardy. And so it may, but perhaps their goals, and the American notion of justice through adversarial proceedings, can be asserted to justify their efforts.

—Lee Allen

Sources and Suggestions for Further Reading

Axelrod, Alan, Charles Phillips, and Kurt Kemper. *Cops, Crooks and Criminologists.* Facts on File, 1996.

Bowman, John S., ed. *The Cambridge Dictionary of American Biography.* New York: Cambridge University Press, 1995.

Cartwright, Gary. *Blood Will Tell: The Murder Trials of T. Cullen Davis.* New York: Harcourt Brace Jovanovich, 1979.

"Former Judge Indicted for Perjury." *Albilene Reporter-News,* 1 February 1998. Available at <http://www.reporternews.com/texas/indict0201.html>.

Haynes, Richard. *Integrating the Theme into Voir Dire, Opening, Cross & Closing.* Front Royal, Va.: National Association of Criminal Defense Lawyers, 2000. Audio cassette.

Marquis Who's Who in American Law. Chicago: Marquis Who's Who, 1979, 338.

Marshall, Thom. "New Player Brings Drama to Sting Trial." *Houston Chronicle,* 30 March 1999. Available at <http://www.chron.com/cs/CDA/story.hts/metropolitan/marshall/223405>.

Naifeh, Steven, and Gregory W. Smith. *The Best Lawyers in America.* Aiken, S.C: Woodward & White, 1991.

_____. *Final Justice: The True Story of the Richest Man Ever Tried for Murder.* New York: Onyx, 1994.

Phillips, David A. *The Great Texas Murder Trials: A Compelling Account of the Sensational T. Cullen Davis Case.* New York: Macmillan, 1979.

Presser, Steven B., and Jamil Zainaldin. *Law and American History.* St. Paul: West, 1987.

"Richard 'Racehorse' Haynes: Biographic Information." Houston Human Rights Committee, 2000. <http://www.culturalbridges.com/rights/RichardHaynes.htm>.

Templer, Le. "David v. Goliath: O'Quinn Accused of Ambulance Chasing." *Wichita Falls Times Record News,* 7 December 1998. Available at <http://www.trnonline.com/archives/1998archives/12071998/battling.htm>.

Thompson, Thomas. *Blood and Money.* Garden City, N.Y.: Doubleday, 1976.

Wice, Brian W. "Convictions—at Any Price." *Houston Post,* 19 March 1981, E1.

HENRY, PATRICK

(1736–1799)

PATRICK HENRY
Library of Congress

FAILED SHOPKEEPER, COUNTRY lawyer, inflamer of revolutionary passions, wartime governor, opponent of the Constitution, and defender of popular and liberal rights, Patrick Henry lived the most political of lives. History knows Henry best for his fiery oratory, notably his charge at St. John's Church in March 1775, "Gentlemen may cry peace, peace—but there is no peace. The war is actually begun! . . . Is life so dear, or peace so sweet, as to be purchased at the price of chains and slavery? Forbid it, Almighty God! I know not what course others may take; but as for me, give me liberty or give me death!" (Henry 1969, 1:266). Beneath the burning coals of his rhetoric, however, Henry was no demagogue. Though radical, his passions were shot through with the more ordered and lawlike sentiments of a backwoods barrister.

To understand Henry, voice of popular revolution, one must also view his political life through the lens of the law, that career of forensic advocacy from which he emerged triumphant onto the political scene and into which he retreated honorably when his political career began to wane.

Henry's education in the law was, at best, cursory; his introduction to the bar, inauspicious. Although early biographers tended to mythologize and exaggerate the rustic qualities of his upbringing, Henry was born into a respectable and educated Virginia family on May 29, 1736. His father, John Henry, gained a college education before becoming a landowner, vestryman, militia colonel, and chief justice in Hanover County; his mother, Sarah Winston Syme, came from a well-off farm family. His uncle, Patrick Henry, was a reverend in the Anglican church. Young Patrick received a good basic education, first in a common school and then from his father, learning history, mathematics, Latin, and Greek. At the time, however, there was no American law school; the boy went to work rather than attending college. His first endeavors, at keeping shop, farming, and tending bar, failed. Having married young at eighteen, he needed to find a trade quickly at which he could make a decent living. In 1760, he turned to law, for which he prepared only a matter of months—according to some reputable estimates, as little as six weeks.

Satisfied as to his own fitness to practice, Henry set out for Williamsburg to meet with the panel of bar examiners. The committee, which contained some of Virginia's most eminent men, seems to have been shocked by Henry's rough edges and his lack of particular knowledge. Although errant in many details of his recollection, Thomas Jefferson later recounted that Henry's approval had been in great doubt. John Randolph, Virginia's attorney general, and GEORGE WYTHE, later to become America's first professor of law, signed off, but not without great hesitation. Peyton Randolph and Robert Nicholas remained unconvinced. After initially refusing a meeting, John Randolph subjected Henry to an extensive examination. Deficient in the specifics of the law, he nonetheless showed an acuity of mind and a sharp understanding of history and legal theory. In a debate over the common law, Randolph took Henry back to his office to check an authoritative tome, only to discover that the younger man had been correct. Marvelling at his "force of natural reason," Randolph went on to exclaim, "Mr. Henry, if your industry be only half equal to your genius, I augur that you will do well, and become an ornament and an honor to your profession" (Wirt 1832, 35).

Henry returned home to practice in Hanover and Goochland counties, and began to make a decent showing of himself. Most of his early cases were the routine stuff of a colonial country lawyer: debt actions, business transactions gone bad, wills and estates. In a slander case, *Winston v. Spencer*, one man called another a "hog stealer." Suing for Winston, Henry won £20, a sum considerably less than the £500 he had sought. Henry took cases where he could find them. One surgeon had not been paid by a woman for "many Chirurgical operations Amputations Incisions & Scarifyings" (Meade 1957, 107). Henry represented a plaintiff in a suit against Henry's cousin, John Payne Jr., who had hired the man to take his place in a military campaign, only to later renege on the payment. That first year saw Henry as lawyer in 176 cases for around 70 clients. Collections always posed a problem—Henry even had his own suit against the reputed "hog stealer"—but overall Henry managed to break roughly even. His practice grew steadily over the next few years as Henry scrapped for cases in surrounding counties, particularly in rural areas where few other lawyers would travel. By 1763, he was handling almost 500 cases for the year, making £225 but leaving far more outstanding. These were mostly small cases, but they prepared Henry for the career-making case that was soon to come.

The *Parson's Cause* forged Henry's reputation as the great orator and lawyer of backwoods Virginia. The case involved a dispute between the Virginia legislature and the official Anglican ministers, who drew their pay from the state. By long practice, ministers had been paid in a set number of pounds of tobacco—a wage scale that fluctuated widely depending on the market value of tobacco. In an effort to save money, however, the assembly had set the price of tobacco for reimbursement purposes in the aptly named Two Penny Acts of 1755 and 1758, moves that greatly undervalued the crop and forced the ministers to take a drastic cut in pay. The clergy gained public sympathy but rapidly undermined this good will by taking their complaint directly to the Privy Council in England rather than to the assembly. They won, but Virginia authorities were not anxious to concede and compensate.

The ministers now sued for damages in local Virginia courts. Reverend James Maury, unable to gain redress from the local tax collectors, hired the King's attorney for Louisa County to pursue his case in neighboring Hanover and won the initial judgment; a hearing on specific damages would follow. At this point, the defense attorney quit and was replaced by Henry. The stakes remained high, so when the case was called in December 1763, the courtroom was packed with ministers (including Henry's uncle), their local opponents, and many onlookers. With little time to prepare and with the main judgment already lost, Henry adopted a radical strategy: He would attack not only the clergy, but also the legitimacy of the king's order as violating natural law and popular sovereignty. In this, he would appeal to popular resentment against royal meddling in local taxation and against the clergy as patrons of royal power. Henry's argument thus had its advantages despite being on the wrong side of the law. It also did not hurt that he would be making his appeal in front of a sympathetic jury, as well as his own father, who was the presiding judge.

Henry started slowly and initially seemed to be over his head. The crowd grumbled; his father shrank in embarrassment. But Henry's demeanor changed as he rose to the cause. Elevating himself into a fearsome oratorical presence, he challenged the legitimacy of an established church and argued that the Two Penny Act had served the common utility. He drew his logic from John Locke's social contract theory, popularized locally by Richard Bland. Henry opined that "a king by annulling or disallowing laws of this salutary nature, from being the father of his people degenerates into a tyrant and forfeits all right to his subject's obedience" (Meade 1957, 5). Some of the crowd began to cry "Treason!"—a claim echoed by Peter Lyons, the opposing counsel. But Henry had made his impact on the assembled jurors and judges. His father and many others were reportedly reduced to tears. The jury took five minutes to return a token judgment of one penny for the plaintiff, as Henry had requested. Henry lost some clients afterward—and would later handle a similar case against his uncle—but his reputation had grown exponentially.

Soon after, Captain Nathaniel Dandridge retained Henry to challenge the seating of James Littlepage in Virginia's House of Burgesses. The charge: Littlepage had illegally influenced voters by plying them with free rum punch. Arguing before the Committee on Privileges and Elections, Henry again mustered a stirring speech, only to lose, largely because the legislators wanted to retain their election practices in the face of a prohibitive law. Significantly, the event signaled a shift in Henry's career—he would now turn his legal oratory increasingly toward a political forum.

The next year, 1765, Henry won election as burgess from Louisa County, an achievement that boosted his law practice. His confidence grew as well. He would often hunt on his way to court and appear before the bench unwashed and bloodsplattered, only to outshine his opponents with his rhetorical skill. His friend Spencer Roane described his style: "He was perfect master of the passions of his auditory, whether in the tragic or the comic line. The tones of his voice, to say nothing of his matter and gesture, were insinuated into the feeling of his hearers, in a manner that baffled all descriptions" (Henry 1969, 2:465). Even Peter Lyons remarked that Henry was the one attorney during whose speech he could not write, but only sit and listen. Despite his penchant for heated oratory, Henry's court manner was exceptionally deferential toward court and opposition, and he maintained good relations with other attorneys.

In 1769, Henry was accepted as a lawyer before the Virginia General Court, an honor that required him to terminate his county practice and forced him to adopt a more conservative court attire. Although he now worked fewer cases, his earnings greatly increased. Henry also broadened his legal interests. The late 1760s saw him defending the rights of dissenting Baptists against religious persecution. On the general court, Henry took to criminal defense, which became his expertise. By 1773, his reputation had grown to the point where Robert Nicholas, who had earlier refused to sign his bar application, now trusted Henry enough to bestow on him his law practice on retirement (Jefferson, Henry's rival, had first demurred). It made little difference for Henry's legal career. Economic recession and the onset of the Revolution had more direct effects: Legal practice became less profitable, the general court was dissolved, and Henry found himself much more embroiled in political and military affairs. During this time, Henry would distinguish himself as a delegate to the Continental Congresses, as the first governor of an independent Virginia, and as a crusader for a national bill of rights.

After the war, with his health declining and debts for his large family mounting, Patrick Henry began a gradual retreat from political life. He completed his fifth and final one-year term as governor in November 1786, and declined to serve a sixth. Instead of attending the Constitutional Convention in Philadelphia, he chose to stay in Virginia and revive his law practice. Once again he built slowly. He handled mostly small civil cases in the first few years of his return. In 1789, he became an attorney for the Prince Edward District Court and took on cases of larger significance. One of his first big cases involved an intrafamily dispute over twelve thousand acres of land. Henry lost the case to EDMUND RANDOLPH, arguing for the plaintiff, but managed to secure an agreement by which his client, Robert Carter, could keep half the land on payment of £450. An ungrateful Carter refused to pay Henry's fee.

In another notable case, Henry defended John Venable, a commissary for the Continental Army. During English general Charles Cornwallis's invasion of Virginia, Venable had stolen two steers from John Hook, a wealthy Tory, in order to feed the troops. Hook now demanded compensation. Henry had little trouble painting Hook as a contemptible villain, coldly denying succor to starved and bloodied soldiers. Adopting his most mocking tone, Henry asked, "But hark! What notes of discord are these which disturb the general joy and silence the acclimations of victory? They are the notes of *John Hook*, hoarsely bawling through the American camp, *beef! beef! beef!*" (Meade 1969, 416). The county clerk had to run from the room to avoid bursting into a public fit of laughter. Hook narrowly escaped tarring and feathering.

Henry also resumed his criminal defense practice to great effect. He won several high-profile murder cases, sometimes playing off jury hostility toward Tory victims killed in ambiguous circumstances, and sometimes winning acquittals in the face of an anxious public. In one trial, Henry defended a constable before a tired and already convinced jury. Henry turned the tide by reminding the jury of the seriousness of the task: "I shall aim at brevity. But should I take up more of your time than you expect, I hope you will hear me with patience when you consider that *blood is concerned*" (Axelrad 1947, 242). According to one witness, Henry's very pronunciation of the word "blood" seemed to overwhelm and revive the court.

Sam Houston: The Lawyer as Frontiersman

Few American lawyers have packed as much excitement into their lives as did Sam Houston (1793–1863). Born in Virginia, Houston lived with the Cherokee Indians for a time after his family moved to Tennessee. Later rejoining white society, Houston fought under Andrew Jackson during the War of 1812 and was seriously wounded in a battle against the Creek Indians, but he managed to establish a lifelong friendship with the general and future president. Houston read law in Nashville under Judge James Trimble and subsequently set up practice in nearby Lebanon, Tennessee, serving for a time as an attorney general.

Elected to the U.S. House of Representatives and later chosen as governor of Tennessee, Houston had a tempestuous family life, being rejected by his first wife and falling in and out of love with a number of both Indian and white women. At one point, he shot a man in a duel. Houston later moved to Texas, where he ended up commanding the forces seeking independence from Mexico and defeating Mexican president and general Antonio de Santa Anna. Houston helped draft the constitution of Texas, which served as a model for other Western states, was twice selected as president of Texas, and became one of the state's first two U.S. senators. Opposed to the institution of slavery, Houston resigned from this post after Texas joined the Confederacy, but he was unsuccessful in taking the state out of the Union.

References

McWhirter, Daniel A. *The Legal 100*. Secaucus, N.J.: Carol, 1998.

Williams, John H. *Sam Houston: A Biography of the Father of Texas*. New York: Simon & Schuster, 1993.

Perhaps Henry's most famous criminal case involved a suspected infanticide. Richard Randolph, an idle gadabout from Virginia's prominent Randolph family, was accused of having fathered a child born to his wife's younger, prettier sister, and then having killed and buried it. No body was ever found, but persistent rumor forced the prosecutor to take action. The prime witnesses were slaves, who could not testify, and much of the other evidence was circumstantial speculation on the sister's uncertain state of pregnancy. Working with JOHN MARSHALL, Henry successfully challenged the evidence as unreliable innuendo. Cross-examining the sister's aunt, who had claimed to have seen the naked girl's pregnant belly through a crack in the door, Henry queried, "Which eye did you peep with?" After the courtroom laughter had subsided, Henry proclaimed, "Great God, deliver us from eavesdroppers!" (Henry 1969, 2:492). Randolph was acquitted.

The most important case from this part of Henry's career was the *Great British Debts Case*, which later reached the Supreme Court as *Ware v. Hyl-*

ton. During the war, Virginia passed a law allowing its citizens to repay their British debts into the state treasury using inflationary currency, but the Treaty of Paris, which ended the war, demanded repayment in full. Although this could not be enforced in the Confederation, the Constitution gave added weight to federal treaties. Virginians resisted the deal, however, especially since it would force many to repay debts twice. Jefferson estimated the total burden at thirty times the money in current circulation. But with the debts unpaid, the British refused to leave the American frontier.

Henry joined John Marshall to defend one such debtor against his British creditors. Preparing extensively, Henry spent hours studying Vattel and Grotius on international law. Contracts between citizens of warring nations are invalid, Henry argued. Lampooning the petty hypocrisy of the creditors, he contrasted the sacrifice of life in a noble war to the preservation of commerce: "Though every other thing dear to humanity is forfeitable, yet *debts*, it seems, must be spared! Debts are too sacred to be touched? It is a mercantile ideal that worships Mammon instead of God" (Meade 1969, 410). Had the Americans lost the war, the British would have arbitrarily seized much of their property. Why now should the winners pay? Virginia had every right to sequester debts during the war. Henry won at both the federal district court and the circuit court level, although the ruling was overturned by the Supreme Court after Henry had left the legal team. Henry's arguments, however, had greatly impressed all involved, particularly Justice James Iredell, who had been predisposed to see Henry as a demagogue. The case also led to new political opportunities. Washington hoped to appoint Henry to the Supreme Court; crossing party lines, Marshall tried to recruit Henry as a vice-presidential candidate (largely to undermine Jefferson). Henry declined both offers. He died on June 6, 1799.

The career of Patrick Henry helps demonstrate the close interrelation of law and politics that is so central to American experience. Henry was no mere legal technician. Although he was capable of finely tuned argumentation, his legal brilliance emerged from his great political perception. He drew his moral voice, his ringing oratory, from the principles of natural law, popular sovereignty, and individual liberty that shaped the most democratic segments of the founding generation.

—*Robb A. McDaniel*

Sources and Suggestions for Further Reading

Axelrad, Jacob. *Patrick Henry: The Voice of Freedom*. Westport, Conn.: Greenwood Press, 1947.

Beeman, Richard R. *Patrick Henry: A Biography*. New York: McGraw-Hill, 1974.

Henry, William Wirt. *Patrick Henry: Life, Correspondence and Speeches*. 2 vols. New York: Scribner, 1891. Reprint, New York: Burt Franklin, 1969.

Meade, Robert Douthat. *Patrick Henry: Patriot in the Making*. Philadelphia: J. B. Lippincott, 1957.

_____. *Patrick Henry: Practical Revolutionary*. Philadelphia: J. B. Lippincott, 1969.

Tyler, Moses Coit. *Patrick Henry*. Boston: Houghton Mifflin, 1898. Reprint, Ithaca: Great Seal Books, 1962.

Wirt, William. *Sketches of the Life and Character of Patrick Henry*. New York: Melrath & Bangs, 1832.

HOPKINSON, JOSEPH

(1770–1842)

JOSEPH HOPKINSON
Archive Photos

JOSEPH HOPKINSON WAS BORN in 1770 in Philadelphia. One of a long line of attorneys and jurists, Hopkinson's impact on the American legal system cannot be overstated. Best known for his service as a federal judge and congressman, Hopkinson participated as a litigator in several major constitutional cases that helped to define the U.S. Constitution and shape our legal system in its formative years. Looking back on the life and career of Joseph Hopkinson, one can clearly see his influences on bankruptcy, admiralty, and constitutional law. In addition, Hopkinson was a Shakespearean scholar and a composer, and, much like his father's friend Benjamin Franklin, can be considered a true Renaissance man, as his life's work can now be seen to have affected many different aspects of American society. Joseph Hopkinson was truly a great man, as well as a great lawyer, in American history.

A Rich Family Tradition

Born into an already distinguished family, Joseph Hopkinson had much to live up to merely because of his noble lineage. His grandfather, Thomas Hopkinson, Jr., was born in England in 1709. About 1730, he traveled to America, where he joined a group of young intellectuals called the "Junto" in Philadelphia. Subsequently, Thomas Hopkinson became judge of the vice admiralty court and governor's council. Along the way, Thomas Hopkinson befriended Benjamin Franklin, with whom he conducted experiments involving electricity. Unfortunately, Thomas Hopkinson died at the young age of forty-two, leaving seven children, including a fourteen-year-old son named Francis. Young Francis was to follow in his father's footsteps and was fortunate enough to have Benjamin Franklin as a lifelong friend as well. Francis Hopkinson was admitted to the New Jersey state bar in 1775, and he later represented New Jersey in the Continental Congress, where he signed the Declaration of Independence in 1776. During the Revolutionary War, Francis Hopkinson continued to serve in the Continental Congress, and in 1779 he was commissioned as judge of the Pennyslvania admiralty court. After the creation of the federal judiciary, which took jurisdiction of all admiralty cases, Judge Hopkinson was commissioned by President Washington to the Eastern District Court of Pennsylvania, which also made him a judge of one of the three federal circuit courts, on which he served until his death in 1791. Francis Hopkinson was survived by his only son, Joseph, who was twenty-one years old at the time of his father's passing.

Renaissance Man

Joseph Hopkinson was admitted to the bar in Philadelphia in the spring of 1791 after having graduated from the University of Pennyslvania and reading law under Philadelphia attorneys William Rawle and James Wilson. Although his legal career was to be lengthy and distinguished, it is important to stress that Hopkinson was truly a multitalented and complex individual who came to represent the unquenchable American spirit of the times. He was, for example, a Shakespearean scholar and was a generous benefactor to the arts throughout his lifetime. In addition, Hopkinson was a talented composer. In 1798, a friend requested that he compose lyrics to accompany "The President's March" to stimulate public interest in the opening of a new theater in Philadelphia. The song with Hopkinson's lyrics came to be known as "Hail Columbia" and rapidly became the most popular national song of the day. Although the enormous popularity of "Hail Columbia" first thrust Hopkinson into the national spotlight, it was his successful, high-profile legal career that ensured his lasting legacy in the nation's history. A Federalist, Hopkinson married Emily Mifflin. Emily, the daughter of a Pennsylvania governor, bore him nine children.

In the National Spotlight

Four years after having been admitted to the bar, Hopkinson defended participants in the Whiskey Rebellion against charges of treason, and in 1799 he successfully pursued a libel suit by Benjamin Rush against William Cobbett. In 1804, Congress voted to impeach Supreme Court Justice Samuel P. Chase. Congress took this action because of its displeasure with the conduct of Justice Chase in several high-profile cases, including a treason trial in which Hopkinson had been involved as counsel. Accordingly, before the Senate trial, Justice Chase retained Hopkinson, among several other attorneys, to defend him. The Senate trial, presided over by Vice-President Aaron Burr, began on February 9, 1805, and lasted nearly one month. During the trial, the House managers attempted to prove that Justice Chase had, among other offenses, prejudged the law in the treason trial, making it impossible for the defense to win.

On February 22, 1805, Hopkinson opened for the defense. He warned the Senate to remember that posterity would judge their decision:

> Then, I trust, the high honor and integrity of this court will stand recorded in the pure language of deserved praise, and this day will be remembered in the annals of our land, as honorable to the respondent, to his judges and to the justice of our country. (Konkle 1931, 103)

Hopkinson then proceeded to argue that Justice Chase was not charged with treason or bribery, so he must be found guilty of high crimes and misdemeanors to be removed from office. Hopkinson also focused on the independence of the judiciary, stating that the people do not have the right to interfere with the regular operations of government, despite the fact that government exists at the pleasure of the people:

> Having delegated this power, having distributed it for various purposes into various channels and directed its course by certain limits, they have no right to impede it while it flows in its intended directions; otherwise we have no government. (Konkle 1931, 105)

After the lengthy trial, the Senate voted to acquit Justice Chase. According to Vice-President Burr, Hopkinson "acquitted himself greatly to his honor" and "displayed much ingenuity and knowledge of his subject" (Konkle 1931, 110). Justice Chase wrote to Hopkinson in March 1805, expressing his "thanks for [Hopkinson's] friendly and important services," and vowed that they would "live in my remembrance as long as memory remains" (Konkle 1931, 111).

Outstanding Causes and Cases

In 1809, Hopkinson, responding to an earlier pamphlet advocating the incorporation of common law precedents into a comprehensive system of statutory law for Pennsylvania, wrote an influential essay entitled "Considerations on the Abolition of the Common Law in the United States," in which he opposed this plan. Hopkinson persuasively argued that the existing common law precedents were more stable, and would actually require the exercise of less judicial discretion, than would a new statutory scheme. Joseph Hopkinson is probably best known, however, for his role in several major U.S. Supreme Court cases, which have left such a lasting mark on our jurisprudence as to be taught in most law schools today.

In *Dartmouth College v. Woodward*, 17 U.S. 518 (1819), Hopkinson, along with DANIEL WEBSTER, represented the trustees of Dartmouth College, who had initially filed suit in New Hampshire state court, seeking to invalidate certain acts of the New Hampshire legislature that modified the charter issued in 1769 that had created the college. Specifically, the New Hampshire legislature passed three acts in 1816 amending the charter of the college, by, among other things, changing the name of the college, changing the number of trustees, and creating a new board of overseers, to be appointed by the governor of New Hampshire. William H. Woodward had served as secretary and treasurer, appointed by the original trustees, and was fired by that body in 1816, while still in possession of various goods and property belonging to the college. After the passage of the three acts by the legislature, the new trustees created by these acts reappointed Woodward as secretary and treasurer. The original trustees then filed suit against Woodward to recover the property of the college being held by him.

After a trial in the Superior Court of New Hampshire, then the highest state court, the jury rendered a special verdict providing that, if the acts of the New Hampshire legislature were valid in law, Woodward was not guilty of any wrongdoing. However, the jury provided that if the acts of the legislature were illegal, then Woodward would be required to pay damages to the original trustees. The superior court found the acts of the legislature to be legal and ruled accordingly on the jury verdict. After this decision, Hopkinson and Webster appealed to the U.S. Supreme Court.

In their presentation to the Supreme Court, Hopkinson and Webster argued that the New Hampshire legislature had only as much power over the charter as the King of England, under whose reign the charter was issued, and to whose rights New Hampshire succeeded after the American Revolution; under common law, the king could not modify such a corporation without its assent. Furthermore, anticipating the counterargument that the king (and, therefore, the legislature) could amend the charter of public corporations, Hopkinson and Webster argued that Dartmouth College was an eleemosynary corporation, and as such was necessarily a private corporation. According to Hopkinson and Webster, the New Hampshire acts violated both New Hampshire state law and Article 1, Section 10 of the U.S. Constitution, which provides that no state shall pass any bill of attainder, ex post facto law, or law impairing the obligation of contracts.

After the presentations by Hopkinson and Webster, along with the arguments of opposing counsel, the Court held that the acts by the New Hampshire state legislature violated the U.S. Constitution, and accordingly that the state court decision must be reversed. The opinion of the Court, written by Chief Justice MARSHALL, generally concurred with the points made in Hopkinson's and Webster's presentations. The Court found that the charter at issue was "plainly a contract to which the donors, the trustees and the crown (to whose rights and obligations New Hampshire succeeds) were the original parties" and that the obligation of said contract could not be impaired without violating the U.S. Constitution. Furthermore, the Court found that the obligation of the contract had indeed been impaired by the acts of the New Hampshire legislature, because, among other things, "the whole power of governing the college is transferred from trustees, appointed according to the will of the founder, expressed in the charter, to the executive of New Hampshire." On that basis, the Court held for the original trustees and against Woodward. After the great victory, the original trustees of Dartmouth College passed a resolution calling for Hopkinson, Webster, and their associate counsel to sit for their portraits to be taken and placed at the college, as an expression of the trustees' gratitude.

In *Sturges v. Crowninshield*, 17 U.S. 122 (1819), a significant step was taken toward the creation of a unified federal bankruptcy system. Hopkinson, who had long been an advocate of a national bankruptcy act, was retained to assist David Daggett in representing the plaintiff, Sturges, in a collection suit against Crowninshield. In the Massachusetts state courts, Crowninshield raised as a defense the discharge he had received under a New York bankruptcy statute. Thus, the central issue before the U.S. Supreme Court was the validity of the New York statute on which Crowninshield relied.

Daggett and Hopkinson initially argued that since the adoption of the U.S. Constitution, no state had the authority to enact a bankruptcy law, as the Constitution vested that power exclusively in Congress. Article 1, Section 8 of the Constitution provides that Congress has power "to establish a uniform rule of naturalization, and uniform laws on the subject of bankruptcies, throughout the United States." According to Daggett and Hopkinson, "every power given by the constitution, unless limited, is entire, exclusive and supreme." In addition, Daggett and Hopkinson maintained that the New York law impaired the obligation of contracts and therefore was unconstitutional.

Counsel for the defendant argued that the mere granting of power to Congress does not vest that power exclusively in Congress. The failure of Congress to legislate on the issue, according to the defendant, amounted to a declaration that Congress did not believe a uniform national system was necessary; thus, the states were justified in passing their own laws. Furthermore, the defendant argued that bankruptcy and insolvency laws historically were not regarded as impairing the obligation of a contract; since these laws were based on the inability of the debtor to pay, it was impossible for the debtor to perform the contract, and thus no impairment could actually occur by virtue of the statute at issue. In effect, the parties to such a contract entered into the contract with the knowledge that the bankruptcy statute was in place; thus, the bankruptcy law was effectively made a part of the contract. Hopkinson replied to this argument by stating that the "idea of a contract made with reference to a law which impairs the obligation of contracts, is absurd and incomprehensible."

The Court agreed with Hopkinson and Daggett and held that the New York law was unconstitutional. The Court first noted that until Congress exercises its power to enact uniform bankruptcy laws, the individual states are not forbidden to pass their own laws on the subject. However, the Court found the New York law to be unconstitutional due to its impairment of the obligation of contracts (by virtue of its discharge provisions). Thus, the groundwork for the passage of a uniform federal bankruptcy act was laid.

In *McCulloch v. Maryland*, 17 U.S. 316 (1819), Hopkinson again played an important role in a case with major constitutional implications. The main issue in this case was the constitutionality of a Maryland law that imposed a tax on "all banks or branches thereof, in the state of Maryland, not chartered by the [Maryland] legislature." Pursuant to this statute, the president, cashier, and directors of any bank violating the law were to be fined $500.00 per offense. When the Bank of the United States opened a branch in Baltimore, and no tax was paid to Maryland, the cashier of the branch (McCulloch) was fined accordingly; the state then sued McCulloch to collect the fines.

After a favorable decision for Maryland in the state courts, McCulloch appealed to the U.S. Supreme Court. His counsel argued primarily that Congress was authorized to raise a revenue and also to pass all laws necessary and proper to execute the powers conferred on it. Furthermore, since the Constitution was the supreme law of the land, the state overstepped its authority in attempting to tax the federal bank, for "an unlimited power to tax involves, necessarily, a power to destroy." Hopkinson was retained by the state of Maryland and argued as follows: (1) the Constitution did not expressly grant Congress the power to incorporate the bank; (2) even if the incorporation of the bank was authorized, the bank had no authority to establish its own branches without the direction of Congress; and (3) the bank and its branches could not claim to be exempt from the "ordinary and equal taxation of property, as assessed in the states in which they are placed" (Konkle 1931, 330–337). This, according to Hopkinson, would be an "overwhelming invasion of state sovereignty."

Chief Justice Marshall, writing for the Court, held that the Maryland law was unconstitutional. After finding that the incorporation of the bank was constitutional, the Court held that "states have no power, by taxation or otherwise, to retard, impede, burden, or in any manner control, the operations of the constitutional laws enacted by congress to carry into execution the powers vested in the general government."

Conclusion

After his lengthy and noteworthy litigational career, Hopkinson served as federal judge of the Eastern District of Pennsylvania, a post to which President JOHN QUINCY ADAMS appointed him in 1828. Hopkinson served as a federal judge until his death in 1842 and was a delegate to the Pennsylvania Constitutional Convention of 1837. Among the cases he decided was the precedent-setting *Wheaton v. Peters* (1837), which is credited with having "established the foundations of American copyright law" (Broomfield 1999, 193).

Why does Hopkinson stand out as such a unique contributor to our legal system? Is it simply because of the time period in which he lived? Granted, Hopkinson was alive during the formative early years of post-Revolutionary America, a time during which the fledgling Constitution was tested and galvanized by several major Supreme Court cases. However, many attorneys were alive during this period, and few can match the impact that Hopkinson had on our current legal system. Is it perhaps due to the fact that Hopkinson made his impact both as a lawyer, a legislator, and a judge? Or, is it due to Hopkinson's multifaceted life, in which he exhibited unique skills not only as a legal scholar, but also as a Shakespearean expert, composer, and benefactor of the arts? These are questions that have no certain answer. However, it is safe to assume that Hopkinson's lasting legacy is due at least in part to his ability to excel in many different areas. Like his family friend Benjamin Franklin, Hopkinson was a true Renaissance man, the type of man that Americans have always admired and remembered. Indeed, Joseph Hopkinson was a man that all lawyers, and all men, would do well to emulate.

—*M. Keith Siskin*

Broomfield, Maxfield. "Hopkinson, Joseph." In *American National Biography,* edited by John A. Garraty and Mark C. Carnes. Vol. 11. New York: Oxford University Press, 1999.

Cook, Charles M. *The American Codification Movement: A Study of Antebellum Legal Reform.* Westport, Conn.: Greenwood Press, 1981.

Konkle, Burton Alva. *Joseph Hopkinson, 1770–1842, Jurist: Scholar: Inspirer of the Arts.* Philadelphia: University of Pennsylvania Press, 1931.

HOUSTON, CHARLES HAMILTON

(1895–1950)

CHARLES HAMILTON HOUSTON
Library of Congress

CHARLES HAMILTON HOUSTON was a legal educator, civil rights litigator, and the foremost African-American lawyer before Thurgood Marshall. Houston was born in Washington, D.C., to William Houston, a lawyer, and Mary Hamilton. He graduated from Amherst College in 1914 as one of six valedictorians and a member of Phi Beta Kappa. After briefly teaching English in the District of Columbia, he entered the army as a second lieutenant in a segregated unit during World War I. Houston's military experience was crucial to his subsequent development as a lawyer and civil rights leader. "The hate and scorn showered on . . . Negro officers by our fellow Americans," Houston wrote, "convinced me that there was no sense in my dying for a world ruled by them." Based on that experience and the example of his father, Houston determined to "study law and use my time fighting for men who could not strike back" (McNeil 1983, 42).

Houston entered the Harvard Law School in 1919 and graduated three years later in the top five percent of his class. He spent a fourth year and earned an S.J.D. degree, the first to be awarded to an African-American. Based on his strong academic performance, Houston won a coveted spot on the *Harvard Law Review* and subsequently became its editor, once again the first African-American to hold that position. During his time at Harvard, Houston became the protégé of Dean Roscoe Pound, one of the most influential legal academics of his day and a proponent of the concept of sociological jurisprudence. Pound played a pivotal role in the development of Houston's legal thinking and his subsequent career. Pound, for example, helped to arrange a Sheldon Fellowship for Houston that permitted the young lawyer to spend a year in Spain studying at the University of Madrid. The experience had a lasting impact because the new friends that he made there cared not at all about his color. He earned his doctorate in civil law and then returned to Washington in 1924 to join his father's law firm, renamed Houston and Houston.

William Houston, the father and founder, built a solid general practice that relied mostly, but not exclusively, on middle-class African-American clients. In subsequent years Charles's cousin, WILLIAM HASTIE, the first African-American to sit on a federal appeals court, joined the firm as well. Charles Houston brought to this practice a quick mind and impressive educational credentials.

Charles Houston learned much from his father. William Houston taught his son an important lesson about loyalty, since even as his firm's fortunes grew he continued to represent the maids, chauffeurs, and lower-echelon government workers and laborers that gave him his start. He also learned that an important part of a lawyer's work was to negotiate to avoid unnecessary, time-consuming litigation. William Houston also taught his son the value of thorough and accurate legal preparation, traits that characterized the younger Houston's subsequent legal career and a lesson that he carried to his students when he became a teacher at Howard University law school.

Houston's contributions to the education of African-Americans lawyers were among his most important achievements. Once again, Roscoe Pound played a critical role. Pound and Harvard law professor and future Supreme Court justice Felix Frankfurter wrote strong letters in support of Houston's successful application to join the Howard faculty. In 1924, the institution was trying to upgrade itself from a part-time, night law school to a full-time, accredited institution. At that time, Howard had trained more than three-fourths of the nation's nearly 950 African-American lawyers.

Thanks to his intelligence and determination, Charles Houston quickly became a faculty leader. He wanted Howard to become the training ground for a cadre of African-American civil rights lawyers. To accomplish that goal, Houston was a stern taskmaster who demanded that his students realize that in the struggle for civil rights they had to be well equipped, not just legally but psychologically, to face the resistance that he knew would confront them. Houston also demanded that his students approach law in the same way that Pound had urged on him: from a sociological and psychological perspective. African-American lawyers, according to Houston, had to become social engineers who used the law as an instrument to change society. Throughout his life, Houston, who flirted with the ideas of communism but never joined the Communist party, also consistently taught that the law had a differential impact on people based on their race, wealth, and position in the social order. Thus, Houston's classroom mixed law and liberal arts and theory and practice in ways that asked students to grapple with the law's social consequences.

Houston had an abiding interest in the fate of all African-American lawyers. In 1927, Howard's board of trustees approved Houston's proposal, funded by a grant from the Rockefeller Foundation, to undertake a *Survey of the Status and Activities of Negro Lawyers in the United States*. Houston produced comprehensive studies of the status of African-American lawyers, of which the most influential was *The Negro and His Contact with the Administration of Justice*. It reported that not only were African-Americans treated as second-class citizens before the law, but they were also often accorded second-class representation through the legal profession. On the basis of these findings, Houston urged better training for African-American lawyers and a corresponding commitment to helping African-Americans realize full citizenship.

Houston invoked his experience as director of the *Survey* to press for substantial changes at Howard. In 1929, the board of trustees responded by appointing him vice dean in charge of the three-year day law school and its library. Houston strove relentlessly to make Howard an accredited law school. That objective met stiff resistance from many faculty members, some of them white, who condemned the project as elitist. Houston, however, recognized that accreditation from the American Bar Association and the American Association of Law Schools would give Howard law graduates a chance to gain real professional legitimacy. After considerable internal turmoil, Houston prevailed; in 1931, both organizations extended their imprimatur to Howard. Thereafter, the law school became a training ground for many of the most influential African-American civil rights lawyers, including THURGOOD MARSHALL, William Bryant, and Oliver Hill.

In 1935, Houston became the first full-time paid counsel to the Legal Defense Fund of the National Association for the Advancement of Colored People (NAACP). Even after he left the NAACP in 1940, Houston continued to have extraordinary influence. He helped to produce major change in education, labor, and housing.

Joseph Welch: A Folksy Attorney with a Sense of Decency

Courtroom skills are often transferable to other settings. One setting, which often fulfills a similar function to that of a courtroom, is the congressional hearing. Although such hearings can be an effective and powerful force for ferreting out incompetency and corruption (consider lawyer Sam Ervin's use of committee hearings in exposing the Watergate scandal), hearings can also sometimes be used to harass or embarrass individuals who, though they may have marched to a different drummer, have committed no crimes.

Few members have been as reckless in their use of the investigating committee mechanisms as Republican Senator Joseph McCarthy of Wisconsin, who was aided by Roy Cohn. At a time when tensions were heightened by the Cold War, McCarthy had charged that the State Department and other governmental agencies had hired scores of Communists, who were serving as foreign spies. In televised hearings, McCarthy widened his accusations to include the U.S. Army. The army hired Boston lawyer Joseph Welch (1890–1960) to defend it. A relatively obscure Boston attorney who had raised himself from poverty in Iowa and was known for his collection of more than 150 bow ties, Welch's folksy but straightforward manner ultimately proved to be Senator McCarthy's undoing.

After first getting McCarthy to show the same kind of evasiveness to questions that McCarthy had attributed to "Fifth Amendment Communists," Welch pressed McCarthy for keeping secret for months a document that purported to show Communist infiltration in the military. On June 9, 1954, Welch further responded to counter questions by McCarthy about the Communist affiliation of a person in Welch's own law firm by publicly asking, "Have you no sense of decency, sir, at long last? Have you no sense of decency?"

The committee room followed with applause, and the next day, newspapers throughout the country repeated Welch's question in bold headlines. By year's end, the Senate voted to censure McCarthy, and he died within three years. The folksy Welch continued to receive fan mail until his death in 1960.

REFERENCE

Emert, Phyllis R. "Joseph Welch: Legal Folk Hero." In *Top Lawyers & Their Famous Cases*. Minneapolis: Oliver Press, 1966, 117–132.

Although Houston did not invent the idea of a planned litigation campaign, during his time with the NAACP he raised it to a new level, especially in the areas of education and rights of the accused. As Gena Rae McNeil, Houston's biographer, notes, he developed a three-pronged litigation strategy. First, he was careful to select cases that presented clear legal issues and that had strong underlying records. Second, Houston knew that it was often best to attack some issues indirectly by building a chain of minor precedents that, once linked together, could undermine a major precedent, such as the concept of "separate but equal" associated with *Plessy v. Ferguson* (1896). Third, Houston also understood that any successful litigation campaign required community support.

Houston's most important victory during his time with the NAACP was *Missouri ex rel. Gaines v. Canada* (1938). Lloyd Gaines was an African-American who sought admission to Missouri's all-white law school in the absence of a facility for African-Americans. The University of Missouri denied Gaines's application on racial grounds, and the state's highest appellate court upheld the denial. Houston, who had been representing Gaines, then appealed to the U.S. Supreme Court for a writ of mandamus ordering his admission. Houston insisted that the equal protection clause of the Fourteenth Amendment required Missouri to do more than merely pay the tuition for an African-American law student to attend an out-of-state school. State-sponsored out-of-state scholarships for African-Americans did not constitute equal protection of the laws. Chief Justice CHARLES EVANS HUGHES, writing for the Court, agreed with Houston's position and ordered Gaines admitted.

Houston's victory in *Gaines* was a pivotal moment in the NAACP's campaign to overturn the separate-but-equal doctrine. The Court did not repudiate segregation, but its decision was a vital step toward the subsequent legal destruction of the doctrine in *Brown v. Board of Education* (1954, 1955). Gaines, however, proved a personal disappointment for Houston. After winning the case, Lloyd Gaines disappeared, never entered law school, and was never heard from again.

During his service to the NAACP, Houston also rallied to the cause of African-American criminal defendants. For example, he succeeded in *Hollins v. Oklahoma* (1935) in having the Supreme Court overturn a death sentence imposed by a jury from which African-Americans had been excluded.

In 1940, mounting health problems prompted Houston to resign from the NAACP, although he remained a valued advisor to the organization and his successor and former student, Thurgood Marshall. In that year, Houston became general counsel of the International Association of Railway Employees and the Association of Colored Railway Trainmen and Locomotive Firemen. In this capacity, Houston tackled another important subject: the selection and recognition of bargaining agents for African-American railway employees.

The Railway Labor Act contained no provision prohibiting discrimination based on race either in the selection of a bargaining agent or in providing minorities adequate representation. Houston, however, believed that such a right could be implied from the language and spirit of the statute, a position that he argued in two seminal cases: *Steele v. Louisville & Nashville Railroad Co.* and *Tunstall v. Brotherhood of Locomotive Firemen and Enginemen* (1944). These cases involved the denial on grounds of race of the right of African-American firemen to work and the abuse of the right of the railway unions to be the statutory exclusive bargaining agent for them.

Houston personally argued both cases before the Supreme Court on November 14 and 15, 1944. Justice William O. Douglas observed afterward that "he was a veritable dynamo of energy guided by a mind that had as sharp a cutting edge as any I have known" (McNeil 1983, 168). For Houston the cases boiled down to a simple matter: a union had to represent white and African-American employees equally.

In December 1944, the justices reversed lower courts' opinions and remanded the cases for further proceedings. Chief Justice Harland Fiske Stone, speaking for the Court, found that a union had a fiduciary duty to protect minority members. Justice Frank Murphy, in a concurring opinion, adopted part of Houston's oral argument to find that "racism is far too virulent today to permit the slightest refusal, in the light of a Constitution that abhors it, to expose and condemn it wherever it appears in the course of a statutory interpretation" (McNeil 1983, 169).

Both of these victories came during an especially complicated time for Houston. President Franklin D. Roosevelt in 1944 appointed him to the President's Fair Employment Practices Committee (FEPC), an advisory body designed to address issues of discrimination in employment. When in 1945 the new president, Harry S Truman, refused to follow an FEPC recommendation to ban discrimination by the District of Columbia's Transit Authority, Houston resigned. In a letter to Truman that he widely circulated, including to foreign ambassadors in Washington, Houston wrote that "the failure of the Government to enforce democratic practices and to protect minorities in its own capital makes its expressed concern for national minorities abroad somewhat specious, and its interference in the domestic affairs of other countries very premature" (McNeil 1983, 174).

Houston's last major legal victory dealt with housing. Many cities, including the District of Columbia, attempted to pin African-Americans in their traditional ghetto housing by enforcing private racial covenants on real property. So important had this line of legal work become to Houston's practice that he hired another African-American attorney and future civil rights litigator, SPOTTSWOOD W. ROBINSON, to assist him. Houston, however, had little success with the courts of the District, whose judges routinely sustained such covenants.

The NAACP had been pressing similar cases in the states, and by 1948 the stage had been set for an appeal to the Supreme Court. In this instance, two cases, one from Missouri, *Sipes v. McGhee*, and the other from Michigan, *Shelley v. Kraemer*, were waiting to be heard. Houston managed to convince the justices to add another case to their list, *Hurd v. Hodge*.

A District of Columbia court in 1947 had ordered James and Mary Hurd, African-Americans, to abandon their home and remove their personal property because the house that they occupied had been sold to them in violation of a restrictive racial covenant. The Court of Appeals for the District of Columbia subsequently sustained this verdict. Houston then moved for a rehearing, which was quickly denied. The denial, however, provided the basis to carry an appeal to the high court along with the *McGhee* and *Kraemer* cases.

Houston's brief for *Hurd*, which was prepared and argued along with white attorney Phineas Indritz, depended extensively on economists and sociologists to document the invidious consequences of promoting private discrimination through restrictive covenants. By all estimates, the brief prepared in *Hurd* represented Houston's most elaborate justification for the concept of the lawyer as social engineer, since it mixed constitutional, statutory, and common law concepts with public policy and social science. Houston urged the justices to understand that restrictive covenants violated public policy, federal law, and most notably the due process clause of the Fifth Amendment. Only six of the justices, however, heard the case; the three others absented themselves because of their personal connections to covenanted properties.

By a vote of 6 to 0 the high court in May 1948 ruled against judicial enforcement of racially restrictive covenants. In his opinion for the majority, Chief Justice Fred Vinson held that the courts could not be used to deny rights of occupancy or ownership on the grounds of race. Vinson and his colleagues found that in the case of the states such a practice violated the Fourteenth Amendment. However, in *Hurd*, which involved a federal rather than a state jurisdiction, the justices rejected Houston's constitutional position that the due process clause of the Fifth Amendment blocked such activity. Instead, the court adopted the position that the Civil Rights Act of 1866 prohibited judicial enforcement of discriminatory agreements. While failing to gain the broader constitutional position he argued, Houston nevertheless recognized that *Hurd* was a victory, since it afforded African-Americans an opportunity to claim another right due them.

Houston's health declined shortly after *Hurd*, and on April 22, 1950, he died of a coronary occlusion in Washington, D.C. Houston left behind a remarkable record of personal and professional success. Without his creative approach of "social engineering" through the law, his determination to prepare a new generation of African-American lawyers, his skills at mentoring those lawyers, his strategic sense of how to advance the African-American civil rights agenda, and his passion for justice, the victories achieved after his death would not have come as they did. As Gena Rae McNeil has argued, Charles Hamilton Houston "turned the Constitution, the laws, and the legal process into weapons in the cause of his people." His legacy was that "there should be no end to struggling, no immobilizing weariness until full human rights were won" (McNeil 1983, 224).

—*Kermit L. Hall*

Sources and Suggestions for Further Reading

Hastie, William. "Charles Hamilton Houston." *Negro History Bulletin* 13 (1950): 207.

Franklin, John Hope. *From Slavery to Freedom: A History of African Americans.* 8th ed. Boston: McGraw-Hill, 2000.

Kennedy, Randall. "The Moses of That Journey." *Constitution: A Journal of the Foundation for the U.S. Constitution* 5 (Winter 1993): 29–35.

Kluger, Richard. *Simple Justice: The History of* Brown v. Board of Education *and Black America's Struggle for Equality.* New York: Alfred A. Knopf, 1975.

McNeil, Gena Rae. *Groundwork: Charles Hamilton Houston and the Struggle for Civil Rights.* Philadelphia: University of Pennsylvania Press, 1983.

———. "To Meet the Group Needs: The Transformation of Howard University School of Law, 1920–1935." In *New Perspectives in Black Educational History,* edited by Vincent Franklin and James D. Anderson. Boston: G. K. Hall, 1978.

Smith, J. Clay, Jr., "Forgotten Hero." *Harvard Law Review* 98 (1984): 482–491.

HUGHES, CHARLES EVANS

(1862–1948)

CHARLES EVANS HUGHES
Library of Congress

Charles Evans Hughes is regarded as one of the most outstanding Americans of the twentieth century. His list of achievements is extensive. He was a reformer, a politician, a diplomat, and a statesman, and he served twice on the U.S. Supreme Court. He was also the foremost and best-known lawyer of his day.

Hughes was born on April 11, 1862. His father, David Charles Hughes, was a Methodist minister who had come to New York City from Wales in 1855. In 1858, the elder Hughes met Mary Catherine Connelly, a school-teacher, and soon decided to marry her. Converting to the Baptist faith to overcome the objections of her parents, the young preacher was assigned to the Glen Falls, New York, parish, where Charles Evans was born. The family subsequently moved to Sandy Hill, Oswego, Newark, and then New York City.

Clearly a precocious child, Hughes learned to read at age three. By age six he had studied German and French at home; by the time he was eight, he was studying Greek, science, and

Shakespeare. He possessed a photographic memory and was able to recite extensive passages from scripture. His mother forced him to work arithmetic sums in his head, without recourse to pencil and paper. His father had collected an extensive library, and there young Hughes read voraciously.

At age six, he was sent to a public school in Oswego. Hughes found the rigid routine of the school stifling and the subject matter—which he had long since mastered—extremely boring. Within four weeks he was petitioning his parents to be allowed to return to home schooling. To this end, the boy wrote out what he called "Charles E. Hughes' Plan of Study," specifying what subjects he planned to study and how much time each day he would give them. His father accepted the plan—which Hughes, as an adult, claimed was merely a device to give him more time to play after his studies (Pusey 1963, 1:7)—and Hughes left the public school for home studies. The boy did not return to public school until he was eleven; at age thirteen, he gained his diploma from Public School 35, one of the best secondary schools in New York City.

In September 1876, Hughes began his studies at what is now Colgate University; he remained there for two years, earning marks that ranged between "superior" and "the maximum." Desiring a larger college with more academic opportunity, he transferred to Brown University in 1878 and eventually graduated from that institution in 1881, at age nineteen. It was at Brown that Hughes developed his interest in poker, baseball, theater, and law. Both of his parents were deeply religious and had educated and trained their son with the hope that he would become a minister; at Brown, however, Hughes gradually realized that he did not "feel the call" to the ministry, and by his last semester there he found himself drawn toward the legal profession. After graduating from Brown, he spent a year teaching at an academy to raise money for law school. In 1882, he entered Columbia University Law School; he graduated in 1884 with highest honors. In the summer of 1884, he passed the New York bar examination with a score of 99.5.

As a student at Columbia, Hughes had been a summer intern at the New York law firm of Chamberlain, Carter, and Hornblower, and upon gaining admission to the bar, he joined that firm as a clerk. He rapidly advanced, and when the firm was reorganized in 1887, he became the lead lawyer in the new firm of Carter, Hughes & Cravath. The firm was successful and Hughes was very busy. (It was at this time that he grew his famous beard to eliminate trips to the barber shop.) In 1888, he married Antoinette Carter, the daughter of the firm's senior partner; the couple remained married until her death fifty-seven years later.

His obsession with perfection in every detail of his work brought Hughes great respect from his fellow lawyers and a substantial income, but it also contributed to a tremendous strain on his health. On the verge of a physical collapse, he left private law in 1891 and accepted a teaching position at Cornell University law school. (More than once, Hughes worked himself to the verge of a breakdown.) The teaching duties were very agreeable to Hughes, and he soon recovered his full health. Unfortunately, the pay was not very good. Unable to support his growing family adequately on a professor's salary, he left the university in 1893 and rejoined his old firm.

Hughes entered public life for the first time in 1905. In 1904, amid charges of corruption, a controversy erupted over the rates the gas trusts were charging New York City for power. When the city government, influenced by the gas lobby, refused to investigate, the state legislature ordered its own investigation and sought a lead counsel. Although unknown to the public, Hughes was tapped for the job. His investigation of the industry revealed enormous price gouging—for example, the city was paying more than three times the rate of large private consumers—and a pattern of fraud, corruption, overvaluation of assets, and adulterated gas. The result of his work was the creation of the New York State Public Service Commission to regulate the activities of the power companies in the public interest.

Hardly had the gas inquiry been completed when Hughes was asked to lead another investigation, this time into malfeasance in the life insurance industry. Again the New York Senate summoned Hughes to be the chief counsel for the investigating committee. Under Hughes's relentless interrogation, leading figures in the insurance business admitted to overcharging on premiums and otherwise using fraudulent data and practices to provide exorbitant salaries for top executives. Hughes also discovered that the insurance industry had donated huge sums of money to political campaigns (including Theodore Roosevelt's 1904 presidential bid) and effectively "bought off" a number of legislators. The revelations forced a thorough reform of the insurance business and also led to New York's first regulations on lobbying and campaign donations.

His role in the investigations brought Hughes praise in the press and public fame, establishing his reputation as a brilliant—if somewhat aloof and austere—man of great integrity. In 1906, this reputation led to his nomination and election as governor of New York. During his two terms as governor, Hughes, a progressive Republican, "fought for campaign and election reform, strengthened child labor laws and wage and hour laws, and introduced the first workers compensation law in America . . . [and] introduced regulation to the telephone and telegraph industry" (McWhirter 1998, 135).

Despite these achievements, Hughes's first love remained the law. He had entered the rough and crude world of New York politics largely due to a sense of public service, and he soon tired of it. When President William Howard Taft offered him a seat on the U.S. Supreme Court in 1910,

Hughes readily accepted, much to the dismay of the Progressives in New York. Hughes served on the Court until 1916. During that time, he wrote 151 opinions, 32 of which were dissents; only nine times were there dissents from his opinions for the Court (Cushman 1995, 308).

By 1916, Hughes was one of the most respected and prominent Republicans in the country. He had been mentioned as a presidential candidate in 1912 but refused to run. In 1916, the Republican party convention drafted him as its candidate to challenge the incumbent, Woodrow Wilson. He immediately resigned from the Court and devoted his full energies to the campaign, but his bid ended in defeat when he lost California by 3,775 votes.

Upon his loss, Hughes retired from public life and resumed his career as a lawyer, becoming the senior partner in the firm of Hughes, Round, Schurman & Dwight. Well known and respected, he was a lawyer's lawyer, and clients flocked to his door, allowing him to take only the cases that held special interest for him. Even so, he was quite busy, arguing twenty-five cases before the Supreme Court in only twenty-eight months.

In 1920, Warren G. Harding was elected president of the United States. In one of his first appointments, he chose Hughes to be secretary of state. Hughes served in that office until 1925; during that time, he negotiated dozens of treaties, among them the disarmament treaty of 1922 and a security pact for Japan in the western Pacific. Hughes's accomplishments as secretary of state earned him the respect of the international community, but financial concerns led him to resign and return once more to private law practice.

Hughes remained in private life until 1929, when President Herbert Hoover named him to serve on the International Court of Justice in The Hague. His time there was short, however, for the health of U.S. Supreme Court Chief Justice Taft began to fail. In 1930, Taft resigned and Hughes was chosen to replace him. As chief justice, Hughes was a centrist "swing" vote bridging the clear liberal and conservative blocs on the Court; although most of his written opinions were conservative in tone, he often voted with the liberal bloc (Hughes 1973, xxv). Hughes himself denied any ideological bias, claiming to take each case on its objective merits (Hughes 1973, 300). Although he voted against a number of the New Deal laws, he also voted to uphold progressive labor legislation such as minimum-wage laws. Hughes also successfully guided the Court through the crisis created by Franklin Roosevelt's "court-packing" scheme.

In 1941, fearing a deterioration of his abilities as he neared eighty, Hughes resigned from the Court and left public life for the last time. He did not return to private law practice but spent his last years in quiet retirement in Washington, D.C. He died of congestive heart failure on August 27, 1948. More than 1,600 people attended his funeral in New York City.

Hughes's work as a lawyer is generally overshadowed by his achievements as a politician, jurist, and diplomat. In fact, he was an outstanding lawyer, highly regarded in his profession for his integrity and his ability to win difficult cases. He began his legal career in commercial law; as his reputation (and his income) grew with his success in that field, he found other lawyers bringing important cases to him. Eventually, Hughes was able to choose the cases he handled and would take only those that he deemed to involve sufficiently important issues.

Much of Hughes's success in law came from his meticulous preparation for his day in court. As a young student, he would rise early to spend the necessary hours mastering every detail of his assignments; this same trait served him well as a lawyer. No detail of the law was too small for him to know, if it might in some way affect his case. In drafting a will for John D. Rockefeller, Hughes had to deal with an obscure technical question and asked a junior partner to research all of the relevant precedents. The partner returned with every precedent in New York legal history, whereupon Hughes, wanting to eliminate any chance of surprise, sent him back for all of the precedents from every state. Hughes "made it his business to know everything that his opponent could say" about a case and to have a ready response for it (if not actually preempt it) (Pusey 1963, 1: 384–385).

Such diligence in preparation made him a formidable adversary in the courtroom. Yet apparently he was never comfortable before going into court; since he never thought anything important simply because he was saying it, he always feared that he had missed something that might harm his case. Early in his career, an older lawyer had advised him to always get a good night's sleep before a day in court, but he was rarely able to take advantage of the counsel. Instead, he would stay up until one or two in the morning preparing for his court appearances; as he aged, he began rising extremely early to prepare instead. Although he argued several times before the U.S. Supreme Court, Hughes rarely was able to sleep before his appearances there.

In the courtroom, Hughes was a spellbinding orator, arguing with great energy and intensity. The nervousness of the night before would be channeled into his speeches, which made them more effective. His photographic memory allowed him to argue at length without reference to the stacks of law books and papers on the table before him. He developed an ability to strip a case down to its essentials, presenting his argument so clearly and logically as to render counterargument almost pointless. A biographer of Hughes has noted that he devised a style and technique "designed to get his case so clearly, quickly, and cogently before the court as to forestall any objections . . . before such objections could arise in a judge's mind" (Pusey 1963, 1:385). Some of the judges before whom Hughes argued learned to take special precautions against the power of his oratory. Justice Benjamin Cardozo once said that "he always reserved judgment for twenty-four hours in any case argued by Hughes to avoid being carried away by the force of his personality and intellect" (Pusey 1963, 1:385).

As a lawyer, Hughes was involved in a number of important cases that involved significant legal principles or social issues. He believed he had a duty to take "worthy" cases (Hughes 1973, xvi), and so represented both business and labor, defended individual rights of expression, promoted a limited but important increase in government's authority to enact programs benefiting social welfare, and supported key constitutional principles.

He argued before the Supreme Court against the government's seizures of transoceanic cable systems at the very end of World War I, calling them an unjustified overreach of government authority. (The cable lines were returned to private ownership and the case rendered moot before the Court could rule.) Similarly, the Supreme Court accepted his arguments that the Food Control Act of 1917, which banned price gouging but failed to set any specific standards, was unconstitutionally vague.

A strong defender of the right of free speech, Hughes took the lead in arguing the defense of the New York Socialists in 1920. Five members of the Socialist party had been elected to the New York Assembly, but in the wave of anti-Socialist hysteria that followed World War I, the assembly refused to seat them until they had proved their fitness to serve. Arguing before the assembly's judiciary committee, which was sitting as a court, Hughes denounced the assembly's demand that the five prove their worthiness to serve as a reversal of basic criminal due process. Moreover, he argued, the people had a right to elect whomever they chose, and "if a majority can exclude the whole or a part of the minority because it deems the political views entertained by them hurtful, then free government is at an end" (Pusey 1963, 1:392). Although the five were still denied their seats, Hughes's brief has been credited with helping to break the hysteria then raging in the United States.

Hughes also played a significant role in the *Prohibition Cases*. Opponents of the Eighteenth Amendment had filed suit arguing that its adoption was unconstitutional, and they asked Hughes to present their case. Ignoring the prospects of a huge fee from the liquor industry for his services, and despite his misgivings about prohibition as a policy, Hughes filed an amicus brief with the Supreme Court supporting the amendment. In it he argued that the Eighteenth Amendment was constitutional; not only did the people have the right to amend the Constitution as they saw fit, he declared, but such a right was vital to the continued viability of the Constitution. The Court accepted this argument and upheld the amendment.

Also noteworthy examples of his skills as a lawyer were the cases that made his reputation: the investigations into the power and the insurance industries in New York. These cases illustrated his ability to assimilate large quantities of information in a very short period of time: Beginning with no knowledge of either the power or insurance business, within a few weeks he knew both of them better than their own executives and was able to repeat the most minute facts as needed. His skills as a cross-examiner were displayed in the relentless interrogation that elicited damning confessions from officials of the businesses under investigation. And although he did not need his oratorical skills in these investigations, his ability to analyze, simplify, and logically present a problem is seen in his reports on the investigations and his recommendations, most of which were adopted into law.

The list of cases in which Hughes was involved is extensive and can only be hinted at here. His impact on twentieth-century America has been great. As a lawyer and a jurist, Hughes is generally regarded as a conservative, but a "progressive Republican" label would be more accurate. He was a staunch defender of civil liberties and supported policies that opened the door for government regulation of the economy in the public good. Particularly in the latter area, Charles Evans Hughes as lawyer and judge "moved the law forward as few others ever had" (McWhirter 1998, 136).

—*Steve Robertson*

Sources and Suggestions for Further Reading

Cushman, Claire. *The Supreme Court Justices: Illustrated Biographies, 1789–1995.* Washington: Congressional Quarterly Press, 1995.

Glad, Betty. *Charles Evans Hughes and the Illusions of Innocence: A Study in American Diplomacy.* Champaign: University of Illinois Press, 1966.

Hendel, Samuel. *Charles Evans Hughes and the Supreme Court.* New York: Columbia University Press, 1951.

Hughes, Charles Evans. *The Autobiographical Notes of Charles Evans Hughes.* Edited by David J. Danelski and Joseph S. Tulchin. Cambridge: Harvard University Press, 1973.

McWhirter, Darien A. *The Legal 100: Individuals Who Have Most Influenced the Law.* Secaucus, N.J.: Carol, 1998.

Pusey, Merlo J. *Charles Evans Hughes.* 2 vols. New York: Columbia University Press, 1963.

Wesser, R. F. *Charles Evans Hughes: Politics and Reform in New York, 1905–1910.* Ithaca: Cornell University Press, 1967.